RIVER ENGINEERING

(Theory & Practice)

Professor Santosh Kumar
Former University Professor
Bihar College of Engineering (Now NIT Patna)
Patna University

KHANNA BOOK PUBLISHING CO. (P) LTD.
Publisher of Engineering and Computer Books
4C/4344, Ansari Road, Darya Ganj, New Delhi-110002
Phone : 011-23244447-48 **Mobile:** +91-99109 09320
E-mail : contact@khannabooks.com
Website : www.khannabooks.com

Dear Readers,

To prevent the piracy, this book is secured with HIGH SECURITY HOLOGRAM on the front title cover. In case you don't find the hologram on the front cover title, please write us to at *contact@khannabooks.com* or whatsapp us at +91-99109 09320 and avail special gift voucher for yourself.

Specimen of Hologram on front Cover title:

Moreover, there is a SPECIAL DISCOUNT COUPON for you with EVERY HOLOGRAM.

How to avail this SPECIAL DISCOUNT:

Step 1: Scratch the hologram
Step 2: Under the scratch area, your "coupon code" is available
Step 3: Logon to *www.khannabooks.com*
Step 4: Use your "coupon code" in the shopping cart and get your copy at a special discount
Step 5: Enjoy your reading!

Thanks,
Khanna Publishing House

Price: ₹ 395.00

RIVER ENGINEERING

Santosh Kumar

ISBN: 978-93-86173-79-9

Edition: 2021

Published by:

Khanna Book Publishing Co. (P) Ltd.
4C/4344, Ansari Road, Darya Ganj, New Delhi-110 002
Phone: 011-23244447-48 **Mobile:** +91-9910909320
E-mail: contact@khannabooks.com

Printed in India by:
SPS Enterprises, Delhi

PREFACE

Rivers have been lifeline of human civilization which now have started behaving differently due to various negative factors more due to human interference than any other reason.

The human concern towards deteriorating condition of river prompted him to take up the study of river behaviour, resulting in the branch of river engineering.

River Engineering relatively is a new branch in the field of water resources engineering.

River behavior, if not impossible is very difficult to understand. From the very beginning we are being told that rivers' function is to carry runoff resulting from rainfall to the seas or oceans.

However, engineers and researchers in the field of water resources realised within last eighty years that nature has given rivers to perform two functions viz. to carry water to the oceans and to carry sediment. During these years people like Lacey, Kennedy, White, Shield, Einstein, Albertson, Grade, Raju and many more got involved in unfolding the mysteries of rivers vis-a-vis water and sediment transport. Consequently, the subject of River Engineers got into being. In our Undergraduate Courses of Bachelor's level the component of river engineering is very thin and scantily mentioned. In India the River Engineering Subject is taught at Post-Graduate level. Lots of old and new literature is available in the subject. Prof. R.J. Garde and Prof. K.G. Raugaraju authored a book titled "Mechanics of Sediment Transportation and Alluvial Stream Problem". Published by New Age International Publishers which in my opinion is a commendable work. While this book is very useful to senior students and researchers, it does not provide workable solutions to those engineers who have to deal with rivers.

Surely, Prof. Garde and Prof. Raju deserve accolade for producing a book of highest merit. I, on my part present this book for those who desire to pursue career in the development of water resources and understanding the role of rivers. I have tried to simplify the complex equations and curves and their use in solving problems related to hydraulics of river and sediment transport.

The book has been divided in three major parts. The first part contains the importance of rivers, hydrology and hydraulics of rivers and river morphology. Second part deals with the sediment transport which includes sediment and its properties, initiation of motion, bed forms, resistance to flow and mechanism of sediment transport. Part three contains important topics related to River Engineering viz., sediment measurement techniques, river gauging, river training, floods and flood control, river ecosystem and finally the issue of interlinking of rivers.

The hydrology and hydraulics of rivers is well established and understood by our civil engineers dealing with river flows. However, the phenomenon of sediment transport has not yet found a solid scientific basis. Most of the knowledge is either empirical or based on extremely controlled laboratory experiments. The different theories prorogated give highly diverse results. Keeping this in mind I have emphasised the use of methods/results given by Indian researchers like Prof. Garde, Prof. Raju and others who have worked under their guidance.

In the first part which is spread over four chapters, basic river hydraulics is dealt. Besides the hydrologic and erosion cycles, in the chapter river morphology topics like meandering, aggradations and degradation, scour and deposition, etc. have been briefly discussed. River hydrology chapter, details of some important rivers is also provided, besides some important hydrologic elements. In the chapter River Hydraulics role of Chezy and Manning's as resistance coefficient is discussed. Flow through transitions and Gradually varied Flow has also been discussed with some numerical problems.

Part two of the book deals with sediment transport mechanism, starting with sediment characteristics. Inspite of the fact that many investigators have worked on this aspect, Shields analysis still is the most valid option. Number of solved numerical problems are included. Bed forms identification is an important exercise in sediment transport as it decides the form resistance. Here Garde and Raju work seems to be best suited for Indian conditions.

For evaluating the resistance to motion in alluvial streams, various methods have been briefly discussed with more emphasis on Prof. Garde and his associates work, as they have mostly investigated keeping in view the Indian conditions. Here also a number solved problems are included.

This part also contains the sediment load estimation. Different methods suggested are discussed in particular the Einstein's method. Besides semi-theoretical methods, chapter on direct measurement techniques is also added.

Part three of the book deals with sundry topics like methods of river training, river gauging, etc. In this part Floods and their control has been dealt in a little more details also includes flood routing. The highlight of this part is inclusion of two short chapter on River Ecosystem and Interlinking of Rivers. The latter being a hot topic and has many pros and cons. A brief mention is given for the two views.

The book has been prepared keeping in view the Post Graduate Scholars in Water Resources as well as those Engineers working in the field and involved in managing rivers. The book contains more than sixty numerical problems, which I hope will be most helpful to students as well as the field engineers.

I am highly privileged having got support from various quarters in preparing the book. Most importantly I would like to show my gratitude towards Dr. Triyugi Prasad, former Dean and Principal Bihar College of Engineering (now National Institute of Technology) for providing his valuable comments on the book and Dr. Dinesh Mishra a renowned river activist for his comments on interlinking of rivers. Also my Ph.D. Scholars Dr. Murlidhar Singh and Dr. Saroj Kumar Verma and former student Er. Arti Sinha deserve a word of thanks for their moral and material support. Ofcourse my wife Prof. Bharti S. Kumar, former Dean of Faculty of Social Science Patna University, who created a good ambience for producing an engineering book. My son Gorki Gautam, Executive Director, Development Bank of Singapore, his wife Sugandhi Govil, Sugandhi Govil, Associate Director, Scotiabank, my daughter Dr. Gogi Kumar, Director Child Neurology and son-in-law Dr. Ajay Agrawal noted Cardiologist in USA have always been a source of inspiration. My father Mr. R.K. Vaish had been a source of inspiration, not to mention that he himself acquired his Master of Arts degree in Economics at the age of 98 years. My younger brother Nirbhay Kumar and his wife Shashi Kumar always acted as reminder to the progress of the book. My grand children Yash, Suhani and Tara with an appreciating glance have always made my day. More than my friends Prof. R.P. Kashyap and Prof. A.K. Sinha deserve a word of appreciation for the camaraderie they showed through all my efforts.

Finally, I acknowledge the help provided by Mr. Pankaj Kumar Choudhary for typing the Script and of course, Mr. Mukul Seth of Khanna Publishers for his exemplary approach and excellent behaviour.

The book is dedicated to the memory of my Mother Maya Devi, most intelligent and witty person and my Brother Dr. Anand Kumar a highly accomplished Nuclear Scientist.

—Author

FOREWORD

The author of this book Dr. Santosh Kumar had been my colleague at Bihar College of Engineering (Patna University), Patna for a number of years. He carried out his undergraduate and Post-graduate studies in reputed institutions of India and abroad. He successfully guided many students for their Masters and Doctoral research. He himself was a diligent researcher and published several of his papers in reputed journals. Most of all, he was a very popular teacher and his students invariably spoke very highly of his lucid presentation of the subject matter. He taught River Engineering and related subjects in both Undergraduate and post-graduate courses. As the Principal of Bihar College of Engineering and as Head of the Department of Civil Engineering, Patna University, the students occasionally met me pleading for Dr. Santosh Kumar to teach them River Engineering and subjects related to it like Open Channel Flow, Sediment Transport and Reservoir Engineering. When I was superannuating and he had still a few years to go before his superannuation, I urged him to write a book on the subject he taught for many years so that the future students and engineers would also be benefitted through his book. I am happy to write a foreword for his book on "River Engineering".

The author has dealt with various topics related to River Engineering in various chapters, altogether sixteen. His exposition on River Morphology is quite extensive which is well-placed. Understanding the morphology of a river is necessary to appreciate its behavior as it flows down from the source to its confluence with another river or a water body. Similarly, he has devoted quite a few chapters in the book in dealing with sediment and its transport through the river.Commonly, it is supposed that the river mainly carries water from its source to its confluence. However, the problems that a river gives rise to or the potential it has for the life and living of mankind are also on account of the sediment it necessarily carries with its flow of water.So, rather extensive dealing with sediment and its transport by the river is well deserved. Similarly, a river engineer has to deal with and understand the river not only qualitatively but also quantitatively. For this, he has to measure the sediment load that a river carries as well as the gauge and discharges of rivers. These aspects of river engineering have also been covered in the book. Also, a river engineer has not only to understand the river and its behavior as it flows from its origin to its confluence but also to intervene in the natural regime of the river to serve the various needs and purposes of people dependent on the river. Such intervention is required for modifying the direction of river flows to serve his various purposes; or in words, to train the river. Similarly, the naturally occurring very high flows in river during certain periods may be damaging and disruptive of the life and living of people. So, he has to adopt measures to attenuate the flows. The author has rightly devoted one chapter to each of these issues. Also, one has to understand that a river is not only an important element of our ecology but also it has its ecosystem. One must understand the ecosystem of the river in order to optimally benefit from this precious natural resource. The author has devoted one chapter to discuss this important aspect. Lastly, the author has dealt with Interlinking of Rivers, a topic which has been of great interest to generalists as well as specialists as a prospective solution to problems of floods and droughts afflicting different parts of a region in a country.

A chapter on River Modelling has brou7ght the book to explain modern techniques being followed for flood forecasting.

Wherever quantitative aspects of the river and its flows are described and dealt with, the author has given numerical problems and their solutions. This will be quite beneficial to the students as well as to design engineers dealing with rivers.

I congratulate the author for writing such a useful book on River Engineering.

Dr. T. Prasad

Former, Dean of the Faculty of Engineering (Patna University),
Head of the Dept. of Civil Engineering (Patna University),
Principal, Bihar College of Engineering Patna &
Director, Centre for Water Resources Studies (Patna University)

CONTENTS

PART II

PART III

List of Symbols

A	:	Area of Cross-section
a	:	Meander belt, Amplitude, Longest axis of particle
b	:	Channel width, Pier diameter, Intermediate axis of particle
c	:	Shortest axis of particle
C	:	Chezy's coefficient
C_D	:	Coefficient of Drag
C_C	:	Coefficient of Curvature
C_L	:	Lift Coefficient
C_u	:	Uniformity Coefficient
C_a	:	Sediment Concentration at distance (a) from bottom
C_d	:	Coefficient of Notch
C_p, C_t	:	Regional Constants
D	:	Depth of Flow, Rainfall duration, Standard Duration of Rainfall
D_{cr}	:	Depth of Flow under critical condition
d	:	Sediment size (diameter), water depth
d_n	:	Nominal diameter
d_{50}	:	Median size of grains
E	:	Evaporation
F_D	:	Drag Force
F_L	:	Lift Force
F_R	:	Flatness Ratio
F_r	:	Froude Number
f	:	Lacey's Silt Factor
f'	:	Friction factor associated with grains
f''	:	Friction factor associated with bed forms
h	:	Water Depth
I	:	Infiltration, Rainfall Intensity
i_B	:	Fraction of bed load in a given size range
i_s	:	Fraction of Suspended Load in a given size range
i_T	:	Fraction of Total Sediment Load in a given size range
K	:	Runoff Coefficient, Frequency Factor

K, K_r	:	Bottom Roughness
L	:	Length of Mainstream from Outlet
L_{ca}	:	Length of Mainstream upto Centroid of Catchment
M	:	Momentum Flux
N	:	Manning's Roughness Coefficient
N_F	:	Froude Number
n	:	Number of Observation
P	:	Precipitation, Wetted Perimeter, Rouse Number
Q	:	Discharge
Q_p	:	Peak Discharge
q	:	Discharge Intensity (Q/b)
q_b	:	Bed Load per unit width
R	:	Runoff, Hydraulic Radius (A/P)
R_e	:	Reynold's Number
R_b	:	Hydraulic Radius related to bank
R_w	:	Hydraulic Radius related to bed
R'_b	:	Hydraulic Radius related to grain resistance
R''_b	:	Hydraulic Radius related to form resistance
R*	:	Shear Reynold's Number
S	:	Standard Deviation, Storage
S_o,S	:	Bed Slope
S_w	:	Water Surface Slope
S_f	:	Energy Line Slope
S_o	:	Sorting Coefficient
SF	:	Shape Factor
S'	:	Slope related to plain bed
S''	:	Additional Slope related to bed form
S_D	:	Delivery Ratio
T	:	Top width, Return Period, Transport of Sediment
t	:	Time of concentration
u	:	Flow velocity
u_d	:	Characteristic velocity
u_*	:	Shear velocity $\sqrt{\tau_0/\rho}$
u_{*c}	:	Critical Shear velocity
u'_*	:	Shear Velocity associated with grain roughness
u''_*	:	Shear Velocity associated with bed undulations
V	:	Velocity of flow, Bulk Volume
$\bar{V}$	:	Average Velocity of Flow
V_*	:	Shear Velocity
V_v	:	Volume of Voids

V_c	:	Critical Velocity
$V_{0.2}$	:	Velocity at 0.2 depth
$V_{0.6}$	:	Velocity at 0.6 depth
$V_{0.8}$	:	Velocity at 0.8 depth
w, w_o	:	Fall Velocity
w(C)	:	Fall Velocity at Concentration C
w_{50}	:	Width of Unit Hydrograph at 50% Q_p.
w_{75}	:	Width of Unit Hydrograph at 75% Q_p.
x	:	Distance on x-axis from origin
y	:	Distance on y-axis/vertical from bottom
y_o, y_e	:	Normal Depth/Equivalent Depth.
y_c	:	Critical depth
z	:	Bed Level Elevation
z_0	:	Exponent of Sediment Distribution Equation
$\gamma, \gamma_f, \gamma_w$	:	Specific weight of Water 9810 N/m^3
γ_s	:	Specific Weight of Sediment (specific Gravity 2.65)
$\Delta\gamma_s$	:	Difference in specific weights of Sediment and Fluid
δ'	:	Thickness of boundary Sub-layer
$\in$	:	Specific energy
$\in_m$	:	Momentum Transfer Coefficient
$\in_s$	:	Sediment Transfer Coefficient
η	:	Packing Coefficient
λ	:	Wave length (meander)
μ	:	Dynamic Viscosity of fluid (water)
ν	:	Kinematic Viscosity of fluid (water)
ρ, ρ_f	:	Density of Fluid(water) 1000 kg/m^3
ρ_s	:	Density of Sediment
τ	:	Shear Stress
τ_0	:	Average bed shear on boundary
τ_*	:	Dimensionless Shear Stress
τ_b	:	Bed Shear
τ'	:	Shear Stress due to grains
τ''	:	Shear Stress due to form
τ_{oc}	:	Critical Shear Stress
ϕ	:	Angle of Repose
ϕ_*, Ψ_*	:	Einstein's Parameters
Ψ_1	:	Einstein's Function

PART I

- River: The Great Source of Life
- River Morphology
- River Hydrology
- River Hydraulics

PART I

Rivers: The Great Source of Life

River Morphology

River Hydrology

River Hydraulics

CHAPTER 1

RIVER: THE GREAT SOURCE OF LIFE

INTRODUCTION

Human history can generally be considered to be water-centered. The early major civilizations developed and flourished on the banks of major rivers such as Nile, Euphrates, Tigris, and Indus. Throughout the history water has been considered a natural resource critical to human survival. Old civilizations which all occurred along rivers, showing ups and downs in the social and cultural expression remarkably well-phased with the ups and downs of river behaviour.

The rivers of India play an important role in the lives of Indian people. The river system provide irrigation, potable water, cheap transportation, electricity and the livelihood for a large number of people all over India. This easily explains why nearly all the major cities of India are located by the banks of rivers. The rivers also have an important role in **Hindu** mythology and are considered **holy** by all Hindus in the country. India's most sacred river is the river Ganga (or the Ganges). The river has such spiritual significance for Hindus that a dip in Ganga is believed to absolve one of all sins. A few drop of Ganga water (**Ganga jal**) on a dying Hindu's lips are said to earn the latter a permanent abode in heaven. The three most revered towns situated on the banks of Ganga are Haridwar, Allahabad (Prayag) and eternal Varanasi (earlier Banaras).

It is not difficult to realise why civilizations and habitats often developed along the banks of several strategically important rivers. People relied on rivers' continued supply of the so essential water without which life is doomed to remain poor and humble, and at the same time on the possibility to dispose of their waste for which the river serves as excellent remover and purifier. It is logical under such conditions that man, several thousands of years ago, cultivated a belief that the mystic Gods of the rivers had to be kept as good friends, and needed their toll to maintain the people's life artery.

To all this, the river responds, not because its Mystic God becomes angry, but because the river's delicate equilibrium is disturbed. Mildly flowing rivers become wild torrents, carrying large masses of sediment, and depositing these at places where man does not want them. Due to this deposition deep channels in the river become shallow, hampering the navigation and endangering intake structure for irrigation. Flash floods threaten the riverain towns and cause scour of banks. A prolongation of the period of low flow in the river occurs, equally deterimental as the floods, inasmuch as agricultural production suffers from lack of water, navigation becomes impossible and waste products of man, animals and industries are no longer removed properly, jeopardizing even a minimum of hygiene.

It is not only the supply of water that was the reason for settlement. Of course, a large number of aspects jointly led towards the preference of people to live near the rivers. There are the easy transport facilities offered by the river, free of charge and cheap to be used. There is existence of a reasonably flat land at the side of the river, the so called **flood-plain**, that has fertile soils and lends itself very well for agriculture, cattle grazing etc.; the thick humus layer and the very small terrain slopes guarantee a natural conservation of the soil. On the other hand, floods occur regularly, so that the flood plains cannot be fully possessed by man; it is part of the river and as such untouchable.

With the progress of civilization, the riverain population becomes more educated, increasing their production and diversifying their interests. They discover and exploit other uses of the river: it proves to be a source for irrigation water, for energy, for building materials like sand or clay for brick manufacture, for cooling their industrial plants, and finally even for recreation. With such a wealth of gifts which nature endows the people, it can only be expected that man enjoys his good life and riches and develops his society. Such development takes place in two dimensions, viz., in an increase of population and increase of demands of each individual member of the population. As a consequence, more and more use is made of the **Great Resource of Life**, the river. Water is extracted and consumed, which for a great part then evaporates and does not return back to the river. The flood plain, more and more turned into agricultural land, is used also to erect cattle stables, to build small factories and even to establish whole townships which frequently suffer damage through floods, so that people demand the flood plain as their full and inalienable property and want to chase the river away. The drainage basin, hitherto covered with thick vegetation, is deforestated so that it can no longer keep the rainwater stored, and neither resist erosion; factories start to discharge their ever increasing waste products into the river thence gradually turning it into a sewer rather than a healthy supply of clean water and fish.

As long as people behave themselves, taking cognizance of the Natural laws that rule the phenomenon the river is a **friend**. But if the balance is interfered with unwisely, the consequences become manifest; they inevitably turn the river into an **enemy**, which we have to combat for our survival, and in many cases it becomes a battle forever.

In order to understand better the complexities of this delicate balance an effort has to be made to analyse the various elements that together make up the phenomenon called RIVER and also to give a quantitative indication of these natural laws that govern the river's behaviour. Without sufficient knowledge of these elements and laws, human interference in the river may be disastrous. A thorough insight on the other hand may result in enhancing potentiality and eliminate disadvantages.

Advantages

The advantages of any river cannot be ever overemphasised for the people living in the river basin. Besides water supply for domestic use, irrigation, industrial use; river flow helps in waste disposal, hydropower production and recreation activities. The sediment deposited is a great supplier of building material and also fertilizes the flood plains. Navigation has been an age-old advantage provided by the rivers. River water fish is considered to be a delicacy. Overall development of plain area along the river banks is a historical reality.

Disadvantages

Though never rivers were visualised as disadvantageous to mankind, due to human interference some disadvantages have creeped in. Scouring and deposition at wrong places, erosion of humus from basin, damage to structures, flood salinity, pollution etc. have degraded the environment in the river basins.

USE OF RIVERS AND THEIR MAIN FUNCTIONS

The use of rivers should be seen in terms of river basin development. This view has come during the last seventy years and has been found to be a technical tool for achieving social change.

The river systems of the world flow today with only a small portion of their total volume harnessed and applied for human good. Development implies some physical changes in stream flow mostly the regulation of river flow by storage, diversion, or land management so that the water is available when and where needed, rather than as dictated by natural fluctuations over days, seasons and years. The engineering means-dams, diversion structures, water spreading devices are available to carry out such regulation in most of the cases.

Physical limits to river water regulation can be estimated with modest accuracy. The total amount of hydropower which a stream is capable of generating can be calculated as it is a function of volume of natural flow and fall. It is possible, as well to calculate the total of land which may be irrigated from a stream, if fully regulated, taking into account the consumptive use made by crops and also used by animal and human population. However, the amount of non-consumptive use for urban purpose is very high as more than 90 percent of water employed in a municipal system is returned to the stream or aquifer, but with some change in its chemical quality. The theoretical limit to the amount of non-consumptive use for urban purpose is very high, so long as appropriate means of treatment and recycling are available. Similar considerations apply to the use of water for navigation, wildlife, and recreational purposes, though evaporation and transpiration losses are sometimes heavy. Every stream, accordingly has a definite maximum potential output of hydroelectric power and maximum possible consumptive use.

Rivers' natural function has always been considered to collect water directly or indirectly originating from precipitation and to transport this water from higher elevation towards places with a relatively lower elevation, mostly the sea. Therefore, what is basically typical of a river is the presence of water which flows under the action of gravity. This water instead of flowing over the land as a sheet, tends to collect in a series of channels with a concentrated flow. Therefore, a river system may be defined as, "naturally formed channels through which water is discharged from the drainage basin to the sea".

However, much more is involved as the flowing water during its journey has the capability to transport particles originating from the erosion of the earth crust. All the rivers, without exception, will carry a greater or lesser amount of eroded particles called **sediment**. Part of the eroded material is soluble in water and will therefore be carried away by the flow in the form of a solution, which will not play any significant role in the process of river behaviour. The remaining solids move sliding, rolling or jumping over the river bed intermittently or continuously, suspended in the flow, temporarily or permanently deposited, exchanged against other particles and generally subjected to abrasion. These particles play a predominant role in the formation of river bed, banks and in appearance and characteristics of the river. They thus fulfil a major function of the river.

These two functions of the river, the **transport of water** and the **transport of sediment,** form the instruction of nature to which our rivers have to comply. Each of these functions is related to certain dynamic equilibrium in physical processes of our earth, the first function to what is called the **hydrologic cycle** which describes the perennial circular course of the water interchanging between the atmosphere and the earth, and the second function to the so called **erosion cycle** which deals with the geological phenomenon of mountain formation and mountain destruction.

THE HYDROLOGIC CYCLE

The endless circulation of water from atmosphere to the earth and its return to the atmosphere through processes like condensation, precipitation, evaporation and transpiration is called the hydrologic cycle. (Fig. 1.1)

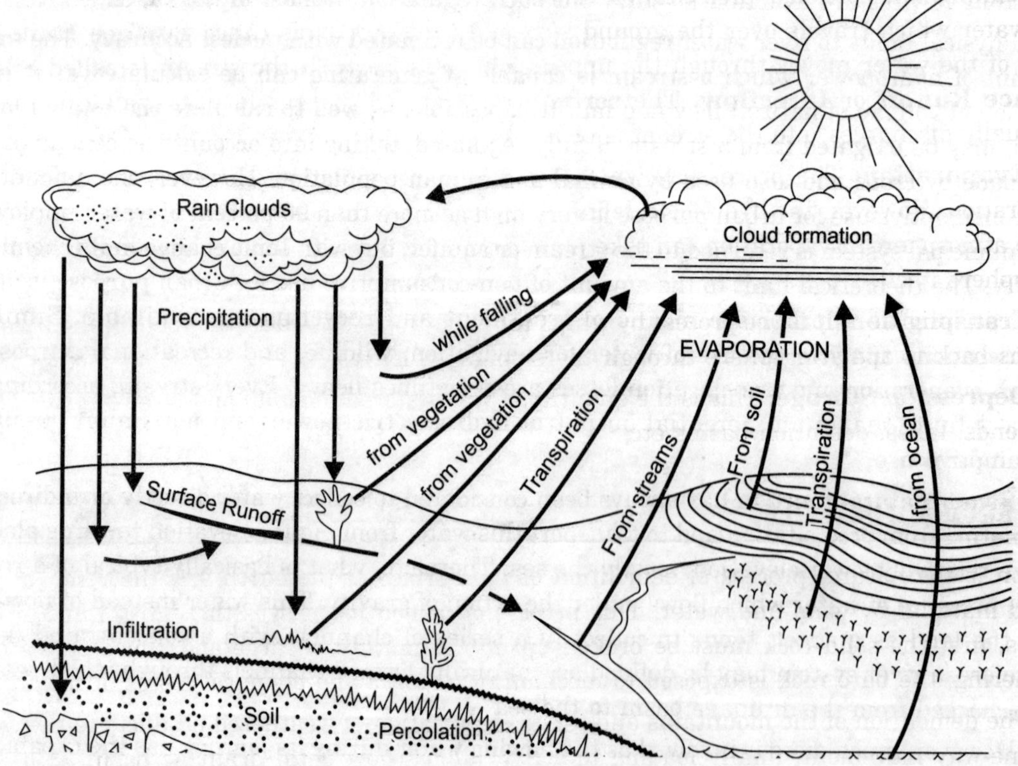

Fig. 1.1: The hydrologic cycle—a descriptive representation. (Ackermann, Colman, and Ogrosky.)

Heating of the ocean water by Sun is the key process that keeps the hydrologic cycle in motion. Water evaporates and then falls as precipitation in the form of rain, hail, snow, sleet or drizzle. On the way to earth some precipitation may evaporate or, when it falls over the land, be intercepted by vegetation before reaching the ground. The precipitation that reaches the land rejoins the cycle in three different ways: Evaporation and Transpiration, Infiltration and Percolation into the ground, and surface Runoff.

The hydrologic cycle is the heart of climate; it is the prime mover of the solar energy around the globe. Without the hydrologic cycle, the tropics would remain unbearably hot and the temperate zones eternally cold. It distributes the available heat and makes large part of the globe liveable.

Various Components of Hydrologic Cycle

As mentioned above, following is brief description of various components of hydrologic cycle.

Precipitation: This is major source of inflow and includes various forms like rain in liquid form and snow, hail etc. in solid form. It varies from time to time and place to place.

Interception: It is that part of precipitation which is intercepted by vegetation and other objects.

Infiltration: It is the process by which water enters the surface strata of the soil and after meeting the soil moisture deficiency percolates down to join the groundwater table.

Runoff: The portion of precipitation which appears in the surface streams is called runoff. The water which travels over the ground surface to the stream is called **Surface Runoff**. Some of the water moves through the upper soil layers to reach the stream is called **Sub-surface Runoff** or **Interflow.** The portion of water which percolates downwards deep eventually discharges into the stream is called **Base Flow** or **Groundwater Flow.**

Evaporation: The process by which liquid water is converted into vapour is called evaporation. However, the hydrologic definition of evaporation is 'net rate of vapour transport to the atmosphere'. Evaporation can take place from water bodies, land surface and from the atmosphere itself.

Transpiration: It is the process by which the moisture absorbed by the roots of the plants returns back to the atmosphere through the stomata of leaves.

Depression Storage: This is the quantity of water stored in small and large depressions like ponds, lakes, detention basins etc.

THE EROSION CYCLE

Erosion is the natural process of demolition of the surface of the earth and the removal of eroded material by wind and water. This process of demolition passes through a number of phases, first the solid rock must be broken up into a mixture of large and small pieces by weathering; the bare rock is exposed to mechanical, organic and chemical forces of nature.

The demolition of the mountains and the transportation of weathered products to the sea is a one-way movement, finally leading to a flat, almost horizontal drainage basin with no mountains or even hills. If this were indeed true, there would be no mountains on our planet.

However the earth is geologically still active, and now and then forms new rocks by uplift, which then causes the erosion to start anew.

The whole **erosion cycle** may take millions of years and during the erosion process the valley go through stages of differential development from youth, through maturity to old age. **Youth** is the period of formation of torrents. Water runs down the steep slopes of mountains and is concentrated into the existing folds. Due to the steep slope there is a high velocity and consequently large kinetic energy, large transport capacity and large erosive power. Such torrents scour the bed rock and form a channel. Gradually the length of the torrent increases as it cuts backwards into the hills; the slope decreases, transport capacity decreases and the rate of scouring also decreases until an equilibrium slope is reached. (Fig. 1.2) Then the walls of the valley are attacked. As the valley walls recede, the river gets space to meander. (Fig. 1.3) The slope of the valley sides is also flattened by erosion until equilibrium is reached and vegetation begins to take root.

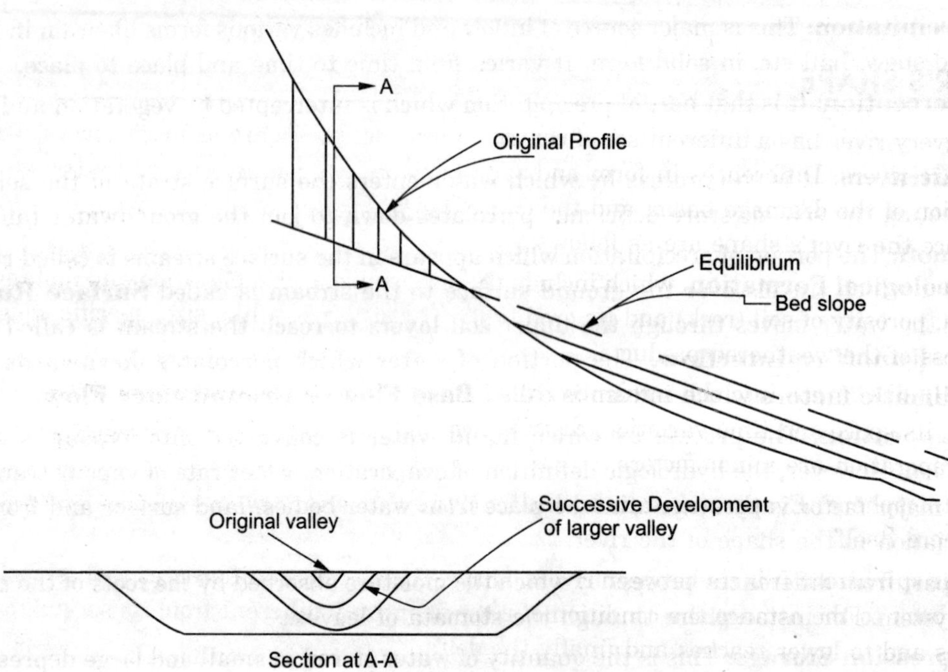

Fig. 1.2

In reality, however, the picture is much more complicated since there is not just one torrent but a whole network of torrents. They tend to produce an overall equilibrium situation with fully developed drainage pattern called **mature river valley**. Finally, it develops into a **Senile Valley** formation (or peneplain) where the whole landscape tends to become plain, with such a gentle slope that the capacity to transport sediment gets reduced to almost zero level. Consequently, it may take millions of years to reach final equilibrium. However, the nature does not leave the time to actually see such a final equilibrium situation because of new tectonic movement which causes a fresh start of the erosion process.

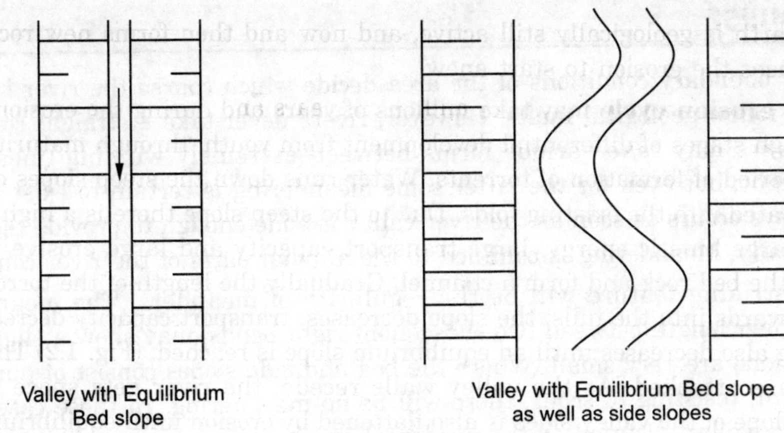

Fig. 1.3

RIVER'S SHAPE

Since every river has a different set of controlling factors, there are as many rivers shapes as there are rivers. Differences in form and type of rivers are mainly caused by the geological formation of the drainage basin, and the climate prevailing in the basin. Main factors which influence the river's shape are as follows:

Geological Formation, which include the size, shape, relief, elevation and distance from the sea, porosity of soil (rock) and its erodibility, characteristics like size, specific weight and hardness of the weathered products.

Climatic factors which influence river's shape are rainfall characteristics like intensity of rain, its space and time variation, distribution, duration and coverage. Temperature (frost) and evaporation are minor factors.

A major factor is the vegetation which has great influence on erosion is also responsible for variation in the shape of the river.

Apart from differences between rivers' shape, there are also differences within each single river system. For instance the condition of river is entirely different from its source to middle reaches and to lower reaches and finally the delta.

The shape of the river also changes with time in historic times, the river started as young river and in course of millions of years of its existence passes through maturity towards old age.

These changes which are governed by nature are more or less regular. Other differences can occur due to outside influences, mostly very irregularly. These include human influences and also climatic changes, tectonic forces causing upheavels, sea level alterations, etc.

It may, therefore, be concluded that the appearance of the river depends on a multitude of factors, each of which is subject to change in course of time.

RIVER'S COURSE

The orographic boundary conditions of the area decide which course the river has to follow. Roughly rivers follow geological faults. However, rivers never take a straight course. Within limitations, rivers may take various forms between extremely winding (meandering) or seemingly straight, but even for the latter some meandering is certain to exist. Meandering practically always occurs as soon as the river valley is wide enough to provide the freedom to move transversally. Meandering is confined to the alluvial parts of the river course only.

Here the striking feature will be the regularity of meanders. The meander length, indicating the river length between two subsequent right bends, may show a slight variation, but such variations are very small. Where the bed and side slopes consist of hard or atleast cohesive material, resisting to scour, there will be no meandering. In these cases the bends will indeed be irregular, dictated by the incidental and haphazardous erodibility of the stony banks.

The meander belt is much narrower than the valley, which implies that only a part of the valley is covered by the river channel. The rest simply is flood plain, a vast plane area inundated during times of high discharge. But this also implies that in the process of deposition in the lower course of the river only part of the valley is accreting through gradual deposition, leaving the rest of the valley low. This problem is solved by nature by sometimes suddenly shifting the whole channel to another part of the valley. In the long run, every part of the valley 'gets its turn'.

THE RIVER'S CROSS-SECTION

No two rivers can have the same cross-section. Also a river has different cross-section in different stretches. The cross-section also changes with time. However, in alluvial rivers some features are common. The shape of the cross-section in an alluvial river is indicated below. (Fig. 1.4)

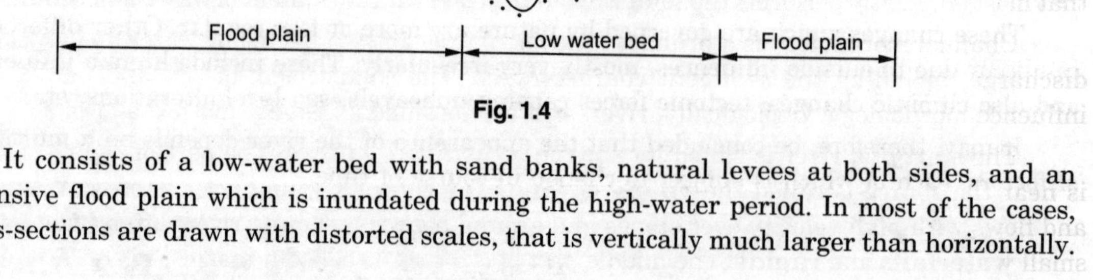

Fig. 1.4

It consists of a low-water bed with sand banks, natural levees at both sides, and an extensive flood plain which is inundated during the high-water period. In most of the cases, cross-sections are drawn with distorted scales, that is vertically much larger than horizontally.

CHAPTER 2

RIVER MORPHOLOGY

The term **river morphology** and its synonym fluvial **geomorphology** are used to describe the shapes of river channels and how they change over time. The morphology of a river channel is a function of a number of processes and environmental conditions including the composition and erodibility of the bed and banks (e.g., sand, clay, bedrock); vegetation and the rate of plant growth; the availability of sediment, the size and composition of the sediment moving through the channel; the rate of sediment transport through the channel and the rate of deposition on the floodplain, banks, bars and bed; and regional aggradation or degradation due to subsidence or uplift.

The science of geomorphology studies the forces that shape the earth surface at the present time. The word is formed from Greek words: **geo** (earth), **morph** (form or shape) and **logos** (study or knowledge).

There are several geological agents which work to shape the face of the earth: water, wind, ice, volcanos and Earthquakes. We as river group are mainly interested in the changes made by water as it flows down the stream channel.

Water, when rain deposits it on an upland, possesses energy in the form of **potential energy**. As the water begins to flow down hill, the potential energy gets converted into **Kinetic energy** or the energy of motion. This kinetic energy is used in eroding away the surface of stream channel and moving the sediments along the stream. Now geo-morphologists have begun to understand that the natural configuration or shape that the river gradually evolves is the one that most efficiently performs the total work of the river (the movement of water and sediment).

Channel morphology is a primary function of time and is affected by water and sediment discharge, including the sediment characterstics. The composition of bed and banks also influence morphology. Geologically, rivers can be classified as young, mature and old.

The start of a river is called its **source** or its **head waters**. The part of the river that is near the source is called the **young** or **youthful river.** A young river is often V-shaped and flows with high velocity over stones and around big rocks. Young rivers often have lots of small **waterfalls** and **rapids**. The middle part of the river is called a **mature river**. A mature river makes a riverbed that is U-shaped. It might be quite deep and run fast. It sweeps over small rocks and boulders, and makes big turns around hills and mountains. It is much wider than a **young river** but not as wide as an **old river.** As the river further flow over flat land, the river becomes wider and slower. A wide slow river is called an **old river**. An old river often floods across the land after there is lots of rain at the headwaters. An old river slowly builds up its banks (levees). It also meanders (twists and turns), and after the floods often leaves lakes behind which are called **oxbows** or **billabongs.** Finally the river ends flowing into an ocean, a lake or a bigger river. The place where the river flows out into a bigger body of water is called the **mouth** of the river. The shape of the mouth depends upon the condition of sea into which it flows. An **estuary** is formed if the sea has strong tides. Sometimes, river flows slowly through sandy or muddy land making lots of small islands as it flows. The mainstream of the river gets broken into many parts that spread out into triangle shape like the Greek letter **Delta (Δ)**. When it happens it is called **Delta of the river**. Deltas are not suitable for human habitation but are very good for birds and other wildlife as well as fishing. Often they are developed as wildlife reserves. The famous deltas are those of Nile, Amazon, Mekong, Mississippi, Danube and Ganga rivers.

Physical Characteristics of the Rivers: Different rivers and different reaches of the same river have different physical characteristics. While a great many factors affect the channel form directly, others affect it indirectly. Lane first identified the most important variables. According to him these factors are not independent but interrelated. These include-stream Discharge, Longitudinal slope, Sediment load and Sediment size, Bed and Banks resistance on flowing water, Vegetation, Temperature, Geology and Human interference.

In practice rivers frequently show complex combinations of various morphological elements. However, stream discharge is the most obvious factor in determining the stream form. Not only the magnitude of the discharge but also its fluctuation is responsible for channel form. The longitudinal slope is set largely by geology and topography of the area. Slope is also related to sediment size. The configuration of the channel cross section and the alignment of the stream are affected by the sediment load and pattern of deposition.

Channel Configuration: River alignment can be categorised in three basic types and their combinations. These are briefly discussed below:

(1) Straight Channels: These usually relatively short reaches and are transitory because even minor irregularities in shape or alignment or a temporary obstruction can create local disturbance that would set up a transverse flow leading to meandering. Straight reaches have negligible sinuosity (the ratio between the Thalweg length and Valley length) at bankful stage. At low stages there are sand-bars along the bank and the Thalweg (points joining the lowest bed levels along the length) meanders in a sinuous path around Sand bars (Fig. 2.1).

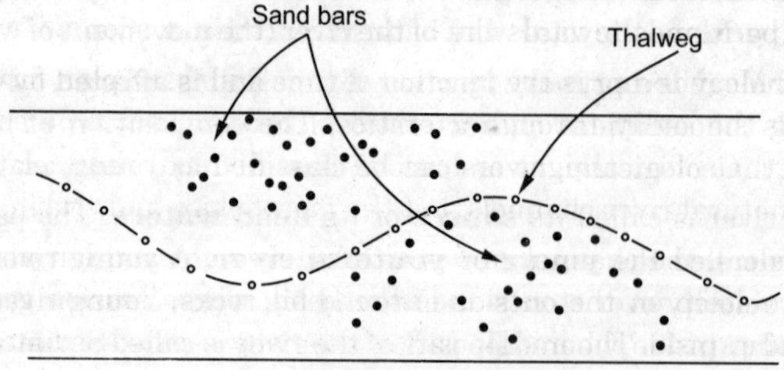

A Typical Straight Channel

Fig. 2.1

(2) **Meandering Channels:** The word meander originates from the river Maeander (Buyuk Menderes) of South West Turkey, which clearly shows the winding course characteristic of a meandering river (Fig. 2.2). The meandering rivers, in plan consists of a series of bends of alternate curvature connected by straight crossing reaches. In these channels, the longitudinal slope is usually relatively flat. Meandering channels are unstable as the banks cave in the downstream reaches of concave bends. There are deep pods in the bends and high velocity along the outer concave Bank. Depths in crossings are relatively shallow compared to bends.

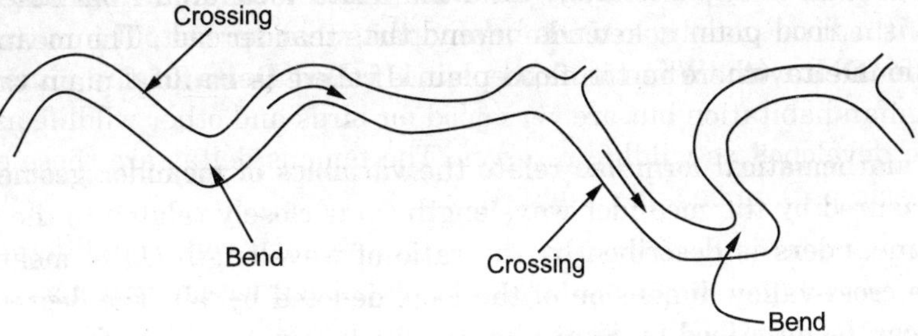

Fig. 2.2: A Typical Meandering River

(3) **Braided Channels:** A braided channels is one which flows in two or more channels around alluvial islands. (Fig. 2.3) Normally there are numerous channels. The stream is wide and the banks are poorly defined and unstable. At low flows there are two or more main channels which cross each other, subsidiary channels, sand bars and islands. At high flows most bars are inundated.

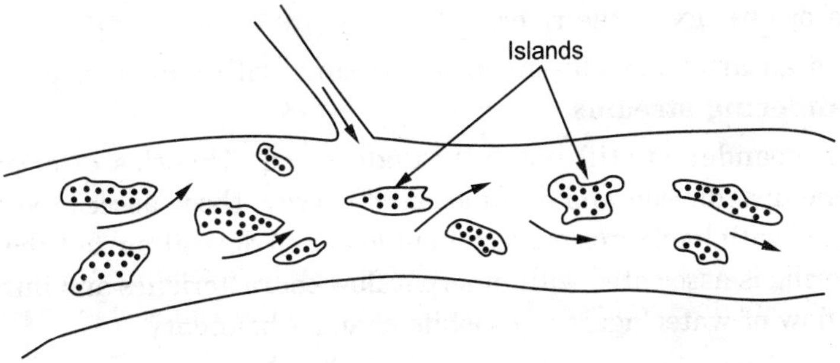

Fig. 2.3: A Typical Braided Channel

Such rivers have relatively steeper slopes and carry a large sediment load. The main stream is deflected by islands towards the banks and cause erosion.

Meandering: Meandering is the term used to describe the plan form of a river channel whose course winds smoothly through a series of bends. This type of pattern is usually distinguished from that of a straight or braided (i.e., divided) channel. Meandering is very common feature of natural river channels, but the morphology and stability of meanders vary.

In river meanders, the channel curves alternately right and left about the down-valley direction. Banks are steep on the outside of the bend, where erosion generally takes place, and are gently sloping inside where deposition normally occurs. Sediment deposited on the inside of the bend forms a **point bar**. The plan form of a meander is frequently characterized as a smooth, symmetrical loop, often as a sine-generated form. However, in practice asymmetric and compound forms are very common.

In contrast to sine-waves, the loops of a meandering stream are more nearly circular. The curvature varying from a maximum at the apex to zero at a crossing point, also called an inflection, because the curvature changes direction in that vicinity. As the loop is not ideal, additional information is needed to characterize it.

A loop at the apex has an outer or **convex** bank and an inner or **concave** bank. The meander belt is defined by an average meander width measured from outer bank to other bank. If there is a flood plain it extends beyond the meander belt. The meander is then free and it can be found anywhere in the flood plain. If there is no flood plain the meanders are fixed.

Various mathematical formulae relate the variables of meander geometry. The size of meanders, measured by the meander wavelength (λ) is closely related to the river discharge. The shape of meanders is described by the ratio of wavelength (λ) to meander breadth or amplitude (the cross-valley dimension of the loop, denoted by 'a'). The degree of meandering for any reach can be described by Sinuosity and Tortuosity.

$$\text{Sinuosity} = \frac{\text{Thalweg Length}}{\text{Valley Length}}$$

$$\text{Tortuosity} = \frac{\text{Thalweg Length} - \text{Valley Length}}{\text{Valley Length}}$$

These parameters of meanders are influenced by the erodibility of the materials of banks and by the **slope** or **energy** of the river.

According to an arbitrary classification streams with sinuosity greater than 1.5 are classified as **meandering streams.**

Why rivers meander is still not fully understood. Theories of origin include those associated with the distribution and dissipation of energy, those associated with helical flow, and those associated with bank erosion, sediment load and deposition, but the consensus seems to be that meandering is associated with inherent flow characteristics and intrinsic instabilities in the turbulent flow of water against a mobile channel boundary.

The pattern of meanders is characterized by three parameters meander length (wavelength λ), meander belt (amplitude a) and width (w). The meander pattern is normally not stationary but moves downstream slowly. In moving down it may change its meander length and meander belt.

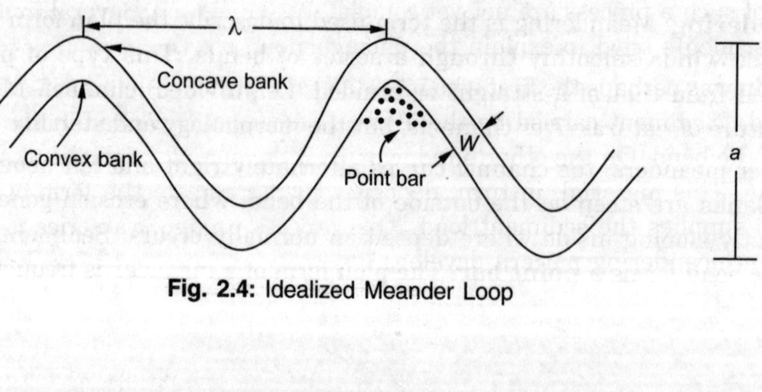

Fig. 2.4: Idealized Meander Loop

REASONS OF MEANDERING

Several investigators have performed laboratory experiments to observe how meanders are initiated and how they get developed in alluvial streams.

Early experiments showed that, under constant conditions, meanders tend to develop a stable, equilibrium form. Classically, river meanders have been represented as migrating in the down valley direction while retaining their equilibrium form. Irregularities of form and occurrence of cutoffs were thought to be caused by variations in bank material. Some river meanders have very low rates of erosion and are now stable. Though they must have been active at some time in the past to have created the meandering pattern. Other meanders exhibit much more active processes, resulting in movement of channel over time. Some of these meanders migrate in orderly manner, but others have been found to evolve in form, with a tendency to become more asymmetric and compound in pattern overtime.

The rate of change in a meandering river reflects the relative strengths of force and resistance in the bed and banks. The forces are influenced not only by the amount of water and the gradient of the reach but also by the pattern of currents within the bend. The pattern of currents was originally represented as a spiral or helicoidal flow, but more complex cells of circulation have since been identified which can influence the distribution of erosion and deposition.

Bank erosion can take place by a number of mechanisms, but it occurs mainly by undercutting the bank through direct removal of material by the river, after which blocks of material fall from the bank. Banks composed of silts, sands and gravels are much more easily eroded than those with high clay content or composed of bed rock.

Deposition takes place in the meander where the energy of flow is insufficient to carry the size or amount of sediment in transport. Coarser material is deposited first. A decrease in sediment size is commonly evident downstream and across the bar. The form and stability of meanders is also a function of the amount and size of sediment transported into a bend from upstream.

While the meander pattern moves downstream slowly, the meander length and belt width may change. In a few cases the meanders grow laterally. As meanders grow a narrow neck is formed, which is often cut through from two sides thus causing the stream to straighten its course. The ends of the meander that have been cut off are likely to be choked with sediment. Water from the main stream seeps into this meander loop and forms what is known as **Oxbow Lake**.

As already mentioned the exact conditions under which a stream meanders and the exact mechanism of such a process are not yet completely understood. Several investigators, on the basis of experiments tried to explain the phenomenon.

Friedkin was perhaps the first who in 1945 performed experiments in a 15m long channel. He concluded, "Sediment carried by the alluvial stream is deposited in the form of a bar at the inside of the bend. On the other hand, caving of the outside of the bend supplies sediment to the stream. This material, in turn, deposits downstream in the form of a bar and bank, caving again supplies the sediment load. This process produces a series of bends along the stream, i.e., a meandering pattern develops."

Inglis in 1949, on the basis of experiments conducted in 36m long tray found, "the process of meandering starts when the stream is overloaded with sediment". Agarwal on conducting experiments in a rectangular channel indicated, "presence of disturbances induce secondary circulation which lead to meandering over the entire length of the channel".

The experiments mentioned above (Friedkin, Inglis and Agarwal) all show that the meander pattern as a whole slowly moves downstream. This tendency has been observed in all the alluvial rivers of the world including Ganga (India), Misisssippi (USA) and Red River (USA). In some rivers however, this phenomena is not very clear. In these cases there is **free meandering** or the gradual lateral enlargement of loops. The examples are river Pembina (Canada) and Tigris (Iraq).

The theories propogated by Friedkin and Inglis also gave some additional conclusions as follows,

- The Meander length (l) and Meander belt (a) increase with increase in the discharge and the slope of the bed.
- The Meander pattern depends upon the sediment load which may cause aggradation or degradation and hence change in slope.
- Changes in the bed and bank material also affect the Meander pattern.

Theories Related to Meandering: Various theories have been put forward to explain the phenomenon of meandering. However, none of these theories has universal acceptance. A brief mention is made here of the available theories.

(1) **Stochastic Theory:** According to Scheidegger (2004), "the meander train is the result of the Stochastic fluctuations of the direction of flow due to the random presence of direction-changing obstacles in the river path."

(2) **Equilibrium Theory:** In the equilibrium theory meanders decrease the stream gradient until an equilibrium between the erodibility of the stretch and the transport capacity of the stream is reached. A mass of water descending must give up **potential energy**, which is used by interaction with the material of the stream bed. The shortest distance; that is, a straight channel, results in the highest energy per unit length, disrupting the banks more, creating more sediment and aggrading the stream. The presence of meanders allows the stream to adjust the length to an equilibrium energy per unit length in which the stream carries away all the sediment it produces.

(3) **Geomorphic/Morphotectonic Theory:** Geomorphic refers to the surface structure of the terrain. Morphotectonic means having to do with deeper, or tectonic (plate) structure of the rock. The features included under these categories are not random and guide streams into non-random paths. They are predictable obstacles that instigate meander formation by deflecting the stream. For example, the stream might be guided into a fault line.

(4) **Earth's Rotation Theory:** According to Gilbert the force produced by earth rotation (called coriolis force) is sufficient to deflect the stream. However, this theory does not get enough support as the force due to earth's rotation is usually very small. Neu has shown that secondary circulation is developed due to earth's rotation, due to which stream may deviate. Part of this deviation may be due to circulation naturally present in the river and not due to earth's rotation.

(5) **Disturbance Theory:** Small disturbances caused in an otherwise straight channel cause asymmetry in flow which might lead to meandering. Werner postulated that meanders are initiated by some disturbance which in turn, starts transverse oscillation in the straight alluvial stream. The transverse oscillation from one bank to the other starts erosion and the first bend forms. This bend often creates sufficient disturbance for the downstream channel and the process once started continues. Werner and Matthes also expressed the concept mathematically.

(6) **Helicoidal – Flow Theory:** Any disturbance which may cause secondary flow or secondary circulation can lead to meandering. The secondary flow is known as Helicoidal flow. The secondary flow has to become unsymmetrical before it could produce meandering. Meandering can occur with a symmetrical secondary flow pattern if the resisting characterstics of bank material change along the length of the stream. Even in straight channels meandering occurs since secondary flow is present which becomes asymmetrical due to friction or obstructions.

(7) **Excess Energy Theory:** Like equilibrium Theory, it assumes that process of meandering is related to the energy content of the stream. According to Schoklitsch, "meander formation might be due to the fact that the slope in such stretches is too great and is not in equilibrium with the size of bed sediment grains." In the same way Inglis asserts, "meandering is nature's way of damping out excess energy during a wide range of varying flow conditions, the pattern depending on the grade of material, the relation between discharge and sediment load and their rate of change." From the above we may conclude, "a channel having excess energy (steeper slope) tries to increase its length by meandering thereby decreasing its slope."

Joglekar contended that not the excess energy but the excess sediment load is the primary cause of meandering. Leopold and Wolman did not agree to the theory of excess sediment load as the main cause of meandering.

(8) **Instability Theory:** Quick argued, "meandring is an instability phenomenon which tends to be self-exaggerating. His main contention is that meandering is due to cyclic change in the direction of rotation of streamwise secondary flow. Erosion occurs when secondary rotation has a downward component of the velocity of the stream boundary and deposition occurs when it has an upward component."

The analysis to evaluate planform is carried out by using equations of motion and continuity equation for water and sediment. Many researchers' works have led to several quantitative criteria for plan forms.

As earlier mentioned, none of these has been substantiated by available data. The empirical criterion still appear to be the most satisfactory means of predicting the plan form.

Bed Level Variation in Alluvial Streams: River alongwith water have to carry sediment. In the process there is erosion and deposition of sediment. There are therefore changes in bed level. These changes may be local or may extend over a long reach. Aggradation and degradation, silting of reservoirs, channel scouring during floods, local scour around structures and in bends are examples of such changes.

The rate of sediment transport is a function of Shear Stress (frictional resistance of bed and sides) on the bed, an increase in shear stress initiates scour and causes a sediment outflow in excess of sediment inflow. On the other hand, if the shear stress is reduced, sediment deposit will take place.

Changes in Bed of Stream during Floods: It has been observed in some rivers that the bed level rises during the floods, while the bed was lowered after the flood receded. However, on a few other streams exactly opposite happenings have been recorded. These changes are normally very rapid.

An example is that of San Juan River (USA) as reported by Leopold and Maddock (Fig. 2.5)

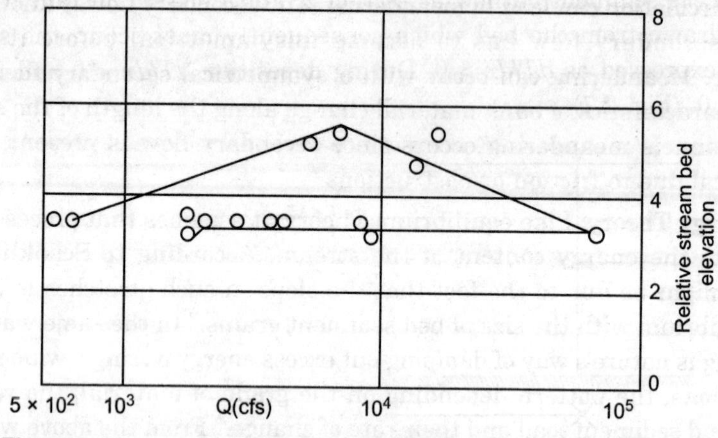

Fig. 2.5: Changes in Stream Bed Elevation of San Juan River (USA)

In the figure, it can be seen that upto a certain discharge the river bed rises, after which the bed got lowered and finally during the falling stage, the bed level was fairly constant.

As against this type of deposition and scour, in the river Rio Grande (USA), bed scoured during the rising stage and the bed elevation rose during the falling stage. (Fig. 2.6)

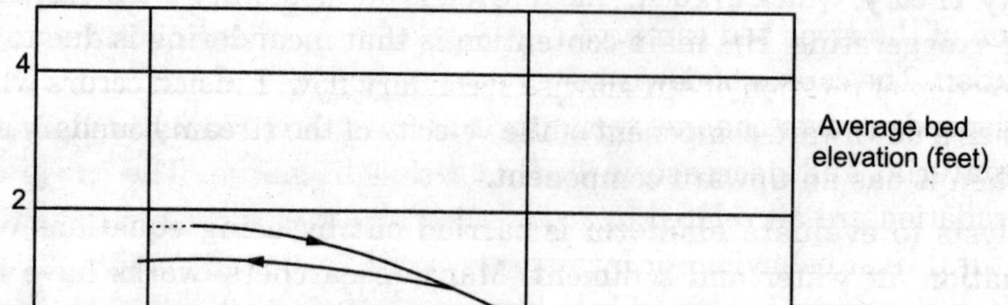

Fig. 2.6: Changes in Stream Bed Elevation in River Rio Grande (USA)

It has been found that the changes in bed level are associated with the changes in the suspended sediment concentration. Whenever, the amount of suspended load brought into a given reach from the upstream reaches was less than its capacity, channel scoured, whereas when the incoming load was greater than its capacity, the channel bed rose.

The study on various rivers in USA, China and other countries revealed that (i) the bed was scoured at bridges where the presence of piers narrowed the section. (ii) the stream bed elevation rose due to deposition where the river was wide. Obviously, in narrowed section where sub-critical flow exists the velocity increases and hence the capacity to carry sediment also increases, reverse occurs in wider sections.

Scour and Deposition: The bed of the stream serves as buffer, in which surplus sand can be stored or from which shortages are borrowed, which is nothing else than an explanation for deposition and scour. The continuity in case of sediment transport is found in changes in bed elevation (degradation or aggradation).

Considering a small reach of the stream of length Δx, in which T_1 is the transport at section 1 and T_2 is sediment outflow at section 2. For a specific instant if $T_2 > T_1$, extra sediment is withdrawn from the bed which consequently must scour, the scour criterion, therefore, can be expressed as $dT/dx > 0$. During deposition $dT/dx < 0$ and for equilibrium condition $dT/dx = 0$. (Fig. 2.7)

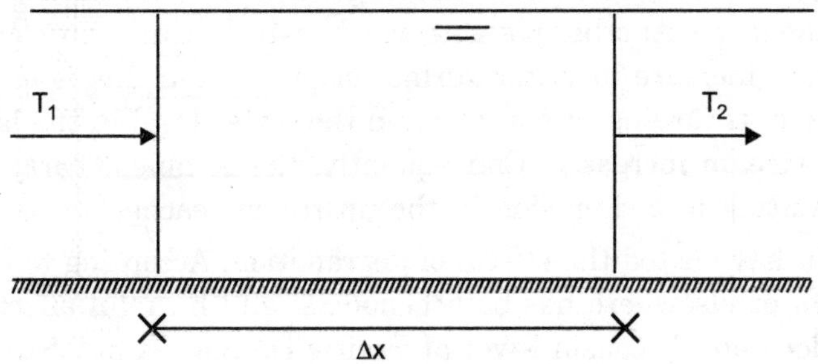

Fig. 2.7

Degradation: Degrading refers to the lowering of a fluvial surface, such as a stream bed or a flood plain, through erosional process. Degradation is characteristic of channel networks in which either bedrock erosion is taking place or in systems that are sediment starved and are therefore entraining more material than is being deposited.

Degradation of the river bed can proceed downstream or upstream depending upon the cause of degradation. The causes of downstream progressing degradation are primarily related to changes in independent river channel variables, such as increase in water discharge, decrease in size of bed material and decrease in bed material discharge. The cause of upstream progressing degradation are all related to an imposed increase in river slope which can occur as a result of natural river behaviour or by man-made changes. Study of various case histories indicates that river slopes are increased by lowering a base level, by decreasing the length of a river, or by removal of a control point. Case histories also show that both downstream and upstream progressing degradation can act in combination along a river system; downstream progressing degradation along the main stream of a river system can initiate upstream progressing degradation on a tributary.

The rate and extent of riverbed degradation resulting from sediment interruption are determined by means of computer based numerical experiments. Momentum and continuity equations for water and sediment flows in a wide prismatic channel are solved numerically using a model for the bed armouring process. The changes in mean bed levels and mean sediment size and the length of degradation, are correlated by multiple regression analysis to the independent dimensionless variables. The depth of degradation depends upon the Froude Number, the geometric standard deviation and the normalised median size of the bed material. The results of analysis are verified with the field data of Missouri River (USA).

Degradation occurs very commonly downstream of large capacity reservoirs when a large percentage of incoming sediment is trapped in the reservoir and practically clear water flows downstream. Degradation also occurs near the confluence of two rivers. Tributaries are in general, steeper than the main stream and carry less discharge. For instance, after regulation of flow in the main stream due to construction of a dam, degradation starts and this results in a chain reaction. Because of the degradation in the main river, the slope of the tributary increases. Therefore, the tributary will acquire sediment carrying capacity in excess of the incoming sediment load. Hence the tributary goes on degrading until the sediment load is equal to the sediment transport capacity. At times this effect extends to sub-tributaries too.

Degradation also starts if the water discharge in a stream is increased, sediment load and size remaining the same. Another possible way by which equilibrium gets disturbed so as to cause degradation is increase in water surface slope, though this is observed rarely. This may happen if a stream is flowing into a lake and the water level in the lake falls, the water surface slope of the stream increases. Consequently, the sediment carrying capacity of the stream increases resulting in bed erosion in the upstream reaches.

Garde and Raju have listed the effects of degradation. According to them, "Degradation downstream of a dam or elsewhere has both beneficial and harmful effects." Their theory is based on the study done on Wisconsin River at Prairie Du Sac Dam (USA) and Saalach River (Munich). These are discussed below–

(i) For a given discharge, the tail-water level is lowered as a result of degradation. In case a hydraulic jump is formed below the spillway, the lowering of tail-water will result in moving of hydraulic jump downstream. It may happen that the hydraulic jump moves beyond the apron and hence endanger the safety of the dam.

(ii) In case of dams on pervious foundation, the lowering of tail water increases the effective head (difference between head and tail water levels). Thus increasing the uplift pressure.

(iii) Increase in effective head provides greater head for power generation.

(iv) Lowering of the stream bed by degradation increases the capacity of the river channel to carry the flood flow, thereby lowering the high flood level of the river. Creating artificial degradation by constructing big reservoirs was suggested for Yellow River (China) and Kosi River (India).

(v) Lowering of water level due to degradation reduces the level of groundwater table in the adjoining areas.

(vi) Lowering of water level may expose pile foundations of bridges, abutment and other structures to atmosphere and this may lead to their deterioration.

(vii) Degradation also causes lowering of water level at the existing irrigation intakes and thus makes the diversion of water for irrigation difficult.

(viii) Degradation may cause substantial lowering of the bed in navigable rivers and in extreme cases locks may become inoperative.

BED MATERIAL COMPOSITION AND DEGRADATION

The bed material, its size and composition have considerable effect on the process of degradation. The ability to erode and transport sediment depends upon the hydraulic characteristics like depth and slope of the stream. The sediment size, on the other hand, determines the resistance to such erosive action.

Let us consider the case of clear water flowing in a stream with **uniform** bed material and having relatively steep slope. Due to its steeper slope more material will be picked up from the upstream portions of the stream and relatively less from the downstream reaches; this results in flattening of the bed slope. This decrease in slope is affected by rotation of the stream bed profile about some control section in the stream, where the water level is kept almost constant. This control section can be a downstream reservoir, sea, gulf, lake, a rock lodge or a sill specially erected for the purpose, where the stream finally discharges. (Fig. 2.8) It can also be an erosion- free reach of the channel with a stable Stage - Discharge relation. Ultimately, the slope will flatten to such an extent that everywhere along the channel the shear stress is critical and sediment movement ceases. This type of degradation of the bed is known as **rotational degradation**.

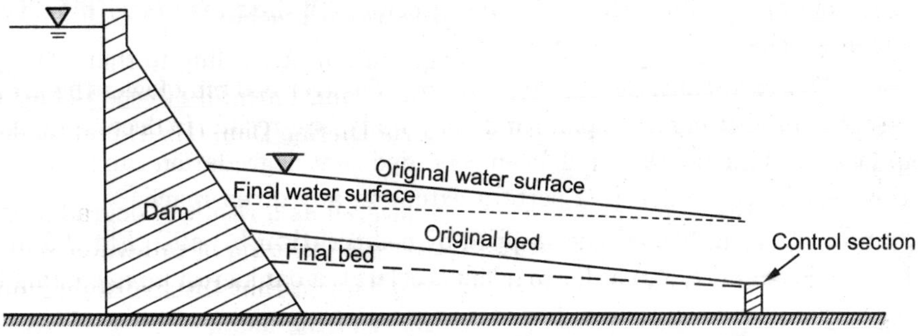

Fig. 2.8: Definition Sketch of for Degradation (Grade-Raju)

Let us now consider the case of clear water flowing in a stream whose bed is composed of **non-uniform** material and the shear stress is such that all the particles are moving. In such cases rotational degradation takes place and the shear stress gradually reduced. However, when the shear stress becomes equal to critical shear stress (τ_c) for the d_{80} or the d_{90} size, the very coarse bed material cease to move and gets accumulated on the bed. Further rotation of the bed stops and the degradation then takes place at nearly constant slope. This is known as **parallel degradation**. As the time passes some more fine material is removed from the bed, but the coarser material settles over the fine layer. The layer of the coarser material is termed as **armour coat**, which ultimately prevents further degradation.

Estimation of Degradation: Various investigators (Tinney, Komura, Kuiper, Mustafa) have studied degradation by using equations of motion and continuity and also using resistance and sediment transport equations. Tinney combined Manning's equation and Du Boys' bed load equation with the continuity equation for sediment for the case of constant discharge and obtained an expression for $\frac{\partial z}{\partial t}$. (z is bed level elevation)

Knowing the initial bed and water surface slopes, one can use the finite difference method to compute the bed profile after time Δt. However, this analysis has a serious drawback that it does not take into account the gradual **coarsening** of material that takes place due to removal of finer material. This also causes the change in resistance offered by the bed during the process of degradation.

Considering the coarsening with time and variation in channel width, important work was done by Kamura and Simon. Prior to this Garde and Hasan, and Gessler tried to predict final bed profile to which the bed will degrade. They made probabilistic analysis as well as conducted experiments to get the final slope and the final depth. Effort was also made to ascertain the nature and thickness of the armour coat required to stabilize the channel bed. Einstein found that an effective armour coat against a flow is developed if a layer of non-transportable particles, one particle thick, covers approximately sixty percent of the bed surface.

Observation, reveal that the final stabilized condition is generally obtained after a long period of degradation. Therefore, transient bed profile is also necessary to be evaluated. Garde and associates on the basis of experiments have shown that coarsening of bed takes place at a fast rate in the beginning, but the process slows down in the final stages prior to reaching of the equilibrium condition. Important contributions were also made by Ilo, Ashida and Michiue to evaluate transient bed profiles. However, the agreement of their results with field conditions has not yet been checked.

Control of Degradation: Severe degradation of a river bed may lower the groundwater table, endanger the stability of bridge piers and quay walls, and results in decreased navigational depth in ship locks and harbours. It has been conceded that degradation cannot be completely stopped. It can only be controlled to a certain extent in any given reach.

Degradation of a river bed can be stopped by bed **fixation** by sills. (Fig. 2.9) In addition banks may have to be stabilized in order to avoid accelerated bank erosion. According to Vanoni channel after degrading to an armoured bed of coarser material (Cobbles and gravel), accelerates bank erosion which subsequently needs stabilization measures. When armouring effects accompany degradation it may be possible to reach the final stage by supplying a sufficient amount of coarse material to the channel reach concerned.

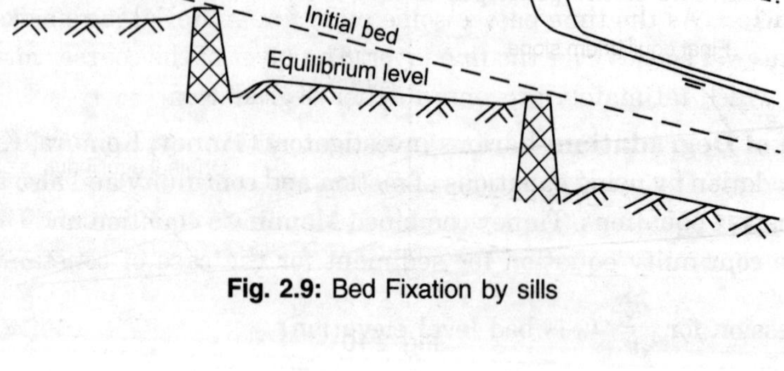

Fig. 2.9: Bed Fixation by sills

Construction of fixed weirs also offers a possibility for stopping degradation since fixed weirs are energy-absorbing structures which decrease the capacity of the flow to transport sediments. These can be applied mainly in head waters and reaches without shipping, especially in cases where accelerated erosion might result in unfavourable sedimentation downstream. They are built in series and their crest level and mutual distances can be determined by an optimization procedure.

Storage of water in a large reservoir results in reduction of flood discharges downstream of the reservoir. The resulting reduced flood flows are not able to transport the coarse material brought into the stream by its tributaries downstream of the dam. This coarse material get deposited in the stream channel and cause an aggrading condition which offsets degradation.

In many rivers of Indian sub-continent, it has been observed that after a few years of degradation, aggradations of the river starts and many times causes the river bed to rise above the original bed. This is according to Garde and Raju, is due to many reasons, prominent among these being,

(i) Opening of barrage gates in summer to flush large amount of sediment into the downstream of stream channel and

(ii) Presence of irrigation intakes which draw comparatively clear water and thus disturb the sediment balance.

Aggradation: As has been already described that when the inflow of sediment from a certain reach is less than the outflow of sediment, deposition will occur and hence the river is aggraded. Aggradation is initiated in a reach of a stream depending upon the way in which equilibrium condition is disturbed.

Aggradation often occurs due to increase in the sediment load at a section without change in discharge and size of the sediment. This condition is explained by Garde and Raju. Referring to the figure 2.10 ACB is the original equilibrium bed profile. The sediment load is increased at C. As the stream between C and B cannot transport the increased sediment load with the prevailing slope, the excess material gets deposited thereby increasing the slope. With the passage of time the region where deposition takes place slowly moves downstream towards B, acquiring steeper slope represented by line C_3B which is able to transport increased sediment load. The changes between C and B also cause aggradation of upstream bed between A and C. As the bed rises at C, the water surface slope upstream decreases, causing deposition. Hence progressive deposition is observed upstream of C and a new equilibrium profile A_3C_3 parallel to AC will be formed. One of the principal causes of increased sediment load is landslides.

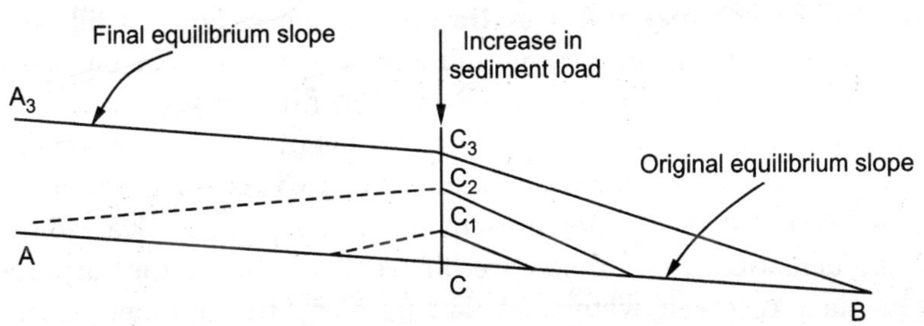

Fig. 2.10

Aggradation also occurs if the water level is suddenly raised at any section. This often happens resulting in silting of reservoirs. With the construction of a dam, a lake is formed on the upstream side of the dam. Because of backwater, the velocity gets reduced as the water flows towards the dam. The coarser material deposits first, farther away from the dam, while finer material is deposited closer to the dam. This process continues and the bed rises gradually. This, in its turn, will affect the slope of the backwater curve which will after sometime spread out. After a very long time the whole area will be filled with sediment. In the ultimate equilibrium, the new river bed will become parallel to its original situation. When this happens the bed load starts to move over the crest. In such case, there will be deposition downstream of the dam and the scouring process described earlier gets reversed. Also, as a result of delta formation at the mouth of a stream, aggradation occurs in the upstream reaches.

The successive stages of aggradation upstream of a reservoir are shown in the following figure 2.11. With continuous deposition of material on the bed the level rises to the top, parallel to original bed.

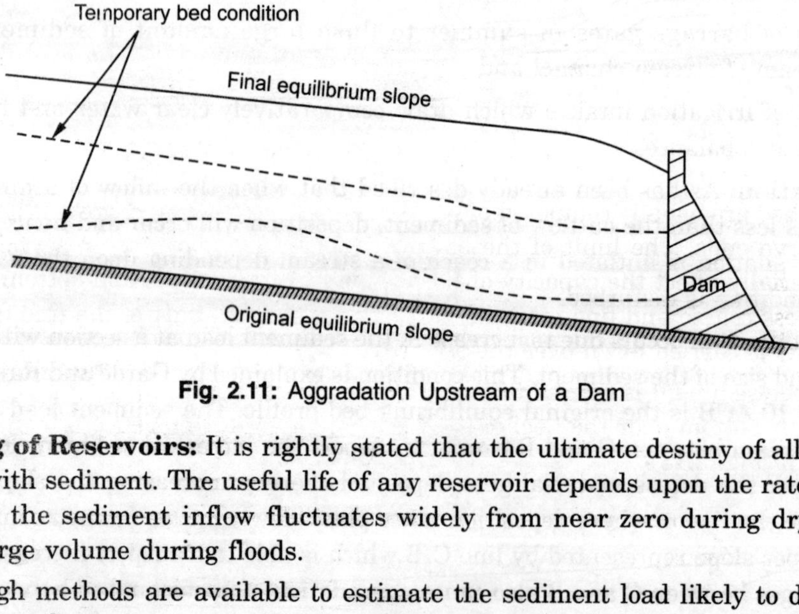

Fig. 2.11: Aggradation Upstream of a Dam

Silting of Reservoirs: It is rightly stated that the ultimate destiny of all reservoirs is to be filled with sediment. The useful life of any reservoir depends upon the rate of sediment inflow. Also, the sediment inflow fluctuates widely from near zero during dry weather to extremely large volume during floods.

Although methods are available to estimate the sediment load likely to deposit in the reservoir, the information is not enough as the main interest is in knowing the pattern of accumulation of sediment in the reservoir. The sediment distribution or deposition at different elevations of the reservoirs has to be estimated.

The stream carries some **suspended sediment** and moves larger solids along the stream bed as **bed load**. Since the specific gravity of sediment is about 2.65, the particles of suspended sediment tend to settle to the channel bottom but upward currents in the turbulent flow counteract this gravitational setting process. When sediment laden water reaches a reservoir, the velocity as well as turbulence are greatly reduced because of the increased cross-sectional area of the channel. Normally the water present in the reservoir is clear while the inflow is muddy (turbid), the densities of two fluids are different and hence the turbid water plunges directly under the clear reservoir water and flowing along the channel bottom towards the dam under the influence of gravity. This condition is known as **Stratified flow** and underflow is called **Density Current**. This results in the larger suspended particles and most of the bed load to get deposited as a **delta** at the head of the reservoir. The smaller particles however remain in suspension for a longer period and finally get deposited farther down the reservoir. The finest of the particles remain in suspension and find their way through outlets.

Earlier it was believed that sediment always deposits in the lower elevations of reservoir rather than over the full range of reservoir depth. Lane has discussed in details the manner in which sediment is deposited in the reservoir. He has divided the deposits into top-set beds, fore-set beds, bottom-set beds and density current deposits. (Fig. 2.12)

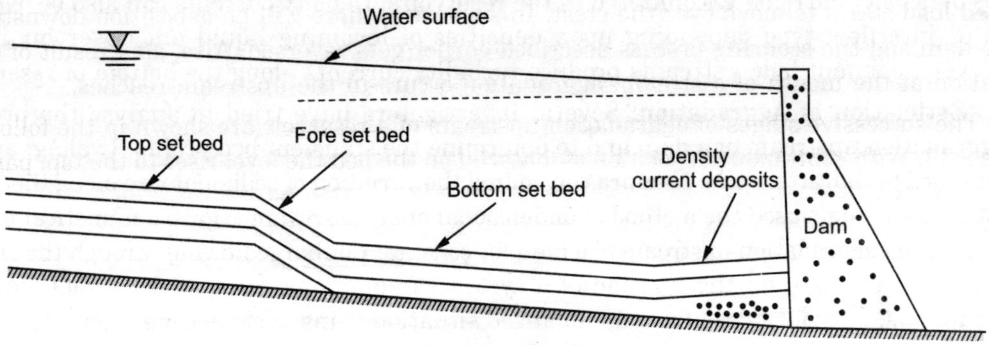

Fig. 2.12

Top set bed are usually composed of large size sediment and extend upto the point where backwater curve ends. The limit of the backwater being far above the reservoir level. This does not materially affect the capacity of the reservoir. Foreset beds and bottom set beds are composed of less coarse and fine material respectively. A large part of the fine material such as silt and clay is carried down over the spillway if retention time is small.

Where the sediment is carried in the form of density current, finer material is deposited on the reservoir bottom near the heel of the dam. The sediment deposits gradually settle and get compacted. (Fig. 2.13)

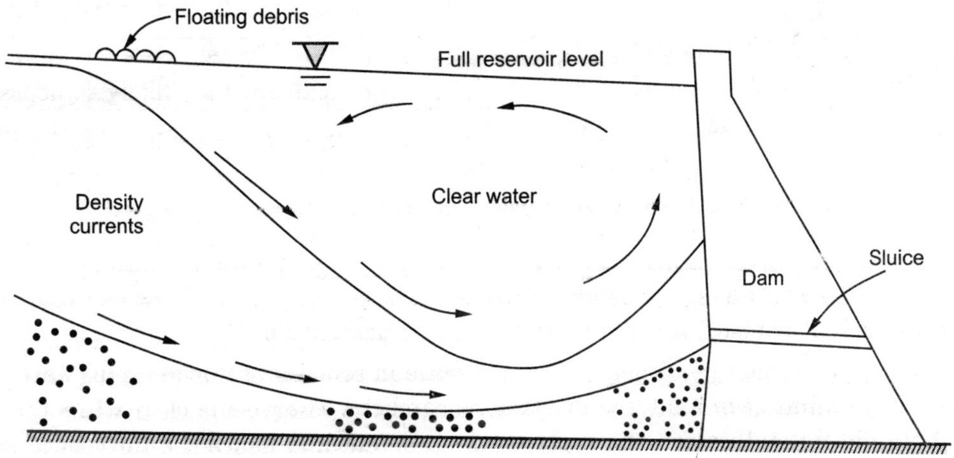

Fig. 2.13

Density currents: Bell has defined **density current** as the 'gravity flow of a fluid through, under or over a fluid of approximately equal density'. The difference in the mass densities of the two fluids is usually very small. Further, it is essential that two fluids are miscible and the density difference be a function of difference in temperature, salt content and/or sediment content of the two fluids.

A sediment laden inflow with density greater than the reservoir water descends to the lower water layers and moves there in the direction of the dam. Such underflows are common types of density currents encountered in the reservoirs. Density currents can also be overflow type or interflow type depending upon densities of incoming liquid and reservoir liquid. However, sediment laden streams produce turbidity currents along the bottom of reservoirs.

Estimation of Aggradation: Several investigators have tried to analyse the problem of aggradation upstream of a dam and to determine the transient bed profile. Iwakagi applied the method of characteristics, Kamura considered the variation of sediment size along the length of the stream. Sugio used the method of dimensional analysis. Swamee gave a numerical method for predicting aggradation upstream of a dam for constant discharge flowing through the stream. The method is based on the solution of a system of equations. He tested his mathematical procedure using typical data from an idealized situation using various time intervals ranging from 0.083 year (about a month) to 0.5 year (6 months) in a stretch of 1 Km. Data collected from laboratory experiments were used to compare observed and predicted bed profiles. The agreement was found to be satisfactory as can be seen in the following figure. (Fig. 2.14)

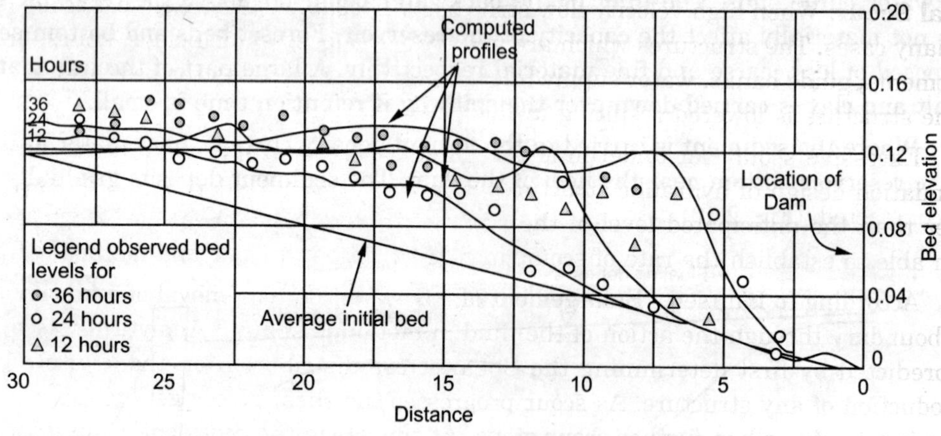

Fig. 2.14: Observed and Computed Bed Profiles Upstream

The laboratory experiments indicated that the process of aggradation is in the form of movement of a bed wave, the height of which increases as the wave moves towards the dam. Such movement is also indicated by the mathematical model.

The aggradation resulting from an increase in sediment or decrease in water discharge at any section has been analysed by some researchers. The results of experiments conducted by them did not tally with their assumed mathematical models. Figure here gives their experimental findings. (Fig. 2.15)

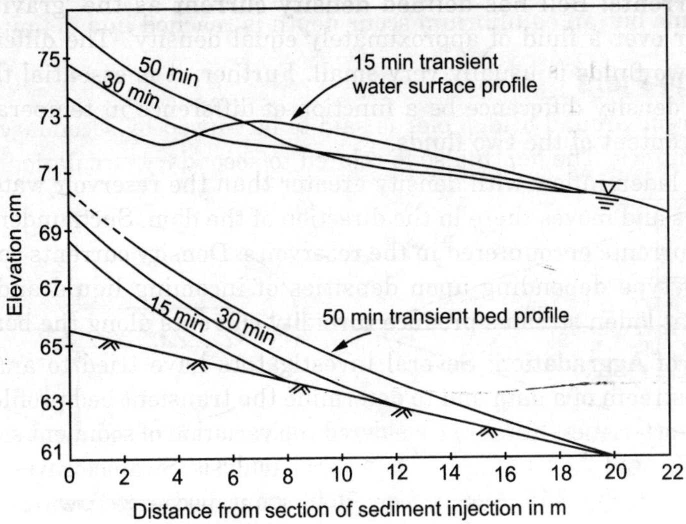

Fig. 2.15: Distance from section of sediment injection in m

Typical Bed and Water surface Profiles during Aggradation due to Overloading

Local Scour: When high velocity flow strikes any hydraulic structure, local scour is observed in many cases. The structures which are vulnerable to local scour include, spurs, bridge piers, abutments, guide banks, water supply inlets etc. In all these cases the bed level in the vicinity of the structure is lowered resulting in flow modification.

Excessive scour can undermine the foundations and lead to failure of the structure. Foundation design of hydraulic structures requires that foundation be taken down to a level lower than the anticipated level of the scour depression. Engineers have to a great extent, been able to establish the rate of scour, maximum depth of scour and methods of protection.

According to Laursen, "Enlargement of a flow section by removal of material comprising the boundary through the action of the fluid in motion is **scour.**" Analytically local scour can be predicted by first determining the Shear-stress distribution on the channel bed due to introduction of any structure. As scour progresses the shear stress gets reduced and reaches the critical value when further scour stops. At this stage the sediment coming in equals the sediment going out. It has not been possible to evaluate scour analytically. Hence the scour problem is often tackled using emperical methods based on dimensional consideration.

Scour equilibrium is reached when either of the following conditions is satisfied.

(1) The channel does not transport any sediment.

(2) The rate of sediment does not vary from one section to another.

(3) Scour around any obstruction (scour hole) remains constant.

Rate of Scour: It has been experimentally found that clear water scour around hydraulic structures increased as a logarithm of time and hence would continue to increase with time at a decreasing rate. Normally, the rate of increase with increase in time becomes so small that for all practical purposes a maximum scour depth will be reached.

In case of sediment-transporting flow it has been shown that scour does not increase infinitely with time but an equilibrium scour depth is reached in a definite time.

Scour at Bridge Piers

The local scour around bridge pier is said to be caused by secondary circulation due to bending of streamlines. The depth also is related to secondary circulation.

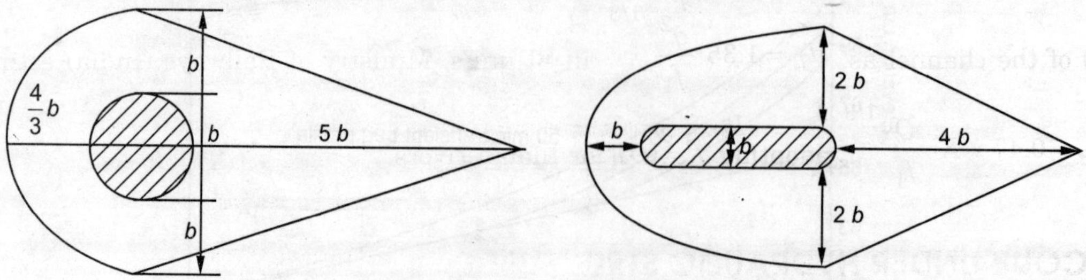

Fig. 2.16: Area needing Protection around bridge pier

The mechanics of local scour around bridge piers has been discussed by various investigators. The strong pressure field developed on the upstream face of a blunt nosed pier causes a horse-shoe vortex moving downstream. The horse-shoe vortex at upstream face and on the sides results in large shear stress on the boundary and causes scour. In case of sharp nosed piers, the pressure field is not strong enough to cause separation of approaching flow and thus vortex is not formed. In this case, large scour holes may develop downstream of the nose because of wake-vortex system.

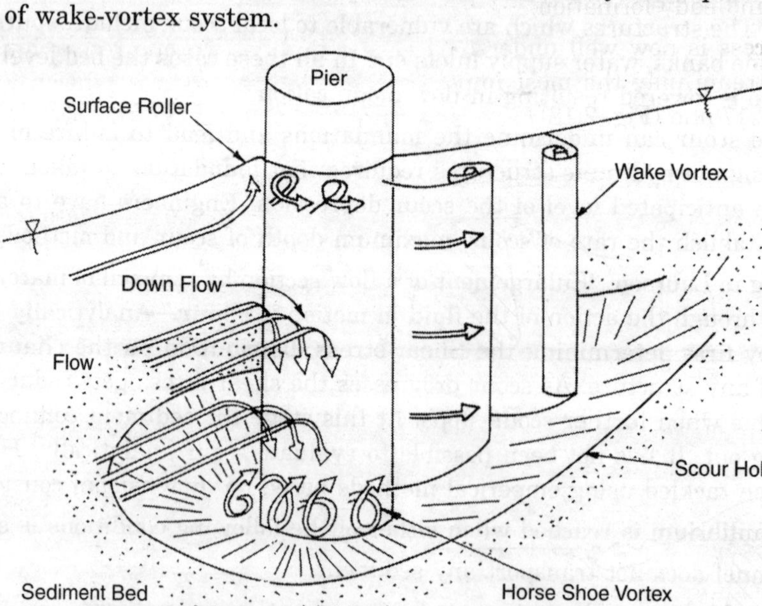

Fig. 2.16(a): Flow structure at a bridge pier

In clear-water scour, it is contended that strength of the horse-shoe vortex system is a function of pier Reynolds Number Vb/v where b is the width or diameter of the pier. The scour depth is given as:

$$d_s = 2.23 \times 10^{-4} \left(\frac{Vb}{\nu}\right)^{0.619}$$

The scour in sediment transporting flows has been evaluated by using Lacey's scour depth formula, $d_L = 0.47 \left(\frac{Q}{f_1}\right)^{1/3}$. Lacey's depth can be expressed in terms of discharge per unit width (q) of the channel as, $d_L = 1.35 \left(\frac{q^2}{f_1}\right)^{1/3}$ in SI units. Ministry of Railways (India) estimated $d_L = 0.47 \times K \left(\frac{Q}{f_1}\right)^{1/3}$ adopting $K = 1.92$ for Indian rivers.

SCOUR UNDER HYDRAULIC STRUCTURES

The scour downstream of structures like dams, weirs and barrages has been disturbing the river engineers everywhere. The local scour here occurs because the flow contains excessive kinetic energy; the general scour or degradation occurs because fairly clear water flows over the dam or the weir and hence picks up sediment from the bed of the downstream river to satisfy its capacity to transport sediment.

The local scour would occur if, there is insufficient dissipation of kinetic energy, there is formation of unstable hydraulic jump below the toe, or there is high apron level resulting in high velocity and eddy formation.

The process is now well understood on the basis of various researches. Formation of rollers downstream play the most important role in local scour as shown in the following figures. (Fig. 2.17 and (Fig. 2.18)

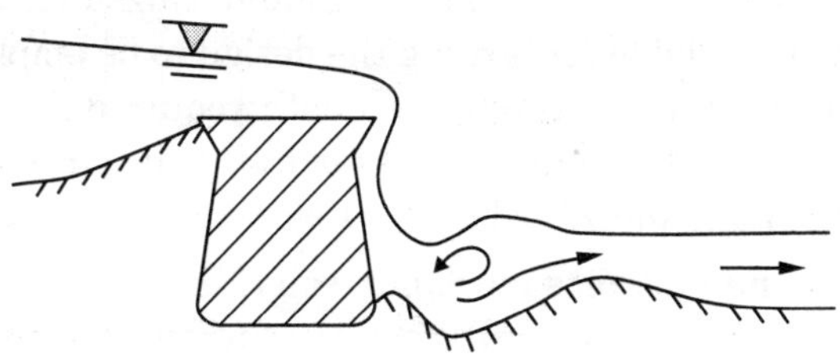

Fig. 2.17: Initiation of Scour

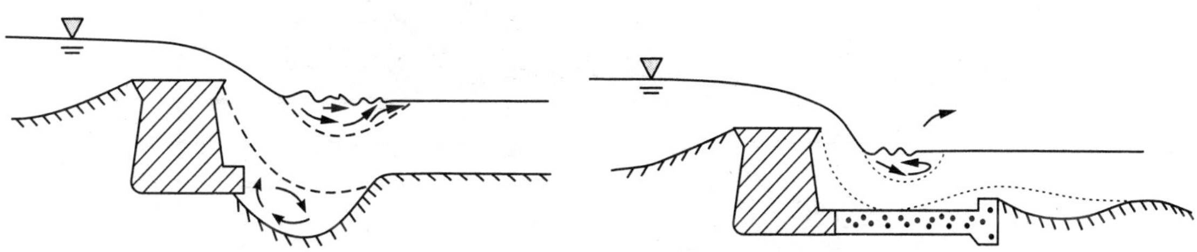

Fully Developed Rollers and Scour Hole

Modified Scour Hole with Apron

Fig. 2.18: Modified Scour Hole with Apron

Figures 2.16 clearly demonstrate that an anticlockwise vortex is formed whose erosive power is very great. The scour material lifted from the vicinity of the structure is deposited downstream. The scour hole gets enlarged with time and the pattern of rollers is also modified. There is an anticlockwise roller near the surface and a clockwise roller near the bed. While the anticlockwise roller causes scour, the clockwise roller helps in deposition of material. If an apron is provided, the resulting clockwise roller helps in depositing the material thus assuring the safety of the structure.

PROTECTION AGAINST LOCAL SCOUR

Various techniques have been developed to reduce the local scour at bridge piers. Flexible mats, sinking of isolated pile in the channel bed upstream of the pier, provision of a thin circular collar above the ground, all have helped in reducing the scour.

But the most popular method of protection has been to provide a loose apron of rock around the pier over the area vulnerable to scour. As scour develops the coarse material covers the sides of the scour hole thereby paving it and preventing further scour. It was found that mean Shear near a cylinder is 12 times the mean shear stress in the approach channel. The maximum shear is about 2.65 times the mean shear, the maximum instantaneous shear stress near the cylinder will be nearly 32 times the mean shear stress in the channel. The corresponding figure for a blunt nose pier is about 10. This information can help us in determining the size of the rocks for scour protection. A more conservative design assumes that the rock size should be such that its critical velocity is equal to twice the maximum flood velocity in the channel.

For river engineers, prevention of scour downstream of large spillways is a problem of great importance. Well established designs of stilling basins are available to prevent scour downstream of the spillway toe. These designs are standardized for different Froude Number ranges. Also information is available concerning the design to be employed in case of variations between the tailwater depth and the conjugate depth required for efficient hydraulic jump. These designs are available in only standard books of hydraulic structures design. Good designs are developed in India by Bligh and Khosla.

For diversion weirs and barrages on Sandy soils Khosla's method is used. These weirs have a sloping floor followed by horizontal floor of concrete, an inverted filter, piles and to avoid scour a launching apron is provided as shown in figure 2.19.

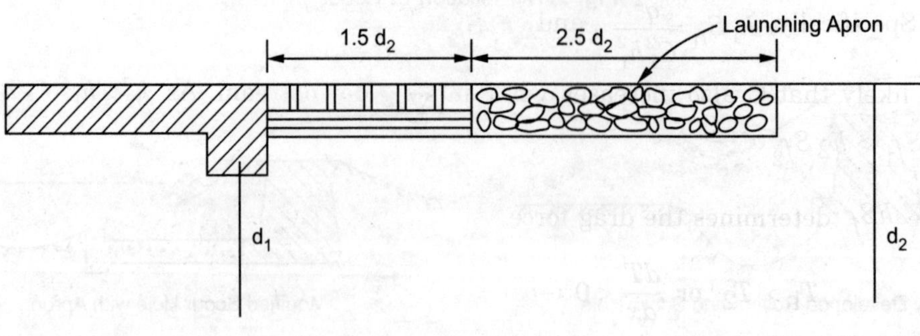

Fig. 2.19

When the scour holes are formed, the stones of the launching apron settle in the holes and cover them.

Scour and Deposition Theory: The bed of the river serves as buffer, in which surplus sand can be stored or from which shortages are borrowed, which is nothing else than an explanation for deposition or scour. Wherein water discharge the law of continuity is applied by backwater effects, for sand transportation the continuity is found in change in the bed elevation.

The Scour Criterion: In this rather simple light, it can be concluded that the theory that scour occurs when drag force on certain location increases can be replaced or supplemented by the simple logic. Considering the figures 2.20 and 2.21.

If, moving from cross-section 1 to cross-section 2 for a specific instant the transport (T) of sediment increases, the extra outflow must be withdrawn from the bed, which consequently must scour. The scour criterion, therefore, can be expressed as,

$$\frac{dT}{dx} > 0 \; ; \; or \; T_1 < T_2$$

If equilibrium conditions in water flow do not exist, i.e. if actual depth differs from equilibrium depth (he), we have backwater and $\frac{dT}{dx} \neq 0$; Obviously if $h = he$, $\frac{dT}{dx} = 0$. and there is no scour neither deposition.

Scour and Deposition Under Backwater and Drawdown Conditions

If equilibrium conditions in flow of water, do not exist, i.e. if the actual depth differs from the equilibrium depth (he), backwater or drawdown condition will occur. Under this condition $\frac{dT}{dx} \neq 0$ resulting in scour or deposition considering the case of backwater curve where if S_f decreases and depth (h) increases in the direction of flow,

According to Chezy's Equation:

$$q = Ch^{3/2} S_f^{1/2}$$

Or, $$\frac{q^2}{C^2h^2} = h.S_f$$

Or, Specifically, $h_1 S_{f1} = \frac{q^2}{C_1^2 h_1^2}$, and $h_2 S_{f2} = \frac{q^2}{C_2^2 h_2^2}$

It is likely that C also increases while moving downstream. As $h_2 > h_1$, $C_1 h_1 < C_2 h_2$ hence, $h_1 S_{f_1} > h_2 S_{f_2}$

Since hS_f determines the drag force,

$$T_1 > T_2 \text{ or } \frac{dT}{dx} < 0 \; (-ve).$$

This would mean that there will be deposition as flow progresses.

Similarly in drawdown curve, the sediment quantity increases in x-direction giving,

$$\frac{dT}{dx} > 0\ (+ve)$$

This would result in scour of the bed as the flow moves.

Meanwhile, the deposition pattern for backwater curve differs considerably from the scour pattern in a drawdown curve condition. To assess that, actual bed load T must be computed for all successive cross-sections along the river and plot the result in a diagram, the T-diagram. The Slope of the T curve yields dT/dx, and its magnitude is the measure for the rate of deposition or Scour.

The result is indicated in the following figure 2.20. It can be concluded that for a backwater curve, the T-diagram is S-shaped, with the highest value of dT/dx at the point of inflection, the Shoaling of the river will be most pronounced there. On the other hand, a drawdown curve yields a continuous T-diagram with the highest value of dT/dx at the most downstream location, just upstream of the course of drawdown. At that location there may be a severe scour in the river bed.

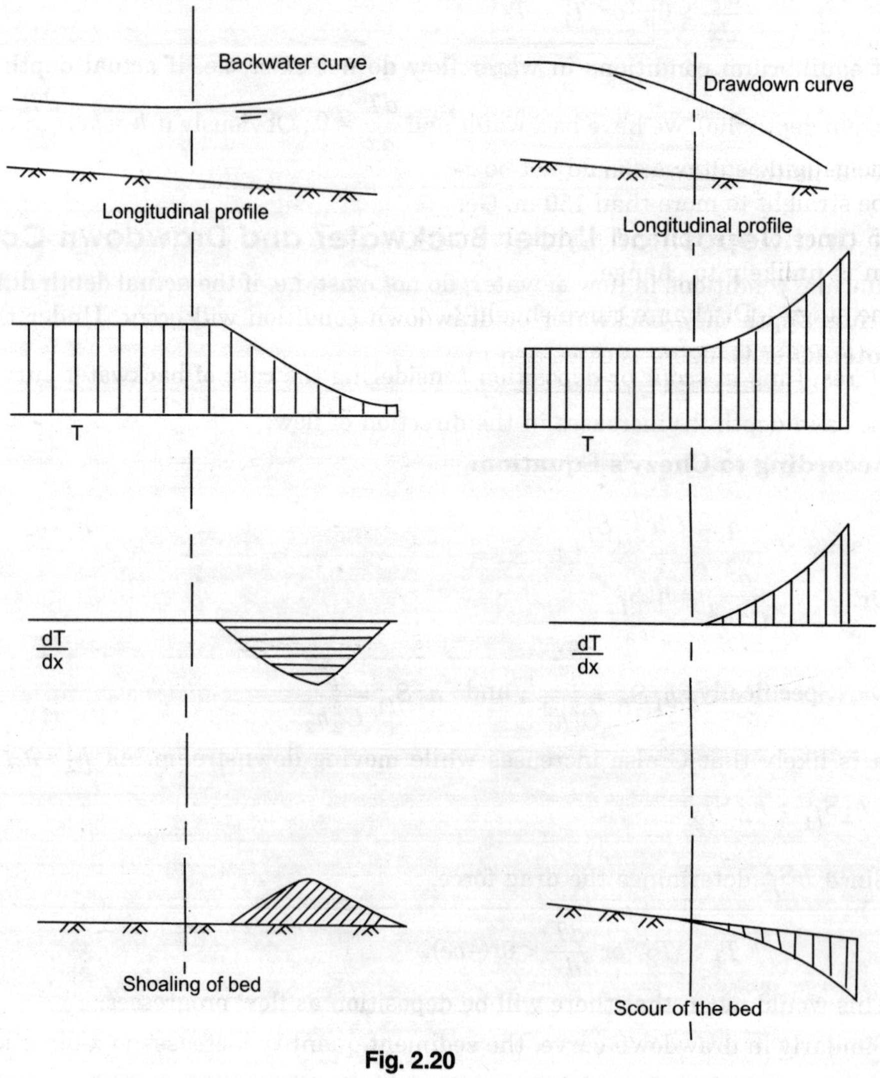

Fig. 2.20

STAGE-DISCHARGE RELATION

A continuous record of streamflow can facilitate establishment of a relation between rate of flow and water level in the stream. In small channels this can be found by use of weir, notch or flumes. In large streams, measurement of discharge is made with current meter. A stage-discharge relation or rating curve is constructed by plotting the measured discharge against water surface elevation or stage. Care must be taken to locate the measuring station at a stable place.

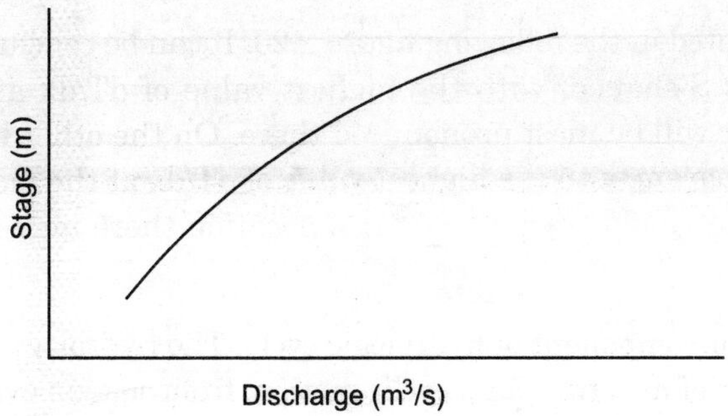

Fig. 2.21

The gauging stations should not be located within the influence of backwater. The reach should be straight to more than 150 m. Generally, the length of the straight portion should be about 15 times of the channel width. It must be ascertained that base is stable with bottom elevation is unlikely to change.

The stage – Discharge curve should be updated periodically.

Note: River Gauging is discussed in chapter 12.

CHAPTER 3

RIVER HYDROLOGY

River flow is a major component of hydrologic cycle. The hydrologic cycle essentially covers the permanent movement of moisture, in a cyclic motion, from sea via evaporation (E), transport by wind, precipitation (P) and river discharge (R) back to the sea. If these magnitudes were constant, the movement is a steady one, and it will be possible to write,

$$E = P - R$$

Assuming that no evaporation takes place in the catchment area, the motion is perfectly circular and the Runoff will be equal to Precipitation. There are, however two types of complications.

(i) Variation in rainfall over time

(ii) Short circuits in circular motion

VARIATION IN RAINFALL

Seasonal and daily variations cause non-permanent or unsteady conditions which affect each part of the cycle. One such seasonal variation is concerned with the fact that in summer the land gets heated more than the sea, thus developing a low pressure region over the land. Humid air from over the sea flows towards the land, where it rises, condenses and falls as rain. In the winter the reverse is true. This same cycle can occur on a daily basis giving breezes towards the shore during the day and towards the sea at night.

Under such unsteady conditions, the above equation is no longer valid. Intermittent periods of rain and dry weather cause the soil in the catchment area to dry out and subsequently absorb part of the rain and so do lakes, marshes and other storage areas. Hence, there is a variation in volume of water stored in the catchment area, which is expressed mathematically by introducing another term in equation, S = accumulation. The equation now will be,

$$R = P - S$$

In which sense S can be either positive (storage capacity being filled or R less than P) or negative (storage being emptied or R more than P).

Short Circuits: Evaporation does not take place only from the sea, but also from the whole catchment area. Rain is also not confined to land surface. Run-off too is not only the open-river-discharge but also includes other forms like groundwater flow. In fact every square meter of the drainage basin is subject to a complex movement of moisture. However, the full picture of the total drainage basin must comply with the law of continuity as expressed by the mathematical formula explained earlier. A simplified scheme of various movements of moisture is given in the following picture and Fig. 3.1.

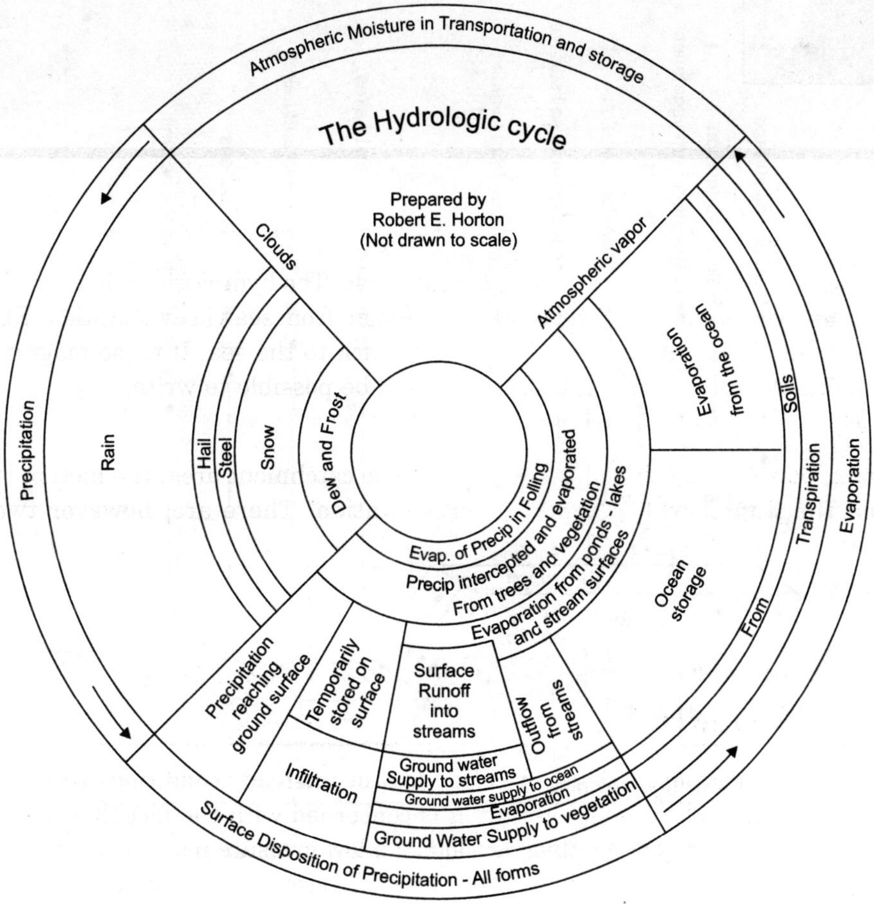

Hydrologic Cycle
(A Qualitative Representation)

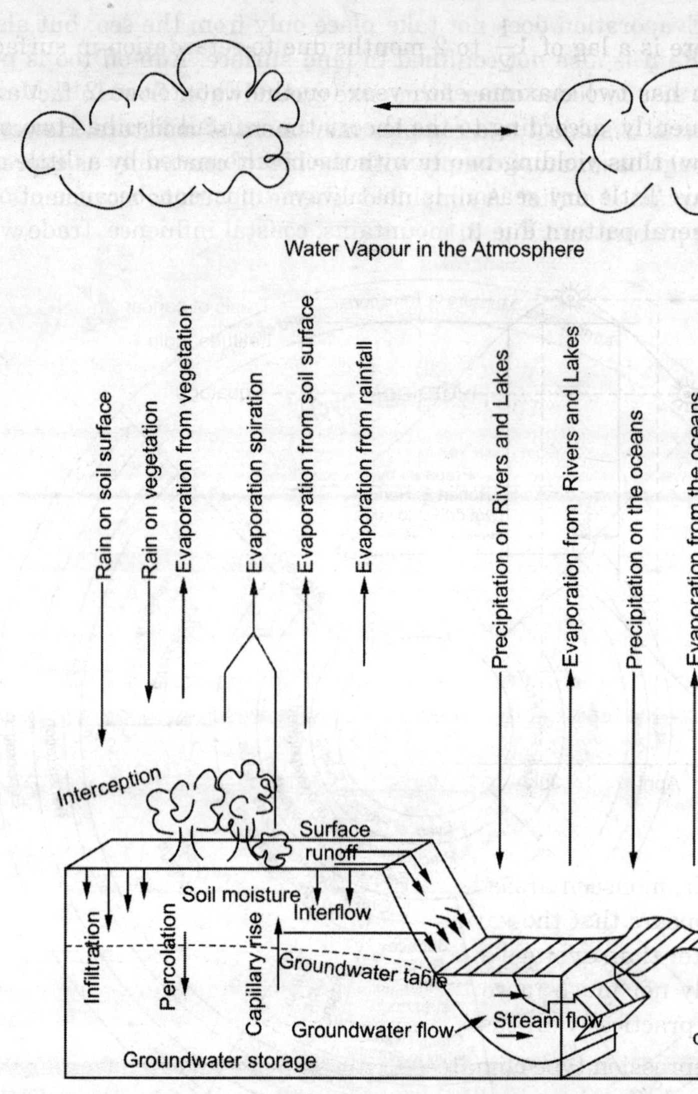

Fig. 3.1: Simplified Scheme of Moisture Movement

Precipitation

Rainfall is nearly always caused by moist air rising, expanding and then cooling. Moist air at a certain temperature and relative humidity forms clouds. As soon as it is cooled below the point of maximum saturation vapour pressure, and if other conditions are favourable, then rainfall will take place. The transport of moist air towards a certain area and the raising of that air mass are mainly caused by low pressure in the area. Low pressure can either occur in a heated area or in the centre of a depression, where it moves with the system of depressions or cyclones.

Monsoon in tropical regions is the example of the first type of rain. In monsoon areas, like India, there is a dry season in the months when the Sun is at a low altitude (in winters); maximum rainfall occurs at times of maximum altitude of the Sun, when the heating is great and air masses rise. There is a lag of $1\frac{1}{2}$ to 2 months due to retardation in surface heating. Between the tropics Sun has two maxima each year (on the Equator on 21st March and on 21st September). Consequently, according to the theory the rainfall also has two maxima (as shown in the figure below) thus yielding two rainy seasons alternated by a 'little dry season' in between. However, this 'little dry season' is not always apparent, because of all kinds of complications to this general pattern due to mountains, coastal influence, trade winds etc.

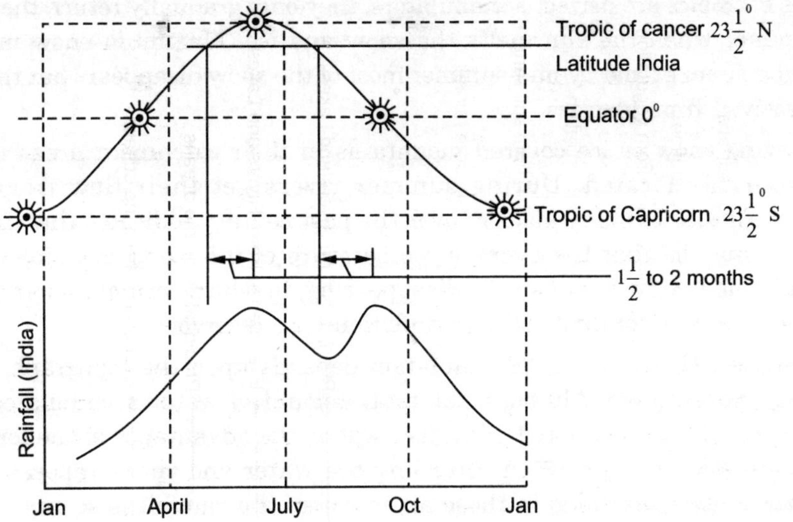

Fig. 3.2

In general, however, monsoon areas have the habit of complying nicely to above theory. In particular, it often appears that the variation from year to year is remarkably small ; wet periods may be 20% wetter than average and dry periods may have 20% less rain volume, but the deviation is normally not much more than that. Rains may occur a few weeks later or earlier, but they are, in practically all cases, bound to come.

Areas subject to depression type climates, on the other hand, can have rain on any days of the year although more depressions are likely in some months than in others. The variations for any particular month from one year to the next may be quite considerable and it is only by taking a long period average (minimum 20 years) that it is possible to say that there are months with statistically more chance to have a rainfall and other months with lower chance.

Other ways by which moist air is made to rise include presence of barriers (hills, mountains) giving orographic rain, local heating causing thunderstorms and passage of weather fronts producing cyclonic rainfall. In coastal regions turbulence can also cause ascent of moist air.

Rainfall is normally expressed as average annual figures computed over a series of years. Such figures appear to vary from place to place, there are arid places with only a few millimeters, whereas other locations get upto 10,000 mm or more rain. But these are very local phenomenon, limited in expanse. Viewed over larger areas, such as entire drainage basins of Indian and the world's large rivers, the extremes level themselves off, and the average rainfall becomes a moderate number with moderate variations between one river and the other.

Another comparison between rain figures refers to one single drainage basin, which is subject to wet and dry years. The annual rainfall in a specific year as deviation from long term average. The deviation here can be substantially higher. Still more important is the variation in monthly figures over the year, not to speak of weekly or daily figures.

Water Accumulation: Water is found as snow and ice, groundwater and surface water on the earth besides in the vapour form in atmosphere.

The Snow and Ice: The solid form of water of the temperate regions and of some very high mountains of tropics are perfect accumulators, they only gradually return the water during spring and summer when the sun melts the snow and ice. Maximum snow melting occurs during spring and summer and by mid-summer most of the snow disappears but then maximum discharge is received from glaciers.

Rivers having snow or ice covered mountains in their catchment areas normally are, therefore, favourably located. During summer rivers get their flow from meltwater. Measurement of the size of many glaciers over the past century indicates that gradually they are shrinking. It may be that the average temperature of the world is rising and that this form of accumulation is slowly but surely disappearing, in which case mankind may be forced to replace it by some kind of artificial accumulation e.g., reservoirs.

Groundwater: Groundwater accumulation depends upon the topography of the area, soil permeability, porosity etc. Although the total amount of water accumulated in the sub-soil is generally less than the amount of surface water, the advantages of the former are that there is a considerable retardation in returning the water and that evaporation is greatly reduced. Also the water percolates in those areas where the rainfall is scanty.

Surface Water: It has usually the greatest accumulation capacity of the three. Surface water consists of the volume of rain stored in lakes, ponds, marshes, man made reservoirs and the river itself prior to or during its runoff towards the sea.

Runoff: The influence of precipitation on surface runoff is obvious, even without the mathematical expression,

$$R = P - I - E$$

More precipitation will normally yield a higher runoff. Obviously, a wet year (with a high annual rainfall) provides a higher discharge and a dry year a low discharge.

Also the variation within a shorter term, for instance monthly figures that indicate seasonal effects in the rains will certainly result in a variable discharge, with maxima occurring shortly after the period of maximum rain (time lag) and a minima at the end of the dry season and just before the rain starts again.

It has been found that a good measure to express the discharge variation within one single year in a quantitative sense is the ratio of maximum discharge and the Minimum discharge Q_{max}/Q_{min} in which daily discharges are used, Q_{max} being the flood peak discharge and Q_{min} lowest daily discharge in the year. Table 3.1 on world rivers contains the values of this ratio for well known rivers. On observing the table we find that difference in the figures are most striking, with the ratio ranging between as low as 2.5 for the Congo over 250 for purely tropical monsoon river like the Benue in Nigeria. The low value of this ratio can be explained by the fact that its drainage basin is partly in the Southern hemisphere with a rainy season from November to March and partly in Northern hemisphere with a rainy season from May to September. However, the differences are not solely due to precipitation; accumulation is probably even more important.

Many times storage conditions in the river basin cause a slower inflow of the rainwater into the river. Gently sloping terrain, well covered with forest and other vegetation, retains rainwater for a longer duration and will release it long after the rain has stopped. The hydrograph for such an area will, therefore, have much smoother appearance i.e. lower peaks than the precipitation pattern would suggest, while considerable retardation will be manifested as shown in the following figure (Fig. 3.3).

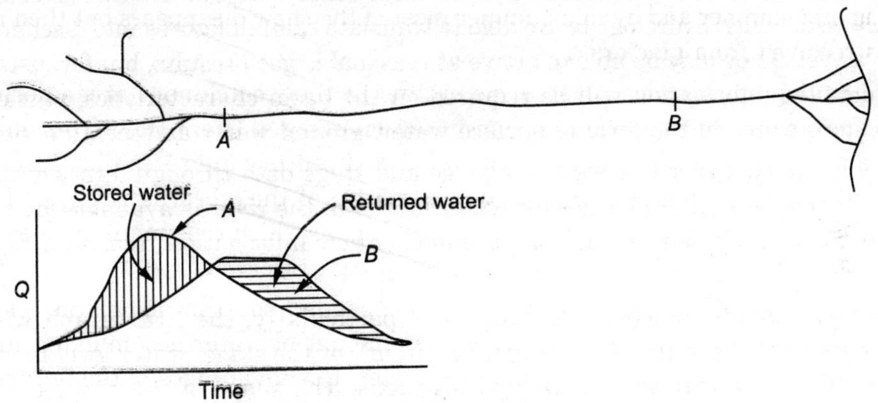

Fig. 3.3: Simplified Hydrograph for retarded flow

On further downstream these effects are more prominent. A river with large flood plains and many tributaries has relatively large storage capacities which further tend to modify the hydrograph, erasing irregularities and promoting retardation.

Another example of the effect of accumulation on discharge refers to monsoon-type river. A portion of the first rains of the year gets infiltrated into the ground. Subsequent rains contribute to bring in higher peak flow. At the end of the rainy season the river level falls gradually because of supply of water from storage as shown below (Fig. 3.4).

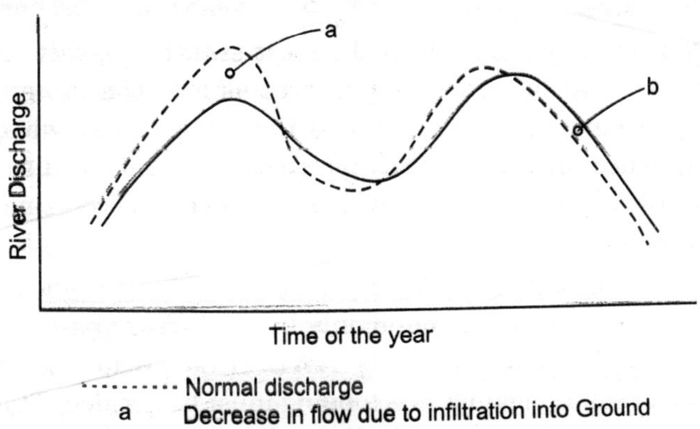

Fig. 3.4: Simplifie

Evaporation in tropical areas is significant. It causes yearly runoff always smaller than the rainfall. The proportion of the total rainfall that runs off is called the Runoff Coefficient

$$K = \frac{R}{P} = \frac{P - S - E}{P},$$

S = Storage or Accumulation

The value of Runoff coefficient K depends upon the period over which it is applied, normally a whole year.

A thorough analysis of the hydrological elements P, S and E leading to an understanding of K (or in terms of river engineering, Q) is in most cases does not interest river engineers. The accuracy with which hydrologists are able to translate rainfall figures into discharge figures is not great as yet. They may be able to arrive at reasonable good results, but for instantaneous conditions detailed information will be required on the basin characteristics, particularly its capacity to store water in the form of surface water, ground water and ice and snow.

It may be much easier to collect discharge and stage data through direct measurement in the river. If the data on discharges (or water levels) in the river is available for too short a period to be used for statistical analysis, complementary information from rain figures may be useful.

Hydrology explains much of the river, and particularly, the hydrograph which gives continuous picture of either the water discharge (in m^3) or the stage (water level in m), plotted along the vertical axis against a horizontal time axis. The shape of the hydrograph greatly depends on the hydrological conditions in the catchment area.

River Hydrometry

For laboratory flumes highly sophisticaed theories have been derived about movement of water which can be applied to river flow also. For river engineering, however, the required accuracy is limited; there are many aspects which lower the precision. Also it is absolutely without significance to endeavour a very high accuracy in discharge information.

Obviously, discharges of a river cannot be measured directly, they are computed by measuring cross-sectional areas and velocities, and both these depend upon the water level in the river.

Levels of the river (or stage) are one of the most essential aspects of the river, both for the general understanding and for practical purposes as for flood protection, navigation etc. All hydraulic structures have direct relation to the water level, whether it is design of revetments, bridges, groynes, inlets or any other structure. It must also be understood that efficient design or planning is only possible when frequency of occurrence of certain stages, both high and low are known.

For example, an embankment for flood protection is built higher than the maximum flood level and such a maximum can be found only by statistical analysis. For this, frequency curves of annual or seasonal High Water Levels (HWL) or Low Water Levels (LWL) are plotted and then desired degree of safety against overtopping must be decided. This also depends upon other factors, such as danger to property, life, livestock etc and may range from say 1: 100 to 1: 10,000. Sometimes for temporary structures like cofferdams, a calculated risk is acceptable. A balance is made between risk and cost of construction.

The compilation of frequency curves is only possible with the help of long period records. The longer the period of reliable records the better are the results. Sometimes continuous records at the same site are not available in such cases if a relation can be established between the records at an existing gauge elsewhere, the gaps can be filled in. In fact, knowledge on relation between the levels of different gauges is not only important for checking or completing records but also for predictions. An early establishment of gauges should, therefore, be undertaken whether or not major projects are envisaged. It is sometimes possible to obtain valuable local information about high water levels from inhabitants or by observation of marks on trees, buildings, roads etc.

When compiling records all earlier information should be expressed in levels at the latest gauge, taking into account the transverse and longitudinal gradients of the river. Where actual level observations cover only a short period, sometimes use can be made of rainfall records that usually cover a much longer period. A reliable correlation between rainfall and river stages is extremely difficult to establish.

The number of gauges required depends upon the desired accuracy and on changes in gradient of the river and, possibly, it's tributaries. Spacing of gauges vary approximately between 10 km to 100 km. The location of gauges should be chosen with regard to points of special importance but free from disturbing influences. Important positions are immediately upstream and downstream of weirs, locks, bridges, inlets etc., and downstream of confluences. It is not suitable to have gauges just upstream of confluences because the level in each tributary affects the other. A bench mark should be established in the vicinity for periodic (once or twice a year) checking the zero. It is usually not necessary for the zero of each gauge on a river to be based on the same datum but it is frequently convenient that it should be so, because then gradient can be directly computed. Also, datum for levels along the river should be fixed parallel to the longitudinal profile and not on horizontal plain.

The frequency at which readings should be taken depends upon the rate of rise and fall in the level. A large river rises and falls slowly and one reading per day is sufficient. In head waters and tributaries which may be subjected to rapid fluctuations in level many readings may be required to be able to draw the hydrograph correctly.

There is a great range of gauge types available, the most common gauge consists of a staff fixed vertically on walls, rock faces, piers or specially driven piles and carrying readable scales. In inaccessible places or places where frequent readings are required, self-recording gauges may be used. These gauges are of variety of types and brands, operating on different principles such as mechanical, pneumatic, hydrostatic, electrical or electronic systems.

Whatever system is used great attention must be paid to its reliability. The elaboration of readings also deserves the greatest care. All readings are primarily to be plotted against a time axis, yielding a hydrograph of stages but much more can be done with them. Analysis of long time records can yield, **envelopes** of maximum and minimum records, **probability** of peak levels and **level relations** between two gauge stations. Following figures illustrate each of the above types.

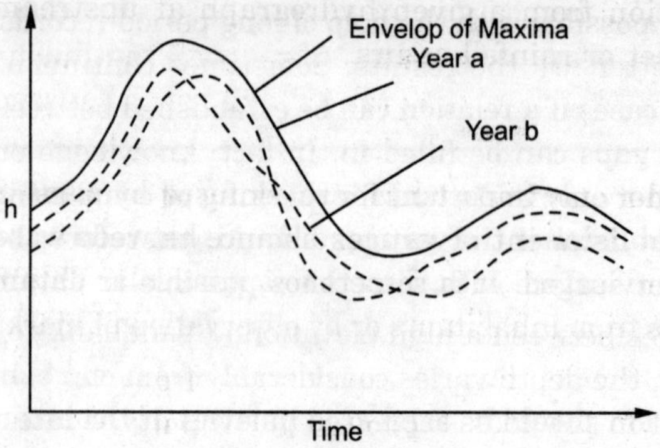

Various Hydrographs

Fig. 3.5

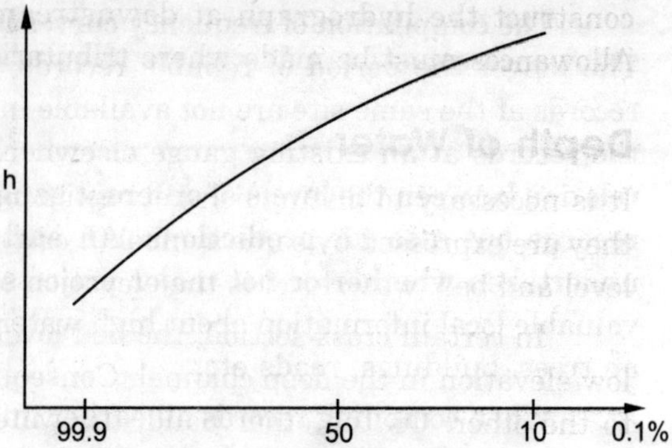

Probability of Peak levels

Fig. 3.6

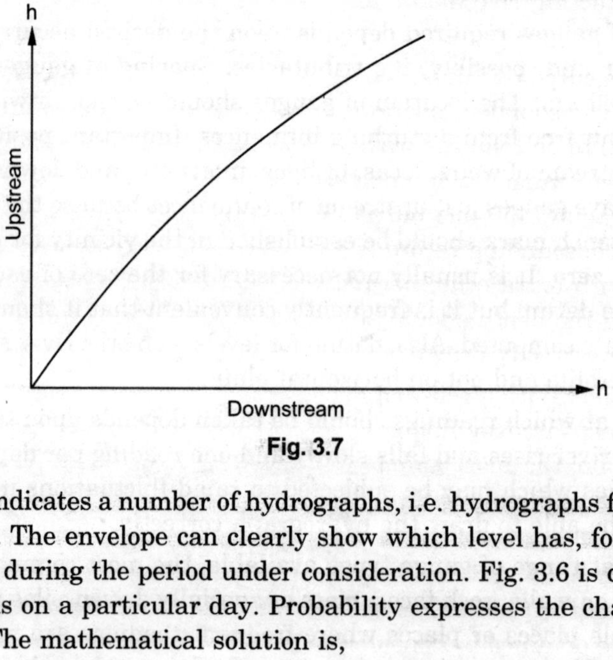

Fig. 3.7

Fig. 3.5 above indicates a number of hydrographs, i.e. hydrographs for a number of years, plotted in one graph. The envelope can clearly show which level has, for a certain day, been the highest recorded during the period under consideration. Fig. 3.6 is drawn for probability of occurrence of levels on a particular day. Probability expresses the chance of occurrence at any year in future. The mathematical solution is,

$$\text{Probability,} \quad P = \frac{n}{n+1} \times \text{frequency}$$

where n is the number of observed years. Fig. 3.7 is the relation curve and it offers the possibility to inform downstream station when to expect a certain level. Time lag and relation of levels can easily be assessed for specific stages. The method is to plot levels at one station against the other. Plotting readings of the two stations observed in one on the same day is not realistic, the reading in upstream station may only be compared with a reading in downstream station after considering the time required for translation wave to travel from upstream station to the downstream station. The time of travel need not be same for all stages. Often, it may happen that during flood stages the travelling speed is slower than for low-flow conditions. Once, the correlation is found and the value of time lag known, it is possible to construct the hydrograph at downstream station from a given hydrograph at upstream. Allowances must be made where tributaries meet or rainfall occurs.

Depth of Water

It is necessary to distinguish between *depth* and *water levels* which are confused by some as they are expressed by same symbol (*h* or *d*). While *depth* is the vertical distance between water level and bed, waterlevel is the elevation of water surface with respect to a particular datum.

In certain cross-section, the bed level ranges between a high elevation at sandbank to a low elevation in the deep channel. Consequently, the depth varies considerably from one bank to the other. On the other hand, the waterlevel in the cross-section is particularly constant (apart from a possible small) transverse gradient.

In river engineering depths are of great importance. We need the depth for computing discharges, but apart from that depth must be known for various other purposes, ranging from navigation to constructing rivetments and from channel studies to foundation problems for bridges.

Depths are measured by taking soundings, either manually by hand lead or electronically by echo-sounders. Echo-sounders operate on the principle of transmitting sound waves from the vessel downward to bottom; the waves are reflected and received again at the vessel. The time interval between transmission and reception is a measure for the depth. The velocity of sound in water is about 1450 m/s but is affected by density which depends on salinity and temperature. The echosounding record is also affected by different types of river bed such as rock hard bottom with extra echo, normal hard bottom, soft bottom, several soft layers etc. Ofcourse, measuring the depth should be combined with some kind of position fixing, so that cross-section can be correctly drawn.

Flow Velocities: With levels and depths known, the next to be evaluated is the velocity of flow. It can be measured by floats, by propeller meters or by resistance meters. Among these floats are by far the most simple and widely used method. However, floats have the disadvantage that they are not accurate. Instead of surface floats, staff floats give better result. The length of staff floats be such that they do not touch the obstacles on the bottom of the river.

An indication of the relation between observed float speed and the average flow velocity in the vertical can be obtained by considering the velocity distribution in the vertical as shown in the figure 3.8. The usual adopted formulae in this respect are,

$$V_Y = 5.75\ V_* \log \frac{30y}{K};$$

$$\overline{V} = 5.75\ V_* \log \frac{12h}{K} \quad \text{and}$$

$$V_* = \sqrt{\frac{\tau_0}{\rho}} = \sqrt{ghI}$$

where V_Y is velocity at distance y from bottom.

$\overline{V}$ = is Average velocity

V* = Shear velocity

τ_o = Bed Shear stress

K = Bottom Roughness

From above formulae, the actual average velocity can be computed from any float observation. Due to all kinds of disturbing factors, it is not certain that formulae are accurately applicable. A great disadvantage of float is that the results from float measurements refer to the measured section as a whole. For many applications, we need the specific velocity in a certain cross-section, which cannot be obtained by floats. The advantage of floats is that they trace the path and show pattern of flow which is in certain cases of great help in analysing the phenomena in the river.

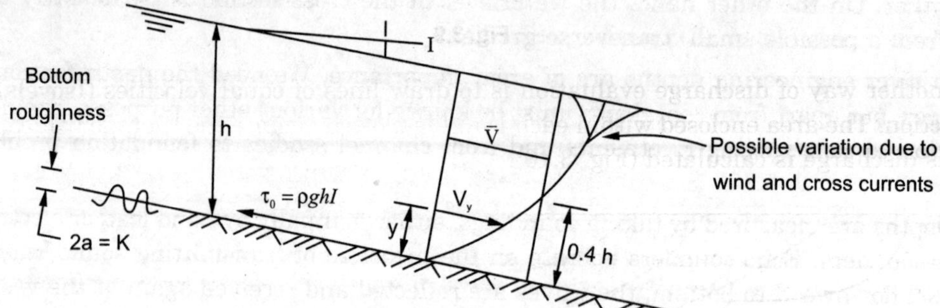

Fig. 3.8

Keeping in mind the drawbacks of float measurement other instruments like propeller type of *Current meters* are used. It measures the number of rotations in a given time; this information is translated into velocity through calibration. The main disadvantage is that they are delicate and vulnerable to damage.

Another instrument which is cheap but robust is known as Plaenta or *Pendulum meter*, a new version of resistance meter. The principle involved is that water flow exerts a force on the end of pendulum causing it to deflect. The angle of deflection is a measure of force and hence of the stream velocity. The main disadvantage of this instrument is that it needs experienced operators.

From the observations of velocity from either of the above methods, average velocity can be computed. However, to economise, it is a common practice to rely on the adopted vertical distribution as well. Referring to previous figure and listing in ascending order of accuracy average velocity , the position for reading the velocity will be as follows,

(a) Single reading at water surface, $\overline{V} = 0.85$ Vs

(b) Single reading at 0.6 h from water surface, $\overline{V} = V_{0.6\,h}$

(c) Two readings at 0.2 h and 0.8 h from water surface $\overline{V} = \dfrac{0.2\text{ h} + 0.8\text{ h}}{2}$

(d) Four or five readings at various depths which are plotted, out of which $\overline{V} = \int \dfrac{V\,dh}{h}$

(e) Accuracy can be further improved by increasing the number of readings beyond 5.

Discharge Evaluation: With the knowledge of depths and velocities, it is possible to evaluate discharge (m^3/s) through the whole cross-sectional area. The river cross-section is divided into a number of strips, preferably of equal widths. Mean velocity and average area of each strip is found out and discharge through each strip is found (Fig. 3.9).

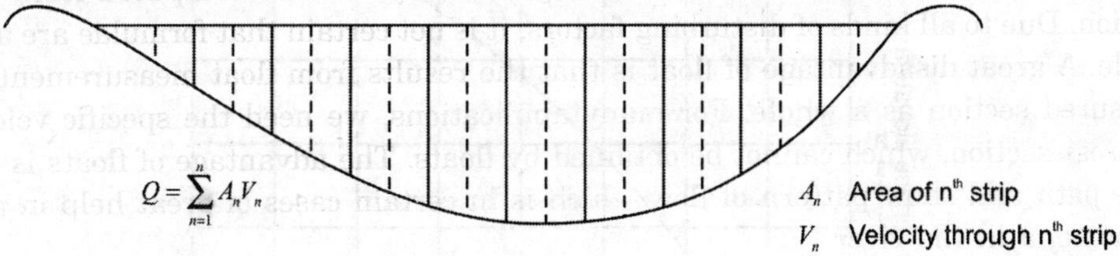

Fig. 3.9

Another way of discharge evaluation is to draw lines of equal velocities (Isovels) in the cross section. The area enclosed within each isovel is plotted against the average value of Isovel and thus discharge is calculated (Fig. 3.10).

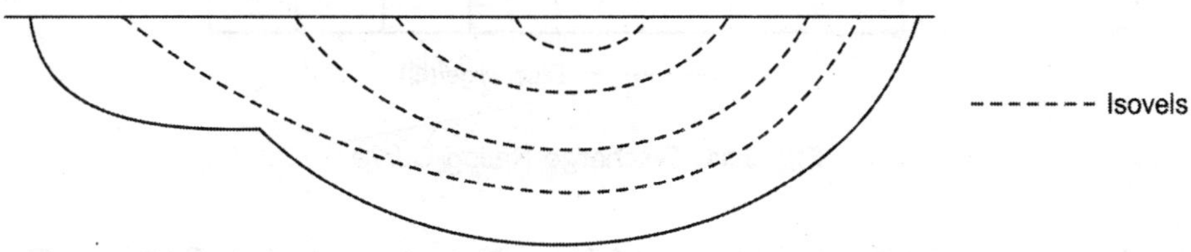

Fig. 3.10

Rating Curve: Obviously, the discharge measurements are time consuming, expensive and troublesome. Yet it is necessary to know the daily variation of the discharge that is to say, a hydrograph of discharge is needed. In order to avoid the necessity to measure the discharge everyday, use can be made of the fact that at some suitably selected cross-sections, there exists a unique relationship between discharge and water level. If enough values of discharge have been measured for different water levels, then a Discharge-Elevation (Q–h) curve known as *rating curve* can be drawn (Fig. 3.11).

The number of values required to obtain a good rating curve depends upon the desired accuracy and the shape of the cross-section. A difficulty arises in measuring higher floods. It will therefore, often be necessary to extrapolate the measured $Q - h$ rating curve in an upward direction. In case the cross-section is not too complicated, and the slope can be measured with the help of two nearby gauges, computation by means of the discharge formula may come to the rescue. Sometimes, extrapolation can be done by converting the rating curve to log-log paper; in that case the rating curve (Q–h – curve) is often a straight line.

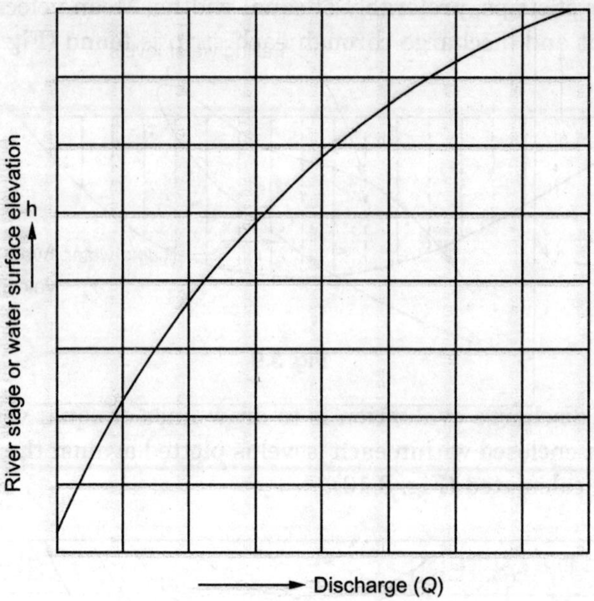

Fig. 3.11: Discharge Rating Curve

Rapidly Rising or Falling Stage of the River and The Rating Curve

Discharge gauging should normally be carried out free from the influence of rapid changes in slope i.e. neither within the backwater curves nor while the level is rising or falling rapidly. When the level rises rapidly there is an increase in the gradient of water surface. For falling stages, the gradient is smaller and Q lower than expected (Fig. 3.12).

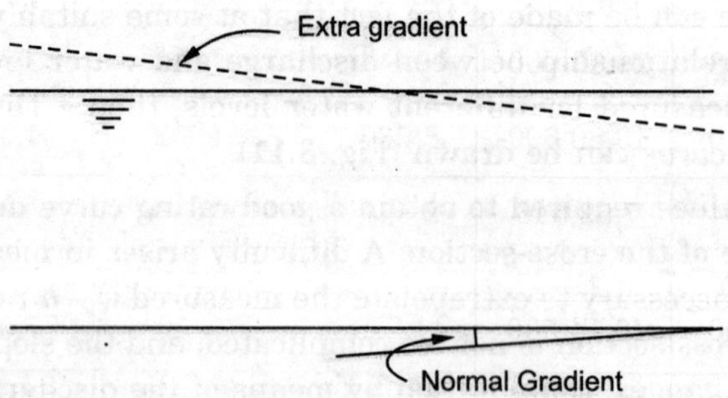

Fig. 3.12

Consequently, for a rise and subsequent fall of the river, the actual Q-h relation does not precisely follow the rating curve, but rather a loop around the rating curve (Fig. 3.13).

The phenomenon is supported by the changes in the bed-roughness caused due to changes in bed forms. In the rising stage ripples are too small resulting in small resistance, opposite happens in falling stage.

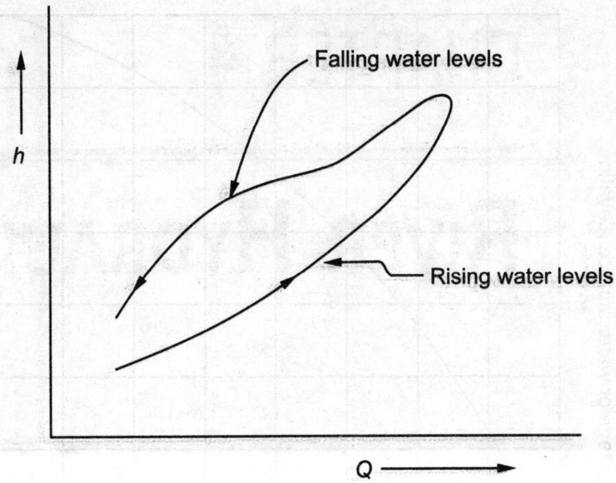

Fig. 3.13

IMPORTANT PARAMETERS OF SOME WORLD RIVERS

Table 3.1

River	Length in Km	Drainage Area Km^2	Water Flow m^3/s	Annual Sediment Load Tonnes	Water Discharge m^3/s		Ratio Q_{max}/Q_{min}
					High	Low	
Nile	6,653	33,49,000	2,830	60 × 10^6	11,335	454	24.96
Amazon	6,400	70,50,000	2,09,000	700 × 10^6	3,40,000	1,80,000	1.88
Missisippi	3,778	29,80,000	16,800	5500 × 10^6	86,800	45,00	19.28
Volga	3,530	13,80,000	8,060	25 × 10^6	24,022	3,918	6.13
Hwang Ho (Yellow)	5,464	7,52,546	2,571	1100 × 10^6	58,000	1,030	56.31
Congo	4,700	40,14,500	41,200	35 × 10^6	75,000	23,000	3.26
Indus (Sindhu	3,610	11,65,000	6,600	214 × 10^6	58,000	1,200	48.3
Ganga (Ganges)	2,525	10,86,000	16,650	329 × 10^6	70,934	1,161	61.09
Rhine	1,232	1,85,000	2,900	1.86 × 10^6	13,000	800	16.25
Kosi (Koshi)	720	74,500	2,166	187 × 10^6	24,200	–	–

CHAPTER 4

RIVER HYDRAULICS

The river's basic function is to collect water directly or indirectly originating from precipitation and to transport this water from areas with higher elevation towards places with a lower elevation mostly the sea.

The flow of water through the river is guided by the principles of physics applied to open channel flow. Most of the formulae developed are for uniform and steady flow. Of course the flow conditions in the river do not exactly comply to these assumptions. Hence, some corrections have to be applied whenever required. Still, these formulae are effectively used except in few extreme situations e.g. in tidal sections.

CHEZY'S FORMULA

In an open channel the uniform flow is characterized by uniform depth throughout its length in all the cross-sections considering prismatic channel.

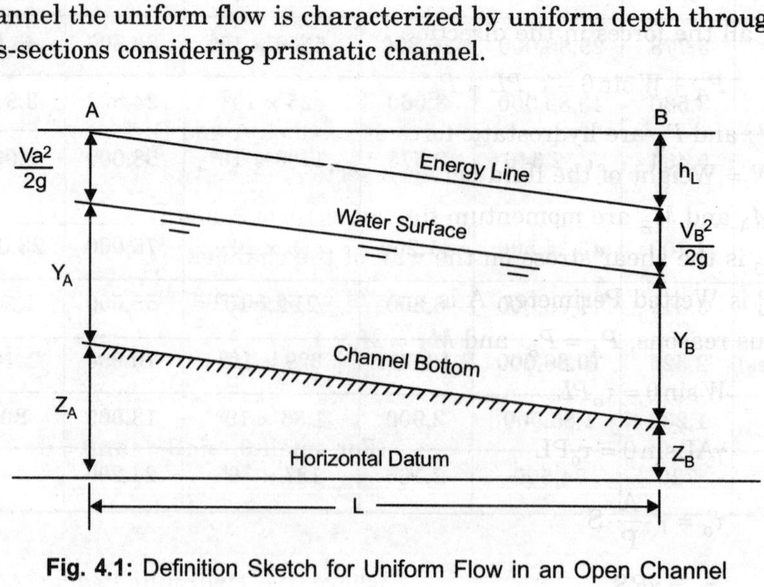

Fig. 4.1: Definition Sketch for Uniform Flow in an Open Channel

Figure 4.1 illustrates conditions for uniform flow of water in an open channel. Writing the energy head equation between sections A and B where each term has units as Newton-meters per Newton (Nm/N).

$$Z_A + y_A + \frac{V_A^2}{2g} = Z_B + y_B + \frac{V_B^2}{2g} + h_L$$

Where, Z is the elevation of channel bottom above an arbitrary horizontal datum, Y is the depth of flow, V is the average velocity and h_L is the head loss between sections A and B.

In uniform flow $y_A = y_B$ and $V_A = V_B$. Hence, $h_L = Z_A - Z_B = SL$, where S is the slope of energy grade line and L is the distance between section A and B.

For developing Chezy's Equation consider a fluid element in an open channel with uniform flow depth (also called Normal Depth y_o or y_n).

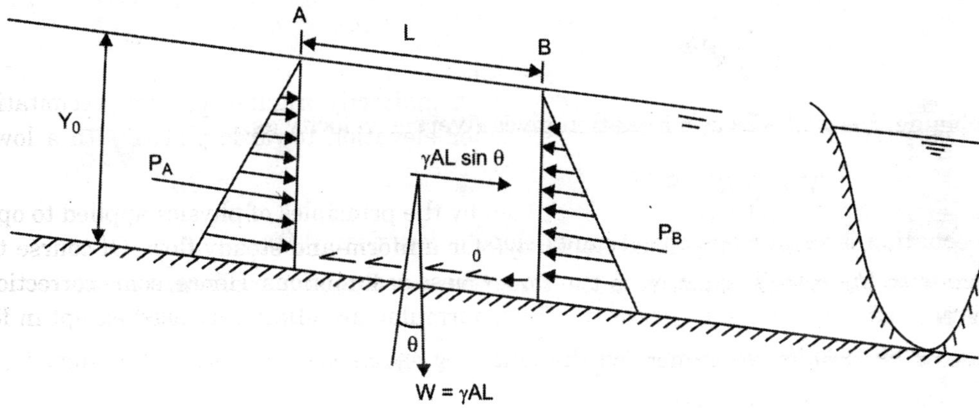

Fig. 4.2

Resolving all the forces in the direction of flow,

$$P_A + W\sin\theta - \tau_o PL - P_B = M_B - M_A$$

Where, P_A and P_B are hydrostatic force at sections A and B.

W = Weight of the fluid between sections A and B.

M_A and M_B are momentum flux at sections A and B.

τ_0 is the shear stress on the wall of the channel.

P is Wetted Perimeter, A is area of cross-section

For obvious reasons, $P_A = P_B$ and $M_A = M_B$

$\therefore \quad W\sin\theta = \tau_o PL$

Or, $\quad \gamma AL\sin\theta = \tau_o PL \quad$ (For small θ, $\sin\theta = \tan\theta = S$

$\therefore \quad \tau_o = \gamma \cdot \frac{A}{P} \cdot S$

Or, $\quad \tau_o = \gamma RS \quad$ where, R = Hydraulic Radius (A/P)

It is well known that shear stress at the boundary is proportional to V^2 and can be related to Darcy-Weisbach Friction factor 'f' as

$$\tau_o = \frac{f}{8}\rho V^2$$

Equating, we get $V = \sqrt{\frac{8g}{f}}\sqrt{RS}$

Or, $V = C\sqrt{RS}$ is Chezy's Equation

Where, C is Chezy's Coefficient with units $m^{1/2}/s$.

Value of Chezy's Coefficient 'C': Many emperical formulae have been developed to determine the value of Chezy's 'C'. Of these Manning's Equation is most widely used. It expresses Chezy's coefficient as,

$$C = \frac{1}{N}R^{1/6}$$

Combining this with Chezy's Equation gives Average velocity as,

$$V = \frac{1}{N}R^{2/3}S^{1/2}$$

The equation is valid when the channel slope is less than 0.10.

Factor N in Manning's equation is the Roughness or Rugosity coefficient or simply the Manning's 'N'.

Value of N: Strikler recommended the following equation to evaluate Manning's N,

$$N = \frac{(d_{50})^{1/6}}{21}$$

Where, d_{50} is the size of sediment in m. such that 50% of material is finer than this size.

Note: The value of N so obtained is approximate and needs to be verified.

Factors affecting the value of C and N: Both C and N are terms representing resistance to flow primarily due to friction. Some important factors affecting C and N are as follows.

(i) Surface roughness depending upon the material characteristics

(ii) Vegetation, particularly in earthen channels.

(iii) Irregularities in the cross-section.

(iv) Presence of hydraulic structures in the channel.

(v) Channel alignment.

If the roughness is not uniform across the channel width, an average value of C or N is adopted or the channel may be treated as two or more contiguous channels, each having its own value of C or N. The discharge is calculated in each part independently to get the total flow. Natural channels with overbank flood plains are often treated in this manner.

Some standard recommended values of 'N' for different Channel Materials

Channel Material	N
Plastic, Glass, drawn tubing	0.009
Neat cement, Smooth metal	0.010
Planed timber, asbestos pipe	0.011
Wrought iron, welded steel, canvas	0.012
Ordinary concrete, asphalted cast iron	0.013
Unplaned timber, vitrified clay	0.014
Cast-iron pipe	0.015
Riveted steel, brick	0.016
Rubble masonry	0.017
Smooth earth	0.018
Corrugated metal pipe	0.022
Firm Gravel	0.023
Natural Channels in good condition	0.025
Natural channels with stones and weeds	0.035
Very poor natural channels	0.060

Colebrook and Whites formula for value of C:

They developed the following relation for the value of C.

$$C = 15 \log \frac{12y}{Kr}$$

Where, Kr is the roughness of the bed including all kinds of obstructions like ripples, sand banks, bends, islands, vegetation, structures etc. Kr varies largely with the regime of flow. However, measuring Kr is almost impossible.

In most cases, therefore, reverse is done i.e. from measured values of V, R and S, C is computed, which on its turn may yield Kr. Obviously, it is much easier to work directly with C, Since Kr becomes of secondary importance.

Velocity Distribution in Alluvial Streams

Velocity distribution in alluvial streams can be expressed by well-known Prandtl-Karman velocity distribution dimensionless equations,

$$\frac{u}{u_*} = 5.75 \log \frac{u_* y}{\nu} + 5.5 \text{ (For smooth boundary)}$$

And

$$\frac{u}{u_*} = 5.75 \log\left(\frac{y}{K_s}\right) + 8.5 \text{ (For Rough boundary)}$$

where, u is the velocity at a distance y from the bed.

Ks is Equivalent sand grain roughness

u^* is the Shear velocity $= \sqrt{\frac{\tau_o}{\rho}}$

τ_0 is Shear stress on bed $= \gamma R S_0$.

Smooth and Rough Boundary: The smooth and rough boundaries are defined on the basis of relative thicknesses of the Equivalent sand grain roughness and boundary sub-layer.

Smooth Boundary: When laminar sub-layer δ' is much larger than K_s, the boundary is called a smooth boundary. As a result of submergence of roughness projections, turbulent eddies do not come in contact with them. The velocity distribution is governed by Shear Reynold's Number. (Fig. 4.3(a))

Rough Boundary: When K_s/δ' is greater than 6.0, hydraulically rough surface is obtained. In such cases laminar sub-layer is completely destroyed and eddies are in direct contact with the projections. The velocity distribution is governed by the parameter y/K_s. (Fig. 4.3(b))

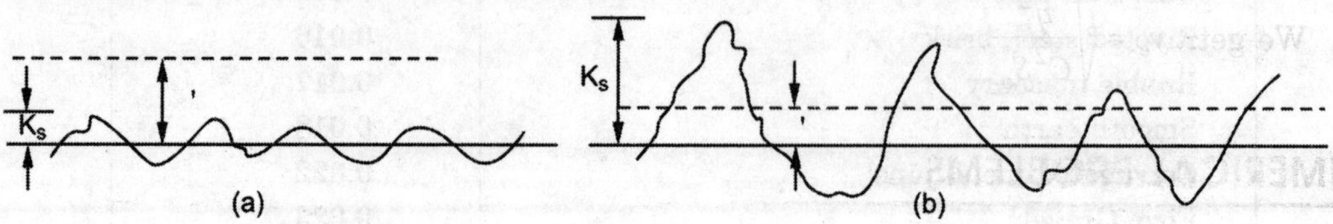

Fig. 4.3

The thickness of boundary sub-layer is calculated by the following formula, $\delta' = \dfrac{11.6\nu}{u_*}$

The Normal Depth or the Equilibrium Depth (y_n, y_o or y_e)

Uniform and steady flow conditions actually reflect a condition of equilibrium. The forces that are exerted upon the water compensate on each other. The motive force Gravity is split into two components, one parallel to the bed and other normal to the bed.

The latter is compensated by the river bed's reaction; the former must be equal to the friction force F. In total therefore $\sum \text{Force} = 0$, so that there is no acceleration experienced. Under these circumstances the total energy line, the water surface line and the bed level all run parallel at distances y and $v^2/2g$.

Consequently, the Energy line slope (S_f), the water surface slope (S_w) and Bed slope (S_0), all are equal, i.e.,

$$S_f = S_w = S_o$$

The whole system is sloping downstream by a slope so as to obtain the energy required to overcome the friction.

Considering a wide rectangular channel of width b and depth of flow y, such that $b \gg y$.

Approximating, $R = \dfrac{by}{b+2y}$, by assuming $b + 2y = b$

We have, $R = y$

Rewriting the Chezy's equation, we have

$$V = C\sqrt{yS_o}$$

Or $$Q = AC\sqrt{yS_o}$$

The required slope to sustain the flow,

$$S_o = \frac{Q^2}{A^2C^2y} = \frac{Q^2}{b^2y^2C^2y} = \frac{Q^2}{C^2b^2y^3}$$

The equivalent (normal) depth is given by

$$y_e^3 = \frac{Q^2}{C^2b^2S_o}$$

Defining, $\frac{Q}{b} = q$ i.e. discharge per unit width also called discharge intensity.

We get, $y_e = \sqrt[3]{\frac{q^2}{C^2S_o}}$

NUMERICAL PROBLEMS

Problem 4.1. Find the velocity and discharge in an open channel of rectangular cross-section of width 10 m, normal depth 1.5m, Bed slope 0.0006 and Chezy's coefficient C = 40 $m^{1/2}/s$. Compute also the value of Manninge N in this channel.

Solution: $A = 10 \times 1.5 = 15\ m^2$

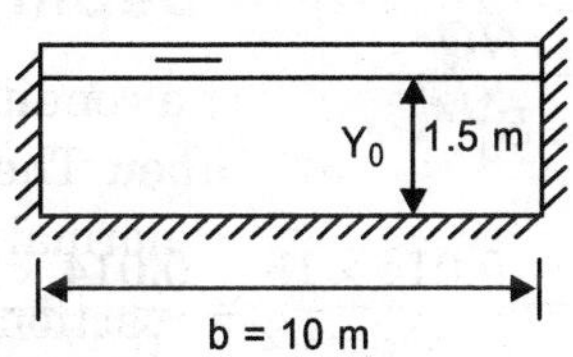

Fig. 4.4

$$P = 10 + 2 \times 1.5 = 13\ m, \quad R = \frac{15}{13}\ m,$$

$$V = C\sqrt{RS_o} = 40\sqrt{\frac{15}{13} \times 0.0006} = 1.052 \text{ m/s}$$

$$Q = A \times V = 15 \times 1.052 = 15.787 \text{ m}^3/\text{s}$$

We know that,

$$C = \frac{1}{N}R^{1/6} \quad \text{Or,} \quad N = \frac{1}{C}R^{1/6} = \frac{1}{40} \times \left(\frac{15}{13}\right)^{1/6} = 0.0256 \text{ m}^{1/2}/\text{s}$$

Problem 4.2. In the above problem find the boundary Shear Stress.

Solution: $\tau_o = \gamma RS_o$, $\quad \gamma$ = unit weight of water in N/m^3

$$= 9810 \times \frac{15}{13} \times 0.0006 = 6.791 \text{ N/m}^2$$

Problem 4.3. A trapezoidal channel has a base width of 20 m and side slopes 1(V): 1(H). The bed slope is 0.0005. If N = 0.014, compute the Normal Depth at a discharge of 18 m^3/s.

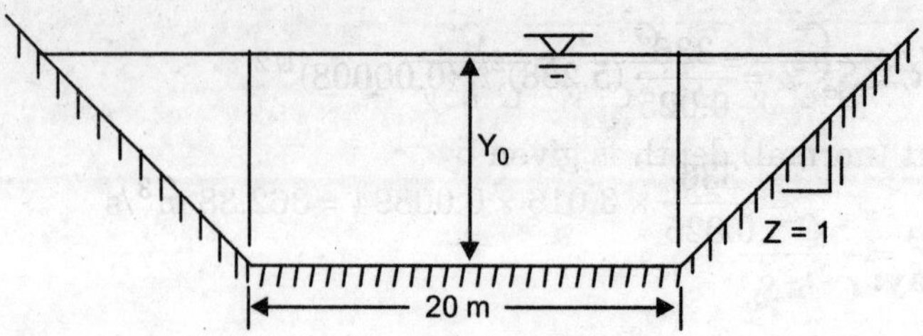

Fig. 4.5

Solution: Let y_0 be the normal depth

$$A = y_o(B + zy_o) = (20 + y_o)y_o$$

$$P = B + 2y\sqrt{1+z^2} = 20 + 2\sqrt{2}y_o$$

$$\therefore \quad R = \frac{(20 + y_o)y_o}{20 + 2\sqrt{2}y_o}$$

From Manning's Equation, $Q = \dfrac{A}{N}R^{2/3}S_o^{1/2} = \dfrac{A}{N}\dfrac{A^{2/3}}{P^{2/3}}S_o^{1/2}$

Or, $$\frac{A^{5/3}}{P^{2/3}} = \frac{NQ}{S_o^{1/2}}$$

Or, $$\frac{[y_o(20 + y_o)]^{5/3}}{(20 + 2\sqrt{2}y_o)^{2/3}} = \frac{0.014 \times 18}{(0.0005)^{1/2}} = \frac{0.014 \times 18}{0.02236} = 11.27$$

By Trial and Error $y_0 = 0.73\ m$ (approximately)

Problem 4.4. A river cross-section has been approximated as shown. Find the total discharge through the river. If the bed slope is 0.00008.

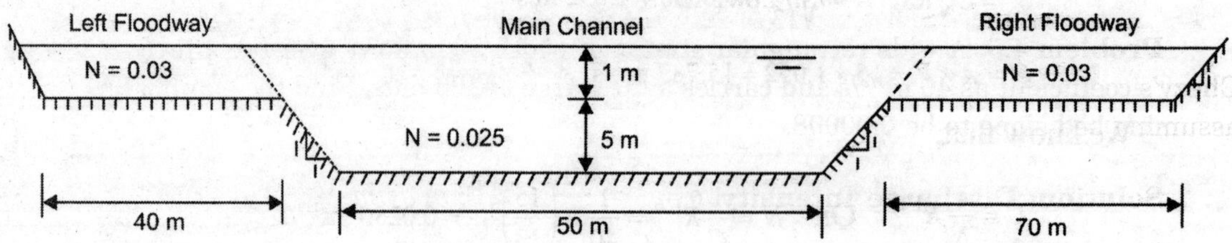

Fig. 4.6

Solution: Main channel: Area $A = \dfrac{62 + 50}{2} \times 6 = 336\ m^2$

Wetted Perimeter $p = 50 + 2\sqrt{50} = 64.14\ m$

Hydraulic Radius $R = \dfrac{A}{P} = \dfrac{336}{64.14} = 5.238\ m$

Or, $Q = \frac{A}{N} R^{2/3} S_o^{1/2} = \frac{336}{0.025} (5.238)^{2/3} (0.00008)^{1/2}$

$$= \frac{336}{0.025} \times 3.016 \times 0.00894 = 362.38 \text{ m}^3/\text{s}$$

Left Floodway:

$$A = 40 \times 1 = 40\ m^2$$

$$P = 40 + \sqrt{2} = 41.414\ m$$

$$R = \frac{40}{41.414} = 0.9658\ m$$

$$\therefore \quad Q = \frac{40}{0.03} \times (0.9658)^{2/3} \times (0.00008)^{1/2}$$

$$= \frac{40}{0.03} \times 0.977 \times 0.00894 = 11.645 \text{ m}^3/\text{s}$$

Right Floodway:

$$A = 70 \times 1 = 70\ m^2$$

$$P = 70 + 1.414 = 71.141\ m$$

$$R = \frac{70}{71.141} = 0.984\ m$$

$$\therefore \quad Q = \frac{70}{0.03} \times (0.984)^{2/3} \times (0.00008)^{1/2}$$

$$= \frac{70}{0.03} \times 0.9893 \times 0.00894 = 20.636 \text{ m}^3/\text{s}$$

Hence, Total Discharge = 362.38 + 11.645 + 20.363

= 394.661 m³/s

Problem 4.5. A wide rectangular stream of width 50 m flows over the alluvium having Chezy's coefficient as 40 $m^{1/2}/s$ and carries a discharge of 108 m^3/s. Find the equilibrium depth assuming bed slope to be 0.00008.

Solution: Discharge Intensity $q = \frac{Q}{b} = \frac{108}{50} = 2.16\ m^3/s/m$

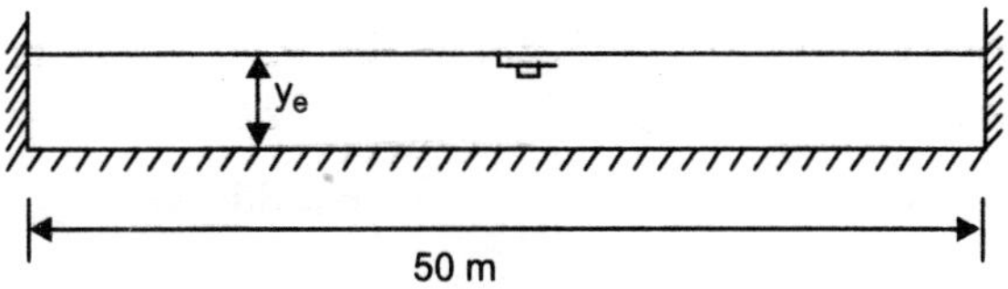

Fig. 4.7

$$y_e = \left[\frac{q^2}{C^2 S_o}\right]^{1/3} = \left[\frac{2.16^2}{40^2 \times 0.00008}\right]^{1/3} = 3.315\ m$$

Unsolved Problems

4.6 A main channel with a floodway is shown below. Compute the discharge if the main channel is of earth ($N = 0.025$) and the floodway has $N = 0.035$. The slope of the channel is 0.0008. **[Ans. 200 m³/s]**

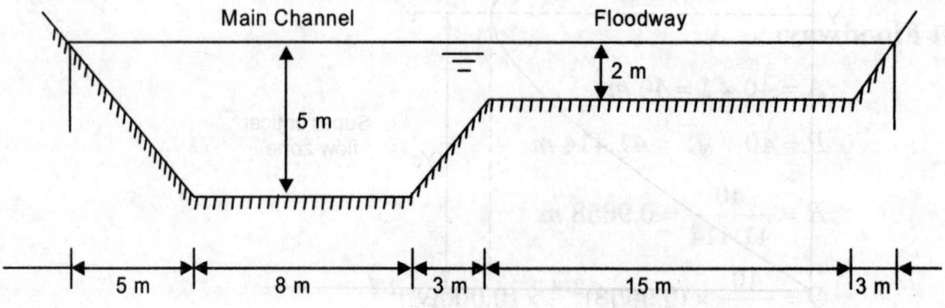

Fig. 4.8

4.7 Estimate the Normal depth in a 3 m wide rectangular channel carrying a discharge of 1.5 m^3/s on a slope of 0.0004. Assume Manning's Roughness coefficient as 0.013.

[Ans. 0.58 m]

4.8 A wide rectangular channel 30 m wide flows over sand with Chezy's C = 45 $m^{1/2}/s$ carrying a discharge of 60 m^3/s on a bed slope of 0.000075. Find the Equilibrium depth.

[Ans. 2.974 m]

FLOW THROUGH CHANNEL TRANSITIONS

Any rise in the bottom of the channel i.e. formation of a hump or narrowing of the channel at any spot is termed as transition. These transitions can be of very short length or else can be relatively longer. As most of rivers flowing in alluvium exhibit sub-critical flow i.e. Froude Number $F_r < 1$, following discussion will be for sub-critical flow only.

Short Transitions: Considering rectangular channels only.

Flow over a Hump: The figure 4.10 shows a channel of rectangular cross-section with a hump at the bottom. A rise in the channel bottom causes a decrease in the specific energy $\left(y + \dfrac{v^2}{2g}\right)$. From the Specific Energy graph (fig. 4.11) it can be easily concluded that a decrease in specific energy will result in fall of water surface at the location of hump for sub-critical flow.

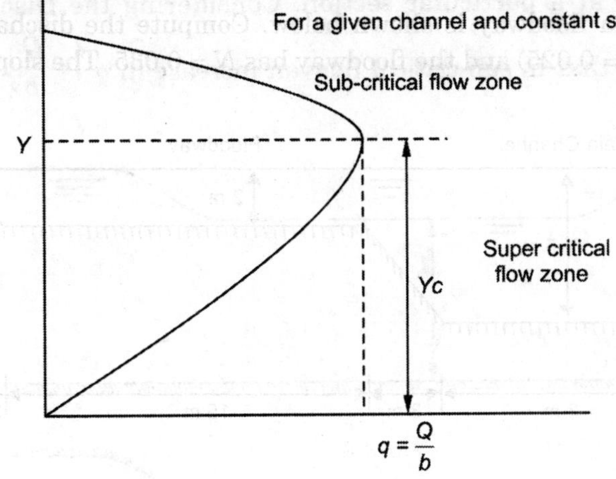

Fig. 4.9

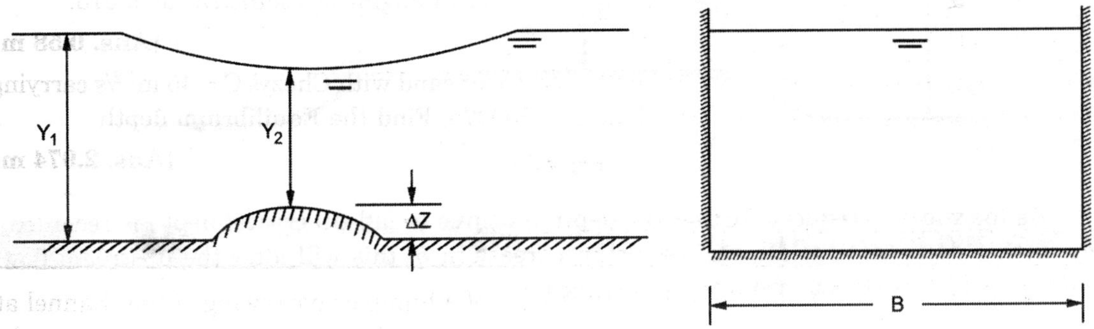

Fig. 4.10

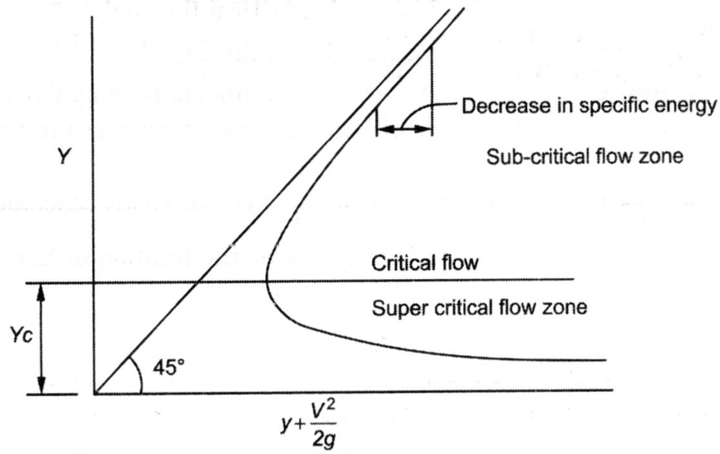

Fig. 4.11

It may be noted that further increase in the height of the hump will result in further fall in the water till the critical depth is reached. Any further rise would cause change in upstream flow condition or backwater effect.

Flow through a constriction: The figure 4.12 shows a channel of rectangular cross-section with reduced width at a particular section. Considering the Discharge Diagram (q *vs* y) fig. 4.9, we can infer that in sub-critical flow an increase in $q \left(= \frac{Q}{b}\right)$, there will be a fall in water level.

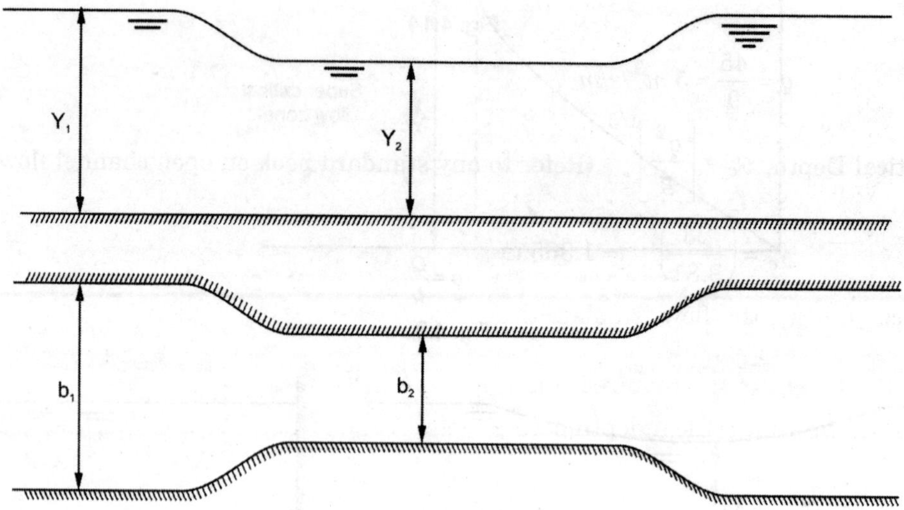

Fig. 4.12

As the width is reduced further the depth continue to fall till critical depth is recorded. Any further decrease in width will result in increase in q, this will alter the upstream flow condition, which is obvious from the y–q diagram.

NUMERICAL PROBLEMS

Problem 4.9. A 9 m wide rectangular channel carries 45 m^3/s water at a depth of 2 m. At what height of a hump the depth over the hump will be critical ?

Solution:

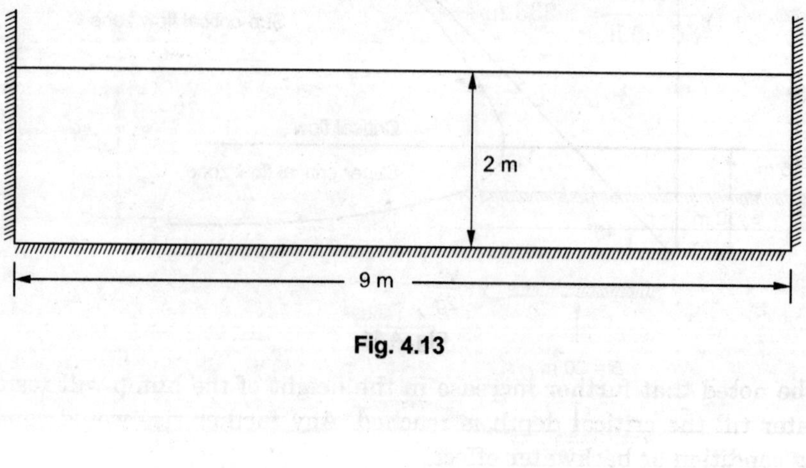

Fig. 4.13

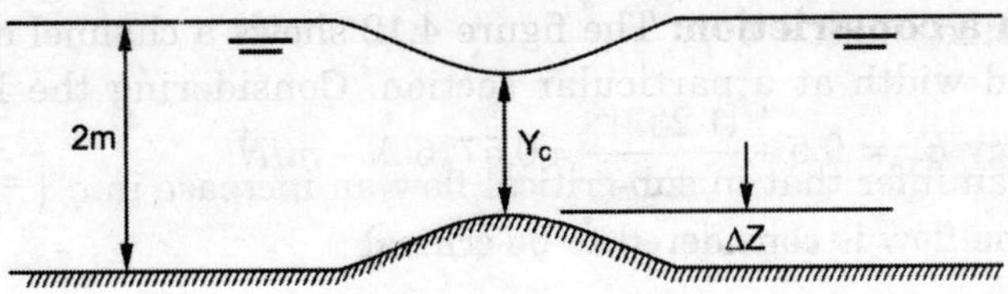

Fig. 4.14

$$q = \frac{45}{9} = 5\ m^3/s/m$$

Critical Depth, $y_c = \left[\frac{q^2}{g}\right]^{1/3}$ (Refer to any standard book on open channel flow)

$$\therefore \quad y_c = \left(\frac{23}{9.81}\right)^{1/3} = 1.365 \text{ m}$$

Since $y_c < y_o$, the flow is sub-critical flow. Hence the water surface at the hump will fall.

Let the height of the required hump = Δz

It is known that critical depth occurs at minimum specific energy ($\in_m$), which is given by,

$$\in_m = \frac{3}{2} y_c = \frac{3}{2} \times 1.365 = 2.048 \text{ Nm/N}$$

Equating Total energy at two sections, we have

$$2 + \frac{45^2}{18^2 \times 2g} = 2.048 + \Delta z$$

$$\therefore \quad \Delta z = 0.27 \text{ m}$$

Problem 4.10. A rectangular channel is 30 m wide and carries a flow of 18.5 m³/s at a depth of 50 cm. A channel contraction is required at a section. Find the greatest allowable contraction in width without altering the upstream flow.

Solution: $V_1 = \frac{18.5}{30 \times 0.5} = 1.233$ m/s

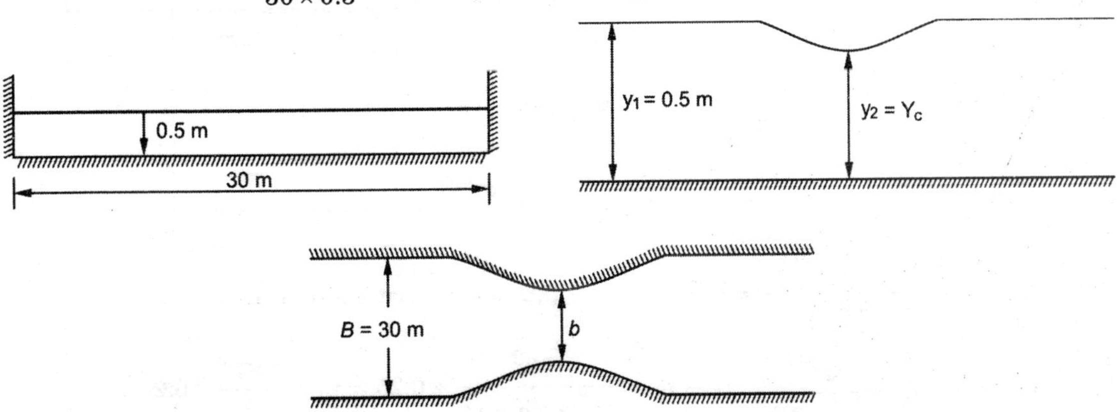

Fig. 4.15

Let the contracted width = b

$$\therefore \quad \text{Total Energy } E_1 = 0.5 + \frac{(1.233)^2}{2g} = 0.5775\ N-m/N$$

At section 2, the flow is considered to be critical

$$\therefore \quad y_c = \left[\frac{q_2^2}{g}\right]^{1/3} = \left[\left(\frac{18.5}{b}\right)^2 \Big/ 9.81\right]^{1/3} \quad \text{Or } q_2 = \frac{18.5}{b}$$

$$\text{Or,} \quad y_c^3 = \frac{34.887}{b^2}, \ or \ b^2 = \frac{34.887}{y_c^3}$$

$$\text{Also,} \quad y_c = \frac{2}{3} \times 0.5775 = 0.385 \text{ m (For no less)}$$

Equating we get,

$$b^2 = \frac{34.887}{(0.385)^3} = 611.338 \quad \text{Or,} \quad b = 24.725 \text{ m}$$

Problem 4.11. A 25 m wide rectangular channel carries a discharge of 100 m³/s at a depth of 2 m.

(a) Calculate the depth over a hump of 25 cm on bed.

(b) Minimum rise in bed level to obtain critical flow.

(c) Flow condition if the height of the hump is 60 cm.

Solution: $Q = 100 \text{ m}^3/\text{s}, \ v_1 = \frac{100}{25 \times 2} = 2 \text{ m/s}, \ q = \frac{100}{25} = 4 \text{ m}^3/\text{s/m}$

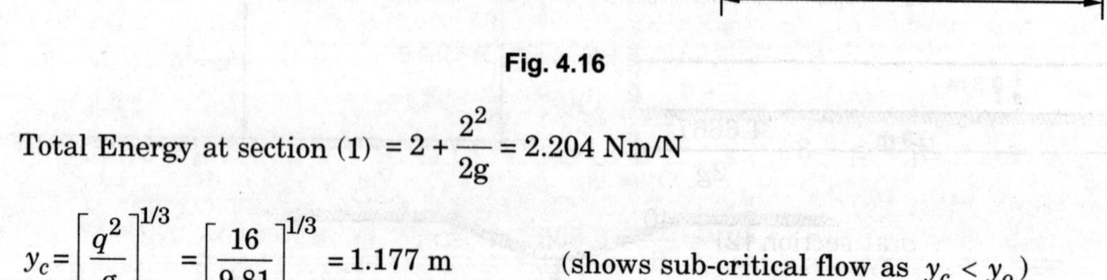

Fig. 4.16

$$\text{Total Energy at section (1)} = 2 + \frac{2^2}{2g} = 2.204 \text{ Nm/N}$$

$$y_c = \left[\frac{q^2}{g}\right]^{1/3} = \left[\frac{16}{9.81}\right]^{1/3} = 1.177 \text{ m} \qquad \text{(shows sub-critical flow as } y_c < y_o)$$

$$\text{(a)} \quad E_2 = y_2 + \frac{Q^2}{b^2 y_2^2 \cdot 2g} + \Delta z = y_2 + \frac{100^2}{25^2 \times 2g \times y_2^2} + 0.25 = y_2 + \frac{0.815}{y_2^2} + 0.25$$

Equating energies for no loss condition

$$y_2 + \frac{0.815}{y_2^2} + 0.25 = 2.204 \quad \therefore \; y_2 + \frac{0.815}{y_2^2} = 1.954$$

Solving by trial and error, $y_2 = 1.657\, m$

(b) Minimum specific energy $\in_m = \frac{3}{2}\, y_c = \frac{3}{2} \times 1.177 = 1.765$ Nm/N

$$E = \in_m + \Delta Z_m \;\; \therefore \;\; \Delta Z_m = 2.204 - 1.765 = 0.439\, m$$

(c) Since $\Delta z > \Delta Zm$, specific energy is not adequate to carry the flow. Let y' is the depth at upstream and $\in_1'$ the specific energy. The depth at section 2 will still be critical.

$$\in_1' = \in_m + \Delta z \;\; \text{or} \;\; \in_1' = 1.765 + 0.6 = 2.365 \text{ Nm/N}$$

Equating

$$\therefore \; 2.365 = y_1' + \frac{0.815}{y_1'^2} \quad \text{by trial } y_1' = 2.197 \text{ m}$$

Problem 4.12. A rectangular channel 8 m wide carries 40 m^3/s water at a normal depth of 3 m. If the channel is contracted to (*a*) 6 m and (*b*) 3.5 m, Examine the flow conditions by computing the upstream depth and depth at contracted section.

Solution: (a) $V_1 = \frac{40}{8 \times 3} = 1.6667\, m/s$

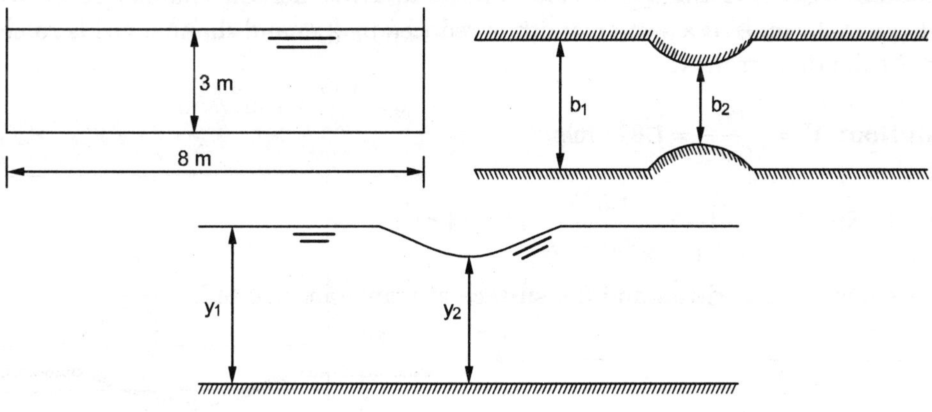

Fig. 4.17

$$E_1 = \in_1 = 3 + \frac{1.6667^2}{2g} = 3.14157\, Nm/N$$

$$q \text{ at section (2)} = \frac{40}{6} = 6.6667 \text{ m}^3\text{/s/m}$$

$$y_{c_2} = \left[\frac{6.6667^2}{9.81}\right]^{1/3} = 1.6546\, m$$

$$\in_2 = \frac{3}{2} y_{c_2} = \frac{3}{2} \times 1.6546 = 2.4819\ m$$

Since $\in_1 > \in_2$, there will be no change in the upstream flow condition.

Equating Total Energy E_1 with energy at section (2), considering no losses.

$$3.14157 = y_2 + \frac{40^2}{(6y_2)^2 \times 2g}$$

Or, $\quad y_2 + \dfrac{2.265}{y_2^2} = 3.14157$ by trial and error, We get, $y_2 = 2.86\ m$

(b) $\quad q_2 = \dfrac{40}{3.5} = 11.4285\ m^3/s/m, \quad y_{c_2} = \left[\dfrac{11.4285^2}{9.81}\right]^{1/3} = 2.37\ m$

$$\in_{min} = \frac{3}{2} y_c = \frac{3}{2} \times 2.37 = 3.555 \text{ Nm/N}$$

Since $\in_1 < \in_{min}$, the flow will not sustain and there will be change in upstream depth.

Let the new upstream depth is y' then,

$$y' + \frac{40^2}{8^2 y'^2 \times 2g} = 3.555 \quad \text{or} \quad y' + \frac{1.2742}{y'^2} = 3.555$$

By Trial, $y' = 3.45$ m

Problem 4.13. A discharge of 60m³/s flows in a rectangular channel 16 m. wide at a normal depth of 2.0 m. If at a section width is reduced by 2 m and channel bed is raised by 20 cm. Find the depth at transition.

Solution: $V_1 = \dfrac{60}{16 \times 2} = 1.875$ m/s

Froude No. $F_r = \dfrac{V_1}{\sqrt{gy_1}} = \dfrac{1.875}{\sqrt{9.81 \times 2}} = 0.423 < 1$

Hence flow is subscritical and the surface at transition will fall.

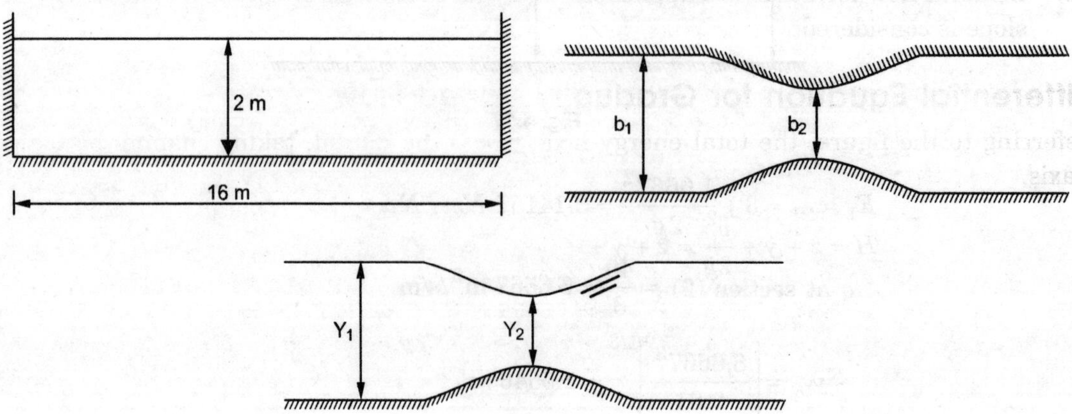

Fig. 4.18

Specific Energy: $\in_1 = y_1 + \frac{V_1^2}{2g} = 2 + \frac{1.875^2}{2 \times 9.81} = 2.179 \text{ N-m/N}$

$$q_2 = \frac{Q}{b_2} = \frac{60}{14} = 4.285 \text{ m}^3\text{/s/m}$$

$$\therefore \quad y_{c_2} = \left[\frac{q_2^2}{g}\right]^{1/3} = \left[\frac{4.285^2}{9.81}\right]^{1/3} = 1.2325\ m$$

$$\in_{c_2} = \frac{3}{2} y_c = \frac{3}{2} \times 1.2325 = 1.8487 \text{ N-m/N}$$

Since, $\in_2 = \in_1 - \Delta z = 2.179 - 0.2 = 1.979$ N-m/N $> \in_{c_2}$, there will be no change in upstream flow condition.

For finding depth at the transition.

$$y_2 + \frac{60^2}{2g\,(14 \times y_2)^2} = 1.979, \quad y_2 + \frac{0.936}{y_2^2} = 1.979$$

By Trial, y_2 = 1.622 m

Long Transitions: In long length transitions there is gradual change in depth. Hence, theory of gradually varied flow is applied.

Gradually Varied Flow: Gradually Varied Flow (GVF) is the non-uniform flow in which only small change in depth occurs in long stretches of the channel. As a result the curvature of streamlines is negligible; the distribution of pressure in the vertical may be assumed as hydrostatic.

Following assumptions are made in the analysis of Gradually Varied Flow.

(a) Channel slope is small.

(b) Channel is prismatic.

(c) Velocity distribution is uniform

(d) Pressure distribution is hydrostatic.

(e) Uniform flow formulae are applicable, except that instead of bottom slope, energy line slope is considered.

Differential Equation for Gradually Varied Flow

Referring to the figure, the total energy head above the datum, taking channel bottom as x-axis.

$$H = z + y + \frac{v^2}{2g} = z + y + \frac{Q^2}{2gA^2}$$

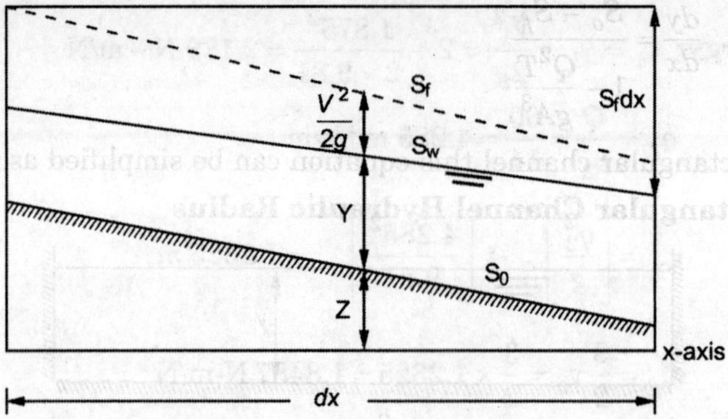

Fig. 4.19

Differentiating the above with respect to x, we have

$$\frac{dH}{dx} = \frac{dz}{dx} + \frac{dy}{dx} + \frac{d}{dx}\left(\frac{Q^2}{2gA^2}\right)$$

Deriving each of the above terms separately,

$\frac{dH}{dx}$ → Represents Energy slope = $-S_f$

$\frac{dz}{dx}$ → denoted bottom slope = $-S_o$

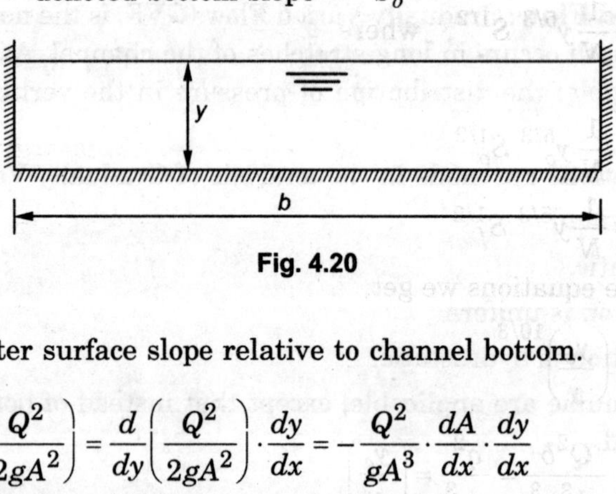

Fig. 4.20

$\frac{dy}{dx}$ → Gives water surface slope relative to channel bottom.

$$\frac{d}{dx}\left(\frac{Q^2}{2gA^2}\right) = \frac{d}{dy}\left(\frac{Q^2}{2gA^2}\right)\cdot\frac{dy}{dx} = -\frac{Q^2}{gA^3}\cdot\frac{dA}{dx}\cdot\frac{dy}{dx}$$

Substituting $\frac{dA}{dy} = T$ (Top width)

We have $\frac{d}{dx}\left(\frac{Q^2}{2gA^2}\right) = -\frac{Q^2T}{gA^3}\cdot\frac{dy}{dx}$

Substituting each of the above in the total head equation we get,

$$-S_f = -S_o + \frac{dy}{dx} - \left(\frac{Q^2T}{gA^3}\right)\frac{dy}{dx}$$

Readjusting results in the following differential equation for Gradually Varied Flow.

$$\frac{dy}{dx} = \frac{S_o - S_f}{1 - \dfrac{Q^2 T}{gA^3}}$$

For a wide Rectangular channel this equation can be simplified as follows,

For wide rectangular Channel Hydraulic Radius

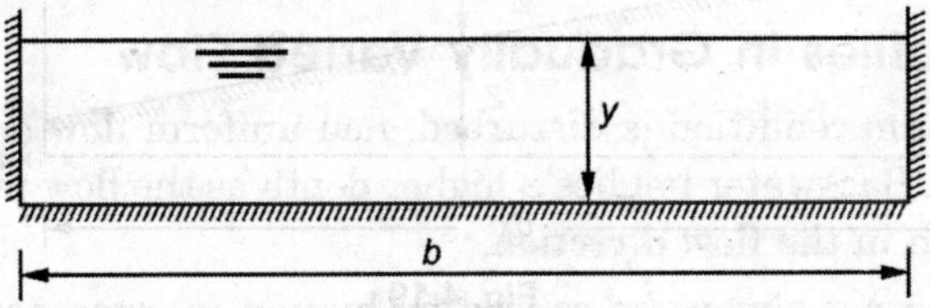

Fig. 4.21

$$R = \frac{A}{P} = \frac{by}{b+2y} \approx y \qquad \text{(since } b + 2y \approx b\text{) for wide channels.}$$

Writing the Manning's Equation

$$Q = \frac{A}{N} R^{2/3} S^{1/2} = \frac{by}{N} y^{2/3} S^{1/2}$$

Or,
$$q = \frac{1}{N} y^{5/3} S^{1/2}, \quad \text{where } q = \frac{Q}{b}$$

We may write,

$$q = \frac{1}{N} y_o^{5/3} S_o^{1/2} \qquad \text{For Uniform Flow and}$$

$$q = \frac{1}{N} y^{5/3} S_f^{1/2} \qquad \text{For Gradually Varied Flow}$$

On dividing above equations we get,

$$\frac{S_f}{S_o} = \left(\frac{y_o}{y}\right)^{10/3}$$

Solving,
$$\frac{Q^2 T}{gA^3} = \frac{Q^2 b}{gb^3 y^3} = \frac{q^2}{gy^3} = \left(\frac{y_c}{y}\right)^3$$

Substituting in the differential equation for GVF.

$$\frac{dy}{dx} = S_o \frac{1 - \left[y_o / y \right]^{10/3}}{1 - \left[y_c / y \right]^3}$$

If instead of Manning's Equation Chezy's Equation ($V = C\sqrt{RS}$) was used,

$$\frac{dy}{dx} = S_o \frac{1 - \left[y_o / y \right]^3}{1 - \left[y_c / y \right]^3}$$

Water Surface Profiles in Gradually Varied Flow

Whenever the equilibrium condition is disturbed, non-uniform flow occurs and backwater or drawdown effects occur. Backwater implies a higher depth as the flow progresses and drawdown means decreasing depth in the flow direction.

These effects need not always be caused by human interference; nature also provides disturbances. For instance, at confluences where two rivers join, one may experience backwater and other drawdown.

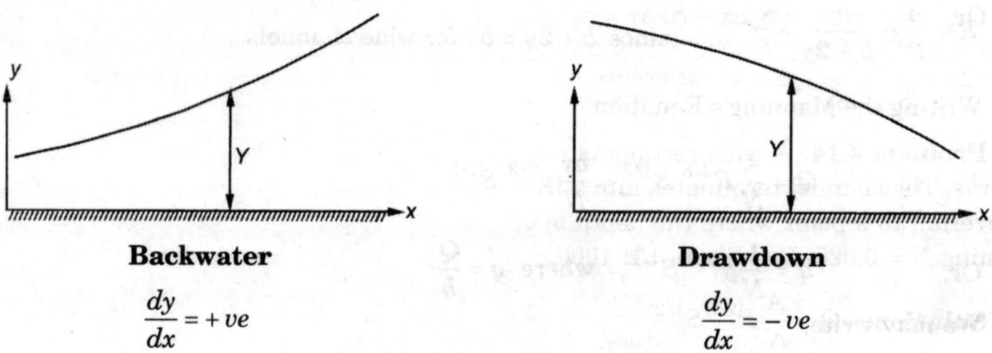

Fig. 4.22

Solution of the Gradually Varied Flow Equation

In gradually varied flow to evaluate the surface profile i.e. find out the depth at various sections, the dynamic equation of GVF has to be integrated. Various methods are available for the purpose e.g. the Step method, the Graphical Integration method and the Direct Integration method. (Details can be had from any standard book on open channel flow.)

Here, the simplest of the methods i.e. the Direct Step Method is mentioned. In the Direct Step Method the channel is divided into a number of smaller reaches and the computation is carried step by step from one end to reach the other end.

Referring to the following figure and considering the Channel reach of length Δx and equating the total head at sections 1 and 2.

$$z_1 + y_1 + \frac{v_1^2}{2g} = z_2 + y_2 + \frac{v_2^2}{2g} + \overline{S_f}\Delta x, \quad \overline{S_f} = \text{Average gradient between section 1 and 2}$$

Solving for Δx.

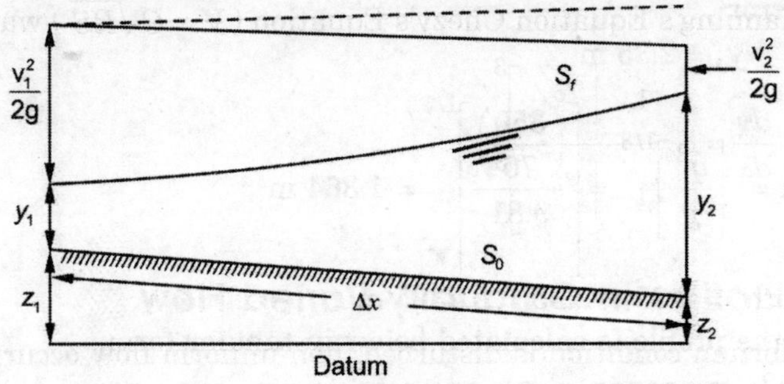

Fig. 4.23

$$(z_1 - z_2) - \overline{S_f}\Delta x = \left(y_2 + \frac{v_2^2}{2g}\right) - \left(y_1 + \frac{v_1^2}{2g}\right)$$

Or,

$$S_o \Delta x - \overline{S_f}\Delta x = \epsilon_2 - \epsilon_1$$

$$\Delta x = \frac{\Delta \epsilon}{S_o - \overline{\overline{S_f}}}$$, $\Delta \epsilon$ is difference of specific energy between the two sections.

Problem 4.14. A wide rectangular channel of base width 70 m carries a discharge of 350 m^3/s. The channel terminates into a free overfall. Compute the length of the profile from free overfall to a point where the depth is 0.95 of the normal depth. Use direct step method assuming N = 0.025. Bed Slope = 1: 1000.

Solution: $Q = \frac{A}{N} R^{2/3} S_o^{1/2}$

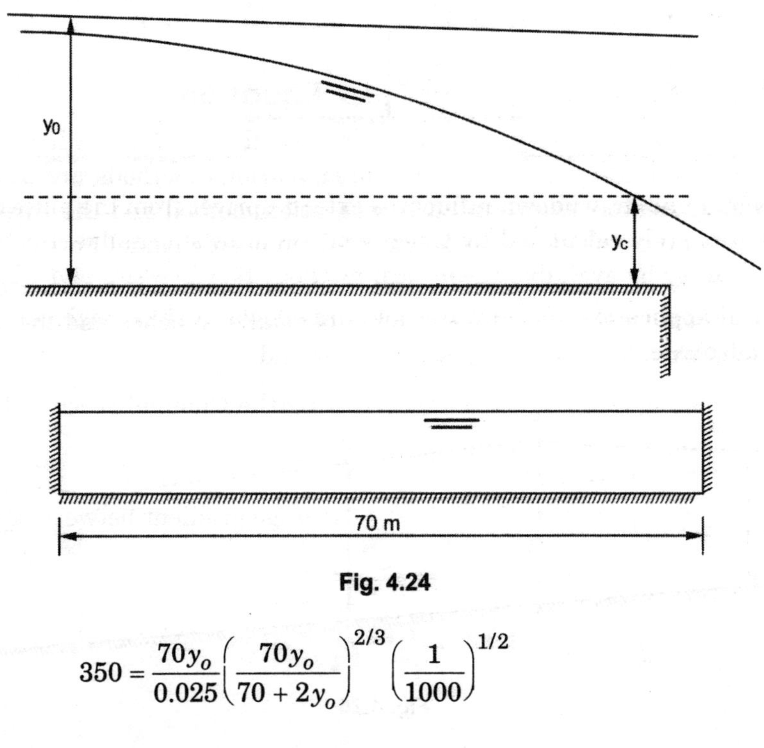

Fig. 4.24

$$350 = \frac{70y_o}{0.025}\left(\frac{70y_o}{70 + 2y_o}\right)^{2/3}\left(\frac{1}{1000}\right)^{1/2}$$

By trial and error

$$y_o = 2.35 \text{ m}$$

$$\text{Critical Depth} = \left[\frac{q^2}{g}\right]^{1/3} = \left[\frac{\left(\frac{350}{70}\right)^2}{9.81}\right]^{1/3} = 1.364 \text{ m}$$

Upstream Depth = 0.95 × 2.35 = 2.2325 m

The length of the profile is calculated below in tabular form.

$$N^2 = 0.000625 \qquad Q = 350 \text{ m}^3/\text{s}$$

SN	y	A	P	R	$R^{4/3}$	$V=\frac{Q}{A}$	V^2	$S_f = \frac{V^2N^2}{R^{4/3}}$	$\overline{S_f}$	$\in = y+\frac{V^2}{2g}$	$\Delta\in$	Δx	L
	m	m^2	m	m	–	m/s	–			N–m/N	Nm/N	m	m
1	1.364	95.48	72.73	1.31	1.43	3.66	13.4	0.005856		2.0469			
2	1.5	105.0	73.0	1.438	1.62	3.33	11.11	0.004855	0.005355	2.0662	0.0193	4.43	4.43
3	2	140.0	74.0	1.89	2.34	2.5	6.25	0.001669	0.003262	2.3185	0.2523	1025	1029.43
4	2.23	156.1	74.46	2.096	2.68	2.242	5.027	0.001172	0.00142	2.4862	0.1677	5919.5	6949

The length of the surface profile will be approximately 6.949 Km.

(**Note:** Taking closer depth intervals would give better result)

A fine example of the occurrence of backwater and drawdown curves is flow in a long narrowed river section as shown in the figure 4.25.

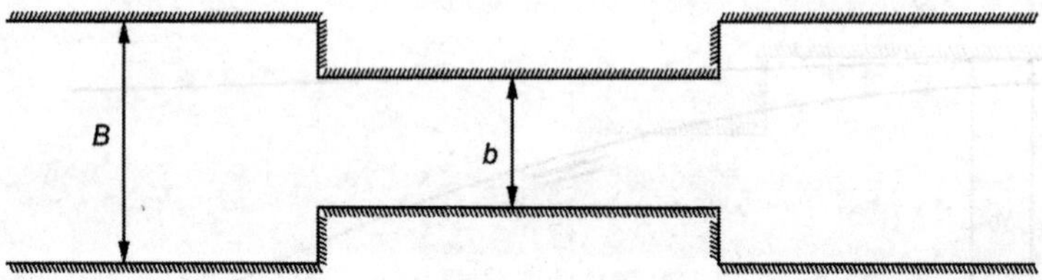

The backwater and drawndown influences extend upriver from the place of disturbances and can be quantitatively calculated by Chezy's or Manning's formulae. Such computations can be done in steps or by available theoretical methods like Bresse's and Chow's methods.

For practical application of backwater and drawdown in river engineering, the step by step method is adequate.

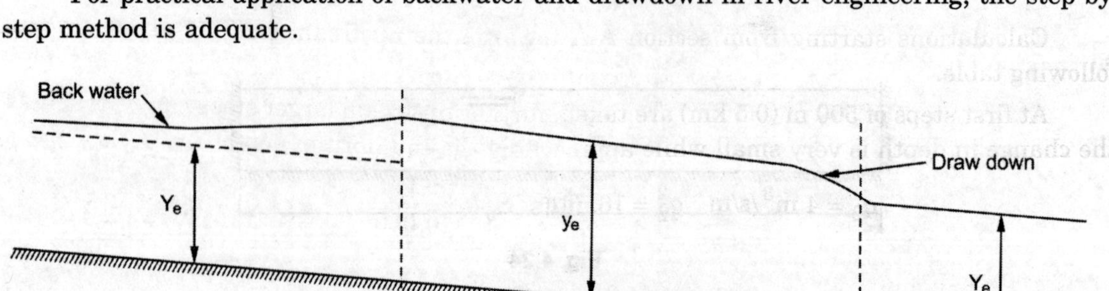

Fig. 4.25

Problem 4.15. In a long narrowed section of the preceding figure compute the drawdown curve, if the discharge is 1000 m³/s. Width of the main channel B = 500 m, width of the contracted section b = 250 m, bed slope S_0 = 1:10,000 and Chezy's C = 40 $m^{1/2}/s$.

Solution: Main Channel: $q_1 = \dfrac{1000}{500} = 2\ m^3/s/m$

$$\therefore \quad \text{Equilibrium Depth } y_{e_1} = \left[\frac{q^2}{C^2 S_o}\right]^{1/3} = \left[\frac{2^2}{40^2 \times 10^{-4}}\right]^{1/3} = 2.92\ m$$

Narrow channel: $q_2 = \dfrac{1000}{250} = 4\ m^3/s/m$

$$\therefore \quad \text{Equilibrium Depth } y_{e_2} = \left[\frac{4^2}{40^2 \times 10^{-4}}\right]^{1/3} = 4.64\ m$$

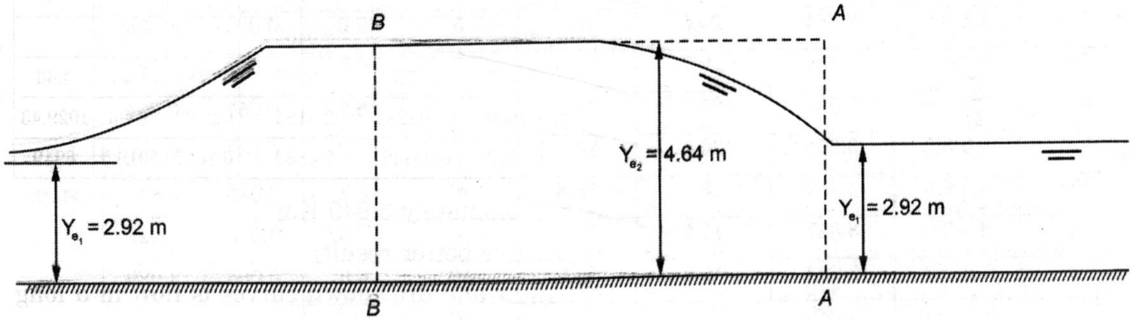

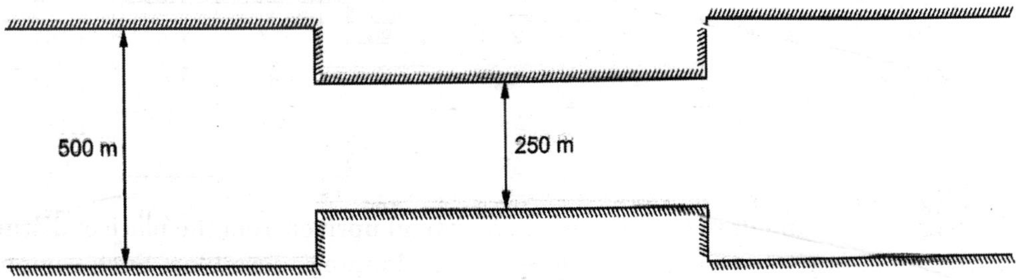

Fig. 4.26

Calculations starting from section A-A towards the upstream side are shown in the following table.

At first steps of 500 m (0.5 km) are taken, further upstream larger steps can be taken as the change in depth is very small while approaching the equilibrium depth.

$$q_2 = 4\ m^3/s/m \quad q_2^2 = 16 \text{ units} \quad S_o = \frac{1}{10,000}$$

Step	Distance u/s of A-A (Km)	Depth at the beginning of step (m)	$S=\frac{q^2}{C^2y^3}$ $\times 10^{-5}$	Change in Elevation Per step		Change in Depth y		Depth at the end of the step	Length of the step
				Water	Bed				
				$(x \times S)$ cm	$(x \times S_o)$ cm	cm	m	m	Km
1	0-0.5	2.92	40	20	5	15.0	0.15	3.07	
2	0.5-1.0	3.07	34.5	17.2	5	12.2	0.122	3.192	
3	1.0-1.5	3.192	30.7	15.4	5	10.4	0.104	3.296	
4	1.5-2.0	3.296	27.9	14.0	5	9.0	0.090	3.386	0.5 Km
5	2.0-2.5	3.386	25.8	12.8	5	7.8	0.078	3.464	
6	2.5-3.0	3.464	24.0	12.0	5	7.0	0.070	3.534	
7	3.0-3.5	3.534	22.7	11.3	5	6.3	0.063	3.597	
8	3.5-4.0	3.594	21.5	10.7	5	5.7	0.057	3.654	
9	4.0-5.0	3.654	20.5	20.5	10	10.5	0.105	3.759	1 Km
10	5.0-6.0	3.759	18.8	18.8	10	8.8	0.088	3.847	steps
11	6.0-7.0	3.847	17.6	17.6	10	7.6	0.076	3.923	
12	7.0-8.0	3.923	16.6	16.6	10	6.6	0.066	3.989	
13	8.0-10.0	3.989	15.7	31.4	20	11.4	0.114	4.103	
14	10.0-12.0	4.104	14.5	29.0	20	9.0	0.09	4.193	2 Km
15	12.0-14.0	4.194	13.5	27.0	20	7.0	0.07	4.263	steps
16	14.0-19.0	4.264	12.9	64.5	50	14.5	0.145	4.408	
17	19.0-24.0	4.409	11.6	58.0	50	8.0	0.080	4.488	5 Km
18	24.0-29.0	4.489	11.0	55.0	50	5.0	0.050	4.538	steps
19	29.0-39.0	4.539	10.7	107.0	100	7.0	0.070	4.608	10 Km steps

In the similar way the backwater curve starting from section B-B can be computed.

SOME SPECIAL FLOW PHENOMENON

In previous discussion various assumptions were made, one of these is that the flow lines are straight and parallel which in effect means that this flow is two dimensional. This, however, is not very much in conformity with reality. In natural water courses, the flow is always three, dimensional.

Still, many of such three-dimensional flows that can be treated with sufficient accuracy by the formulae relating to two-dimensional flow, for example, formulae relating to energy gradient and friction losses, velocity distribution, Bernoulli's law, acceleration and retardation, discharge over notches and weirs etc. Particularly, in all those cases where streamlines can be assumed to be straight two-dimensional approach is well taken. It is known, as soon as the streamlines deviate from the straight, additional energy losses are unavoidable.

Flowing water cannot decelerate quickly, therefore, abrupt changes in direction of flow cannot occur, kinetic energy is not readily reconverted into potential energy. Only if the changes are gradual flow follows the wall, otherwise flow separates from the wall and eddies are formed between the wall and first regular streamline. (Fig. 4.27)

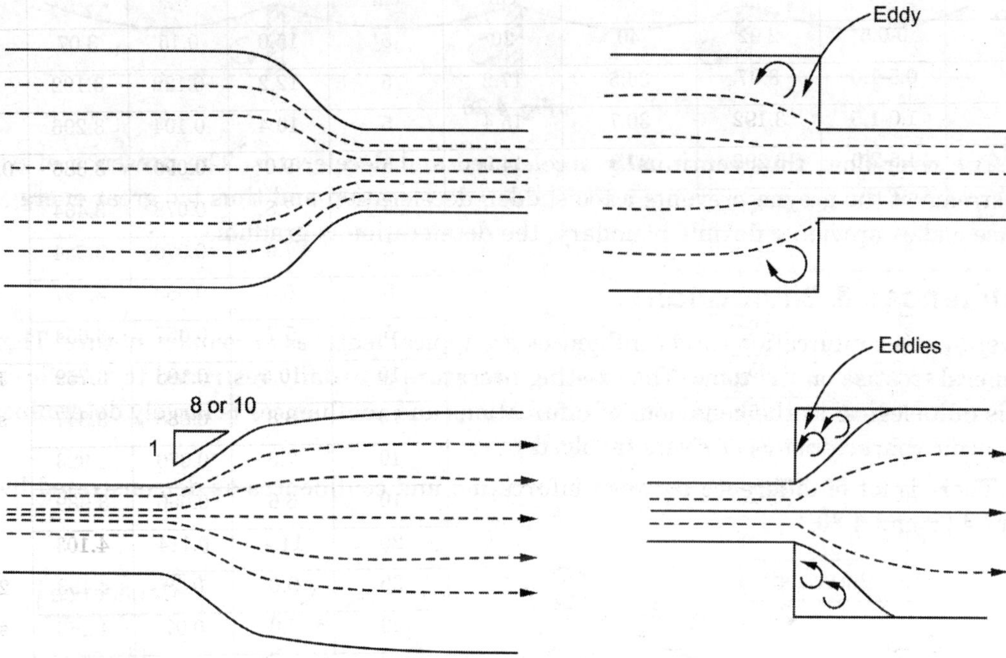

Fig. 4.27 Accelerating and Decelerating Flow

The eddies derive their energy from the main stream and use it up in extra friction loss. These eddies have elliptical shape, when the ratio between the major and minor axes becomes too great, the eddy splits up in several smaller ones. The eddies can be compared with ball-bearings; as they support the flowing water in absence of a fixed wall. The centrifugal force of the eddy which is proportional to $\frac{v^2}{r}$, provides the support; if r becomes too large, the force becomes too small and the eddy breaks up into smaller units of smaller r values.

At times the eddy grow out of its fixed wall and cause a narrower section for the main stream. The main stream is therefore accelerated, the water surface falls and a transverse gradient is established.

Eddies in River Engineering Problems: Eddies occur frequently in river engineering problems. Some examples are given here.

(1) Spurs for Bank Protection: Suprs or Groynes are used in rivers to protect the river bank or marginal bunds (embankment) against heavy current and also to reduce the net width so that the depth of the net cross-sections is increased. The net width, the distance between the outer streamlines varies: it is narrowest at or just downstream of the spur, and widest just upstream from the spur. (Fig. 4.28)

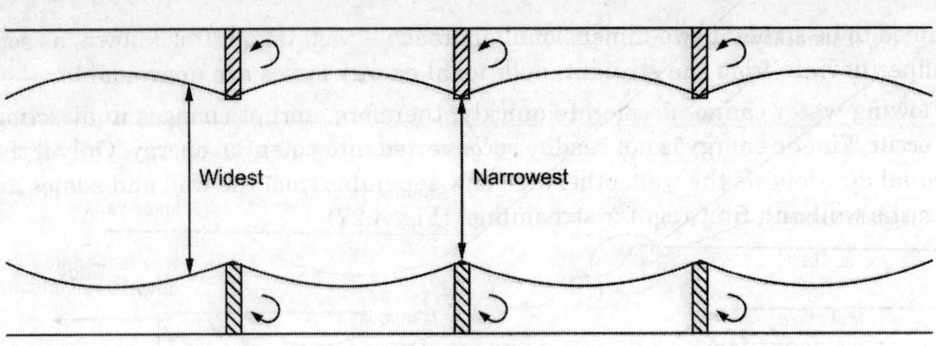

Fig. 4.28

The river flow, thus continually accelerated and decelerates. The presence of eddies downstream of the groyne prevents a too sudden deceleration and thus too great energy loss because eddies provide a flexible boundary, the deceleration is gradual.

Confluences & Bifurcations

In river systems bifurcations and confluences are typical features of complex nature. There is no general treatise on the topic. The existing literature is usually restricted to specific cases. This is quite logical as the behaviour of bifurcations and confluences is largely determined by the specific characteristics of rivers involved.

There is lot of difference between bifurcation and confluences as demonstrated by the figures 4.29 and 4.30.

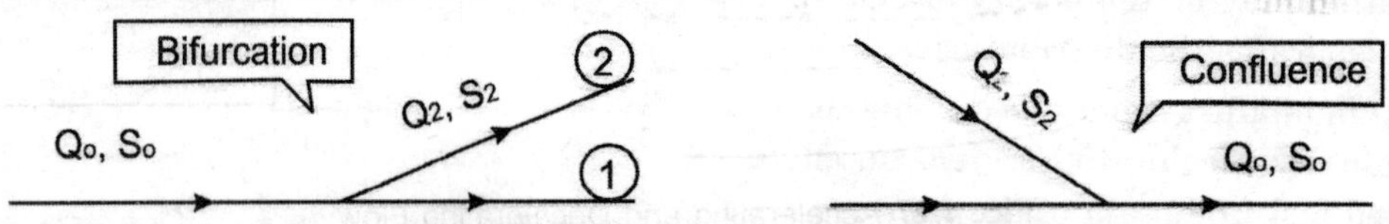

Fig. 4.29

River (1) is assumed to be larger than the river (2) Following points can be made,

(1) At bifurcation the discharge division Q_1 and Q_2 is governed by the conveyance and the geometry of the channel.

(2) At confluence difference between Q_1 and Q_2 is the dominating factor, if $Q_1 > Q_2$ strong backwater effects in (2) will be observed. This will affect the supply of sediment also from (2) to the main river.

Confluence: A confluence is a place where two flows merge with different flow and sediment characteristics merge together-confluences are common occurrences along the natural rivers. Normally, a lateral flow confluences into a main flow at various angles. The confluence angle influences the flow and sediment transport at the confluence region. The bed erosion occurs because of imposed turbulence. The bank opposite to the direction of lateral flow may get stressed. In addition, the main flow width in downstream of the confluence is increased due to addition of discharge.

A confluence is characterized by the presence of (i) a stagnation zone (ii) a separation zone (iii) a mixing layer and (iv) a flow recovery zone (Fig. 4.30)

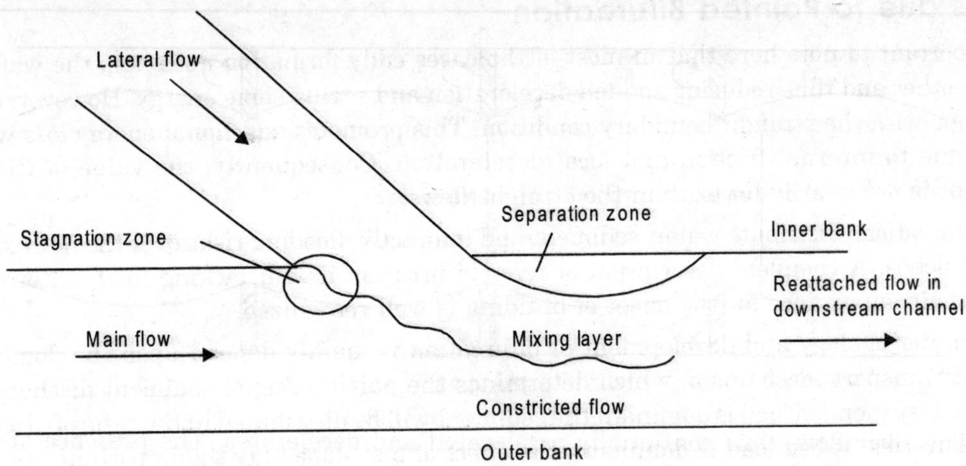

Fig. 4.30 Different flow zones identified at an open-channel confluence

A secondary circulation or helicoidal flow is induced by the lateral flow leads to formation of a scour-hole along the central portion of the confluence. The eroded soil poses problem by depositing in the downstream locations. The lateral flow transfers momentum while merging with the main flow. The momentum from lateral flow depends upon its discharge and flow velocity. This causes deceleration of flow and rise of level at upstream of the confluence.

(2) River Bifurcations: River bifurcation occurs when a river flowing in a single stream separates into two or more separate streams called **distributaries**, which continue downstream. If distributaries merge again, then the bifurcation forms an **island**. River bifurcation may be temporary or semi-permanent depending upon the strength of formation which separates the distributaries.

If in a bifurcations the dividing point of the land is rounded or made blunt, the flow will be gradually accelerated and so no eddies are formed. However, some deposition shall be observed just upstream of the rounded point.

In order to solve the problem of this kind of deposition, a sharp pointed division can be used. The streamlines will follow the two sides. However, they would differ in pattern with changing discharge. The configuration of the sharp point entry can be suitably chosen to give a stable position over the whole year. In this case eddy formation cannot be avoided. Eddies change position with low and high flows. (Fig. 4.31)

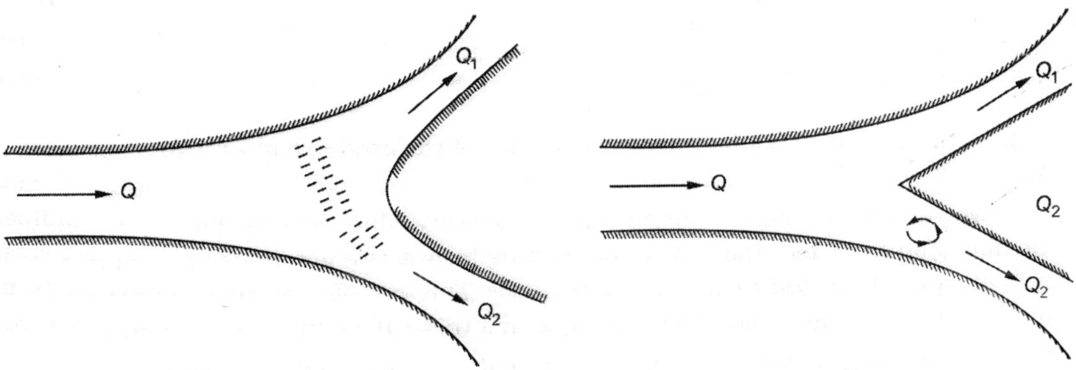

Fig. 4.31

Eddies due to Pointed Bifurcation

It is important to note here that in most of the cases eddy formation does help the water to flow smoother and thus reducing sudden deceleration and saving some energy. However, eddies never-cope with the straight boundary condition. This promotes additional energy loss which is both due to internal friction and local deceleration. Consequently, the value of Chezy's coefficient is necessarily lower than the straight flow.

Bifurcations distribute water, sediment and indirectly, flooding risks over the downstream river branches. A complete description of river bifurcation is still lacking in the literature, though their importance for the onset of braiding is well recognized.

The morphology and development of bifurcation is mainly depend upon the dominant sediment transport mechanism, which determines the partitioning of sediment discharge in branches. If suspended load is dominant the sediment will be distributed in the ratio of discharge in distributaries. If bed load is dominant, the effect of bed slope play the important role.

However, there is a lack of detailed insight into the flow dynamics within river bifurcations, the resulting effect on sediment transport through bifurcating channels, and thus the impact on bifurcation stability over time. The hydraulics of river bifurcation must he studied with reference to three parameters: discharge ratio, width-to depth-ratio and bed roughness.

Hydraulics of Flow Through Bends

A typical feature of meandering rivers is the Bend. The flow around the bends has attracted the attention of research workers for about a century and half.

As the water enters from a straight reach into the bend, besides the gravitational and frictional force, two more forces come into play,

(i) The centrifugal force directed outwards.

(ii) The actual motive force which causes particles to deviate from the straight line. There is only one conceivable force that is capable of doing this, viz. a gradient of water surface in lateral direction.

The Centrifugal force per unit volume can be expressed as, $\frac{\rho u_x^2}{r}$, acting out wards and the transversal gravity force expressed by $\rho g i_y$ acting inwards. Where, u_x is velocity at radius r, assumed constant in the vertical, i_y is water surface gradient = $\partial h/\partial r$.

For equilibrium these forces must be equal,

Hence, From Euler's Equation,

$$\rho g i_y = \rho \frac{u_x^2}{r} \quad \text{Or,} \quad i_y = \frac{u_x^2}{gr}$$

This would require that the water level outside of the bend is higher than inside of the bend. (Fig. 4.32)

However, at the surface, u_x is larger than the average which implies that, at the surface, the centrifugal force is larger than the counteracting transversal gravity force, resulting in a net force outwards. Along the bed reverse takes place. This variation along the vertical makes the water particles at the surface flow outwards, and those along the bed move inwards.

This results in a helicoidal secondary current superimposed upon the normal flow.

Presence of secondary flow modifies the flow pattern considerably, since the high velocity filament now moves closer to the outer bank.

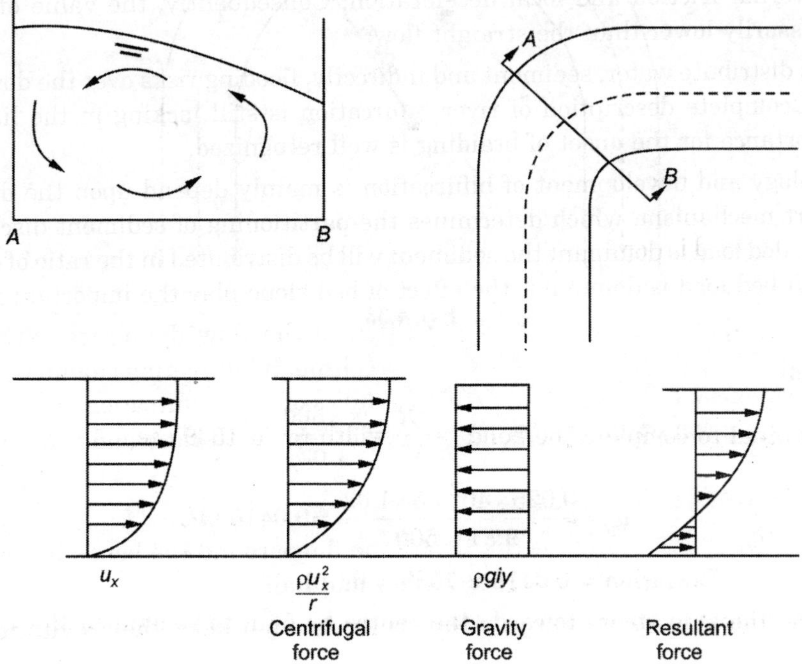

Fig. 4.32

Mathematically, the problem of spiral flow can be solved after some simplifications of the differential equation of this flow. From the analysis, it can be concluded that,

(1) The transverse gradient of the water surface at a certain point of the cross section is,

$i_y = 1.06 \frac{V^2}{g.r}$, where,

The factor 1.06 represents Kinetic Energy correction factor. V is the average velocity.

(2) The deviation of the surface velocity from the average velocity direction appears to be,

$u_y/u_x = 0.025 \frac{u^2}{g.r.2x}$, where u is the average velocity in vertical under consideration ($u = C\sqrt{hi_x}$)

r = radius of average streamline in this vertical and

i_x = longitudinal slope of water surface in this vertical.

Problem 4.16. A ship is travelling round a semi-circular bend of average radius of 500 m with average depth of 5m and longitudinal velocity of 1.02 m/s. How much the ship should steer towards the centre to remain in the middle. Assume Chezy's Coefficient C = 40 m$^{1/2}$/s.

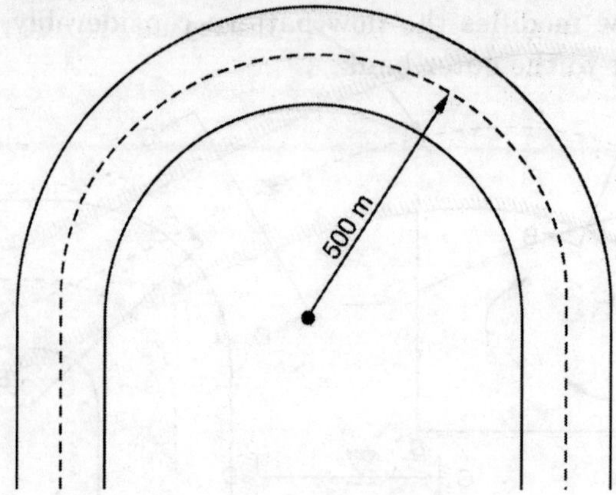

Fig. 4.33

Solution:

$$\text{Time required to complete the bend} = \frac{\pi R}{V} = \frac{\pi \times 500}{1.02} = 1539 \text{ sec.}$$

$$u_y = \frac{0.025 \times 40^2 \times 5 \times 1.02}{9.81 \times 500} = 0.0416\ m/s$$

$$\text{Deviation} = 0.0416 \times 1539 = 64 \text{ m.}$$

Therefore, the ship steers towards the centre by 64m to remain in the middle of the bend.

Bends in Alluvial Channels

Centrifugal force acting on the flow of water around a bend produces a superelevation of the water surface at the concave bank (outer bend) and lowering of water surface at the convex bank (inner bend). The resultant velocity moves the bed load towards the convex-bank and builds up the point bar at that location consequently; a deeper section develops near the concave bank. (Fig. 4.34)

Crossings

Crossing sections are located between bends of reverse curvature. Crossing sections in alluvial rivers are approximately rectangular in contrast to the triangular sections in the bend. It has been observed that at high stages of the river, crossings get aggraded while bends scour deeper. At low discharges bend fills and crossing gets eroded. (Fig. 4.34)

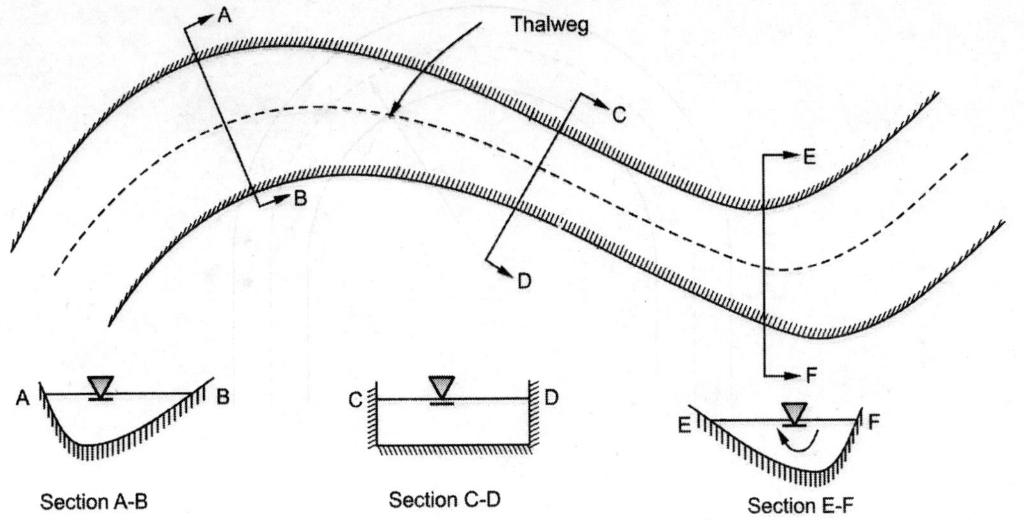

Fig. 4.34

Meander Cut offs

As the meandering continues with time, and as the concave bank continues to recede, old bends become elongated and a narrow neck of land develops as shown. (Fig. 4.35)

Meandering and Oxbow Lake

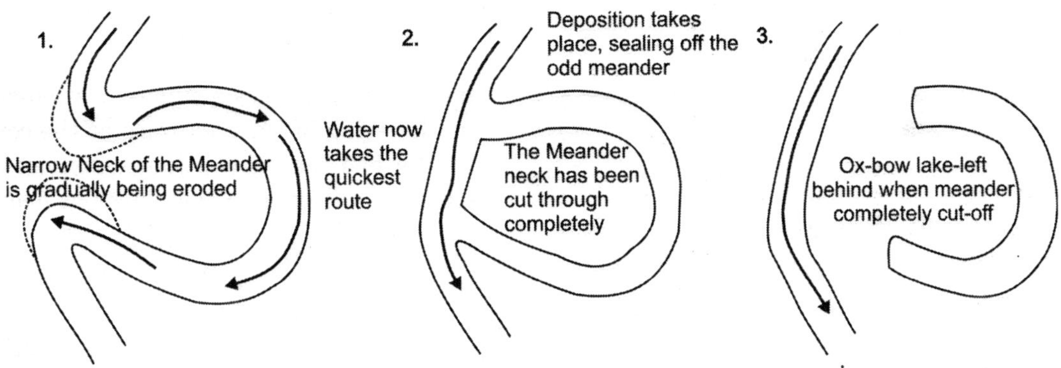

Fig. 4.35

When the bend and bank resistance become too large for continued stretching of loop, it is easier for the flow to cut across the neck than to flow along the bend. This causes the flow to abandon the meander and to continue straight downslope. Cutoffs are a natural part of the evolution of a meandering river, and have also been used to artificially shorten the length of meandering rivers for navigation. The stagnant part of this river sometime forms an 'oxbow lake'.

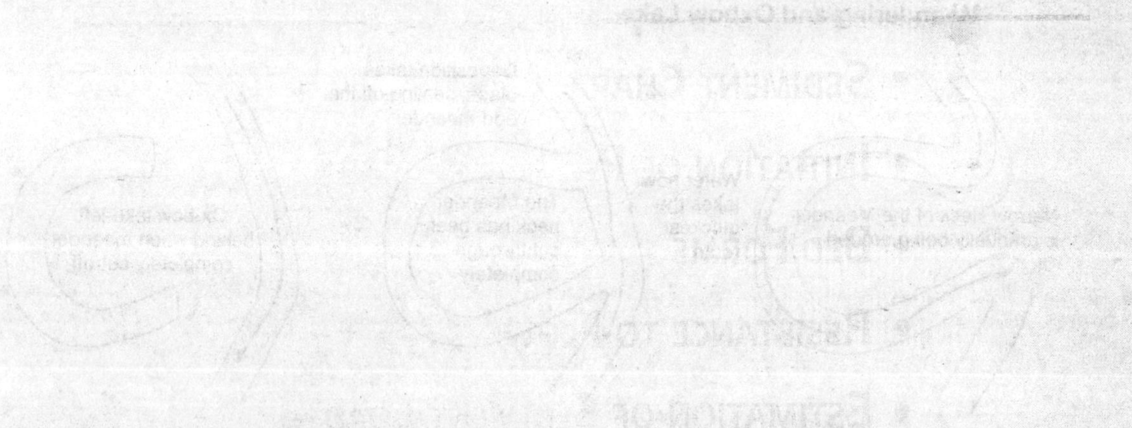

PART II: Sediment Transport

- Sediment Characteristics
- Initiation of Particle Motion
- Bed Forms
- Resistance to Flow
- Estimation of Sediment Load
- Sediment Measurement Techniques

INTRO[illegible]

It has been seen [illegible]
element of [illegible]
omitted, [illegible]
discharge 10 [illegible] point error.

Completely analogous to this is the [illegible]
matters most. Sediment transport has [illegible]
but only less [illegible]
of river engineering. [illegible]
deformation [illegible]
transport.

Here it must be [illegible]
system will be followed [illegible]
Qualitative and particularly quantitative [illegible]
sediment transport will [illegible]
in history.

The main objective of sediment [illegible]
conditions, erosion, scour or deposition [illegible]
involved. The rate of sediment transport [illegible]
can be determined [illegible]
low degree of accuracy so that the [illegible]
transport rates has to be considered.

The main reason for empirical [illegible]
of transport process. The interaction of [illegible]
known by empiricism and a boundary [illegible]
simple mathematical equations. Most [illegible]
therefore, on experiments and measurements [illegible]

CHAPTER 5

SEDIMENT CHARACTERISTICS

INTRODUCTION

It has been seen that, for river engineering, the discharge of water is the most important element of the hydrological cycle. Obviously, the other hydrological elements also cannot be omitted, but because of its direct 'bearing' on river's characteristics, we readily turn to the discharge (Q) as the main parameter.

Completely analogous to this, in the erosion cycle is the transport of sediment that matters most. Sediment transport has been the subject of investigation for many centuries, but only less than a century ago have modern hydraulics given proper attention to this aspect of river engineening. It was during 1930's that understanding grew about the formation and deformation of the river bed. This was possible with the development of study of sediment transport.

Here it must be realized that every man-made intervention in natural conditions of the system will be followed by change in sediment transport and thence in the changes in the bed. Qualitative and particularly quantitative knowledge of the mechanism and consequences of sediment transport will decrease, the chances of failures, of which there have been so many in history.

The main objective of sediment transport hydraulics is to predict whether an equilibrium condition, erosion (scour) or deposition (silting) will occur and to determine the quantities involved. The rate of sediment transport, expressed as mass, weight or volume per unit time can be determined from field measurements or from calculations. Both methods only have a low degree of accuracy so that the sensitivity of the design to possible variations in the calculated transport rates has to be considered.

The main reason for empirical character of sediment transport knowledge is the complexity of transport process. The interaction of a turbulent flow, the characteristics of which are only known by empiricism, and a boundary consisting of loose sediments cannot be described by simple mathematical equations. Most of our knowledge of sediment transport is based, therefore, on experiments and measurements both in the field or in laboratories.

PROPERTIES OF SEDIMENT

The sediment characteristics, such as its relative density, size, shape, fall velocity, porosity etc. play a decisive role in various stages of phenomenon of sediment transport. These properties are governed by a large extent to the origin of sediment and process of its formation.

Sediment is a naturally occurring material that has broken-down by process of weathering and erosion, and is subsequently transported by the action of wind, water, or ice, and/or by the force of gravity acting on the particles. Sediments are most often transported by water, wind or glaciers. According to the mode of transport sediments are named as follows,

Alluvium: When transported by water (Fluvial processes)

Loess: If transported by wind/air (Aeolian processes) and

Glacial Drift: These are carried by glaciers.

River channel and deposits and beach sands are examples of fluvial transport and deposition. Desert sand dunes and loess (loose fine soil) are examples of aeolian transport and deposition. Glacial moraine deposits and till (stiff impervious clay) are ice-transported sediments.

Classification of Sediment

Sediment can be classified based on its grain size and/or its composition. Sediment size is measured on a log 2 scale, called the ϕ (phi) scale, which classifies particle size from **boulder** to **colloid**, as mentioned below:

ϕ Scale	Size Range (mm)	Size Range (inch)	Class	Popular Names
< - 8	> 256	> 10.1	Boulder	
-6 to -8	64-256	2.5 – 10.1	Cobble	
-5 to -6	32 – 64	1.26 – 2.5	Very coarse Gravel	Pebble
-4 to -5	16-32	0.63-1.26	Course Gravel	
-3 to -4	8- 16	0.31-0.63	Medium Gravel	
-2 to -3	4-8	0.157 – 0.31	Fine Gravel	
-1 to -2	2-4	0.079 – 0.157	Very Fine Gravel	Granule
0 to -1	1-2	0.039 – 0.079	Very coarse Sand	
1 to 0	0.5 – 1	0.02 – 0.039	Coarse sand	
2 to 1	0.25 – 0.5	0.01 – 0.02	Medium Sand	Sand
3 to 2	125 – 250 μm	0.0049 – 0.01	Fine Sand	
4 to 3	62.5 – 125 μm	0.0025 – 0.0049	Very fine Sand	
8 to 4	3.9 – 62.5 μm	0.00015 – 0.0025	Silt	
> 8	< 3.9 μm	<0.00015	Clay	Mud
> 10	< 1 μm	< .000039	Colloid	

Cohesive and Non-Cohesive Sediment Particles

Sediments are broadly divided into cohesive and non-cohesive categories. In case of cohesive soils like loam, clay or silt, the particles in the soil bond to one another. Due to this bond cohesive sediment offer resistance to erosion depending upon the strength of cohesive bond. If the bond is strong, it may outweigh the influence of the physical characteristics of individual particles. But once the erosion has taken place it would behave like non-cohesive sediment in respect of further transport.

On the other hand non-cohesive material like sand and gravel, the particles consist of discrete particles and movement of these particles is solely the function of their physical properties. These properties include the size, shape and density of the particles. Though non-cohesive particles are unattached, they may be bound together by the roots of vegetable cover.

Particle Size

Natural Sediment are irregular in shape and therefore definition of size by a single length dimension is necessarily most incomplete. Such classification is made arbitrarily due to convenience of measurement. For rationalizing the size of the sediment various definitions have been, put forward.

(1) **Nominal diameter:** (dn) It is defined as the diameter (d) of a sphere that has the same volume:

For spherical particles, $dn = d$

For natural particles, $dn > d$

(2) **Tri-axial Size:** If Sediment particle is near an ellipsoid having a, b, and c as its longest, intermediate and shortest mutually perpendicular axes respectively, then

Representative diameter $= \sqrt[3]{abc}$ or Index diameter $= b$

(3) **Sieve diameter:** It is defined as the minimum square aperture through which a particle will just pass.

(4) **Fall Diameter:** It is the diameter of a sphere that has a specific gravity of 2.65 and has the same settling velocity as the given particle in quiescent, distilled water at a temperature of 24°C.

Sieve Analysis: Sieve analysis or gradation test is a procedure to assess the particle size distribution of a granular material. The size distribution is often of critical importance to the way the material performs in use.

Procedure: The gradation test is performed on a sample of aggregate in a laboratory. A typical Sieve analysis involves a nested column of sieves with wire mesh screen.

A representative weighed sample is poured into the top sieve which has the largest screen opening. Each lower sieve in the column has smaller openings than the one above. At the base is a round pan, called the receiver.

The column is typically placed in a mechanical shaker. The shaker-shakes the column, usually for some fixed amount of time. After the shaking is complete, the material on each sieve is weighed. The weight of the sample on each sieve is then divided by the total weight of the sample to give a percentage retained on each sieve.

The results of the sieving are presented in a graph of percent passing versus the sieve size. A cumulative frequency curve i.e. the percent by weight greater than a certain size against the logarithm of that size is prepared. From this curve various representative sizes of the sediment can be read off. (Fig. 5.1)

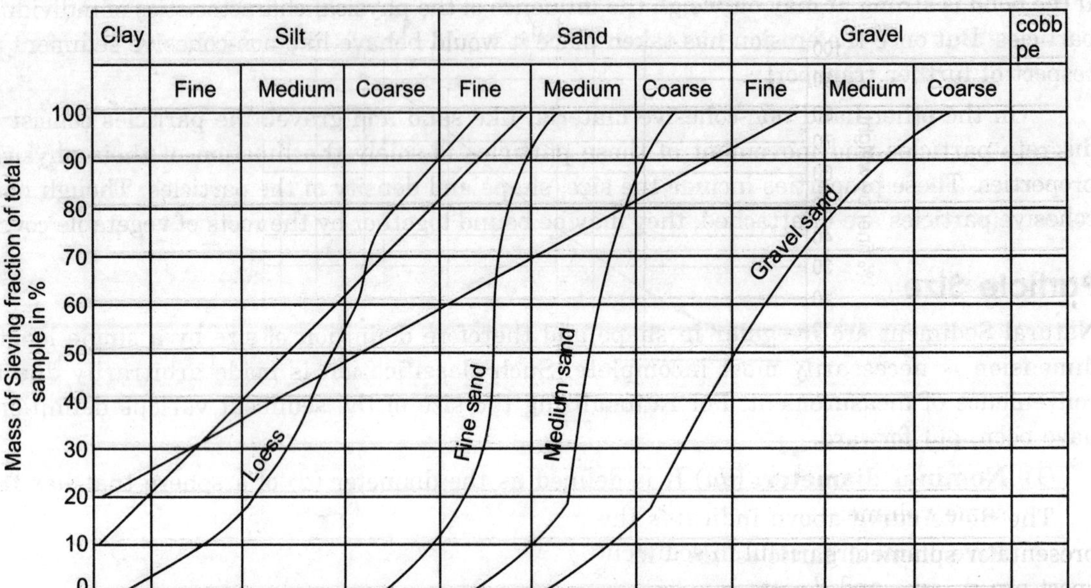

Fig. 5.1

Besides the cumulative frequency curves, simple frequency polygons can be of help in understanding the size distribution of sediment.

Histogram: A histogram can be plotted from the size analysis data which has its ordinates as percentage of total weight and size as abscissa. By joining the top mid-points, frequency curve is obtained. (Fig. 5.2)

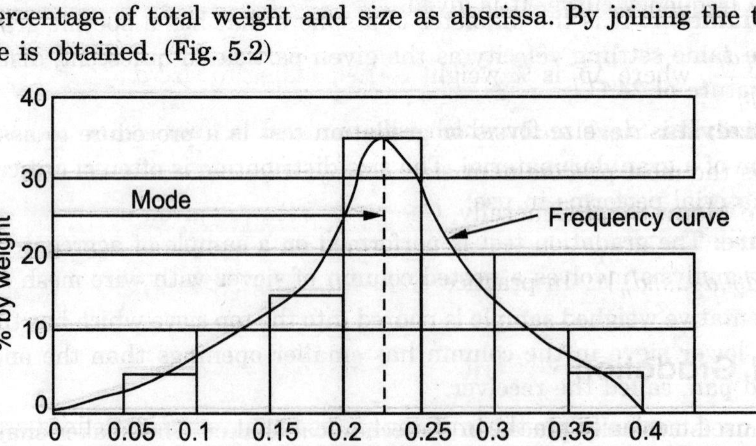

Fig. 5.2

Using Cumulative Frequency Curve

The cumulative frequency curve is obtained by plotting sediment diameter on x-axis and percent finer (or coarser than) a given size on y-axis. Ordinarily, it is drawn on a semi-log graph paper. (Fig. 5.3)

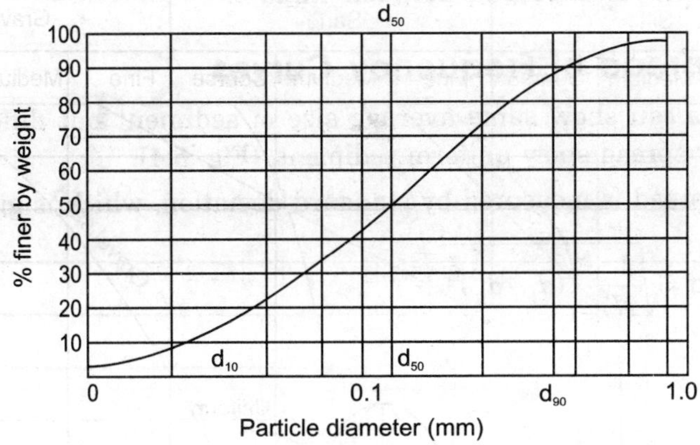

Fig. 5.3

The Sieve curve above indicates the grain size distribution, and provides values of representative diameters useful in sediment transport analysis. Important parameters in this respect are d_{50}, d_{10} and d_{90} etc.

Central Tendency: An important characteristic of the frequency curve is the central tendency, which is defined as the tendency of one size grade to be present in larger percent than other size grades. This tendency can be expressed in terms of arithmetic mean size, median size, geometric mean size and mode. The dominant size range is called chief ingredient and others as admixtures.

Arithmetic Mean Size(d_a): It is defined as the distance from y-axis of the centroid of area enclosed by frequency curve. It is given by,

$d_a = \frac{\Sigma \Delta p_i d_i}{\Sigma \Delta p_i}$, where Δp_i is % weight corresponding to size d_i.

Median Size: It is d_{50} size for which 50% material is finer.

Mode: It is the most predominant size.

Geometric Mean Size: Generally, Geometric Mean is given by,

$GM = [d_1, d_2, d_3 ..... d_n]^{\frac{1}{n}}$. In practice $GM = [d_{84} \cdot d_{16}]^{1/2}$

Measures of Gradation

Some commonly used measures are the uniformity coefficient, which is defined as, $Cu = d_{60}/d_{10}$, when Cu > 4 to 6 shows a well graded soil. The Cu < 4 shows poorly graded soil. For uniformly graded soils Cu will be nearly 1.

Another coefficient to measure gradation is coefficient of curvature C_C, which is defined as,

$$C_C = \frac{{d_{30}}^2}{d_{60} \times d_{10}}$$

For well graded soil C_C should be between 1 and 3.

The degree of spread of Frequency Curves

Two frequency curves can show same average size of sediment but different Spread. The material with smaller spread show uniform sediment. (Fig. 5.4)

The degree of spread is measured by standard deviation, which is given by,

$$\sigma = \sqrt{\frac{1}{N} \sum_{i=1}^{N} (d_i - d_a)^2}$$

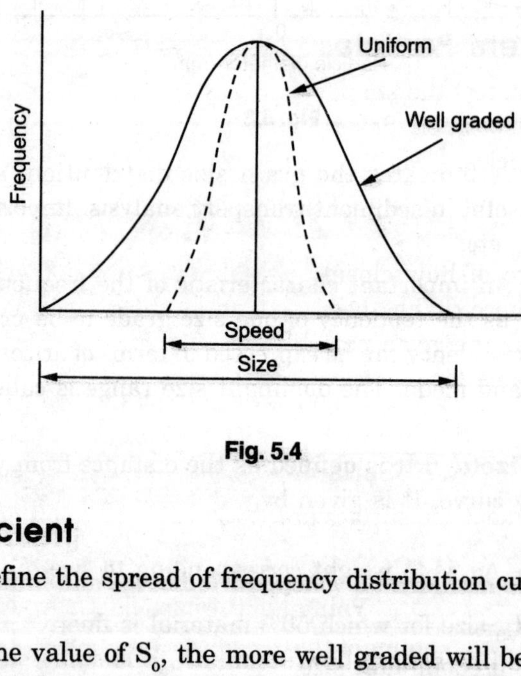

Fig. 5.4

The Sorting Coefficient

It is also a method to define the spread of frequency distribution curve. It is defined as,

$S_o = \sqrt{\dfrac{d_{75}}{d_{25}}}$, the larger the value of S_o, the more well graded will be the soil.

Density and Specific Weight of Normal Sediment

Most Sediments originate from disintegration or decomposition of rock. The density of most sediment particles (< 4mm) varies between narrow limits. Since quartz is predominant in natural sediments the average density of sediment can be assumed to be 2650 kg/m^3 (specific gravity 2.65). Submerged specific gravity of sediment is assumed to be 1.65.

Porosity

Porosity is defined as the percent pore space in the total bulk volume of the sediment. Therefore, porosity (n),

$$n = \frac{\text{Bulk Volume} - \text{Grain Volume}}{\text{Bulk Volume}} = \frac{\text{Volume of Voids}}{\text{Total Volume}} = \frac{V_V}{V}$$

From coarse to fine material porosity varies between 39 to 54 percent.

Bulk Density

Bulk density is defined as the dry weight of soil per unit volume of soil. Bulk density considers both the solid and pore space, whereas particle density considers only the mineral solids. Bulk density depends on the size of the sediment. As the sediment size increases, bulk density also increases. The average bulk specific gravity of sediment can be assumed as below,

Soil Type	Sand	Silt	Clay
Bulk specific Gravity	1.5	1.2	0.9

Shape of the Sediment Particles

Beside the grain size (diameter) the shape of the particles is also of importance, as it affects the process of erosion and deposition. Several definitions have been put forward to characterize the shape of sediment particles.

Sphericity

Sphericity is the measure of how closely the shape of an object approaches that of a mathematically perfect sphere. It has been defined as the ratio of surface area of a sphere (having the same volume as the given particle) to the surface area of the particle. Normally, the sphericity is less than one for particles other than spheres.

$$\text{Sphericity} = \frac{\text{Surface area of a sphere of equal volume}}{\text{Surface area of the particle}}$$

As it is difficult to find out the surface area of the particle another definition of sphericity was put forward, as follows,

$$\text{Sphericity} = \left[\frac{\text{Volume of the particle}}{\text{Volume of the Circumscribing sphere}}\right]^{1/3}$$

This definition is reduced to,

$$Sphericity = \frac{dn}{a}$$

Roundness: It is the measure of how closely the shape of an object approaches that of a mathematically perfect circle. It is defined as, "ratio of average radius of curvature of the edges and the radius of circle inscribed in the maximum projected area of the particle.

Since roundness and sphericity are not suited for practice, another criterion was introduced as the **Shape factor** which gives sufficient results for practical application.

Shape Factor: It is based on mutually perpendicular three axes as follows, it is defined as, $SF = \frac{c}{\sqrt{ab}}$, where *a*, *b* and *c* are major, intermediate and minor axes respectively. The SF for a sphere will be 1 and for other particles less than 1. For natural sand particles $SF \approx 0.7$.

Some more parameters are defined in connection with the shape of particles, as below;

Flatness Ratio: It is described as,

$FR. = \frac{a+b}{2c}$, it is greater than 1 and varies between 1.05 to 10 for natural sediment.

Modulus of Flatness: It is given as, $= \frac{c}{b}$, *if* <0.6 shows Flat Particles.

Modulus of Length: It is given as, $= \frac{a}{b}$, *if* >1.8 shows Long Particles.

In Sediment transport studies Shape Factor is most used parameter as it is applied to the fall velocity study of particles.

Fall Velocity: The fall velocity of a sediment is an important parameter in the study on suspension and sedimentation of sediment particles. The fall velocity is defined by the equation giving equilibrium between gravity force, resistance to the fall of the particle and buoyant force. The equation can be written as follows,

$$\underbrace{\frac{\pi}{6} d^3 (\rho_s - \rho_w) g}_{\substack{\text{Gravity} \\ \text{(Submerged weight)}}} = \underbrace{\frac{1}{2} C_D \rho_w . \frac{\pi}{4} d^2 . w^2}_{\text{Resistance}}$$

Where, C_D is Drag coefficient

d is representative diameter of the particle

ρ_s density of sediment

ρ_w density of water

g acceleration due to gravity.

w is fall velocity.

Under steady state condition, the fall velocity, also known as terminal velocity can now be written as,

$$w^2 = \frac{4}{3} . \frac{1}{C_D} g d \Delta \text{ where } \Delta = \frac{\rho_s - \rho_w}{\rho_w}$$

Value of C_D: Drag is a phenomenon related to viscosity. The Drag coefficient has been defined as,

$$C_D = \frac{Drag}{\frac{1}{2}\rho V_0^2 A_C}$$, where *Ac* is some characteristic area of the body.

A steady fluid flow is controlled by inertial and viscous forces and, therefore, the drag coefficient C_D is a function of Reynold's Number (R_e or R_N) and also of the shape of the particle. (expressed by $SF = C/\sqrt{ab}$).

For spherical particles and low Reynold's Number (Say $Re < 1$), C_D can be expressed as,

$$C_D = 24/Re, \text{ where, } Re = \frac{w d \rho_w}{\mu}$$

μ is the Dynamic Viscosity of water.

$$\therefore \quad w = \frac{1}{18\mu} d^2 (\gamma_s - \gamma_w) = \frac{\Delta d^2 g}{18\nu} \ (Stoke's\ Law)$$

Where, γ_s and γ_w are the specific weights of sediment and water respectively.

ν = Kinematic Viscosity of water.

For Circular discs, $C_D = \frac{20.37}{Re}$

This is valid in Laminar range i.e. for very low Reynold's number.

For Higher Reynold's Numbers: For a single spherical particle in fluid, the drag coefficient C_D is a unique function of Reynolds Number. For non-spherical particles also attempts have been made by defining the shape of the particle in various ways.

It may be observed that for large Reynolds Numbers C_D becomes constant and therefore, fall velocity varies as,

$$w = \sqrt{g d \Delta}$$

This would mean that for all ranges of Reynold's Number, w varies with $d^{0.5}$ to d^2.

To account for the shape of the particle, Albertson found that effect on fall velocity is appreciable in higher ranges of Reynold's Number. He gave relation between C_D, Re and Shape Factor SF. (Fig. 5.5)

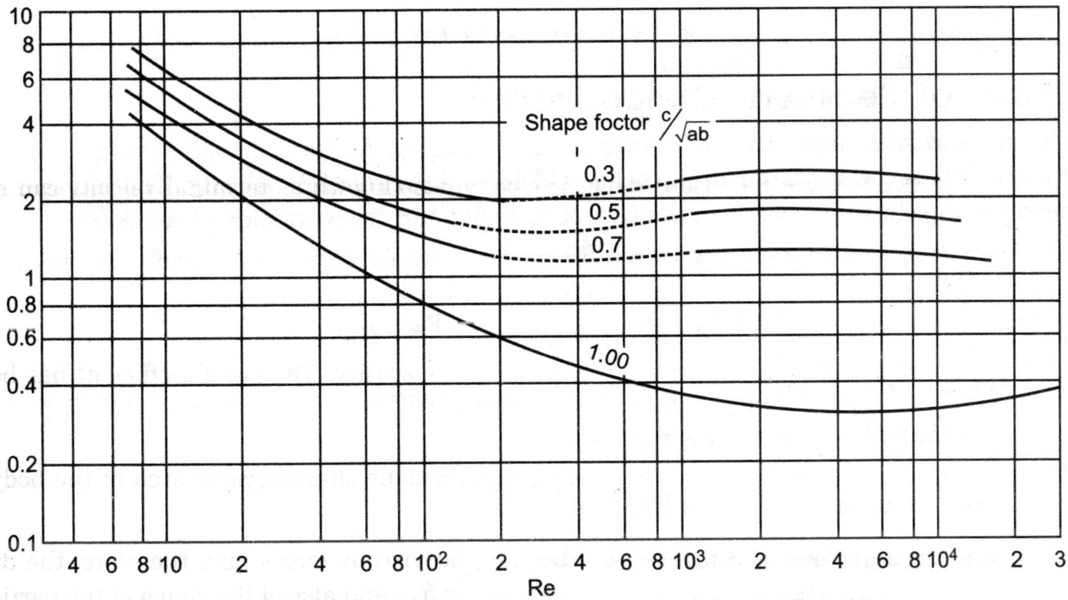

Fig. 5.5 Drag coefficient vs. Reynolds number for different shape factors. [After Albertson (1953)]

Fall Velocity as a function of grain size, shape and temperature based on above analysis a useful graph has been obtained. (Fig. 5.6)

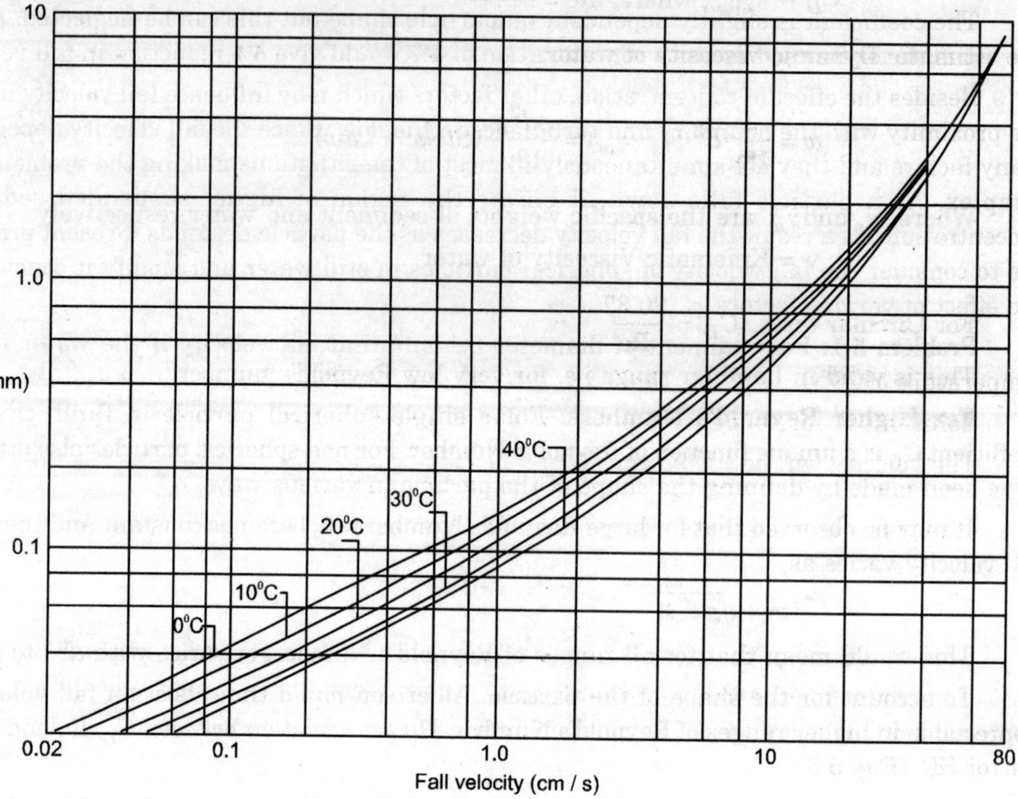

Fig. 5.6: Fall velocity vs. Particle size

Effect of Sediment Concentration

The presence of a large number of other particles tends to decrease the fall velocity of a single particle. However, a cluster of particles will have a greater fall velocity. The increase and decrease in velocity is due to imposition of currents and concentration of sediment.

Based on systematic experiments Richardson and Zaki gave some useful expressions.

$$\frac{w(c)}{w} = (1-c)^{\alpha} \qquad 0 \le C < 0.3$$

Where, $w(c)$ is the fall velocity of a grain in suspension with concentration c by volume. w is the fall velocity for a single grain.

α is a function of Reynold's Number $\left(\frac{wd}{\nu}\right)$

Some experimental results are as follows,

$Re < 0.2$ $\qquad \alpha = 4.65$

$0.2 < Re < 1$ $\qquad \alpha = 4.35\, Re^{-0.03}$

$1 < Re < 200$ $\alpha = 4.45\ Re^{-0.1}$

$Re > 500$ $\alpha = 2.39$

The coefficient is slightly dependent on particle shape but this can be neglected. As per one estimate for fine sediments a concentration of 1% would give 5% reduction in fall velocity.

Besides the effect of concentration, other factors which may influence fall velocity include the proximity with the boundary and turbulence in the flow. Since the fall velocity depends on many factors and they act simultaneously in most of the situations making the problem very complex. As a particle falls down, it enters the region of higher suspended sediment concentration. As a result the fall velocity decreases as the particle descends. Present practices are to consider the fall velocity of spherical particles in still water and modify it considering the effect of various factors.

Problem 5.1: For sediment of diameter 0.1 mm find fall velocity if the water is at a temperature of 20°C.

Solution: Refer to figure 5.6

The velocity will be = 0.95 cm/s (approximately)

CHAPTER 6

Initiation of Particle Motion (Also known as Threshold of Movement or Incipient Motion.)

One of the classic problems in sediment transport is to predict the flow strength at which sediment movement first begins. This condition for incipient movement is usually expressed in terms of a **critical shear stress** or threshold shear stress, which can be denoted by τ_{oc}.

The equilibrium of a particle on bed of a stream is disturbed, if the resultant effects of the disturbing forces (Drag and Lift force, Viscous Forces on the particle surface) become greater than the stabilizing forces of Gravity and cohesion. Cohesion is only important for sediments in the clay and silt range or fine sands with appreciable silt content.

When the flow of a fluid over a flat surface of loose grains is gradually increased, a condition is reached when a few grains here and there begin to move with the fluid owing to the forces exerted by flowing fluid.

Theoretical work on the initiation of motion has started with the effort of Brahms (1753) who gave a sixth power relation between critical flow velocity and weight of the particle.

$$V_c = kW^{1/6}$$

where k is an empirical constant and W is weight of the particle and V_c is critical velocity also known as competent velocity at the top of the particle.

This may also be expressed as, $V_c = k'd^{1/2}$, where V_c is critical velocity also known as competent velocity at the top of the particle.

k' is another empirical constant and D is particle diameter.

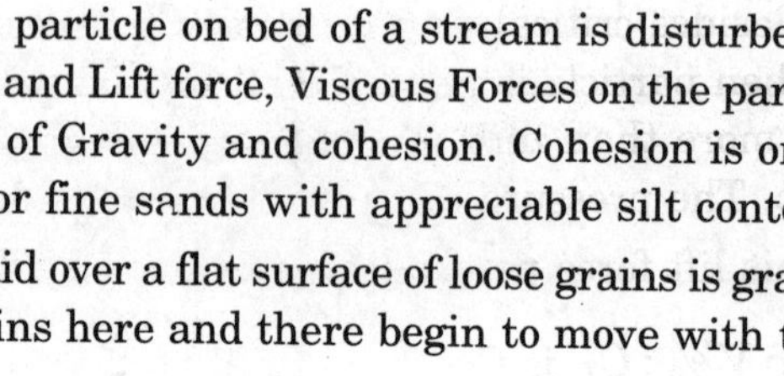

Fig. 6.1

Various investigators have given dimensionless expressions based on critical velocity concept.

Neill's Relation: He gave following relation for critical velocity.

$$\frac{V_C}{\sqrt{\Delta gd}} = 1.414\left(\frac{D}{d}\right)^{1/6}, \text{ where } D \text{ is the depth of flow.}$$

Garde's Equation:

$$\frac{V_C}{\sqrt{\Delta gd}} = 0.5\log\left(\frac{D}{d}\right) + 1.63$$

Yang's Expression:

$$\frac{V_C}{w} = \frac{2.5}{\log \mathrm{Re}^* - 0.06} + 0.66$$

where, Re* is shear Reynold's Number $\frac{u_* d}{\nu}$ and u_* is shear velocity, $u_* = \sqrt{\frac{\tau_0}{\rho}}$,

$\tau_0 = \gamma RS$

All the three formulae for critical velocity are derived for hydrodynamically rough boundaries.

Lift Force Concept: Besides critical velocity theory another worth mentioning concept is the Lift force concept. When particle is resting on floor, the velocity at the bottom is zero, while velocity at the top is more than zero. Hence there is high pressure under the particle and low pressure at the top. The pressure difference causes the lift force.

According to White this lift force per unit area is given by,

$$F_L = C_L \, \rho \, V^2/2 \, ; C_L \text{ is Coefficient of Lift}$$

C_L is about 0.178 (for rough beds), V is velocity of flow at distance $0.35d_{35}$ from the theoretical bed.

CRITICAL TRACTIVE FORCE THEORY

Among the various approaches, the critical tractive force theory seems to be the most rational. The moving fluid exerts forces on the particles resting on the bed. The picture may be of the kind shown below,

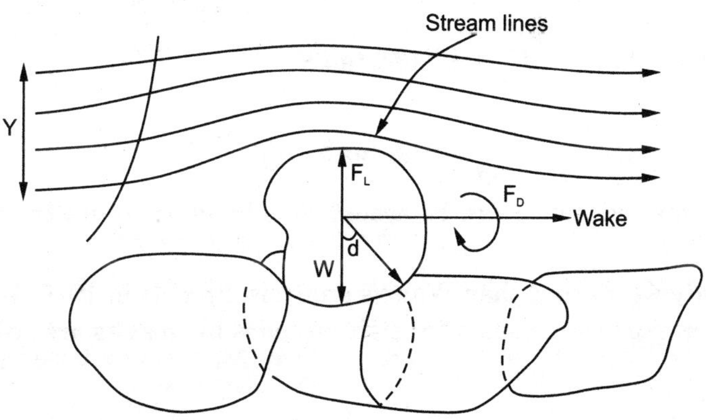

Confining our attention to an assembly of non-cohesive particles of density (ρ_s) greater than that of fluid (ρ).

As the fluid passes the fluid particle streamlines are deflected.

The particle experiences Drag as well as Lift Forces. An increase in velocity causes shedding of eddies and a wake is formed downstream. The size of the wake depends upon the shape and size of the exposed particle.

Theory: White in 1940 gave a thorough discussion on the equilibrium of a grain on the bed of the stream. Neglecting the Lift component, two forces remain to be considered viz.

Submerged weight of the particle = $\frac{\pi}{6}(\gamma_s - \gamma)d^3$

Fluid drag force per particle = $\frac{\tau_0}{N} = \frac{\tau_0}{\left(\eta/d^2\right)} = \frac{\tau_0 d^2}{\eta}$

where, $\eta = Nd^2$, called Packing coefficient.

N = Number of particles per unit area.

Assuming $\tan\phi$ as the coefficient of Friction, where ϕ is angle of repose.

At the critical stage of motion (Incipient motion), $\tau_0 = \tau_{0c}$

$$\frac{\tau_{0c}\, d^2}{\eta} = \frac{\pi}{6}(\gamma_s - \gamma)d^3 \tan\phi$$

or

$$\tau_{0c} = \eta\, \frac{\pi}{6}\, d\,(\gamma_s - \gamma)\tan\phi$$

(valid for high speed flows, $Re^* > 3.5$, *where* $Re^* = \frac{u_* d}{\nu}$, $u^* = \sqrt{\frac{\tau_0}{\rho}}$

For Low speed flow case ($Re^* < 3.5$) pressure force is small and viscous forces predominate. The critical shear stress can be expressed as,

$$\tau_{0c} = \alpha\eta\, \pi/6\, d(\gamma_s - \gamma)\tan\phi$$

where α is a coefficient for part exposure of particle on the horizontal floor of the channel.

In practice: For an estimated value of $\eta = 0.4$ and $\alpha\eta = 0.31$ to 0.39.

For $Re^* > 3.5$, $\frac{\tau_{oc}}{(\gamma_s - \gamma)d} = 0.052\tan\phi$

and for $Re^* < 3.5$, $\frac{\tau_{oc}}{(\gamma_s - \gamma)d} = 0.18\tan\phi$

As an approximation, $\tan\phi$ can be assumed to be equal to unity. (i.e. angle of repose = 45°)

Shield's Analysis: Earlier than White's analysis, Shields in 1936 studied the beginning of motion of sediment particles. Even after eight decades his results are still undisputable and the best available.

Shields considered two forces one required to dislodge the particles F) and Hydrodynamic Force (F_1) exerted by the fluid. Obviously, for incipient condition of motion $F = F_1$, Now

$$F = \alpha_1 (\gamma_s - \gamma) d^3 \text{ and } F_1 = C_D \frac{\rho}{2} u_a^2 \, \alpha_2 d^2$$

where, α_1 is a coefficient which is function of shape of the particle, coefficient of friction and other sediment characterstics.

α_2 is another coefficient such that $\alpha_2 d^2$ gives the projected areas of the particle.

C_D is drag coefficient corresponding to u_a

u_a is the characteristic velocity (say u_d as shown)

Using Karman-Prandtl equation for velocity distribution,

$$\frac{u_d}{u_*} = f_1\left(\frac{u_* d}{\gamma}\right) = f_1\left(\text{Re}^*\right)$$

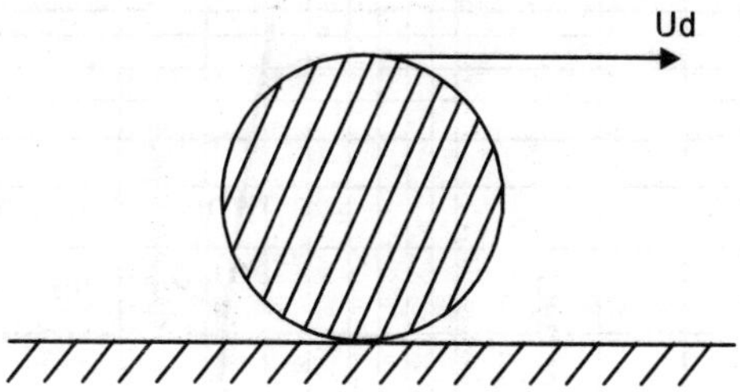

Fig. 6.3

where, u_* called shear velocity $= \sqrt{\tau_0 / \rho}$

and $C_D = f_2\left(u_d \, d/\gamma\right)$

If will follow that, $C_D = f_3(\text{Re}^*)$ $\therefore$ $F_1 = f_3(\text{Re}^*) \frac{\rho}{2} u_*^2 \, f_1^2 \, (\text{Re}^*) \alpha_2 d^2$

Equating, F and F_1, for critical condition,

$$\alpha_1 (\gamma_s - \gamma) d^3 = f_3(\text{Re}_x^*) . \frac{\rho}{2} u_{*c}^2 \, f_1^2 \, (\text{Re}_c^*) \alpha_2 d^2$$

Rearranging the above equation we get

$$\frac{\rho {u_*}_c^2}{(\gamma_s - \gamma) d} = \frac{2\alpha_1}{\alpha_2} f\left(\text{Re}^*\right), \text{ where } \text{Re}_c^* = \frac{u_{*c} d}{\nu}$$

Substituting, $u_{*c} = \sqrt{\frac{\tau_{oc}}{\rho}}$

We get, $\frac{\tau_{oc}}{(\gamma_s - \gamma) d} = f(\text{Rec}^*)$

Shields obtained variation of $\frac{\tau_{oc}}{(\gamma_s - \gamma) d}$ with (Re_c^*) based on experimental data.

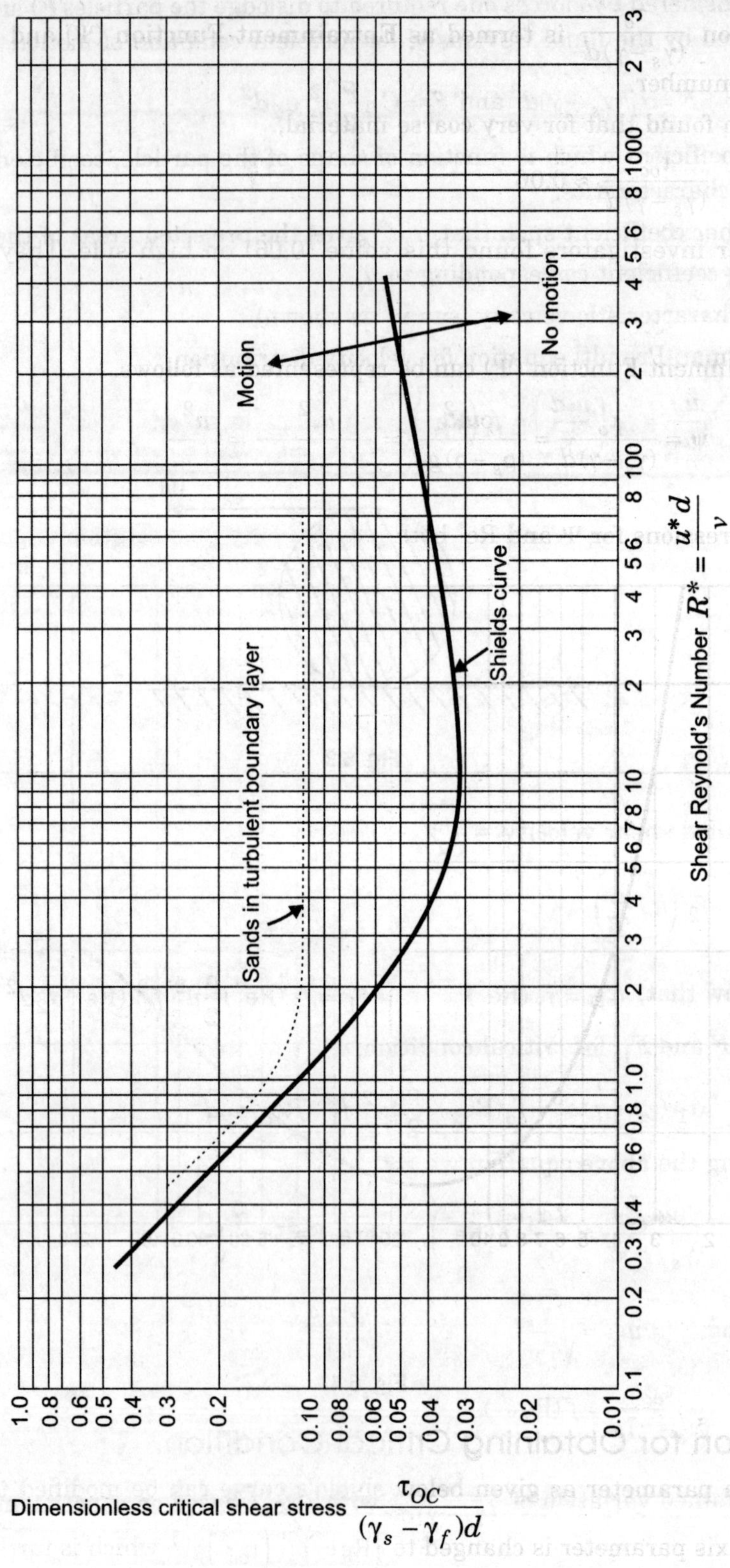
Motion
No motion
Shields curve
Sands in turbulent boundary layer
Shear Reynold's Number $R^* = \frac{u^* d}{\nu}$
0.1 0.2 0.3 0.4 0.6 0.8 1.0 2 3 4 5 6 7 8 10 2 3 4 5 6 8 100 2 3 4 5 6 8 1000 2 3
1.0 0.8 0.6 0.5 0.4 0.3 0.2 0.10 0.08 0.06 0.05 0.04 0.03 0.02 0.01
Dimensionless critical shear stress $\frac{\tau_{oc}}{(\gamma_s - \gamma_f)d}$

The function $\frac{\tau_o}{(\gamma_s-\gamma)d}$ is termed as **Entrainment Function** (Ψ) and Rec* as critical shear Reynold's number.

It has been found that for very coarse material,

$$\frac{\tau_{oc}}{(\gamma_s-\gamma)d} \approx 0.06$$

Some other investigators found this value (0.06) on high side. They recommended,

$$\frac{\tau_o}{(\gamma_s-\gamma)d} \approx 0.03\,.$$

The Entrainment Function (Ψ) can be represented as follows.

$$\psi = \frac{\tau_o}{(\gamma_s-\gamma)d} = \frac{\rho u_*^{\,2}}{(\rho_s-\rho)\,gd} = \frac{u_*^{\,2}}{\left(\frac{\rho_s-\rho}{\rho}\right)gd} = \frac{u_*^2}{\Delta gd}$$

As the expressions for Ψ and Re^* both have u_*, only trial solution is possible to get τ_{oc}.

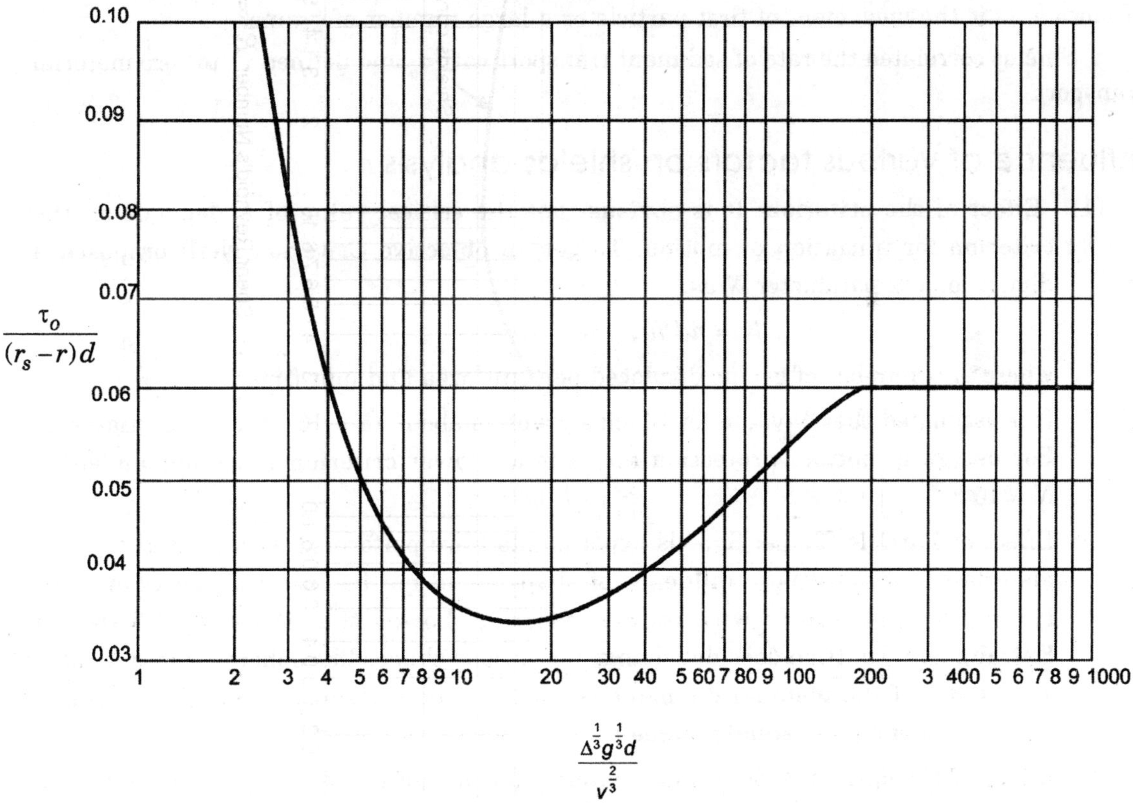

Fig. 6.4

Direct Solution for Obtaining Critical Condition.

By introducing a parameter as given below shield's curve can be modified to yield a direct solution. The x-axis parameter is changed to $\left(\text{Re}\,c^*\right)^{2/3}\left(\tau_{oc}^{\ *}\right)^{-1/3}$ which is further modified as,

$$\left(\mathrm{Re}\,c^*\right)^{2/3}\left(\tau_{oc}^*\right)^{-1/3} = \left[\frac{u_*cd}{\nu}\right]^{2/3}\left[\frac{\Delta gd}{u_*c^2}\right]^{1/3} = \Delta^{1/3} g^{1/3} d \Big/ \nu^{2/3}$$

The transformed graph is given in the Fig. 6.4 and values in the table below.

$\frac{(\gamma_5-\gamma)d^3}{\rho\nu^2}$	13.2	70	400	840	3030	2.5×10^4	4.21×10^4	1.17×10^5	5.8×10^5	6×10^6	1.6×10^7
$\frac{\Delta^{1/3} g^{1/3} d}{\nu^{2/3}}$	2.36	4.12	7.36	9.44	14.40	29.20	34.78	49.00	83.90	181.2	252
$\frac{\tau_{oc}}{(\gamma_5-\gamma)d}$	0.10	0.060	0.040	0.036	0.033	0.016	0.038	0.042	0.050	0.060	0.060

While talking of Initiation of motion, the difficulty arises in the very definition of initiation of motion. Is it the movement of first particle or a large number of grains?

Shields correlated the rate of sediment transport with τ_o and defined τ_{oc} to zero material transport.

Influence of various factors on shields analysis

(1) **Effect of the criterion:** It is obvious that the critical value of τ_o depends on the criterion for initiation of motion. To get an objective Criterion Neill proposed a dimensionless parameter N as,

$$N = nd^3/u_*$$

where, n = number of grains displaced per unit area and unit time.

It is estimated that N-value for Shields graph is about 15×10^{-6} for coarse material. For design of bottom protection etc, a much lower criterion is recommended as $N = 10^{-6}$.

(2) **Effect of Particle Shape:** Shields experiments were performed with several types of materials and systematic influence of shape could not be observed. Tests at Delft Hydraulics Laboratory with coarse material showed that the critical value of Entrainment Function does not change for various shapes like spheres, cubes, broken stones etc., if the nominal diameter is used for comparision. (nominal diameter = diameter of sphere of equal volume.)

(3) **Effect of Gradation:** Wide graded material has an influence on τ_{oc}. In practice it is observed that the gradation has an influence for $d_{90}/d_{10} > 5$ only, because the larger grains are more exposed and smaller grains are shielded by the larger ones. Therefore, d_{50} seems to be a good measure for most samples.

For a wide particle gradation the effect of armoring will occur which means that while fine particles are eroded an armor layer of coarse particles is formed, which prevents the bed from further erosion.

(4) Effect of Ratio of Depth of flow (*h*) and *d* : Factor (*h/d*): For small values of h/d a deviation from Shield's graph is possible. For smaller h/d (<10), more stability is expected. This happens because small h/d gives limitation on size and frequency of large eddies.

(5) Influence of Bed Slope: For particles on a large longitudinal slope, the value of τ_{oc} will be reduced as the Force component parallel to the bed will increase.

Cohesive Sediment

Cohesive character of any soil tends to increase the resistance against erosion. Because of the presence of cohesion the critical velocity as well as the critical tractive stress for such materials is greater than that for alluvial material of the same size without fines. Generally, in the presence of cohesion, lumps of particles move as a unit.

Some investigators have found that the resistance due to cohesive force is proportional to the shear strength of the soil which obviously acts in the opposite direction to the fluid flow force. The equation

$$\tau_{oc} = \alpha\eta \frac{\pi}{6} d(\gamma_s - \gamma) \tan\phi$$

may now be modified for cohesive sediment as,

$$\tau_{oc} = \alpha\eta \frac{\pi}{6} d(\gamma_s - \gamma) \tan\phi + CSy$$

Where Sy is the shear strength of the soil and C is a constant of proportionality.

For coarse sediment CSy is almost zero, while for very fine sediment the first term is very small.

An empirical data on critical mean velocities are given below,

Material	loose	Moderately compact	Compact
Sandy Clay	0.45 m/s	0.90 m/s	1.25 m/s
Clay	0.35 m/s	0.80 m/s	1.20 m/s
Lean clay Soil	0.30 m/s	0.70 m/s	1.05 m/s

Also the shear velocity u_* will have value ranging between 1.0 cm/s (consolidated period few days) to 3.0 cm/s (consolidation period few weeks)

For an exact determination of critical shear stress for cohesive soil a special test for each soil will be required.

Numerical Problems

Problem 6.1. A sediment particle has three mutually perpendicular dimensions as 2.1 mm, 1.1 mm and 0.4 mm. and nominal diameter 1.0 mm. Find its shape factor, sphericity, modulus of flatness and modulus of length.

Solution: Given, a = 2.1 mm, b = 1.1 mm, c = 0.4 mm. and dn = 1.0 mm

$$\text{Shape Factor (SF)} = \frac{c}{\sqrt{ab}} = \frac{0.4}{\sqrt{2.1 \times 1.1}}$$

$$= 0.263 \ \textbf{Ans.}$$

$$\text{Sphericity} = \frac{dn}{a} = \frac{1}{2.1} = 0.476 \text{ Ans.}$$

$$\text{Modulus of Flatness} = \frac{c}{b} = \frac{0.4}{1.1} = 0.3636 \text{ Ans.}$$

$$\text{Modulus of length} = \frac{a}{b} = \frac{2.1}{1.1} = 1.909 \text{ Ans.}$$

Problem 6.2 Find out the fall velocity of 1 mm diameter particle with specific gravity (S) = 2.65, Kinematic Viscosity (ν) = lcS. If concentration (c) = 0.15, find the change in fall velocity.

Solution: From the graph, Fall velocity w_0 = 15 cm/s

$$\therefore \quad \text{Reynold's Number Re} = \frac{w_0 d}{\nu} = \frac{15\times0.1}{1/100} = 150$$

$$\text{From graph } C_D = 0.75$$

we know that,

$$w_0^2 = \frac{4}{3}\frac{1}{C_D}.g.d.\Delta = \frac{4}{3}\times\frac{1}{0.75}\times981\times0.1\times1.65 = 287.76$$

$$\therefore \quad w_0 = 16.96 \text{ cm/s. Ans.}$$

Now,

$$\frac{w(c)}{w_o} = (1-0.15)^{\alpha}$$

For Re 150,

$$\alpha = \frac{4.45}{\text{Re}^{0.1}} = \frac{4.45}{(150)^{0.1}} = 2.696$$

$$\therefore \quad \frac{w(c)}{w_o} = (1-0.15)^{2.696} = 0.645$$

or

$$w(c) = 0.645\times16.96 = 10.93\ cm/s \text{ Ans.}$$

Problem 6.3 Find out the critical velocity for a particle of diameter 1.0 mm of specific gravity 2.65 when the depth of flow is 1.5 m and channel slope 1:10,000 and kinematic viscosity (ν) = $1cS$, by.

(a) Neill's method (b) Garde's Relation and (c) Yang's formula.

Solution: (a) **Neill's Relation:** $V_C = \sqrt{\Delta gd}\times1.414\,(D/d)^{\frac{1}{6}}$

$$V_c = \sqrt{1.65\times9.81\times1\times10^{-3}}\times1.414\times\left[\frac{1.5}{1\times10^{-3}}\right]^{1/6}$$

$$= 0.608\ m/s = 60.8\,cm/s.$$

(b) **Garde's Equation:** $V_C = \sqrt{\Delta\,gd}\ [0.5\log(D/d)+1.63]$

$$= 0.1272\,[0.5\log1500+1.63] = 0.408\,m = 40.8 \text{ cm/s Ans.}$$

(c) **Yang's Expression:** $\tau_o = \gamma\,DS = 9810\times1.5\times\dfrac{1}{10,000} = 1.4715\,N/m^2$

$$u* = \sqrt{\frac{\tau_o}{\rho}} = \sqrt{\frac{1.4715}{1000}} = 0.038\,m/s = 3.8\,cm/s$$

$$R_e^* = \frac{u*d}{\nu} = \frac{3.8\times0.1}{1\times10^{-2}} = 38$$

$$\therefore V_c = \left[\frac{2.5}{\log \text{Re}^* - 0.06} + 0.66\right] w_0 = \left[\frac{2.5}{1.5797-0.06} + 0.66\right] w_0$$

$$= 2.305\times15 = 34.575 \text{ cm/s} \quad \textbf{Ans.}$$

w_o = Fall Velocity for 1 mm particle from graph = 15 cm/s.

Problem 6.4 Water flow in a wide rectangular channel ($S_o = 10^{-4}$) at a depth of 50 cm with bed material having diameter of 1.0 mm. Find whether the channel is stable or not? (Take $\upsilon = 10^{-6}\,m^2/s$, Specific Gravity = 2.65)

Solution: $\tau_0 = \gamma D S_o = 9810\times0.5\times10^{-4} = 0.4905\,N/m^2$

$$u_* = \sqrt{\frac{\tau_o}{\rho}} = \sqrt{\frac{0.4905}{1000}} = 0.02214\,m/s$$

$$\text{Re}^* = \frac{u_* d}{\nu} = \frac{0.02214\times1\times10^{-3}}{10^{-6}} = 22.14$$

Now, $$\frac{\tau_o}{(\gamma_s - \gamma)d} = \frac{0.4905}{9.81(2650-1000)\times10^{-3}} = 0.0303$$

On Shields diagram point (22.14, 0.0303) falls below the curve, hence the channel is stable.

Problem 6.5 The velocity of flow in a wide rectangular channel is 0.5 m/s, the depth of flow 0.5 m, size of the bed material 1.0 mm specific gravity of material 2.65 and bed slope 1:7000, $\nu_{water} = 10^{-6}$ m²/s. Will the bed get eroded?

Solution: $\tau_0 = \gamma D S_o = 9810\times0.5\times\frac{1}{7000} = 0.7\,N/m^2$

$$\therefore \frac{\tau_o}{(\gamma_s - \gamma)d} = \frac{0.7}{(2.65\times1000-1000)\times9.81\times1\times10^{-3}} = 0.0432$$

$$\text{Re}^* = \frac{u_* d}{\nu} = \frac{d\sqrt{gDS}}{\nu} = \frac{1\times10^{-3}\sqrt{9.81\times0.5/7000}}{10^{-6}} = 26.47$$

On Shields diagram point (26.47, 0.0432) falls above the curve, hence the bed will get eroded.

Problem 6.6 Find the slope of a stable channel for following condition d = 25 mm, D = 1.07 m specific gravity of bed material = 2.68 consider channel as wide.

Solution: Using the figure 6.4, we get

$$\frac{\Delta^{1/3} g^{1/3} d}{\nu^{2/3}} = \frac{1.68^{1/3} \times 981^{1/3} \times 2.5}{(10^{-2})^{2/3}} = 636.36$$

From the graph, $\frac{\tau_o}{(\gamma_5 - \gamma)d} = 0.06$

$\therefore$ $$\tau_o = 0.06 \times 1680 \times 0.025 = 2.52\ N/m^2$$

$$\tau_o = \gamma\ DS_o \text{ or } S_o = \frac{\tau_o}{\gamma D} = \frac{2.52}{9810 \times 1.07}$$

or $S_0 = 2.4 \times 10^{-4}$ **Ans.**

Problem 6.7 Find the shear stress required to move the following sediment, d = 0.5 mm, $\rho_s = 2650\,kg/m^3$, $\rho = 1000\,kg/m^3$, $\nu = 10^{-6}\,m^2/s$.

Solution: $$\frac{\Delta g d^3}{\nu^2} = \frac{1.65 \times 9.81 \times \left(\frac{0.5}{1000}\right)^3}{\left(10^{-6}\right)^2} = 2023$$

From Table $\frac{\tau_o}{(\gamma_s - \gamma)d} = 0.034$

$$\therefore\ \tau_o = 0.034 \times (\gamma_s - \gamma)d = 0.034 \times 1650 \times 9.81 \times 0.5 \times 10^{-3} = 0.275\,N/m^2$$

Problem 6.8 Water flows at a depth of 0.3 m in a wide stream with slope 1 × 10^{-3}. The median diameter of the bed material is 1.0 mm, compute and find if the grains are stationary or moving?

Solution: $$\tau_o = \gamma\,DS = 9810 \times 0.3 \times \frac{1}{1000} = 2.943\,N/m^2$$

$$u_* = \sqrt{\frac{\tau_o}{\rho}} = \sqrt{\frac{2.943}{1000}} = 0.05425\ m/s$$

$$\text{Re}^* = \frac{u_* d}{\nu} = \frac{0.05425 \times 10^{-3}}{10^{-6}} = 54.25$$

and $$\frac{\tau_o}{(\gamma_s - \gamma)d} = \frac{2.943}{1.65 \times 1000 \times 9.81 \times 10^{-3}} = 0.1818$$

From shields graph point (54.25, 0.1818) fall in the region of motion,
Hence, grains will be moving.

Problem 6.9 Find the shear stress required to move the following particles.

(a) d = 1 mm, $\rho_s = 1.05 \times 1000\,kg/m^3$, $\rho = 1.2\,kg/m^3$, $\nu = 1.5 \times 10^{-5}\,m^2/s$

(b) d = 1 mm, $\rho_s = 4.2 \times 1000\,kg/m^3$, $\rho = 1000\,kg/m^3$, $\nu = 1.1 \times 10^{-6}\,m^2/s$

Solution: (a) $$\frac{\Delta g d^3}{\nu^2} = \frac{\left(\frac{1050 - 1.2}{1.2}\right) \times 9.81 \times (125) \times 10^{-9}}{2.25 \times 10^{-10}} = 4.76 \times 10^6$$

From the table, $\dfrac{\tau_{oc}}{(\gamma_s - \gamma)d} = 0.048$

$$\therefore \quad \tau_{oc} = 0.048 \times (1050 - 1.2) \times 9.81 \times 5 \times 10^{-3} = 2.469\, N/m^2$$

(b) $$\frac{\Delta g d^3}{\nu^2} = \frac{\frac{3200}{1000} \times 9.81 \times 10^{-9}}{1.1^2 \times 10^{-12}} = 259438 \approx 26{,}000$$

From the table, $\dfrac{\tau_{oc}}{(r_5 - r)d} = 0.0362$

$$\therefore \quad \tau_{oc} = 0.0362(4200 - 1000) \times \frac{1}{1000} \times 9.81 = 1.136\, N/m^2$$

Problem 6.10 **Find the depth of flow at which sediment of 1.0 mm diameter starts moving in a wide rectangular channel set at a slope of 10^{-4}. Relative density of sediment is 2.65 and kinematic viscosity of water is 10^{-4} m²/s.**

Solution: $$\frac{\Delta^{1/3} g^{1/3} d}{\nu^{2/3}} = \frac{(1.65)^{1/3}(9.81)^{1/3} 10^{-3}}{(10^{-6})^{2/3}} = \frac{2.529 \times 10^{-3}}{10^{-4}} = 25.29$$

$$\tau_{oc}^{*} = \frac{\tau_{oc}}{(\gamma_s - \gamma)\, d} = 0.035. \text{ From Sheilds curve.}$$

$$\therefore \quad \tau_{oc} = (2650 - 1000) \times g \times 10^{-3} \times 0.035 = 0.5665\, N/m^2$$

Now, $$\tau_{oc} = \gamma\, DS \text{ or } D = \frac{\tau_{oc}}{\gamma S} = \frac{0.5665}{9810 \times 10^{-4}} = 0.577\, m. \quad \textbf{Ans.}$$

Problem 6.11 **Find the depth and discharge intensity which will just move soil grains of 0.5 mm diameter on a slope of 2×10^{-4} and $\nu_{water} = 10^{-6}$ m²/s.**

Solution: $$\frac{\Delta^{1/3} g^{1/3} d}{\nu^{2/3}} = \frac{(1.65)^{1/3}(9.81)^{1/3} \times 0.5 \times 10^{-3}}{(10^{-6})^{2/3}} = \frac{2.529 \times 10^{-3}}{10^{-4}} = 12.645$$

$$\frac{\tau_{oc}}{(\gamma_s - \gamma)\, d} = 0.033 \text{ from graph}$$

$$\therefore \quad \tau_{oc} = 1650 \times 9.81 \times 0.5 \times 10^{-3} \times 0.033 = 0.267\, N/m^2$$

$$\tau_{oc} = \gamma\, DS,\ D = \frac{0.267}{9810 \times 2 \times 10^{-4}} = 0.136 \text{ m.}$$

$$q \text{ (discharge per unit width)} = \frac{D}{N} D^{2/3} S^{1/2}$$

$$N = \frac{(d)^{1/6}}{21} = \frac{(0.5 \times 10^{-3})^{1/6}}{21} = 0.0134$$

$$\therefore \quad q = \frac{0.136}{0.0134} \times (.136)^{2/3} (2 \times 10^{-4})^{1/2} = 0.038\, m^3/s/m.$$

CHAPTER 7

BED FORMS (REGIME OF FLOW)

Knowledge of sediment transport is most often used to determine whether erosion or deposition will occur, the magnitude of this erosion or deposition, and the time and distance over which it will occur. The estimation could be made only by empirical methods. Bottom shear stress, water depth and bed roughness have been considered as the most important parameters. Description of particle motion under the action of flow is also largely empirical. It is therefore, not difficult to understand why there is only a limited theoretical basis for the relation between flow and sediment transport.

Most of the present knowledge is obtained from experiments and general physical arguments. For the initiation of motion a reasonable picture was obtained in this way. At greater values of the bed-shear stress sediment transport will increase and deformation of the bed will occur. As the deformation is time-dependent and nature is always unsteady, an equilibrium situation will be hardly found in practice.

TRANSPORT MECHANISM

According to transport mechanism two major modes of sediment transport in rivers and channels may be distinguished,

1. **The Bed Load**: The sediment entrained in a flow can be transported along the bed as bed load in the form of sliding, rolling or jumping.
2. **Suspended Load:** This is sediment movement in the flow as Suspended load advected by the main flow. The settling tendency of the particles is continuously compensated by the diffusive action of the turbulent flow field.

A sharp distinction between bed load and suspended load is not possible. In literature sometimes **Saltation load** is also mentioned. This is the mode where particles which are the part of material bouncing along the bed. This mode can be considered as bed load. The bed load can, therefore, be considered as contact load plus the saltation load. Generally, very fine particles (< 50 μm) do not settle and always remain in suspension, this mode of transport is termed as **Wash Load**. Wash load is not important for changes in river bed but only for sedimentation in stagnant water bodies. However, it can have some influence on turbulence and viscosity and therefore have some influence on the flow.

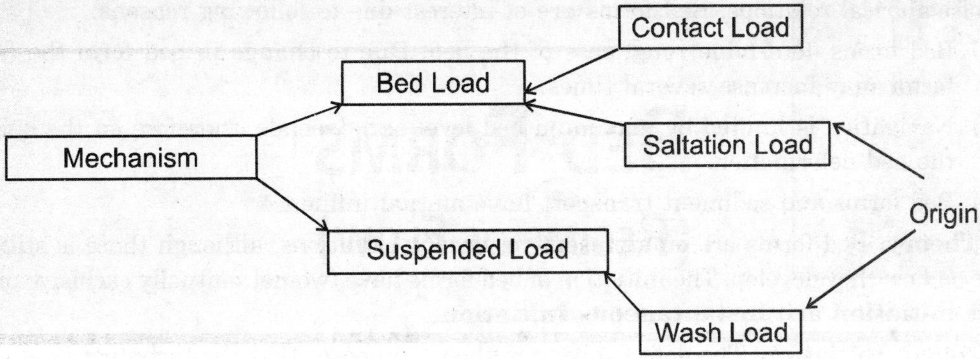

Fig. 7.1

Rouse Number

The location in the flow in which a particle is entrained is determined by the Rouse Number which is determined by the density ρ_s and diameter d of the sediment particle, and the density ρ and kinematic viscosity ν of the fluid.

Rouse Number, $P = \dfrac{w}{\kappa u_*}$

where, w is settling velocity, κ = Von Karman's Constant (0.4) and u^* is shear velocity.

The following table gives the approximate required Rouse Number (P) for transport as Bed Load, Suspended Load and Wash Load.

Mode of Transport	Rouse Number (P)
Initiation of Motion	> 7.5
Bed Load	> 2.5 < 7.5
Suspended Load: 50% Suspended	> 1.2 < 2.5
Suspended Load: 100% Suspended	> 0.8 < 1.2
Wash Load	< 0.8

Rouse Number (P) is non-dimensional number in fluid dynamics which is used to define a concentration profile of suspended sediment and which also determines how sediment will be transported in a flowing fluid. Von Karman's Constant is often used in turbulence modelling to calculate fluxes of momentum. Its value has been universally accepted as equal to 0.4.

Bed Forms

A bed form is a feature that develops at the interface of fluid and movable bed, the result of bed material being moved by fluid flow. The distinctive pattern into which an erodible granular bed forms under some conditions of water flow is a matter of great interest for a River Engineer.

Much literature exists on the classification and dimensions of bed forms, mainly in the form of empirical relations. Bed forms are of interest due to following reasons:

(1) Bed forms determine roughness of the bed. Due to change in bed form the friction factor may increase several times.

(2) Navigation is limited by maximum bed level and depends, therefore on the height of the bed deformation.

(3) Bed forms and sediment transport have mutual influence.

Theory: Bed forms are omnipresent in various situations, although there is still some debate on how they develop. The initiation of bed forms have two-not mutually exclusive models: **defect initiation** and **instantaneous initiation.**

Defect Initiation: The defect initiation theory proposes that the turbulent sweeps that are generated in turbulent flows entrain sediment that upon deposition generates defects in non-cohesive material. These deposits then propagate downstream via a flow separation process, thus developing bed form fields. Once a critical height of grains is reached, flow separation occurs. Sediment is detached only to form a new defect at the downstream.

Instantaneous Initiation: In general, the defect propagation theory plays a bigger role at low sediment transport rates since for high rates defects may be washed away and bed forms generally initiated across the entire bed spontaneously. Instantaneous occurs at larger flow strengths, where sediment transport is general and widespread. This form of bed form initiation begins with imprinting of a cross-hatch pattern on the flat sediment bed, which leads to Chevron-shaped forms that migrate independently of the initial pattern.

It has been observed that when the average shear stress on the bed of an alluvial channel exceeds the critical shear stress, the individual particles start moving. Consequently, the bed gets disturbed and acquires different Bed Forms also called bed irregularities, sand waves or defects in bed. Another name suggested by Garde and Albertson as 'Regimes of Flow.'

A generally accepted classification of Bed Forms at different Froude Numbers is as follows:

[A] In the **Lower Flow Regime** when Froude Number $F_r = \dfrac{V}{\sqrt{gD}}$ is < 0.4 to 1.0.

Under this condition the stream bed may take the form changing from flat bed to ripples to dunes.

(1) **Flat Bed:** At values of the bed shear stress just above the critical shear stress (τ_{oc}), sediment transport without deformation of the bed is possible. Grains are mainly transported by rolling and bouncing. The water surface remains fairly smooth. Boundary acts as a **rigid** boundary.

(2) **Ripples:** When the average shear stress is just above the critical shear stress, small regular undulations appear on the bed having sediment size < 0.6 mm. These are in the form of waves having wavelengths in the order of 5 to 10 cm and height in the order of 1.0 cm. The sediment moves mainly as bed load. The material rolls along the upstream face of ripple and falls over the downstream face. The ripples appear to be moving downstream at a very low speed. Gradually, they become irregular and three-dimensional in character. (Fig. 7.2)

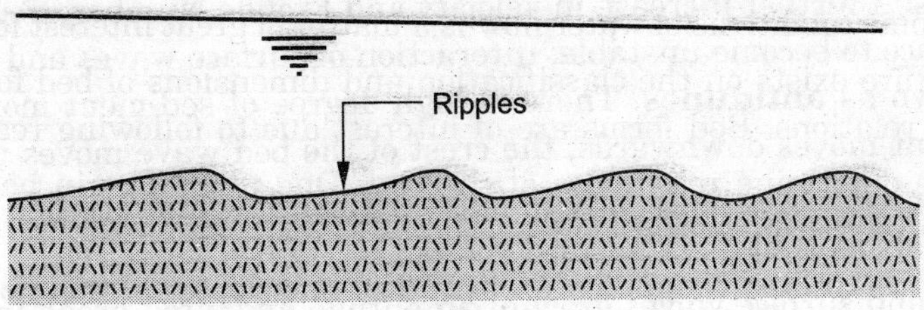

Fig. 7.2

(3) **Dunes:** When discharge is further increased, consequently increasing the shear stress, ripples grow into dunes for all sediment sizes. Dunes are found to be more two-dimensional than ripples and show greater wavelengths and heights. Sometimes small ripples are noticed on the upstream face of the dunes. Water surface is not so smooth. The size of the dunes vary largely, which may be 2 to 3 m long and 0.40 m high as recorded in laboratory flumes. In natural streams they may be upto 100 m long and upto even 15 m high. (Fig. 7.3)

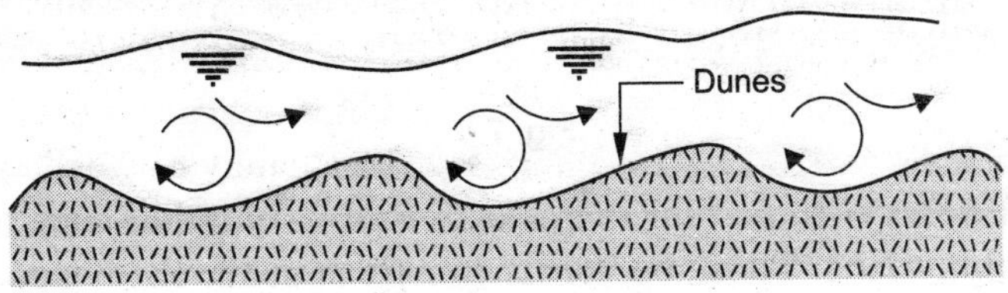

Fig. 7.3

The crest of dunes is perpendicular to the flow, the form is more or less triangular with a gentle slope along which the particles are transported and a steep downstream slope where particles are deposited. The angle of this slope is roughly the angle of repose of material.

[B] In the **Upper Flow Regime:** When Froude Number $F_r = \frac{V}{\sqrt{gD}}$ is $\gtrsim$ 0.4 to 1.0, the dunes are washed away and the bed gets near to the flat bed progressively changing into **antidunes** and **chute** and **pools**.

(4) **Flat Bed:** As the velocity further increases, the dunes are flattened, gradually disappear and the bed becomes flat. Sediment transport rate is high. This state can also be termed as transition from lower flow regime to upper flow regime. (Fig. 7.4 and 7.5)

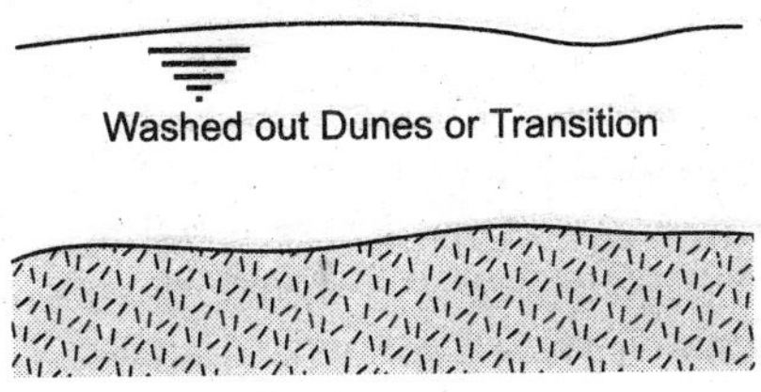

Fig. 7.4

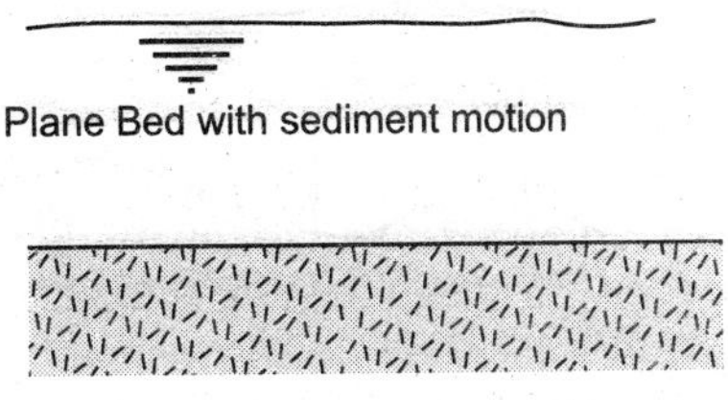

Fig. 7.5

(5) **Antidunes:** A further increase in velocity and Froude Number around 1.0 causes the water surface to become unstable. Interaction of surface waves and bed results in bed forms known as **antidunes**. There is high degree of sediment movement. Although the sediment moves downwards, the crest of the bed wave moves upstream.

Antidunes occur essentially only in supercritical flow and are hence to be found out only in canals as well as in natural rivers.

Antidunes and surface waves grow in amplitude and often break in a similar way as the ocean waves.

In between plane bed and antidunes another bed form has been identified as **antidunes standing wave**. This is sometimes considered as transitional phase. (Fig. 7.6)

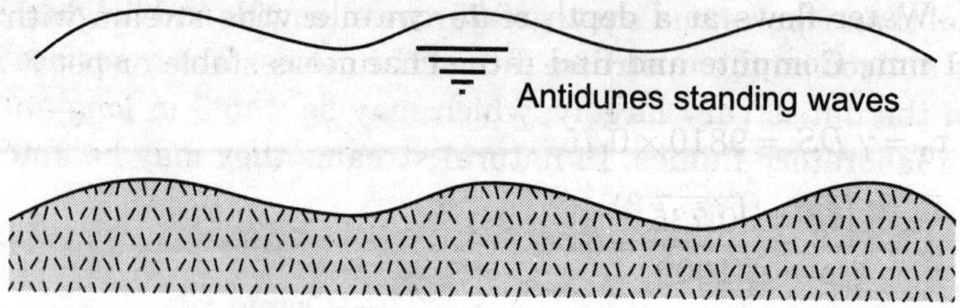

Fig. 7.6

(6) **Chute and Pools:** With further increase in Froude Number, antidunes turn to chute-and-pool combinations. These bedforms consist of sediment heaps followed by chutes (sliding channels). Two successive heaps and chutes make a pool. As a result, a succession of subcritical flow in pools and supercritical flow in the chutes are prevalent. However, formation of chutes and pools rarely occurs in an alluvial river. (Fig. 7.7 and 7.8)

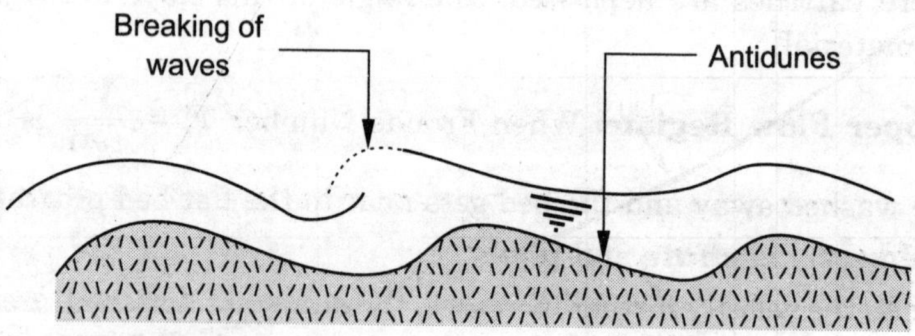

Fig. 7.7

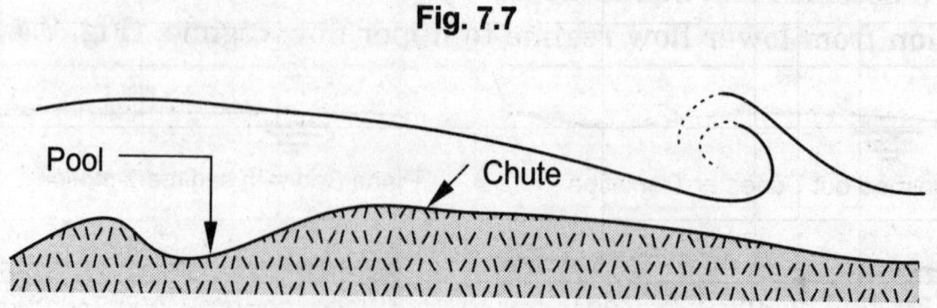

Fig. 7.8

Classification Criteria

A number of researchers have tried to develop theoretical explanations for the origin of ripples and dunes and their advance forms of antidunes and chutes and pools. The theoretical model results have not been very convincing when compared with the experimental and empirical correlations. Liu's postulates, perhaps, had been the first in this respect. He asserted that the instability of the interface between sand and water is responsible for formation of ripples. Also the flow should be capable of transporting sediment for the formation of ripples.

Liu correlated $\frac{u_*}{w}$ *and* $\frac{u_* d}{\nu}$ and established a criterion for the "Beginning of Ripple Formation". (Fig. 7.9)

Probem 7.1. Water flows at a depth of 75 cm in a wide stream with slope 10^{-4}. The grain diameter is 1 mm. Compute and find if the channel is stable or not ?

Solution: $\tau_0 = \gamma\, DS. = 9810 \times 0.75 \times 10^{-4} = 0.735\ N/m^2$

$$u_* = \sqrt{\frac{\tau_0}{\rho}} = \sqrt{\frac{0.735}{1000}} = 0.027\ m/s$$

$$\frac{u_*}{w} = \frac{.027}{.15} = 0.18,\ \text{Re}^* = \frac{0.027 \times 10^{-3}}{10^{-6}} = 27.$$

In the Liu's curve the channel shows stable position, but Shield's criteria shows unstable channel.

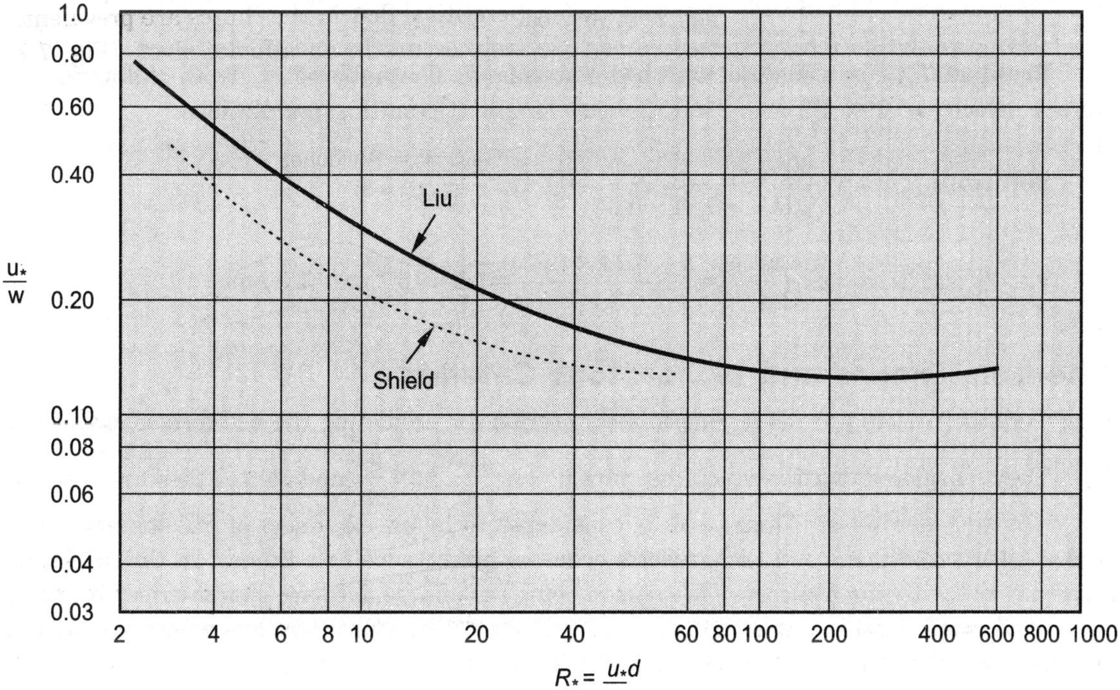

Fig. 7.9 Liu's Criteria for Ripples

Kennedy's Analysis

Kennedy assumed potential flow over a sinusoidal erodible bed to evaluate variations in bed. His work is a relation between the wavelength (λ) of the deformation and the Froude Number (N_F). The results of theoretical models have not been very convincing so that we have to rely again on empirical correlations.

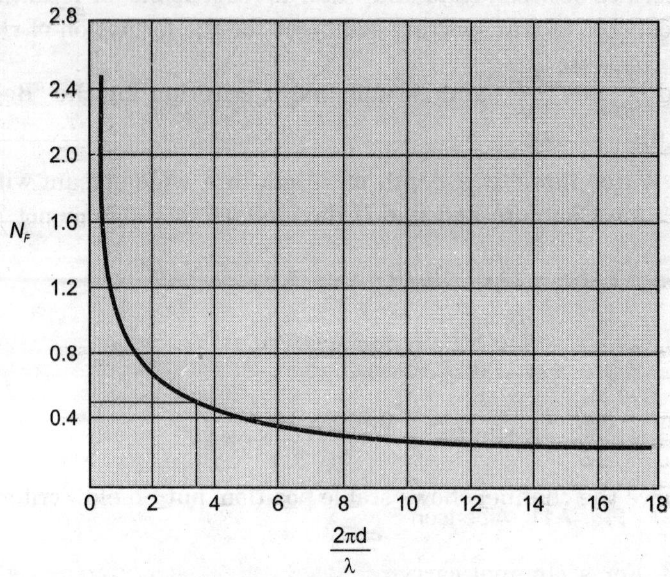

Fig. 7.10 Kennedy's Criteria

Problem 7.2. For a channel with bed material of 1.0 mm diameter, depth of flow 50 cm, average velocity of flow 1.2 m/s. Find the wavelength of resulting undulations.

Solution: $$N_F = \frac{V}{\sqrt{gD}} = \frac{1.2}{\sqrt{9.81 \times 0.5}} = 0.541, \quad \frac{2\,\pi\,d}{\lambda} = 3.4$$

$$\therefore \qquad \lambda = \frac{2 \times \pi \times d}{3.4} = \frac{2 \times 3.14 \times 10^{-3}}{3.4} = 1.8 \times 10^{-3}\,m \ = 1.8\,mm.$$

Albertson, Simons and Richardsons Criterion

They were the first to provide a generalised criterion for predicting the bed forms (regimes of flow). They considered two dimensionless parameters $\frac{u_* d}{\nu}$ and $\frac{u_*}{w}$ and plotted these on abscissa and ordinate respectively. Their work is considered to be an extension of Shields and Liu's works. Albertson-Simons and Richardson's criterion predicts well for flumes. In the field data it has not met with much success. The reason being that flume data are characterised by steep slopes and small depths, it does not seem to hold good for natural streams where the depths are large and slopes are mild. (Fig. 7.11)

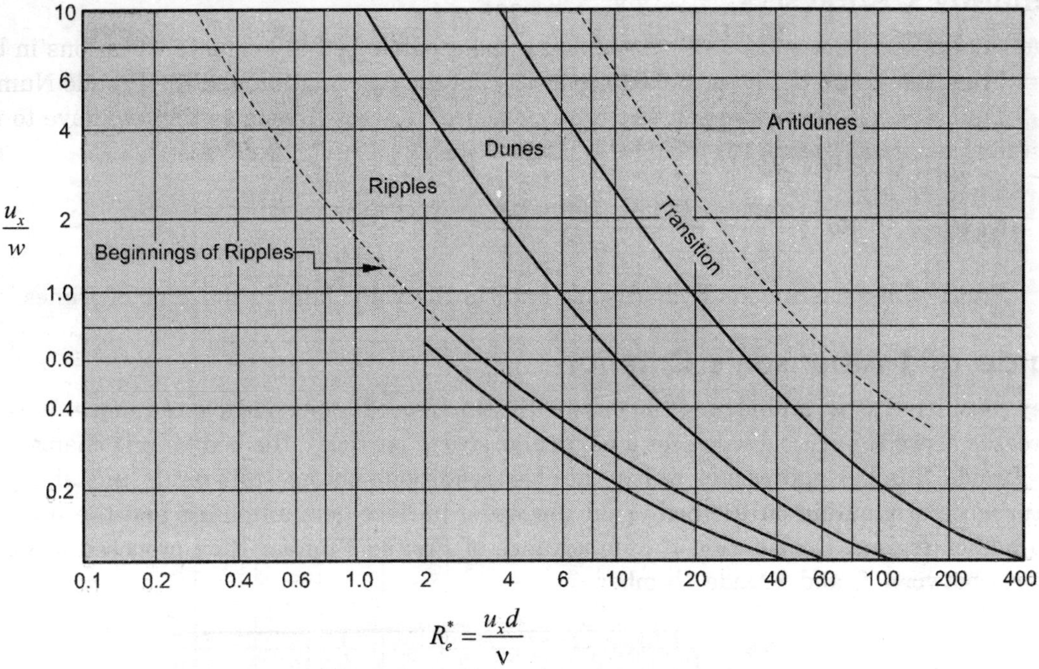

Fig. 7.11 Albertson-Simons-Richardson's Bed Criteria

Problem 7.3. For a channel carrying 1 mm diameter sediment at a depth of 50 cm. Temperature 20°C. The velocity of flow is estimated as 1.2 m/s and Chezy's coefficient C = 42 m$^{1/2}$/s. Find the Bed Form.

Solution: Considering Albertson-Simons-Richardson's Criteria,

$$\frac{u}{u_*} = \frac{C}{\sqrt{g}} = \frac{42}{\sqrt{9.81}} = 13.28$$

$$\therefore \quad u_* = \frac{1.2}{13.28} = 0.09 \; m/s$$

Fall velocity from wv_sd graph = 0.15 m/s (Fig. 5.5)

$$\text{Re}^* = \frac{u_* \, d}{\nu} = \frac{0.09 \times 10^{-3}}{10^{-6}} = 90 \qquad (\nu_{water} = 10^{-6} \text{ m}^2/\text{s})$$

$$\frac{u^*}{w} = \frac{0.09}{0.15} = 0.6$$

Plotting the point on the graph, it falls on the Antidune zone.

Problem 7.4. Find the possible bed form in the following channel, d = 150 μm, Depth of flow = 2 m, velocity = 0.6 m/s and Chezy's C = 63 m$^{1/2}$/s.

Solution: $$u = C\sqrt{RS}, \quad u^* = \sqrt{\frac{\tau_0}{\rho}} = \sqrt{\frac{\gamma RS}{\rho}} = \sqrt{gRS}$$

$$\frac{u}{u_*} = \frac{C\sqrt{RS}}{\sqrt{gRS}} = \frac{C}{\sqrt{g}} = \frac{63}{\sqrt{9.81}} = 20.114$$

$$\therefore \qquad u_* = \frac{u}{20.114} = \frac{0.6}{20.114} = 0.0298 \; m/s.$$

From the graph d_{vs} w, w = 0.015 m/s

$$\therefore \qquad \frac{u^*}{w} = \frac{0.0298}{0.015} = 1.988$$

Now, $$\text{Re}^* = \frac{u_* d}{\nu} = \frac{0.0298 \times 150 \times 10^{-6}}{10^{-6}} = 4.47.$$

From, Albertson-Simons-Richardson's criteria the point falls in the zone of Dunes.

Garde and Albertson's Criterion

They considered τ^* as an index of the ease with which a sediment particle can move. When τ_* increases above the critical value for a particular size of particles, the bed form is changed. As the Froude Number approaches unity, the flow conditions become inherently unstable. Any disturbance originating on the bed or on the water surface gets amplified and the bed goes into higher regime. Considering the importance of Froude Number they proposed a regime criteria between τ_* and Froude Number.

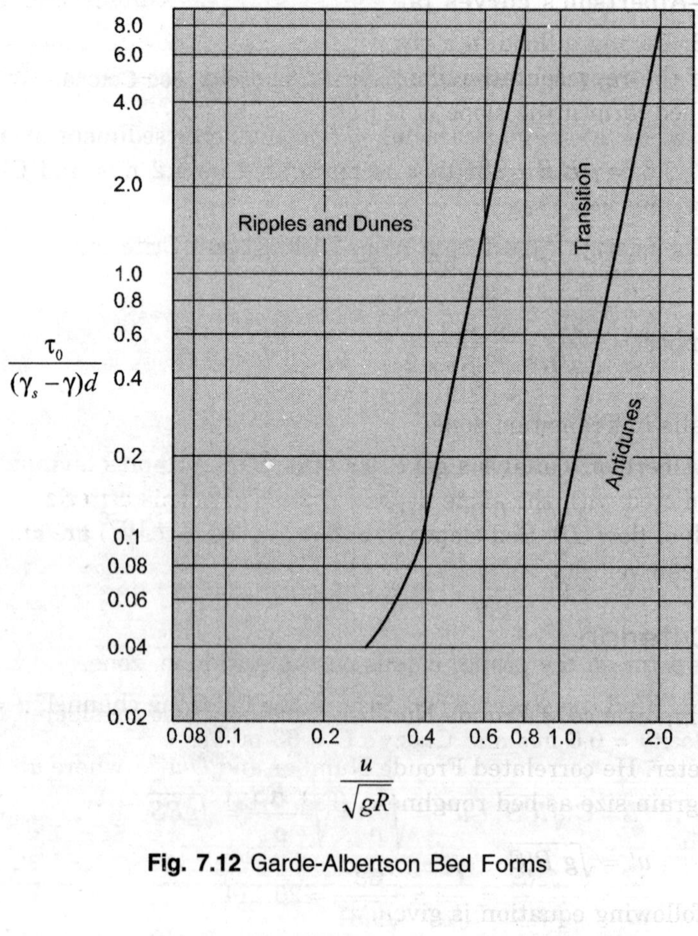

Fig. 7.12 Garde-Albertson Bed Forms

Problem 7.5: Evaluate the possible bed forms in a wide channel flowing at a depth of 1.5 m and average velocity 1.1 m/s, Chezy's coefficient is 60 $m^{1/2}/s$. The representative particle diameter is 0.5 mm.

Solution: Considering Garde - Albertson's criteria.

$$u = C\sqrt{RS}, \quad u^2 = C^2 RS$$

$$\therefore \quad S = \frac{u^2}{C^2 R} = \frac{1.1^2}{60^2 \times 1.5} = 0.000224 \qquad \text{(For wide channels R = D)}$$

$$\tau_0 = \gamma R S_o = 9810 \times 1.5 \times 0.000224 = 3.296 \text{ N/m}^2$$

$$\therefore \quad \tau_* = \frac{\tau_0}{(r_s - r)d} = \frac{3.296}{(2.65 - 1) \times 9810 \times 0.5} = 0.407$$

(γ for water is 9810 N/m^3 and specific gravity of grains' material is 2.65)

$$\frac{u}{\sqrt{gD}} = \frac{1.1}{\sqrt{9.81 \times 1.5}} = 0.286$$

Point on Garde–Albertson's curves fall in the zone of Ripples and Dunes

Problem 7.6: During a flood in a river the velocity of flow was measured as 2.5 m/s at a depth of 2 m. If the representative diameter of the bed material is estimated as 0.6 mm. What will be the bed form if the slope of the channel is 0.00025.

Solution: $\tau_0 = \gamma R S = 9810 \times 2 \times 0.00025 = 4.9 \text{ N/m}^2$

$$\therefore \quad \tau_* = \frac{\tau_0}{(r_s - r)d} = \frac{4.9}{1.65 \times 9810 \times 0.6 \times 10^{-3}} = 0.5$$

$$\text{Froude Number} = \frac{u}{\sqrt{gD}} = \frac{2.5}{\sqrt{9.81 \times 2}} = 0.564$$

The point falls in Transition zone.

Garde and Albertson's analysis gave good results for ripples and dunes. The antidune regime is not predicted with the same degree of accuracy. This criteria can be used if mean velocity (U), depth of flow (D), Bed slope (S) and grain diameter (d) are known. It can also be used to predict mean velocity.

Engelund's Criterion

Considering the importance of Froude Number, Engelund also considered it $\left(F_r = \frac{U}{\sqrt{gR}}\right)$ as one of the parameter. He correlated Froude Number and $U/u'*$, where $u'*$ is the value of $u*$ by assuming the grain size as bed roughness, (Fig. 7.13)

$$u'_* = \sqrt{g R' S}$$

For R' the following equation is given.

$$\frac{U}{\sqrt{g R' S}} = 5.75 \log \frac{R'}{2d_{65}} + 6.0$$

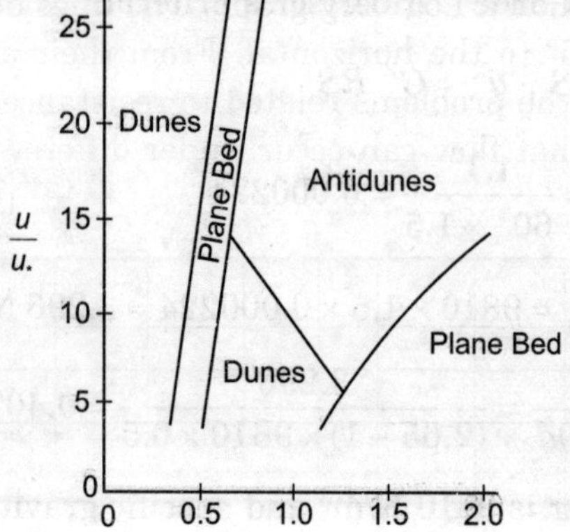

Fig. 7.13 Engelund's Bed Forms

Problem 7.7: For a channel with bed material of diameter 0.5 mm, depth of flow 0.5 m, average velocity 90 cm/s, using Engelund's criteria, find the bed form.

Solution: Froude Number $F_r = \frac{0.9}{\sqrt{9.81 \times 0.5}} = 0.406$

$$\frac{V}{u'_*} = 5.75 \log \frac{R'}{2d_{65}} + 6$$

$$= 5.75 \log \frac{0.5}{2 \times 0.5 \times 10^{-3}} + 6 = 21.52$$

From the Engelund's Bed Form criteria, the point (0.406, 21.52) falls in the Dunes regime.

Problem 7.8: For the following channel and flow condition, find the bed form, use Engelund's criteria. Average velocity 1.5 m/s, bed material d_{65} = 0.35 mm. Depth of flow 45 cm.

Solution: Froude Number $= \frac{1.5}{\sqrt{9.81 \times .45}} = 0.714$

$$\frac{V}{u'_*} = 5.75 \log \frac{0.45}{2 \times 0.35 \times 10^{-3}} + 6 = 22.14$$

From Engelund's criteria, the point (0.714, 22.14) falls in antidune regime.

Note: Engelund's Bed Form criteria has been found to be giving fairly good results.

Garde and Ranga Raju Regime-Criterion

They proposed a regime-Criterion using $\frac{R}{d}$ and $S/[(\gamma_s - \gamma)/\gamma]$ as the two parameters and the resulting data was plotted on a Log -Log graph. The lines demarcating the regimes are at an inclination of less than 45° to the horizontal. From their analysis it was concluded that this criterion can be used for the problems related to resistance as it does not involve velocity of flow. It is also concluded that flow can occur under different regimes at a constant shear stress.

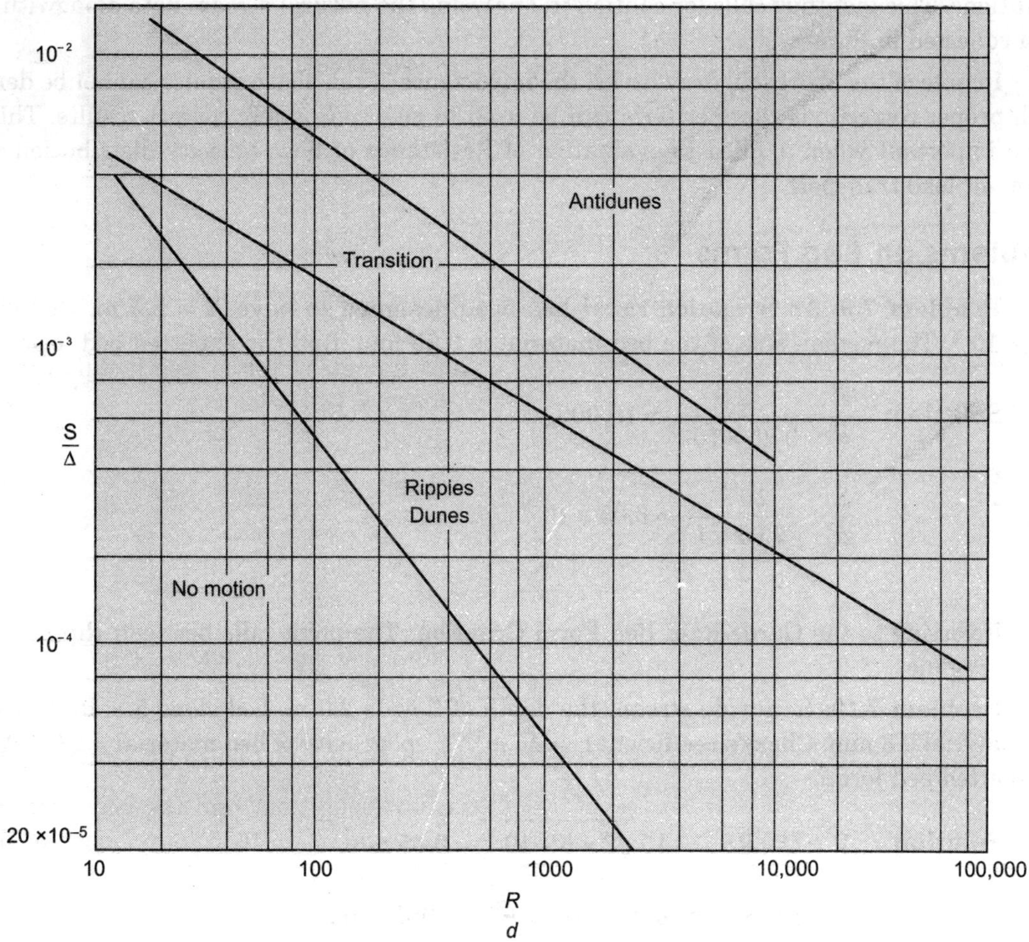

Fig. 7.14 Garde-Raju Bed Forms

Simon and Richardson's Criterion and Stream Power Concept

Stream power is the rate of energy dissipation against the bed and banks of a river or stream per unit downstream length. It is given by the equation,

$$\Omega = \gamma\, Q\, S = \gamma\, b.\, D.\, u\, S = \tau_0\, bu$$

$$\therefore \quad \text{Stream Power per unit width } = \frac{\tau_0 bu}{b} = \tau_0\, u.$$

Simon and Richardson used stream power and sediment size as two parameters for predicting bed forms. The check on accuracy of the criterion did not show satisfactory results.

Some Important Observations

The river flow is non-uniform, unsteady and three dimensional. Hence it becomes, almost impossible to perform theoretical analysis. Therefore, one has to depend upon empirical, experimental and local experience of people.

The criteria described above are mostly the result of flume experiments under idealised conditions. This fact thus calls for caution in analysing the natural stream data alongwith the data collected in flumes.

Inspite of the abovesaid drawbacks, the importance of the above studies cannot be denied. With proper corrections these criteria can be used to give reasonably correct results. This is much important when applied to evaluation of Resistance of flow, velocity distribution and sediment load transport.

Problems on Bed Forms

Problem 7.9. An irrigation canal has been designed to have R = 2.5 m. Bed slope = 1×10^{-4}. The median size of the bed material is 0.25 mm. find the expected bed form.

Solution: $$\frac{R}{d} = \frac{2.5}{0.25 \times 10^{-3}} = 10{,}000$$

$$\frac{S}{\Delta} = \frac{10^{-4}}{\left(\frac{2.65 - 1}{1}\right)} = 6.05 \times 10^{-5}$$

Referring to the Garde-Raju Bed Form Criterion. The point falls between Ripples and Dunes regime.

Problem 7.10: In a wide stream the depth of flow is 2.0 m, bed slope 5×10^{-5}, size of bed material 0.3 mm. Chezy's coefficient $C = 45\ \text{m}^{1/2}/\text{s}$, sp, gravity of bed material = 2.65. What is expected bed form?

Solution : $$V = C\sqrt{RS} = 45\sqrt{2 \times 5 \times 10^{-5}} = 0.45 \text{ m/s}$$

$$\tau_0 = \gamma\, RS = 9810 \times 2 \times 5 \times 10^{-5} = 0.981 \text{ N/m}^2$$

Now, $$\tau_* = \frac{\tau_0}{(\gamma_s - \gamma)\, d} = \frac{0.981}{(2.65 - 1)\, 9810 \times 0.3 \times 10^{-3}} = 0.202$$

$$F_r = \frac{V}{\sqrt{gD}} = \frac{0.45}{\sqrt{9.81 \times 2}} = 0.1$$

Referring to the Garde-Albertson bed form criterion. The point shows Ripple and Dune regime.

CHAPTER 8

RESISTANCE TO FLOW: CHANNEL ROUGHNESS

The resistance to flow in a channel of fixed geometry carrying clear water in steady uniform flow can be predicted quite accurately. In varied flow also this can be done fairly well.

However, it hardly needs to be emphasized that in a channel with erodible boundaries the resistance problem is much more complex.

The shape of the channel in alluvium changes with flow conditions; bed forms changes and alterations in the channel cross-section. These changes affect the **drag** caused by the surface roughness and introduce form drag caused by the bed features, as well as energy losses due to secondary currents.

The problem is further complicated by the movement of sediment along the bed and in suspension, since the mixture of water and sediment does not behave as clear water.

The discussion on the resistance problem in alluvial channels will be aided by a brief survey of the problem in channels of fixed boundary. Assuming that the bed of alluvial streams falls under the category of rough boundaries, following four equations need to be recalled. These are,

Chezy's Equation, $u = C\sqrt{RS}$ ...(1)

Manning's Equation, $u = \frac{1}{n} R^{2/3} S^{1/2}$ ...(2)

Prandtl-Karman's Equations,

$$\frac{u}{u_*} = 5.75 \log (y / Ks) + 8.5 \quad ...(3)$$

and $$\frac{u}{u_*} = 5.75 \log (R / Ks) + 6.25 \quad ...(4)$$

where, u = velocity at a distance of y from the boundary.

C = Chezy's coefficient (a resistance coefficient)

n = Manning coefficient (another resistance coefficient)

Ks = Equivalent sand grain roughness

S = slope of water surface

R = Hydraulic Radius (Area/Wetted Perimeter)

$$u_* = \text{Shear velocity } (\tau_0 / \rho) = \sqrt{\frac{\gamma\, RS}{\rho}} = \sqrt{g\, RS}$$

$$\therefore \quad \frac{u}{u_*} = \frac{C\sqrt{RS}}{\sqrt{g\, RS}} = \frac{C}{\sqrt{g}} \qquad \text{...(5)}$$

$$\text{or} \quad \frac{C}{\sqrt{g}} = 5.75 \log (R / Ks) + 6.25 \qquad \text{...(6)}$$

Above relation displays that the resistance to the flow depends upon hydraulic radius (or depth for wide channel) and surface condition. Also comparing Chezy's and Manning's equation, we get.

$$C = \frac{1}{n} R^{1/6}$$

For estimating the value of n for different bed materials, Strickler's formula is popular. He gave,

$$n = K_s^{1/6} \big/ 25.6$$

$$\text{or,} \quad n = (d_{50})^{1/6} \big/ (21 \text{ to } 25.6) \text{ in SI units.}$$

A graph between R/K_s and $\frac{R^{1/6}}{n\sqrt{g}}$ or $\frac{C}{\sqrt{g}}$ gives reasonable approximation, particularly between R/K_s equal to 7.5 to 250.

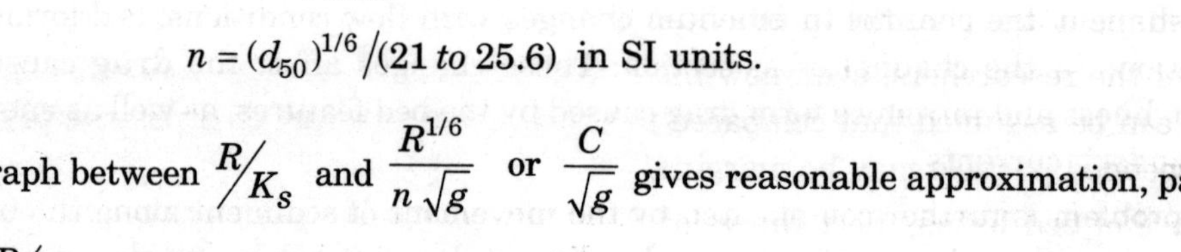

Fig. 8.1

Resistance to Flow in Alluvial Channels

The presence of sediment in water results in changes in bed form by the acts of erosion and deposition, hence changing the total resistance to the flow. The total resistance in general case of an alluvial channel can be considered to be due to,

Grain Resistance and
Form Resistance

Presence of sediment in suspension also has some marginal effect on resistance.

Grain Resistance: (Grain Roughness): The Grain Roughness is associated with the skin drag that is generally defined as the force exerted by the flow and includes both viscous and pressure drags that arise due to flow over individual particles on bed.

Bed Form Resistance (Form Roughness): It is caused by the form drag created by the difference between the high pressure upstream and low pressure downstream of the bed form. This drag force occurs when flow separation occurs behind the bed form.

Presence of Suspended Sediment: It seems natural that suspended sediment will affect the resistance and hence the velocity of flow. However, the finding in this respect are not consistent. According to one of the earlier research by Flammont, "It appears from experimental results, other things remaining constant, the mean velocity of water charged with silt is **greater** than that for clear water." The increase in velocity is attributed to the fact that presence of suspended sediment dampens the turbulence, thus decreasing the value of roughness coefficient.

None of the researchers, even now have been able to give a clear verdict on this issue. However, it can be assumed that compared to Grain and Form part of resistance to flow, the effect of suspended particle may be marginal.

Presence of bed forms affect the velocity of flow, various investigators have attempted to correlate the mean velocity, the hydraulic radius (or depth), the size of the sediment and the bed slope. Changes in these parameters finally reflect in the resistance (resistance coefficient) of the flow.

Broadly, there are two approaches to the problem of alluvial channel resistance.

1. Overall Resistance Approach.
2. Division of Resistance Approach.

Overall or Total Resistance Approach

Here the overall resistance is directly related to the flow velocity, fluid and sediment characteristics. Following is the brief description of relations offered by various investigators considering steady and uniform flow.

(1) Lacey's Approach

This is one of the earliest approaches based on river behaviour at dominant discharge. This equation is not applicable to all stages (discharge) of the river. The equation resembles with the Manning's Equation.

$$u = 10.8\, R^{2/3}\, S^{1/3}$$

The drawback is that the role of sediment size is not considered.

(2) Japanese Approach

Some engineers from Japan suggested the following relation for velocity,

$$\frac{u}{u*} = 5.75 \log R/_{Ks} + 6.0$$

They also tried to evaluate Ks, for which they applied following equations,

$$Ks = 10\, \tau_*^{0.769}$$

and $$\log\left(\frac{Ks}{d}\right) = 3.48\left(1 - 0.225\, \tau_*^{-\frac{1}{2}}\right)$$

These, however did not provide good results.

(3) Garde and Raju Formula

They proposed a functional relationship for the mean velocity.

$$\frac{u}{\sqrt{\Delta\, gD}} = \phi\left[R/_d, \frac{S}{\Delta}, \frac{g^{1/2}\, d^{3/2}}{\nu}\right]$$

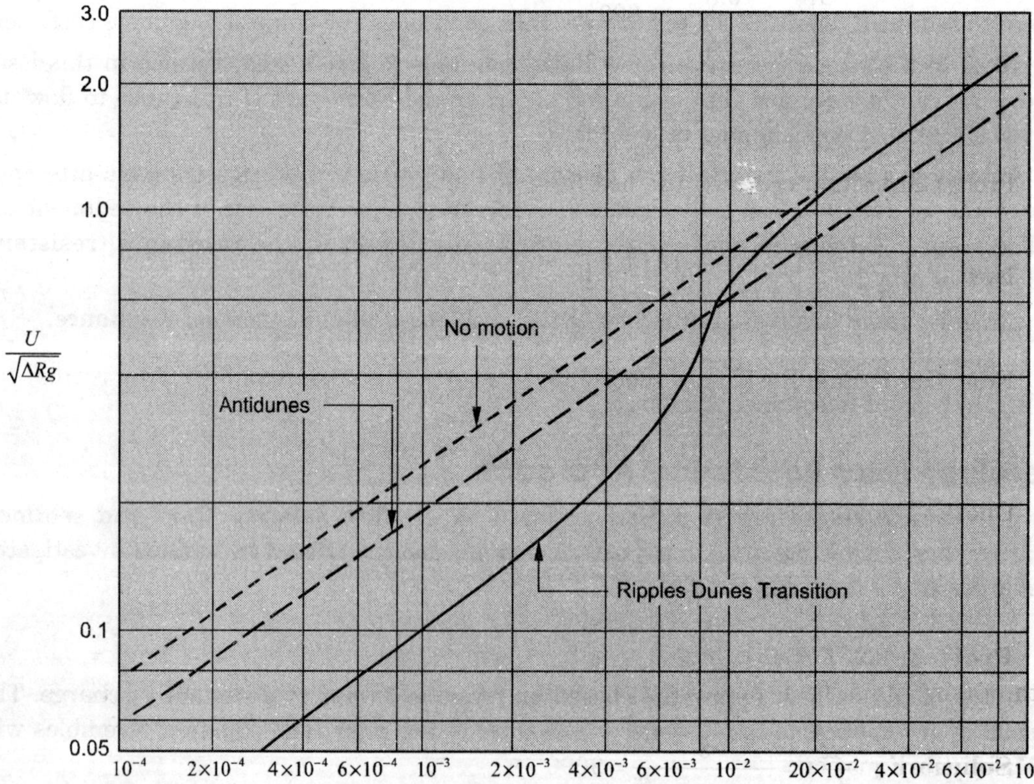

Fig. 8.2: Garde-Raju Resistance Relation

As a first approximation viscous effects were ignored and following relation was proposed,

$$\frac{u}{\sqrt{\Delta\, gD}} = K\left(\frac{R}{d}\right)^{2/3}\left(\frac{S}{\Delta}\right)^{1/2}$$

(This equation also resembles Manning's equation) where K is dependent upon the bed forms. Following values for K have been suggested for various regimes.

Bed Form	K
Plane Bed with no motion	7.66
Bed with Ripples & Dunes	3.20
Transition / Antidunes Regime	6.00

Problem 8.1. Find the average velocity and Chezy's coefficient for the following flow conditions, d = 1.0 mm. specific gravity of Sand 2.65, Depth of flow D = 0.8 m, Slope of the channel 1: 4000.

Solution: First of all find the bed form,

$$\frac{R}{d} = \frac{0.8}{1\times 10^{-3}} = 800$$

$$\frac{S}{\Delta} = \frac{1}{4000\times 1.65} = 1.51\times 10^{-4}$$

From Garde-Raju criterion the bed form is found to be Ripple and Dune regime.

Now, $\left(\frac{R}{d}\right)^{1/3}\left(\frac{S}{\Delta}\right) = (800)^{1/3}\times 1.51\times 10^{-4} = 1.4\times 10^{-3}$

From Garde-Raju Resistance relation for 1.4×10^{-3}, the value of $\frac{V}{\sqrt{g\,\Delta R}}$ is read as 0.15

$$\therefore \qquad V = 0.15\sqrt{9.81\times 1.65\times 0.8} = 0.539 \text{ m/s}$$

Chezy's Equation is $V = C\sqrt{RS}$

$$\therefore \qquad C = \frac{V}{\sqrt{RS}} = \frac{0.539}{\sqrt{0.8\times {}^{1}\!/_{4000}}} = 38.13\ m^{1/2}/s.$$

Problem 8.2. For an alluivial stream of average width 120 m and slope S = 0.000217, depth of flow 3.0 m, find the discharge, using Garde-Raju criterion, take d_{50} = 0.33 mm.

Solution: $\frac{R}{d_{50}} = \frac{3}{0.33\times 10^{-3}} = 9090$

$$\frac{S}{\Delta} = \frac{0.000217}{1.65} = 1.315\times 10^{-4}$$

From the Garde - Raju bed form criterion, the bed form is Ripples and Dunes.

$$\text{Now, } \left(\frac{R}{d}\right)^{1/3}\left(\frac{S}{\Delta}\right) = (9090)^{1/3} \times 1.315 \times 10^{-4} = 0.00\,274 = 2.74 \times 10^{-3}$$

From Garde - Raju Resistance criterion,

$$\frac{V}{\sqrt{\Delta\, gR}} = 0.18$$

$$V = 0.18 \times \sqrt{1.65 \times 9.81 \times 3} = 1.254 \quad m/s$$

Discharge, $Q = A \times V = B \times D \times V$

$$= 120 \times 3 \times 1.254 = 451.44 \text{ m}^3/\text{s}$$

Paris' Formula: From a large experimental flume data as well as field observations Paris gave following criterion for subcritical flow in alluvial streams,

$$\frac{C}{C_o} = 1 - 0.47 \log\left(\frac{\tau_*}{\tau_{*c}}\right) + 0.12\left\{\log\left(\frac{\tau_0}{\tau_{*c}}\right)\right\}^2$$

where, τ_{*c} is the critical shear stress as per Shield, C is the Chezy's coefficient and C_0 is the Chezy's coefficient for critical flow condition. For C_0 he suggested,

$$C_o = \sqrt{32} \log\left(10\,\frac{D_{cr}}{d_{35}}\right)$$

where D_{cr} is the depth under critical condition for the slope S. For D_{cr} following equation was suggested,

$$D_{cr} = \frac{\tau_{*c}\, d_{35}\, (\gamma_s - \gamma)}{S \quad \gamma}$$

From the above mean velocity was found which was in good agreement with the field values.

Resistance of Bank and Bed

Till now it has been assumed that resistance of the channel bed and channel banks is same. However, in some situations the resistance of bed may be different from the resistance offered by the banks. For example this may be due to vegetation on banks or some structures constructed on banks. In such cases hydraulic Readius (R) of bed and wall is defined separately as R_b for bed and R_w for banks/wall. Here it is assumed that velocity is uniformly distributed over the whole cross-section.

Einstein and Barbarossa formulated their 'divided hydraulic radius' approach. This approach first assumes that the hydraulic radius (R) in an alluvial channel can be divided into two major component, i.e., the hydraulic radius related to the bank and floodplain, and the other related to the bed, i.e.,

$$R = R_b + R_w$$

where, R = Hydraulic Radius $= \frac{A}{P}$, $R_b = \frac{A_b}{P_b}$ *and* $R_w = \frac{A_w}{P_w}$ in which A is the flow area and P the wetted perimeter; the subscripts b and w denote the bed and the wall or bank, respectively.

As for the flow in bed region, the mobile bed resistance depends on many interrelated factors. One of these factors is **Skin resistance** - a resistance produced by boundary surface - and is dependent on the depth of flow relative to the size of roughness elements on the boundary surface. The other main component of flow resistance is the **Form drag** associated with the bed features that set up eddies and secondary circulations.

It is now widely accepted that one needs to include both the skin (grain resistance) and form drags for estimating flow resistance in an alluvial channel with bed forms. According to Einstein's theorem, the bed hydraulic radius R_b can be further divided into two components, i.e.,

$$R_b = R_b' + R_b''$$

where, R_b' is hydraulic radius associated with grain friction and R_b'' hydraulic radius associated with sand wave resistance. Therefore, we have,

$$\tau_b = \rho\, g\, R_b\, S$$

where τ_b is bed shear stress.

In the above equation in a uniform alluvial channel flow, S, ρ *and* g are constant.

Consequently, we are limited to only a single relationship to identify roughness components and corresponding shear forces (i.e., bank or bed force and bed form force) i.e., dividing the hydraulic radius.

Current Practice

The current practice is to treat the total bed shear stress as the sum of two shear stress components corresponding to the grain and bed form resistance, i.e.,

$$\tau = \; = \tau' + \tau''$$

For constant $\rho\, g\, S$ value on both sides this will lead only to, $R = R' + R''$

As this was not favoured by many investigators arguing that grain and form resistance often affect one another.

Instead of $\rho\, g\, S$ assumed to be constant, if $\rho\, g\, R$ is assumed to be constant then, equation becomes,

$$S = S' + S''$$

where, S' = Bed slope (energy slope) that the flow would have for plane bed (grain resistance)

S'' = Additional bed slope (energy slope) required for undulations.

Considering, $\tau = \rho\, g\, R\, S$

also in terms of Darcy - Weisbach friction factor,

$$\text{Velocity } V = \sqrt{\frac{8g}{f}}\,\sqrt{RS} \quad \text{or,} \quad f = \frac{8g\,RS}{V^2}$$

and $\quad f' = \dfrac{8g\,RS'}{V^2}$ and $\quad f'' = \dfrac{8g\,RS''}{V^2}$

Here, f' and f'' are the friction factors associated with grain roughness and bed form roughness respectively. In the same way as above, the total friction factor f can be written as, $f = f' + f''$

Further, in terms of Chezy's coefficient, using $C = \sqrt{\dfrac{8g}{f}}$ or $f = \dfrac{8g}{C^2}$, we get

$\dfrac{1}{C^2} = \dfrac{1}{(C')^2} + \dfrac{1}{(C'')^2}$ or in terms of Manning's Resistance coefficient, $n = n' + n''$

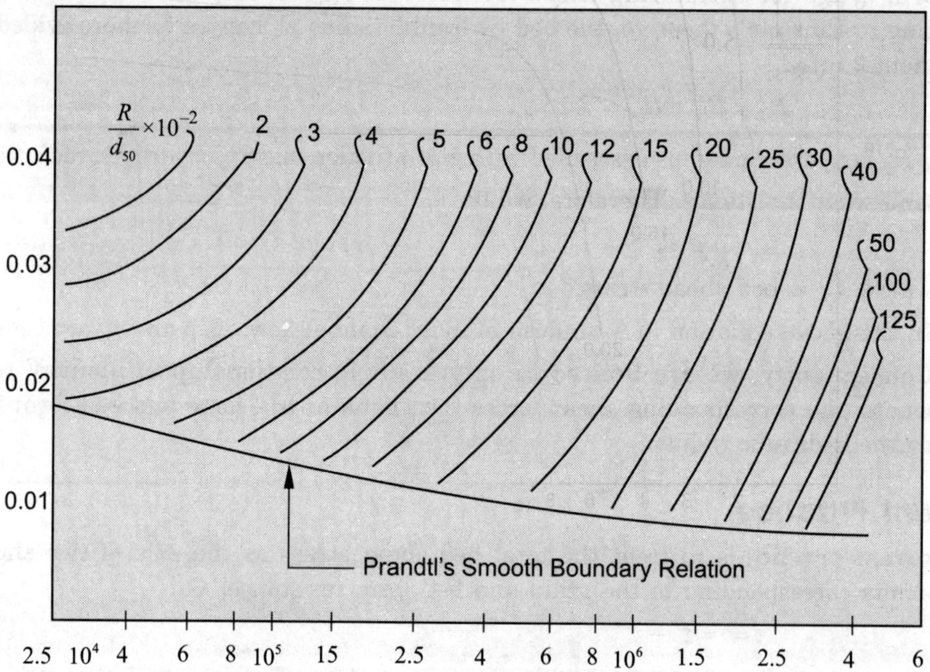

Fig. 8.3: Friction Factor Predictor

For estimation of f' and f'' for grain roughness and bed form roughness respectively a relationship between f', Re $\left(VR/\nu\right)$ and R/d_{50} and another relationship $\dfrac{R_b}{d_{50}}$ is also available to evaluate f''. Use of these two relations to predict stage discharge relation for rivers was good with field values. (Fig. 8.3 and Fig. 8.4)

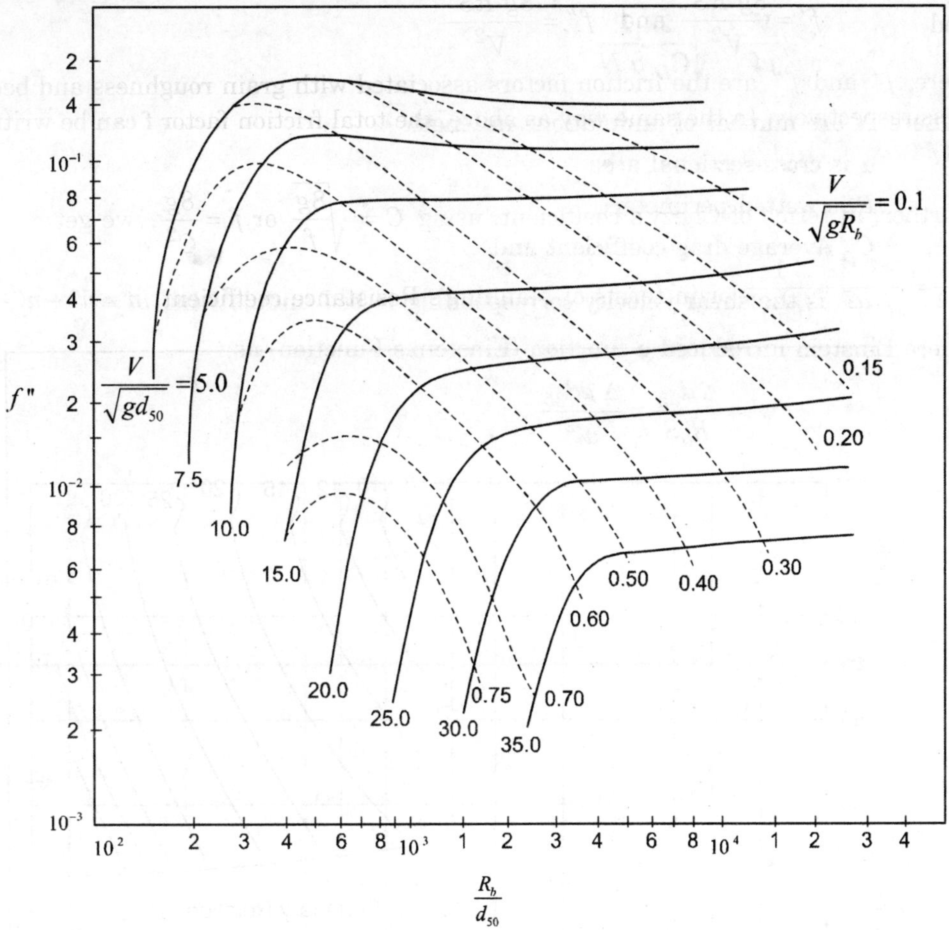

Fig. 8.4

Einstein-Barbarossa Method

Their was the first rational solution to the problem of resistance in alluvial channels. They proposed following equations,

$$\frac{V}{u'_*} = 5.75 \log\left(\frac{12.27\, R'_b}{d_{65}}\right), \textit{ where } \quad u'_* = \sqrt{gR'_b\, S}$$

Above equation is valid for rough boundaries and hence a correction factor was introduced to make the equation applicable for fine material. Above equation becomes,

$$\frac{V}{u'_*} = 5.75 \log\left(\frac{12.27\, R'_b\, \chi}{d_{65}}\right)$$

They however recommended that χ can be assumed to be equal to 1, without introducing much error.

The second type of resistance which exists in addition to the grain resistance is due to bed forms (bed undulations). For this following equation was developed,

$$\frac{V}{u''_*} = \sqrt{\frac{2\lambda_1 P}{C_D\, a\, N}}$$

where, N are number of undulations in length λ_1

a is cross-sectional area

P is wetted perimeter

C_D Average drag coefficient and

u''_* is the shear velocity corresponding to bed undulations, $u''_* = \frac{\tau''_o}{\rho}$

Here Einstein introduced a function (Einstein's Function) as,

$$\psi' = \frac{\Delta\, d_{35}}{R'_b S} = \frac{\Delta\, g d_{35}}{u'^2_*}$$

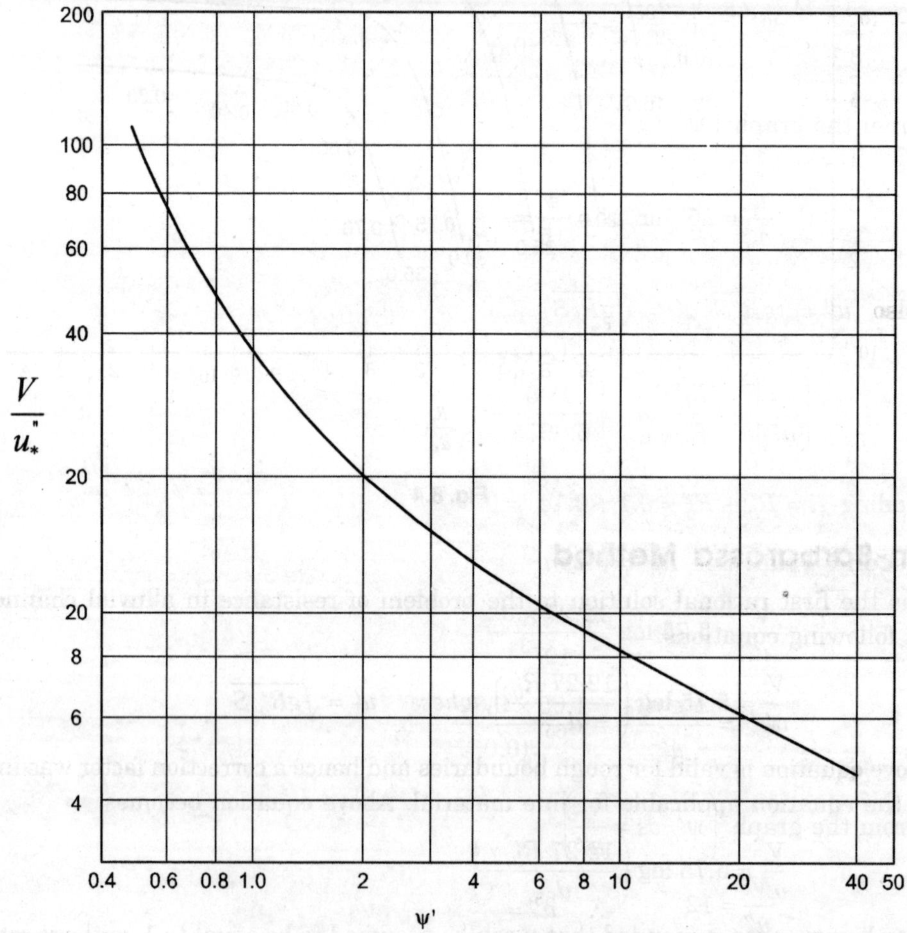

Fig. 8.5: Einstein-Barbarossa Relation

Problem 8.3. Find R'_b from the following data of an alluvial channel. d_{35} = 1 mm, D = 50 cm, velocity of flow = 1.2 m/s. Assume channel to be a wide rectangular channel.

Solution: The solution is of trial and error.

Using Einstein - Barbarossa Method.

Assume R_b = 0.5 m

First Trial: Let $R_b' = 0.1m$

$$\frac{V}{u_*'} = 5.75 \log\left(\frac{12.27\, R_b'}{d_{65}}\right) \qquad (Assume\ \chi = 1)$$

$$= 5.75 \log \frac{12.27 \times 0.1}{1 \times 10^{-3}} = 17.76$$

$$u_*' = \frac{V}{17.76} = \frac{1.2}{17.76} = 0.0675 \text{ m/s}$$

$$\therefore \qquad \psi' = \frac{\Delta\, g d_{35}}{u_*'^2} = \frac{1.65 \times 9.81 \times \frac{1}{1000}}{(0.675)^2} = 3.545$$

From the graph $\left(\psi' \ vs \ \frac{V}{u_*''}\right)$,

$$\frac{u}{u_*''} = 15 \quad \text{or} \quad u_*'' = \frac{4}{15} = \frac{1.2}{15} = 0.08 \text{ m/s.}$$

Also $u_*'' = \sqrt{gR_b''S}$ $u_*' = \sqrt{gR_b'S}$

$$\therefore \qquad \left[\frac{u_*''}{u_*'}\right]^2 = \frac{R_b''}{R_b'} \quad \text{or} \quad \left[\frac{0.08}{0.0675}\right]^2 = \frac{R_b''}{R_b'} \quad \text{or} \quad R_b'' = 0.14 \text{ m.}$$

Adding $R = R_b' + R_b'' = 0.1 + 0.14 = 0.24\ m < 0.5\ m.$

Second Trial: Let $R_b' = 0.2\ m.$

$$\frac{V}{u_*'} = 5.75 \log \frac{12.27 \times 0.2}{10^{-3}} = 19.49 \qquad \therefore \quad u_*' = 0.061 \text{ m/s}$$

$$\psi' = \frac{\Delta\, g\, d_{35}}{u_*'^2} = \frac{1.65 \times 9.81 \times 10^{-3}}{(0.061)^2} = 4.35$$

From the graph $\left(\psi' \ vs = \frac{V}{u_*''}\right)$

$$\frac{V}{u_*''} = 12 \qquad \therefore \quad u_*'' = \frac{1.2}{12} = 0.1 \text{ m/s}$$

$$R_b'' = R_b' \left(\frac{u_*''}{u_*'}\right)^2 = 0.2 \left(\frac{0.1}{0.061}\right)^2 = 0.537 \text{ m}$$

Adding, $R_b' + R_b'' = 0.2 + 0.537 = 0.737 \text{ m} > 0.5 \text{ m}$

Third Trial: Let $R_b' = 0.175\, m.$

$$\frac{V}{u_*'} = 5.75 \log \frac{12.27 \times 0.175}{10^{-3}} = 19.158$$

$$\therefore \quad u_*' = \frac{1.2}{19.158} = 0.0626\, m/s$$

$$\psi' = \frac{\Delta\, g\, d_{35}}{u_*'^2} = \frac{1.65 \times 9.81 \times 10^{-3}}{0.0626^2} = 4.13$$

From graph, $\frac{V}{u_*''} = 14.5 \quad \therefore \quad u_*'' = \frac{1.2}{14.5} = 0.0827 \text{ m/s}$

$$R_b'' = R_b' \left(u_*''/u_*'\right)^2 = 0.175 \left(\frac{0.0827}{0.0626}\right)^2 = 0.305 \text{ m.}$$

Adding, $R_b' + R_b'' = 0.48 \approx 0.5\, m.$

$\therefore$ Correct value for R_b' would be 0.18 m.

Engelund's Method

He also proposed the splitting up of the Shear Stress and hydraulic radius. For grain resistance he proposed the following equation,

$$\frac{V}{u_*'} = 5.75 \log \left(R'/_{2d_{65}} \right) + 6.0$$

He also established a relation between,

$$\tau_*' = \frac{\tau_0'}{(\Delta \gamma_s)\, d_{35}} \quad and \quad \tau_* \; \frac{\tau_0}{(\Delta \gamma_s)\, d_{35}}$$

For finding the bed form (regime) the relation between, Froude Number $\frac{V}{\sqrt{gD}}$ and $\frac{V}{u_*'}$ is used.

To determine the mean velocity V, following procedure is followed,

(1) First the regime is assumed

(2) R′ is obtained from Engelund's relation between τ_*' and τ_*

(3) Mean velocity is found from the relation $\frac{V}{u_*'}$ as given above.

(4) Finally the regime is checked with the help of Froude Number – $V/_{u_*'}$ criteria

(5) If required second trial is made.

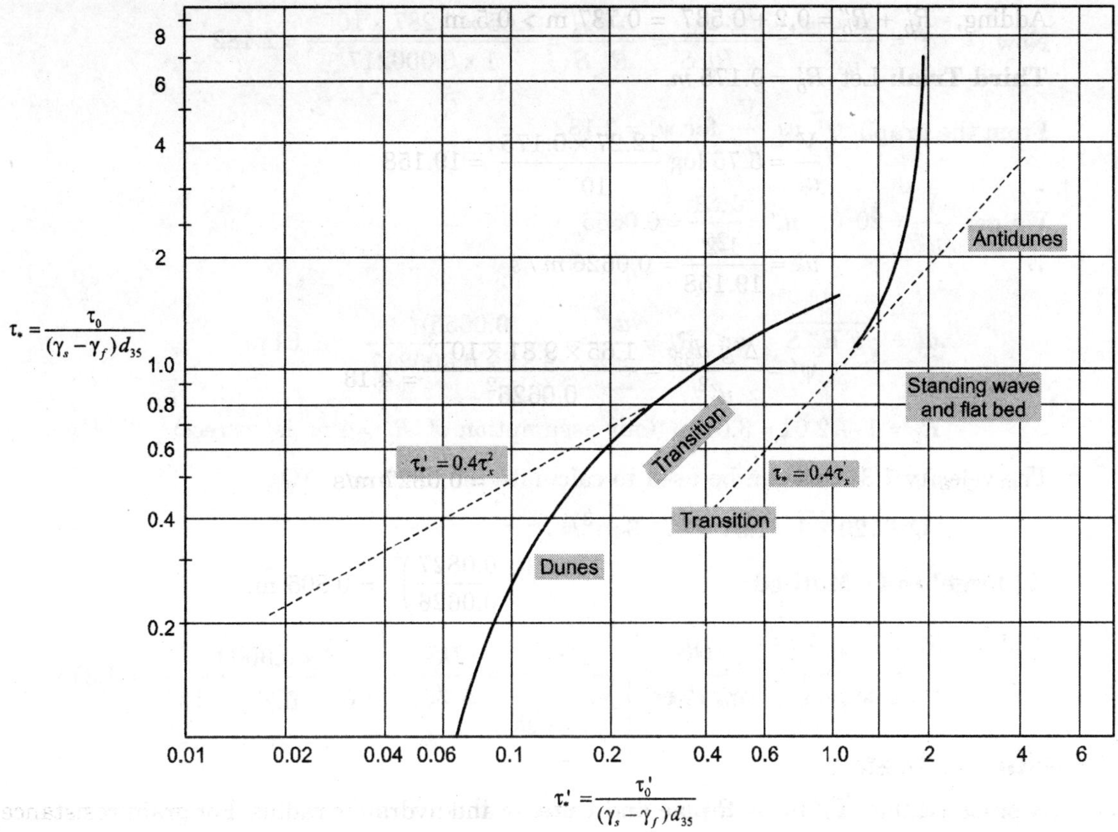

Fig. 8.6

Problem 8.4. for an alluvial stream of average width of 120 m and slope 0.000217, depth of flow 3.0 m. Find the discharge by following methods.

(1) Einstein - Barbarossa Method

(2) Engelund's Method

(3) Garde - Raju Method.

Given, d_{35} = 0.287 mm, d_{50} = 0.33 mm, d_{65} = 0.38 mm and ν = 10^{-6} m²/s.

Solution:

[1] Einstein - Barbarossa Method:

Consider the channel to be wide. $\therefore \quad D = R = R_b = 3m$

Assume $R_b' = 1m$. $\quad \therefore V = \frac{1}{n} R_b'^{2/3} S^{1/2}$ (Manning's Equation)

$$= \frac{1}{n} (1)^{2/3} (0.000217)^{1/2}$$

For n, use $n = \frac{(d_{65})^{1/6}}{24} = \frac{(0.38 \times 10^{-3})^{1/6}}{24} = 0.01127$

$$\therefore \quad V = \frac{1}{0.01127} \times 0.01473 = 1.31 \text{ m/s}$$

Now, $\psi' = \dfrac{\Delta g\, d_{35}}{u_*'^2} = \dfrac{\Delta g\, d_{35}}{g\, R_b'\, S} = \dfrac{\Delta\, d_{35}}{R_b'\, S} = \dfrac{1.65 \times 0.287 \times 10^{-3}}{1 \times 0.000217} = 2.182$

From the graph ψ' *vs* $\dfrac{V}{u_*''}$ for $\psi' = 2.182$

We get, $\dfrac{V}{u_*''} = 20 \quad \therefore\ u_*'' = \dfrac{1.31}{20} = 0.0655$

$$u_*'' = \sqrt{g\, R_b''\, S} \quad \text{or} \quad R_b'' = \frac{u_*'^2}{g\, S} = \frac{(0.0655)^2}{9.81 \times 0.000217} = 2.01\ \text{m}$$

$\therefore \quad R_b = 1 + 2.01 = 3.01$ m (our assumption of $R_b' = 1\ m$ is correct)

The velocity 1.31 m/s can be used to calculate the discharge, (Q),

$$Q = 120 \times 3 \times 1.31 = 471.6\ \text{m}^3/\text{s}\ .$$

[2] Engelund's Method:

$$\tau_* = \frac{\tau_0}{\Delta\gamma_s\, d_{35}} = \frac{\gamma_f DS}{\Delta\gamma_s\, d_{35}} = \frac{DS}{\left[\dfrac{\Delta\gamma_s}{\gamma_f}\right] d_{35}} = \frac{DS}{\Delta\, d_{35}} = \frac{3 \times 0.000217}{1.65 \times 0.287 \times 10^{-3}} = 1.374$$

Assume regime of flow as Ripple and Dune in this case.

From the relation τ_* *vs* τ_*' for Ripple & dune $\tau_*' = 0.65$

Now, $\tau_*' = \dfrac{\tau_0'}{(\Delta\gamma_s)\, d_{35}} = \dfrac{R'\, S}{\Delta\, d_{35}} = \dfrac{R' \times .000217}{1.65 \times 0.287 \times 10^{-3}}$

$$\therefore \quad R' = \frac{0.65 \times 1.65 \times 0.287 \times 10^{-3}}{0.000217} = 1.418\ \text{m.}$$

$$\therefore \quad u_*' = \sqrt{g\, R'S} = \sqrt{9.81 \times 1.418 \times 0.000217} = 0.0549\ m/s.$$

$$\frac{V}{u_*'} = 5.75 \log\left(\frac{R'}{2 \times d_{65}}\right) + 6.0$$

$$V = 0.0549 \times 5.75 \times \log\left(\frac{1.418}{2 \times .38 \times 10^{-3}}\right) + 6 = 1.364\ \text{m/s}$$

Check: $\dfrac{V}{\sqrt{gD}} = \dfrac{1.364}{\sqrt{9.81 \times 3}} = 0.25$, $\quad \dfrac{V}{u_*'} = \dfrac{1.364}{0.0549} = 25$

Considering Engelund's Bed Form relation we find that point 0.25, 25 falls in the Dunes area, hence our assumption is correct.

[3] Garde - Raju Method:

First of all we find the flow regime

$$\frac{S}{\Delta} = \frac{0.000217}{1.65} = 1.315 \times 10^{-4}$$

and $$\frac{R}{d} = \frac{0.000217}{0.33 \times 10^{-3}} = 9090$$

The point 1.315×10^{-4} and 9090 falls in the area of Ripples and Dunes.

Now, $$\left(\frac{R}{d}\right)^{1/3} . \frac{S}{\Delta} = (9090)^{1/3} \times 1.315 \times 10^{-4} = 2.74 \times 10^{-3}$$

From Garde - Raju's Graph.

For $$\left(\frac{R}{d}\right)^{1/3} \frac{S}{\Delta} = 2.74 \times 10^{-3}$$

$$\frac{V}{\sqrt{\Delta g R}} = 0.18$$

or $$V = 0.18\sqrt{1.65 \times 9.81 \times 3} = 1.254 \text{ m/s.}$$

$\therefore$ Discharge, $Q = 120 \times 3 \times 1.254 = 451.44 \text{ m}^3/\text{s}$.

Comparison of Results from the above three criteria.

Method	Einstein's	Engelund's	Garde's
Discharge Q (m^3/s)	471.6	491.04	451.55

Problem 8.5. For an alluvial channel with uniform sand of diameter d = 0.15 mm, average velocity = 0.6 m/s, Depth of flow = 2 m. Evaluate Chezy's coefficient.

Solution: Let $R_b' = 25\%$ *of* R_b i.e. equal to 0.5 m.

$$\therefore \quad \frac{V}{u_*'} = 5.75 \log \frac{12 \times 0.5}{0.15 \times 10^{-3}} = 26.46$$

$$\therefore \quad u_*' = \frac{0.6}{26.5} = 0.02264 \text{ m/s}$$

Now, $$\psi' = \frac{\Delta\, gd}{u_*'^2} = \frac{1.65 \times 9.81 \times 0.15 \times 10^{-3}}{(.02264)^2} = 4.73$$

From Einstein - Barbarossa curve

$$\frac{V}{u_*''} = 13 \qquad \therefore \quad u_*'' = \frac{0.6}{13} = 0.046 \text{ m/s}$$

Check:

$$\frac{V}{u_*''} = 13 \qquad \therefore \quad u_*'' = \frac{0.6}{13} = 0.046 \text{ m/s}$$

$$u_*''^2 = g\,R_b''\,S \qquad \therefore \quad \frac{R_b''}{R_b'} = \frac{u_*''^2}{u_*'^2} = \frac{0.046^2}{.02264^2}$$

$$u_*'^2 = g\,R_b'\,S \qquad\qquad = 4 \qquad \text{(Assumption of } R_b' \text{ is valid).}$$

$$\text{Now,} \quad u_* = \sqrt{u_*'^2 + u_*''^2} = \sqrt{0.02264^2 + 0.046^2} = 0.051 \text{ m/s}$$

$$\text{Chezy's } C = \frac{V\sqrt{g}}{u_*} = \frac{0.6 \times \sqrt{9.81}}{0.051} = 36.848 \text{ m}^{1/2}/\text{s}$$

Alam and Kennedy's Approach

They also split the friction factor f into two parts, $f = f' + f''$

$$\text{where } f = \frac{8\,g\,R\,S}{V^2}, \quad f' = \frac{8\,g\,R\,S'}{V^2} \quad \text{and} \quad f'' = \frac{8\,g\,R\,S''}{V^2}$$

or $\qquad S = S' + S''$

f' and f'' are friction factors associated with grain roughness and bed form roughness.

As a result the slope is split into two parts S' is the slope that the flow would have, if the bed was plane and S'' is the additional slope resulting from the drag of bed undulations.

For evaluating f' and f'', they alongwith others provided two graphs. One between f', $\frac{VR}{\gamma}$ and $\frac{R}{d}$ and the other between f'', $\frac{R_b}{d_{50}}$ and $\frac{V}{\sqrt{g\,d_{50}}}$. (*Figs.* 8.3 & 8.4)

Problem 8.6: Prepare Stage-Discharge Curves in the range of 0.5 m to 4.5 m depths for a channel width of 120 m having a bed slope of 0.000217. The sieve analysis shows, $d_{35} = 0.287$ mm, $d_{50} = 0.33$ mm and $d_{65} = 0.38$ mm.

Solution: [1] Einstien - Barbarossa Method:

$$n = \frac{d_{65}^{1/6}}{24} = \frac{(0.38 \times 10^{-3})^{1/6}}{24} = 0.0112$$

$$V = \frac{1}{n} R_b'^{2/3}\, S^{1/2}$$

$$= \frac{1}{0.0112} \times (R_b')^{2/3} \times 0.000217^{1/2} = 1.315\,(R_b')^{2/3} \text{ m/s}$$

$$\psi' = \frac{\Delta \times g \times d_{35}}{(u_*')^2} = \frac{\Delta \times g \times d_{35}}{g\,R_b'\,S}, \quad \text{since, } u_*' = \sqrt{g\,R_b' S}$$

$$= \frac{\Delta\,d_{35}}{R_b'\,S} = \frac{1.65 \times 0.287\,10^{-3}}{R_b' \times 0.000217} = \frac{2.182}{R_b'}$$

$$R_b'' = \frac{(u_*'')^2}{gS} = \frac{(u_*'')^2}{9.81 \times 0.000217} = 469.75\,(u_*'')^2$$

(a) Assume, $R_b' = 0.5\ m$. $V = 1.315 \times (0.5)^{2/3} = 0.828$ m/s

$$\psi' = \frac{2.182}{0.5} = 4.364$$

From graph, $\frac{V}{u_*''} = 13$, $u_*'' = \frac{V}{13} = \frac{0.828}{13} = 0.0636$ m/s

$$R_b'' = 469.75 \times (0.0636)^2 = 1.9 \text{ m}$$

$\therefore$ $R = R_b' + R_b'' = 0.5 + 1.9 = 2.4$ m.

Discharge, $Q = 120 \times 2.4 \times 0.828 = 238.464\ \text{m}^3/\text{s}$

(b) Assume $R_b' = 1.0\ m$, $V = 1.315 \times (1)^{2/3} = 1.315$ m/s, $\psi' = \frac{2.182}{1} = 2.182$

From the graph, $\frac{V}{u_*''} = 19$

$\therefore$ $u_*'' = \frac{1.315}{19} = 0.069$ m/s

$$R_b'' = 469.75 \times (0.069)^2 = 2.236 \text{ m}$$

$$R = R_b' + R_b'' = 1 + 2.236 = 3.236 \text{ m}$$

Discharge, $Q = 120 \times 3.236 \times 1.315 = 510.64\ \text{m}^3/\text{s}$

(c) Assume $R_b' = 2$ m, $V = 1.315 \times (2)^{2/3} = 2.087$ m/s, $\psi' = \frac{2.182}{2} = 1.091$

From the graph, $\frac{V}{u_*''} = 38$ $\therefore$ $u_*'' = \frac{2.087}{38} = 0.0549$ m/s

$R_b'' = 469.75 \times (.0549)^2 = 1.415$ m $\therefore$ $R = 2 + 1.415 = 3.415$ m

Discharge, $Q = 120 \times 3.415 \times 2.087 = 855.25\ \text{m}^3/\text{s}$

(d) Assume $R_b' = 3$ m, $V = 1.315 \times (3)^{2/3} = 2.735$ m/s, $\psi' = \frac{2.182}{3} = 0.727$

From the graph, $\frac{V}{u_*''} = 60$ or $u_*'' = \frac{2.735}{60} = 0.0455$ m/s

$\therefore$ $R_b'' = 469.75 \times (0.0455)^2 = 0.972$ m

$\therefore$ $R = 3 + 0.972 = 3.972$ m

Discharge, $Q = 120 \times 3.972 \times 2.735 = 1303.6\ \text{m}^3/\text{s}$

(e) Assume $R_b' = 4$ m, $V = 1.315 \times (4)^{2/3} = 3.313$ m/s, $\psi' = \frac{2.182}{4} = 0.5455$

From the graph, $\frac{V}{u_*''} = 80$

or $u_*'' = \frac{3.313}{80} = 0.0414$ m/s

$\therefore$ $R_b'' = 469.75 \times (0.0414)^2 = 0.805$ m

or $$R = 4 + 0.805 = 4.805 \text{ m.}$$

Discharge, $Q = 120 \times 4.805 \times 3.313 = 1910.275 \text{ m}^3/\text{s}$

(f) Assume $R_b' = 4.5$ m, $V = 1.315 \times (4.5)^{2/3} = 3.583$ m/s, $\psi' = \dfrac{2.182}{4.5} = 0.4848$

From the graph, $\dfrac{V}{u_*''} = 100$

$$u_*'' = \frac{3.583}{100} = 0.0358$$

$$\therefore \quad R_b'' = 469.75 \times (0.0358)^2 = 0.602 \; m$$

or $$R = 4.5 + 0.602 = 5.102 \text{ m.}$$

Discharge, $$Q = 120 \times 5.102 \times 3.583 = 2193.656 \text{ m}^3/\text{s.}$$

[2] Engelund's Method:

$$\tau_* = \frac{\gamma\, DS}{\Delta\gamma_s\, d_{35}} = \frac{0.000217 \times D}{1.65 \times 0.287 \times 10^{-3}} = 0.458\, D$$

$$\frac{R}{d_{65}} = \frac{R}{0.38 \times 10^{-3}} = 2613.5\, R$$

$$\frac{S}{\dfrac{\Delta\gamma_s}{\gamma}} = \frac{0.000217}{1.65} = 1.315 \times 10^{-4}$$

$$\tau_*' = \frac{R'S}{\Delta d_{35}} \quad \text{or} \quad R' = \frac{\Delta\, d_{35}\, \tau_*'}{S} = \frac{1.65 \times 0.287\; 10^{-3}\, \tau_*'}{0.000217} = 2.18\, \tau_*'$$

(a) Assume, $R = D = 0.5$ m. (For wide channels $R \approx D$)

$$\tau_* = 0.458 \times 0.5 = 0.229$$

$$\frac{R}{d_{65}} = 2631.5 \times 0.5 = 1315.75$$

From Garde - Raju criteria for Regime the bed form is Ripple and Dune.

For, $\tau_* = 0.229$ and from Engelund's Resistance Relation, $\tau_*' = 0.12$

$$\therefore \quad R' = 2.18 \times 0.12 = 0.26 \text{ m.}$$

Now, $$\frac{V}{u_*'} = 5.75 \log\left(\frac{R'}{2d_{65}}\right) + 6$$

$$= 5.75 \log\left(\frac{0.26}{2 \times 0.38 \times 10^{-3}}\right) + 6 = 20.57$$

$$\therefore \quad V = 20.57 \times \sqrt{g\, R'\, S} = 20.57 \times \sqrt{9.81 \times .26 \times 0.000217}$$

$$= 0.484 \text{ m/s}$$

Discharge, $Q = 120 \times 0.484 \times 0.5 = 29 \text{ m}^3/\text{s}$

(b) Assume, $R = D = 1$ m. $\tau_* = 0.458 \times 1 = 0.458$

$$\frac{R}{d_{65}} = 2631.5 \times 1 = 2631.5$$

Regime is Ripples and Dunes.

For, $\tau_* = 0.458$, $\tau_*' = 0.17$ $\therefore$ $R' = 2.18 \times 0.17 = 0.3706$ m.

$$\frac{V}{u_*'} = 5.75 \log\left(\frac{R'}{2d_{65}}\right) + 6$$

$$= 5.75 \log\left(\frac{0.3706}{2 \times 0.38 \times 10^{-3}}\right) + 6 = 21.456$$

$$V = 21.456 \times \sqrt{9.81 \times 0.3706 \times 0.000217} = 0.603 \text{ m/s}$$

Discharge, $Q = 120 \times 0.603 \times 1 = 72.36 \text{ m}^3/\text{s}$

(c) Assume, $R = D = 2\,m$. $\tau_* = 0.458 \times 2 = 0.916$

$$\frac{R}{d_{65}} = 2631.5 \times 2 = 5263$$

This also shows Ripple and Dune regime.

$$\tau_*' = 0.35 \;\therefore\; R' = 2.18 \times 0.35 = 0.763 \text{ m.}$$

Now,
$$\frac{V}{u_*'} = 5.75 \log\left(\frac{R'}{2 \times d_{65}}\right) + 6$$

$$= 5.75 \log\left(\frac{0.763}{2 \times 0.38 \times 10^{-3}}\right) + 6 = 23.25$$

$$V = 23.25 \times \sqrt{9.81 \times .763 \times 0.000217} = 0.93 \text{ m/s}$$

Discharge, $Q = 120 \times 0.93 \times 2 = 223.2 \text{ m}^3/\text{s}$

(d) Assume, $R = D = 3$ m. $\tau_* = 0.458 \times 3 = 1.374$

$$\frac{R}{d_{65}} = 2631.5 \times 3 = 7894.5$$

Here also it is Ripple Dune-regime.

$$\tau_*' = 1.0, \quad R' = 2.18 \times 1 = 2.18 \text{ m.}$$

$$\frac{V}{u_*'} = 5.75 \log\left(\frac{2.18}{2 \times .38 \times 10^{-3}}\right) + 6 = 25.88$$

$$V = 25.88 \times \sqrt{9.81 \times 2.18 \times 0.000217} = 1.763 \text{ m/s}$$

Discharge, $Q = 120 \times 1.763 \times 3 = 634.68 \text{ m}^3/\text{s}$.

(e) Assume, $R = D = 4$ m. $\tau_* = 0.458 \times 4 = 1.832$

$$\frac{R}{d_{65}} = 2631.5 \times 4 = 10{,}526$$

This also shows Ripple and Dunes (near to flat bed). From graph,

$$\tau'_* = 1.3 \quad \therefore \; R' = 2.18 \times 1.3 = 2.834 \text{ m.}$$

Now, $$\frac{V}{u'_*} = 5.75 \log\left(\frac{R'}{2 \times d_{65}}\right) + 6$$

$$= 5.75 \log\left(\frac{2.834}{2 \times 0.38 \times 10^{-3}}\right) + 6 = 26.53$$

$$V = 26.53 \times \sqrt{9.81 \times 2.834 \times 0.000217} = 2.06 \text{ m/s}$$

Discharge, $Q = 120 \times 2.06 \times 4 = 988.8 \text{ m}^3/\text{s}$.

(f) Assume, $R = D = 4.5$ m. $\tau_* = 0.458 \times 4.5 = 2.061$

$$\frac{R}{d_{65}} = 2631.5 \times 4.5 = 11{,}841.75$$

The Regime is start of Transition. From graph

$$\tau'_* = 1.7, \quad R' = 2.18 \times 1.7 = 3.706 \text{ m.}$$

$$\frac{V}{u'_*} = 5.75 \log\left(\frac{3.706}{2 \times .38 \times 10^{-3}}\right) + 6 = 27.206$$

or $$V = 27.206 \times \sqrt{9.81 \times 3.706 \times 0.000217} = 2.416 \text{ m/s}$$

Discharge, $Q = 120 \times 2.416 \times 4.5 = 1304.64 \text{ m}^3/\text{s}$.

[3] Garde - Raju Method:

$$\frac{S}{\Delta} = \frac{0.000217}{1.65} = 1.315^{-04} = 0.0001315$$

(a) Assume, $R = D = 0.5$ m. $\therefore \; \frac{R}{d_{50}} = \frac{0.5}{0.33 \times 10^{-3}} = 1515$

Regime is Ripple and Dune

Now, $$\left(\frac{R}{d}\right)^{1/3} \times \frac{S}{\Delta} = (1515)^{1/3} \times 0.000135 = 1.55 \times 10^{-3}$$

From Garde - Raju Resistance Relation.

$$\frac{U}{\sqrt{\Delta Rg}} = 0.14$$

$$\therefore \quad U = 0.14\sqrt{1.65 \times 9.81 \times 0.5} = 0.4 \text{ m/s.}$$

Discharge, $Q = 120 \times 0.4 \times 0.5 = 24 \text{ m}^3/\text{s}$

(b) Assume, $R = D = 1\ m.$ $\frac{R}{d_{50}} = \frac{1}{.33 \times 10^{-3}} = 3030$

Regime is Ripple and Dune

Now, $\left(\frac{R}{d}\right)^{1/3} \times \frac{S}{\Delta} = (3030)^{1/3} \times 0.000135 = 1.953 \times 10^{-3}$

$\therefore \quad \frac{U}{\sqrt{\Delta Rg}} = 0.17$

or $\quad \therefore \quad U = 0.17\sqrt{9.81 \times 1 \times 1.65} = 0.68$ m/s.

Discharge, $\quad Q = 120 \times 0.68 \times 1 = 81.6\ m^3/s$

(c) Assume, $R = D = 2$ m. $\frac{R}{d_{50}} = \frac{2}{.33 \times 10^{-3}} = 6060$

Regime is Ripple and Dunes.

Now, $\left(\frac{R}{D}\right)^{1/3} \times \frac{S}{\Delta} = (6060)^{1/3} \times 0.000135 = 2.46 \times 10^{-3}$

$\therefore \quad \frac{U}{\sqrt{\Delta gR}} = 0.19$

$U = 0.19\sqrt{1.65 \times 9.81 \times 2} = 1.08$ m/s.

Discharge, $Q = 120 \times 1.08 \times 2 = 259.2\ m^3/s$.

(d) Assume, $R = D = 3$ m. $\frac{R}{d_{50}} = \frac{3}{.33 \times 10^{-3}} = 9090$

Regime is Ripple and Dunes.

Now, $\left(\frac{R}{d}\right)^{1/3} \times \frac{S}{\Delta} = (9090)^{1/3} \times 0.000135 = 2.816 \times 10^{-3}$

$\therefore \quad \frac{U}{\sqrt{gR\Delta}} = 0.2$

$\therefore \quad U = 0.2\sqrt{9.81 \times 3 \times 1.65} = 1.393$ m/s.

Discharge, $\quad Q = 120 \times 1.393 \times 3 = 501.48\ m^3/s$.

(e) Assume, $R = D = 4$ m. $\frac{R}{d_{50}} = \frac{4}{.33 \times 10^{-3}} = 12{,}121$

Regime is Ripple and Dunes.

Now, $\left(\frac{R}{d}\right)^{1/3} \times \frac{S}{\Delta} = (12{,}121)^{1/3} \times 0.000135 = 3.10 \times 10^{-3}$

$\therefore \quad \frac{U}{\sqrt{g\,\Delta\,R}} = 0.21$

$U = 0.21\sqrt{9.81 \times 1.65 \times 4} = 1.689$ m/s.

Discharge, $Q = 120 \times 1.689 \times 4 = 810.72 \text{ m}^3/\text{s}.$

(f) Assume, $R = D = 4.5$ m. $\frac{R}{d_{50}} = \frac{4.5}{.33 \times 10^{-3}} = 13,636$

Regime is Ripple and Dunes.

Now, $$\frac{R}{d}^{1/3} \times \frac{S}{\Delta} = (13,636)^{1/3} \times 0.000135 = 3.22 \times 10^{-3}$$

$$\therefore \quad \frac{U}{\sqrt{g\,\Delta\,R}} = 0.22$$

$$U = 0.22\sqrt{9.81 \times 1.65 \times 4.5} = 1.877 \text{ m/s}.$$

Discharge, $Q = 120 \times 1.877 \times 4.5 = 1013 \text{ m}^3/\text{s}.$

		Depth in m					
	Method	**0.5**	**1.0**	**2.0**	**3.0**	**4.0**	**4.5**
Velocity $m\ (V)$	Einstein - Barbarossa	0.825	1.315	2.087	2.735	3.313	3.583
	Engelund	0.484	0.603	0.93	1.763	2.06	2.416
	Garde - Raju	0.40	0.68	1.08	1.393	1.689	1.877
Discharge m^3/s	Einstein - Barbarossa	238	510	855	1303	1910	2193
	Engelund	29	72	223	634	989	1304
	Gard - Raju	24	82	259	501	810	1013

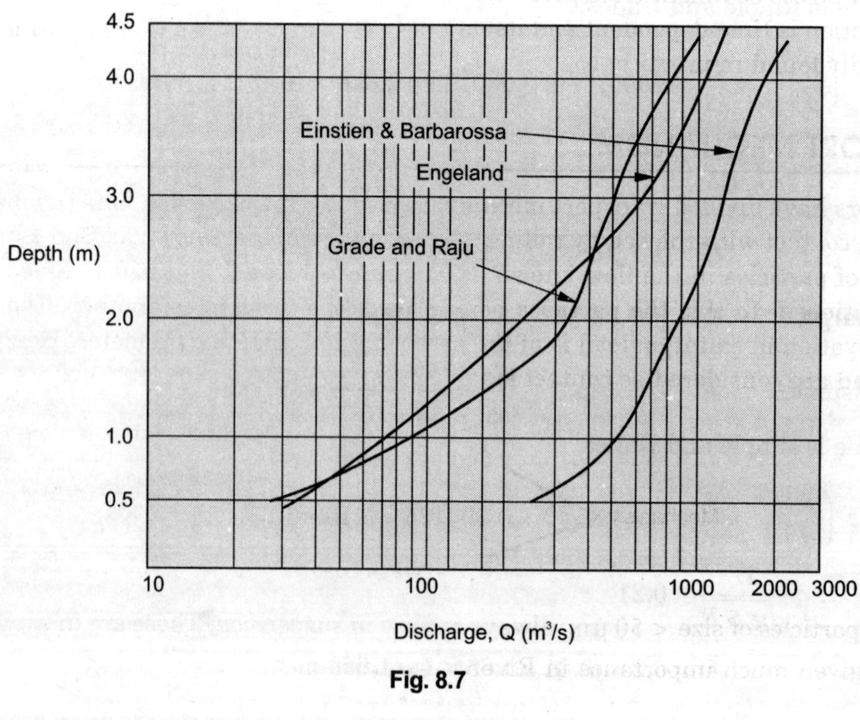

Fig. 8.7

CHAPTER 9

ESTIMATION OF SEDIMENT LOAD

We have already discussed the initiation of motion or incipient motion condition earlier in chapter 6. It is to be noted that when the Shear stress on the bed of any alluvial channel exceeds the critical tractive stress, the particles on the bed start moving. In this connection the bottom shear stress, water depth and bed roughness are most important parameters.

Description of particle motion under the action of the flow is largely empirical and therefore there is only limited theoretical basis for the relation between flow and sediment transport.

Most of the existing knowledge is obtained from experiments and general physical arguments. For initiation of motion a reasonable picture has been obtained. At greater values of bed-shear stress sediment transport will increase and deformation of the bed will occur. As the deformation is time-dependent and its nature is always unsteady, an equilibrium situation will be hardly found in practice.

TRANSPORT MECHANISM

Investigators have divided transport mechanism into two major modes. One the movement of particles in contact with the bed by rolling, sliding and jumping, known as **Bed Load**. Second movement of particles in the flow known as **Suspended Load**. Sometimes **Saltation Load** is also mentioned. In this the particles bounce from one position to another. The maximum particle elevation in saltation load is of the order of 2 to 3 time the diameter. Hence this part and bed load are considered as contact load.

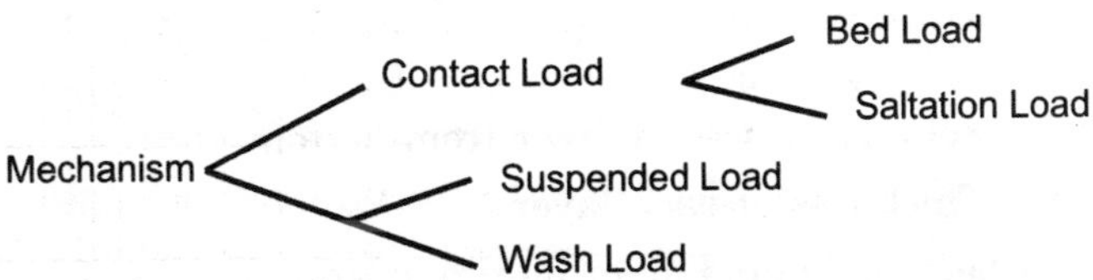

Fine particles of size < 50 μm always remain in suspension. These are in small quantity, hence not given much importance in River Engineering.

Estimation of Bed Load

Bed load transport is of fundamental importance in river engineering. Although there are many bed load transport equations, there is no consensus on which equation is the best and how to select a particular equation for a particular river. Often there are large discrepancies in the bed load transport values yielded by different equations and between those and observed values.

The first bed load equation was developed by Du Boys. Since then several equations have been proposed by various investigators for prediction of bed load. These equations are either purely empirical or semi-theoretical. Few have been developed on dimensional considerations.

Du Boys bed load relation: He assumed that the bed material moves in a series of layers parallel to the bed, the velocity of each layer varying from maximum for the top layer on the bed to zero at some depth. His flow model is shown here,

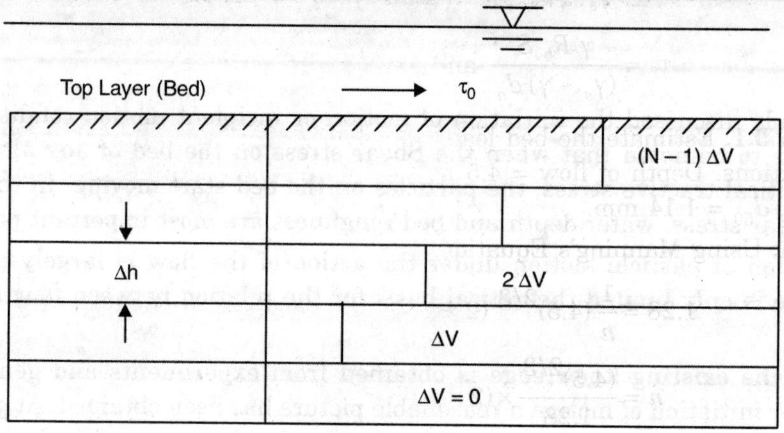

Fig. 9.1

If N is the number of layers in motion and Δh is the thickness of each layer and lowest layer is assumed to be at rest, ΔV will be the velocity of second layer and $(N - 1)\Delta V$ of the surface sediment layer. He gave relation for bed load transport in weight per unit width per unit time as q_B,

$$q_B = \gamma_s \, N \, \Delta h \, (N-1)\frac{\Delta V}{2}$$

Solving further he achieved the following equation for q_B

$$q_B = A\,(\tau_o - \tau_{oc})\,\tau_o$$

where A is defined as, sediment coefficient.

$$A = \frac{\gamma_s \;\; \Delta h. \;\; \Delta V}{2\tau_{oc}^2}$$

where ΔV = velocity of second layer from bottom

Δh = Thickness of each layer

Value of A has been estimated according to grain diameter.

Schoklitsch gave the value of A on the basis of Laboratory experiments with uniform grains of various kinds of sand as,

$$A = \frac{0.54}{(\rho_s - \rho)g}$$

Emperical Relations: There are many emperical equations available but the most commonly used is Meyer-Peter-Muller equation (MPM Equation). Also, Einstein gave a reasonable formula for estimation of bed load.

Meyer - Peter - Muller Formula: These investigators performed a large number of experiments in a wide flume with coarse sands. They gave the following equations.

$$\left(\frac{n_s}{n}\right)^{3/2} \tau_* = 0.047 + 0.25\ \phi^{2/3}$$

where,
$$\phi = \frac{q_B}{\gamma_s}\sqrt{\frac{\rho}{\rho_s - \rho}} \times \left(\frac{1}{g\,da^3}\right)^{1/2}$$

and
$$\tau_* = \frac{\gamma R_b S}{(\gamma_s - \gamma)\, d_a} \quad \text{and} \quad n_s = \frac{d_{90}^{1/6}}{26}$$

Problem 9.1. Estimate the bed load transported in a wide alluvial channel under the following conditions. Depth of flow = 4.5 m, velocity of flow 1.28 m/s, Bed slope = 2×10^{-4}, d_{90} = 2.85 mm, d_{50} = 1.14 mm.

Solution: Using Manning's Equation,

$$1.28 = \frac{1}{n}(4.5)^{2/3}(2 \times 10^{-4})^{1/2}$$

or
$$n = \frac{(4.5)^{2/3}}{1.28} \times (2 \times 10^{-4})^{1/2} = 0.03$$

$$n_s = \frac{(d_{90})^{1/6}}{26} = \frac{(2.85 \times 10^{-3})^{1/6}}{26} = 0.01448 \text{ m}$$

$$\tau* = \frac{\gamma R_b S}{(\gamma_s - \gamma)\, da} = \frac{R_b S}{\left(\frac{\gamma_s - \gamma}{\gamma}\right) da} = \frac{4.5 \times 2 \times 10^{-4}}{1.65 \times 1.14 \times 10^{-3}} = 0.4784 \text{ N/m}^2$$

$$\left(\frac{n_s}{n}\right)^{3/2} = \left(\frac{0.01448}{0.03}\right)^{3/2} = 0.3353$$

$$\therefore \quad \left(\frac{n_s}{n}\right)^{3/2} \times \tau* = 0.3353 \times 0.4784 = 0.16$$

Now, from equation

$$\left(\frac{n_s}{n}\right)^{3/2} \times \tau* = 0.047 + 0.25\ \phi^{2/3}, \qquad 0.16 = 0.047 + 0.25\ \phi^{2/3}$$

$$\phi^{2/3} = 0.452, \quad \phi = 0.303$$

From the equation,

$$\phi = \frac{q_B}{\gamma_s}\sqrt{\frac{\rho}{\rho_s - \rho}} \times \left(\frac{1}{g\,da^3}\right)^{1/2}$$

$$0.303 = \frac{q_B}{2650} \times \sqrt{1/1.65} \times \left[\frac{1}{9.8 \times (1.14 \times 10^{-3})^3}\right]^{1/2}$$

$$0.303 = \frac{q_B}{2650} \times 0.778 \times 8303$$

$$\therefore \quad q_B = \frac{0.303 \times 2650}{0.778 \times 8303} = 0.124 \text{ kg/m/s.}$$

Einstein's Approach: This is a semi-theoretical approach. For the hydraulic flow condition, Einstein used two dimensionless parameters. The two functions are given below,

$$\phi = \frac{q_B}{\gamma_s}\left(\frac{\rho}{\rho_s - \rho}\right)^{1/2}\left(\frac{1}{g\,d^3}\right)^{1/2}$$

and $$\psi = \frac{\rho_s - \rho}{\rho}\,\frac{d}{R_b' S}$$

He further introduced two parameters as,

$$\phi_* = \phi\,\frac{i_B}{i_b} \quad \text{and} \quad \psi_* = \xi\, Y\left(\frac{\beta}{\beta_x}\right)^2$$

where, i_B = Fraction of bed load in a given grain size

i_b = Fraction of bed material in a given grain size

ξ = Hiding Factor of grains in a mixture

β and β_x are logarithmic functions.

Y is a correction factor

Considering all the factors Einstein gave a curve between $\phi*$ *and* $\psi*$. It may be noted that for uniform grains $\phi* = \phi$ *and* $\psi* = \psi$.

Problem 9.2: Solve the previous problem by Einstein's method.

Solution: $$\psi = \frac{(\rho_s - \rho)d}{\rho\, R_b'\, S} = \frac{1.65 \times 1.14 \times 10^{-3}}{4.5 \times 2 \times 10^{-4}} = 2.09$$

From the $\phi* - \psi*$ curve

$$\phi = 1.95$$

$$\phi = \frac{q_B}{2650}\left(\frac{1}{1.65}\right)^{1/2}\left[\frac{1}{9.81 \times (1.14 \times 10^{-3})^3}\right]^{1/2}$$

$$q_B = 0.741 \text{ kg/m/s.}$$

Suspended Load Transport

It is an advanced stage of bed load transport. Suspended load is carried in the lower to middle part of the flow. It is now fairly conclusive that **turbulence** in the flow is responsible for suspension of particles in the stream. The suspended load generally consists of smaller particles, like clay, silt and fine sands.

With the help of velocity profile and sediment concentration profile suspended load can be determined by integration, (Fig. 9.2).

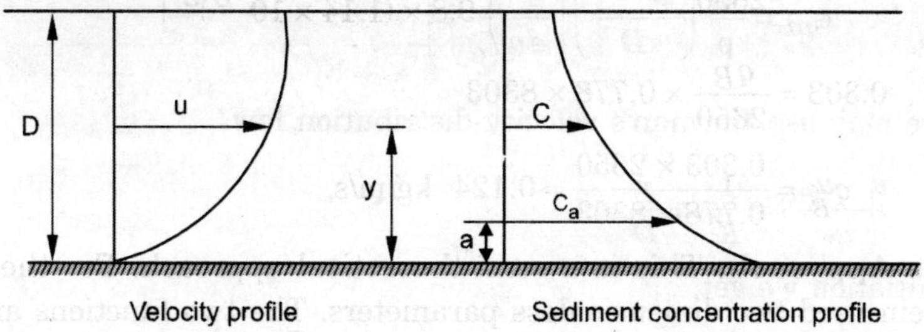

Fig 9.2

Suspended Load $S = \int_0^D C\,(y).\, u(y)\, dy$

In most cases estimates based on theoretical expressions will be necessary. The basic equation describing the concentration distribution in a uniform steady flow is as follows,

$$w_o\, C + \in_S \frac{\partial c}{\partial y} = 0 \qquad \text{(Sediment diffusion Equation)}$$

where, w_0 = Fall velocity, C = Volume concentration of sediment

$\in_s$ = Turbulent diffusion coefficient.

The first term $w_0 C$ represents the settling tendency of the flow and the second term shows the diffusive action of the turbulence. $\delta c/\delta y$ is concentration gradient. Because of the concentration gradient water moving upward carry a larger amount of grains than moving downwards.

Above equation can be written as,

$$\frac{dC}{C} = -\frac{w_o}{\in_S}\, dy$$

On integration,

$$ln \frac{C}{Ca} = -\int_a^y \frac{w_o}{\in_S}\, dy$$

where C is concentration at y and Ca is concentration at (a) from the bottom.

Assuming that w_0 and $\in_0$ are constant with respect to depth y, then,

$$ln\, {}^{C}\!/\!_{Ca} = -\frac{w_o}{\in_S}\,(y - a)$$

or $$ {}^{C}\!/\!_{Ca} = e^{-w_o\,(y - a)/\in_S}$$

It is well known that the shear stress in Turbulent Flow is given by the equaion,

$$\tau = \in_m \frac{\partial\,(\rho\, u)}{\partial\, y}$$

where $\in_0$ is momentum transfer coefficient.

Also, Shear stress is assumed to vary linearly, we have,

$$\tau = \tau_o (1 - y/D), \quad \tau_o = \gamma D S$$

$$\therefore \quad \epsilon_m = \frac{\tau_o}{\rho}\left(\frac{D-y}{D}\right)\left(\frac{1}{du/dy}\right)$$

For $\frac{du}{dy}$ we may use Karman's velocity distribution law.

$$\frac{u - u_m}{u*} = \frac{1}{K} ln \frac{y}{D}$$

On differentiation we get,

$$\frac{du}{dy} = \frac{u*}{K}\frac{1}{y} \qquad \therefore \quad \epsilon_m = u* \, K \, y\left(\frac{D-y}{D}\right)$$

Assuming that, $\epsilon_m = \epsilon_s$

The concentration equation becomes,

$$\frac{dC}{C} = -\frac{w_o}{u*K}\frac{D}{y(D-y)}$$

Hence, $$ln \frac{C}{Ca} = -\frac{w_o}{u*\,K}\int_a^y \frac{D\,dy}{y(D-y)}$$

On integration,

$$\frac{C}{Ca} = \left[\frac{D-y}{y}\frac{a}{D-a}\right]^{z_o}$$

where, $z_o = \frac{w_o}{u*K}$ termed as exponent of sediment distribution equation.

Evaluating z_0: Take log of the above equation.

$$\log\frac{C}{Ca} = z_o\left[\log\left(\frac{D-y}{y}\right)\left(\frac{a}{D-a}\right)\right]$$

The exponent when theoretically calculated is different from the exponent obtained by plotting against $(D-y)\,y^{-1}.a.(D-a)^{-1}$ on a log-log paper. The slope of the line drawn would give the observed value of z_0. From the plot it is observed that equation is applicable only in main flow and not near the bed.

Sediment distribution is nearly constant in vertical for $z_0 < 0.031$ and suspension is insignificant for $z_0 > 5$.

Problem 9.3. For an alluvial stream plot y/D vs. $\frac{C}{Ca}$ for z = 0.1, 0.5, 1.0 and 5 when a/D = 0.1..

Solution: Using $$\frac{C}{Ca} = \left(\frac{D-y}{y}\cdot\frac{a}{D-a}\right)^z$$

$$\frac{a}{D} = 0.1 \qquad \text{or,} \quad a = 0.1\,D$$

$$\therefore \quad \frac{a}{D-a} = \frac{0.1\,D}{D - 0.1\,D} = \frac{0.1\,D}{0.9\,D} = \frac{1}{9}$$

Let $y = nD$, then

$$\frac{D-y}{y} = \frac{D-nD}{nD} = \frac{1-n}{n}$$

$n \rightarrow$	0.25	0.5	0.75	1.0
$(D-y)/y \rightarrow$	3	1	1/3	0

Calculation:

C/Ca $Y/D = n$ ↓	$\left(\frac{D-y}{y}\right)\left(\frac{a}{D-a}\right)$	C/Ca For $Z = 0.1$	C/Ca For $Z = 0.5$	C/Ca For $Z = 1$	C/Ca For $Z = 5$
0.25	$3 \times \frac{1}{9} = \frac{1}{3}$	0.896	0.577	0.333	0.0041
0.50	$1 \times \frac{1}{9} = \frac{1}{9}$	0.802	0.333	0.111	0.0000169
0.75	$\frac{1}{3} \times \frac{1}{9} = \frac{1}{27}$	0.719	0.192	0.037	0.000
1.0	0	–	–	–	–

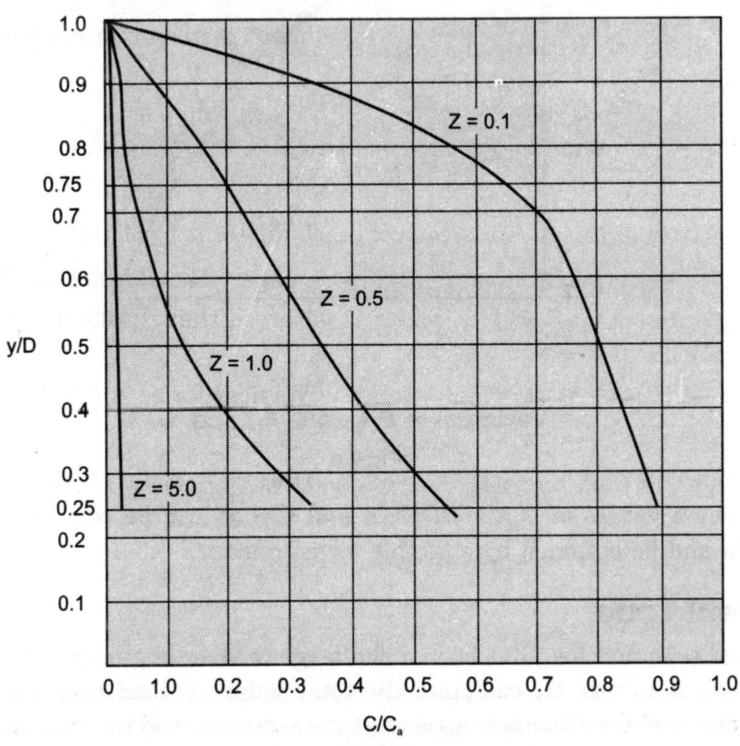

Fig 9.3

Approximate Method for Suspended Load

Lane and Kalinske suggested that if $\in_s$ and $\in_m$ vary with depth y, a constant value of,

$$\in_s = \in_m = D\sqrt{gD\,S}\,/\,15 \text{ can be assumed.}$$

The diffusion equation integration will give

$$\therefore \quad \frac{C}{Ca} = \exp\left\{(-w_o/u_*)\left(y/D - \frac{a}{D}\right)^{15}\right\}$$

The total suspended load becomes.

$$q_s = UD\,Ca \int_o^1 \frac{u}{U} \exp\left\{-15\,(w_o/u_*)\,(Y - A)\,dY\right\}$$

where, $Y = \dfrac{y}{D}$, $A = \dfrac{a}{D}$

The equation can be simplified further, to give,

$$q_s = q\,Ca\,P\ \exp\{15\,(w_o/u_*)A\}$$

Here, P is a function of $\dfrac{w_o}{u*}$ and u_*/KoU.

For U, Manning's Equation is used, which would give u^*/KoU in terms of $n/D^{1/6}$. Figure below shows the plot of P vs w_o/u_* and $nD^{1/6}$ in SI units.

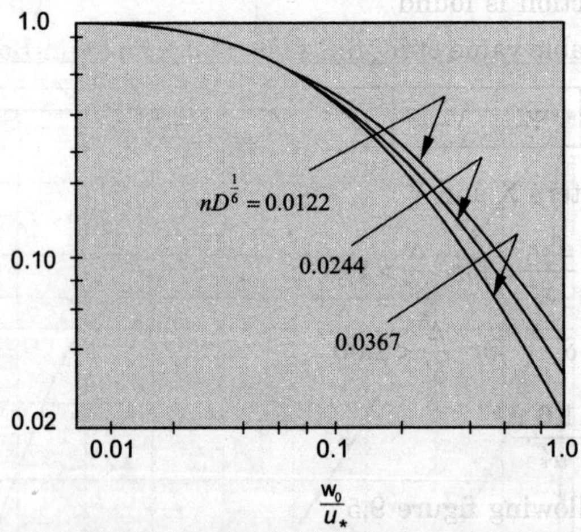

Variation of P with w_o/u_* and $nD^{1/6}$.

Fig 9.4

For the known values of w_o/u_*, $nD^{1/6}$, q and Ca, qs can be computed. The reference concentration Ca and be obtained by a simple measurement.

Total Sediment Load

Prediction to total sediment load has been a challenge to river engineers. Two approaches are typically used: one is to directly calculate the total sediment load from measured flow and sediment properties, and the other is to separate total sediment load into bed load and suspended load and calculate them independently.

Einstein (1950) developed a method to determine the total sediment load in open channels. The method uses the Einstein's bed load function and suspended sediment concentration profile from Rouse. Recent developments through series expansions have improved the accuracy of estimation of Einstein's integrals.

Einstein's Method: Einstein (1950) developed a method to determine the total sediment load in open channels. The knowledge of concentration at a (= $2d$) enables construction of the curve of concentration distribution in the vertical. Subsequent integration of (concentration X velocity) curves yields following relation,

$$i_s\, q_s = i_B\, q_B\, (PI_1 + I_2)$$

where, i_s is the fraction of suspended load in a given size range and,

$$P = 2.3 \log \frac{30.2\, D}{\Delta} \text{ where } \Delta = \frac{d_{65}}{x}$$

x being a correction factor introduced by Einstein and Barbarossa. It was suggested that the correction factor x can be taken equal to 1 (one) without involving much error.

The total load in a given size range is given by

$$i_T\, q_T = i_B\, q_B\, (PI_1 + I_2 + 1)$$

where i_T is the fraction of total load in a given size range.

Step by step Method for preparing a sediment rating curve using Einstein's Method:

(1) Average cross-section is found

(2) Assume a reasonable value of R', find R by using Einstein-Barbarossa method as below:

No.	R′	$R^{2/3}$	V	Ψ′	V/u_*'	u_*'	R″	R = R′ + R″	Stage	Area	Q

(3) Find the parameters X and Y

where, $X = 0.77 \dfrac{d_{65}}{x}$, $for\ \dfrac{\Delta}{\delta'} > 1.80$

and $X = 1.39\, \delta'$, $for\ \dfrac{\Delta}{\delta'} < 1.80$

δ' is given by $= \dfrac{11.6\, \nu}{u_*}$

(4) For Y use the following figure 9.5

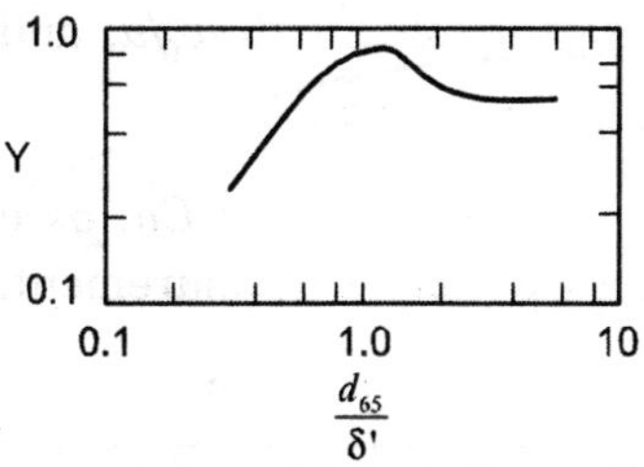

Variation of Y with $\dfrac{d_{65}}{\delta'}$

Fig 9.5

(5) Find $\beta_x = \log (10.6\, x / \Delta)$ and $\beta = \log 10.6$

upto this step is the hydraulic computation which are to be done for different R' values to cover expected range of stage in the river and should be entered in the table below:

1	2	3	4	5	6	7	8	9	10	11	12
R'	u'_*	δ'	d_{65}/δ'	x	Δ	V	Ψ'	V/u_*''	u_*''	R''	R

13	14	15	16	17	8	19
Stage	Area	Q	X	Y	β	β_x

(6) Divide the sample into 4 to 6 size ranges and find the geometric mean size d of each range and also i_b for each range.

(7) For any size d, following steps to be followed.

(8) Find d/x and read ξ from the following figure 9.6.

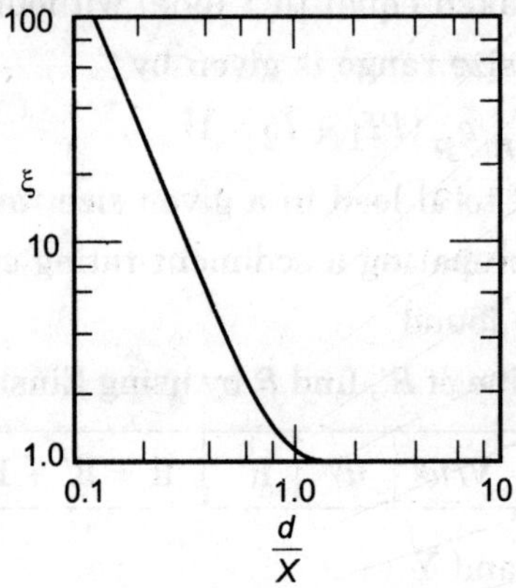

Variation of ξ with $\dfrac{d}{x}$

Fig 9.6

(9) Find Ψ and Ψ_* from the following equations,

$$\Psi = \frac{(\rho_s - \rho) \times d}{\rho\, R'\, S} \quad \text{and} \quad \Psi_* = \xi\, Y\, \Psi \left[\beta/\beta_x\right]^2$$

(10) Read ϕ_* for the above value of Ψ_* from the given Fig. 9.7.

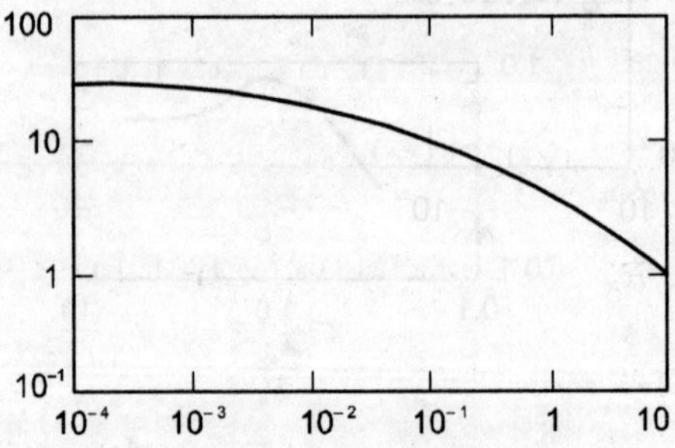

Einstein's $\phi_* - \Psi_*$ Relation

Fig 9.7

(11) Compute the bed load rate $i_B\, q_B$ for the equation

$$i_B\, q_B = \phi_*\, i_b\, \rho_s\, g^{3/2}\, d^{3/2} \left(\frac{\rho_s}{\rho} - 1\right)^{1/2}$$

(12) Compute $A = \frac{2d}{R}$ and $z = \frac{w_0}{u_*\, K_0}$, $K_0 = 0.4$.

(13) For known values of A and z, Read I_1 and I_2 from the following graphs. (Figs. 9.8 and 9.9)

(14) Calculate, $P = 2.3 \log (30.2\, D/\Delta)$

(15) Find, $i_t\, q_t = i_B\, q_B\, (PI_1 + I_2 + 1)$

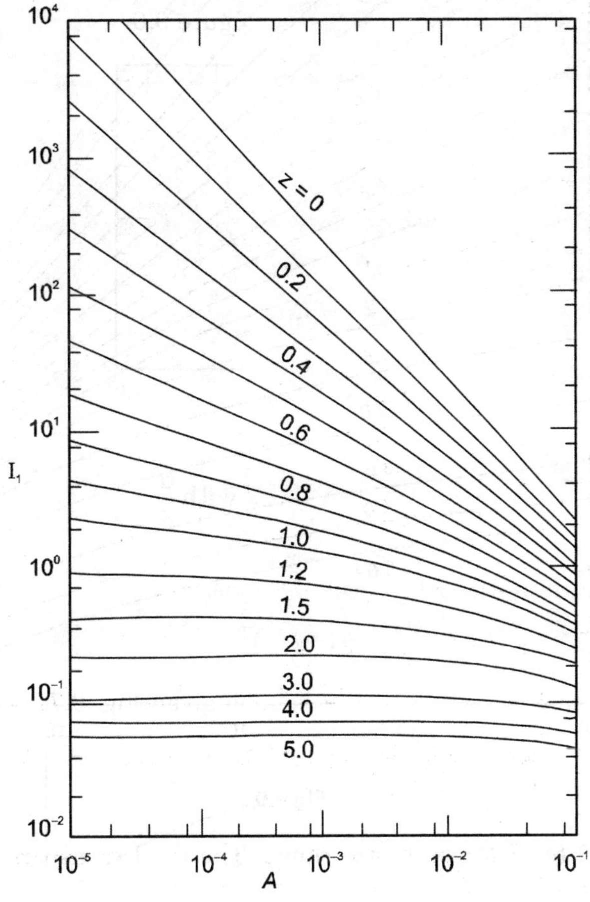

Fig 9.8

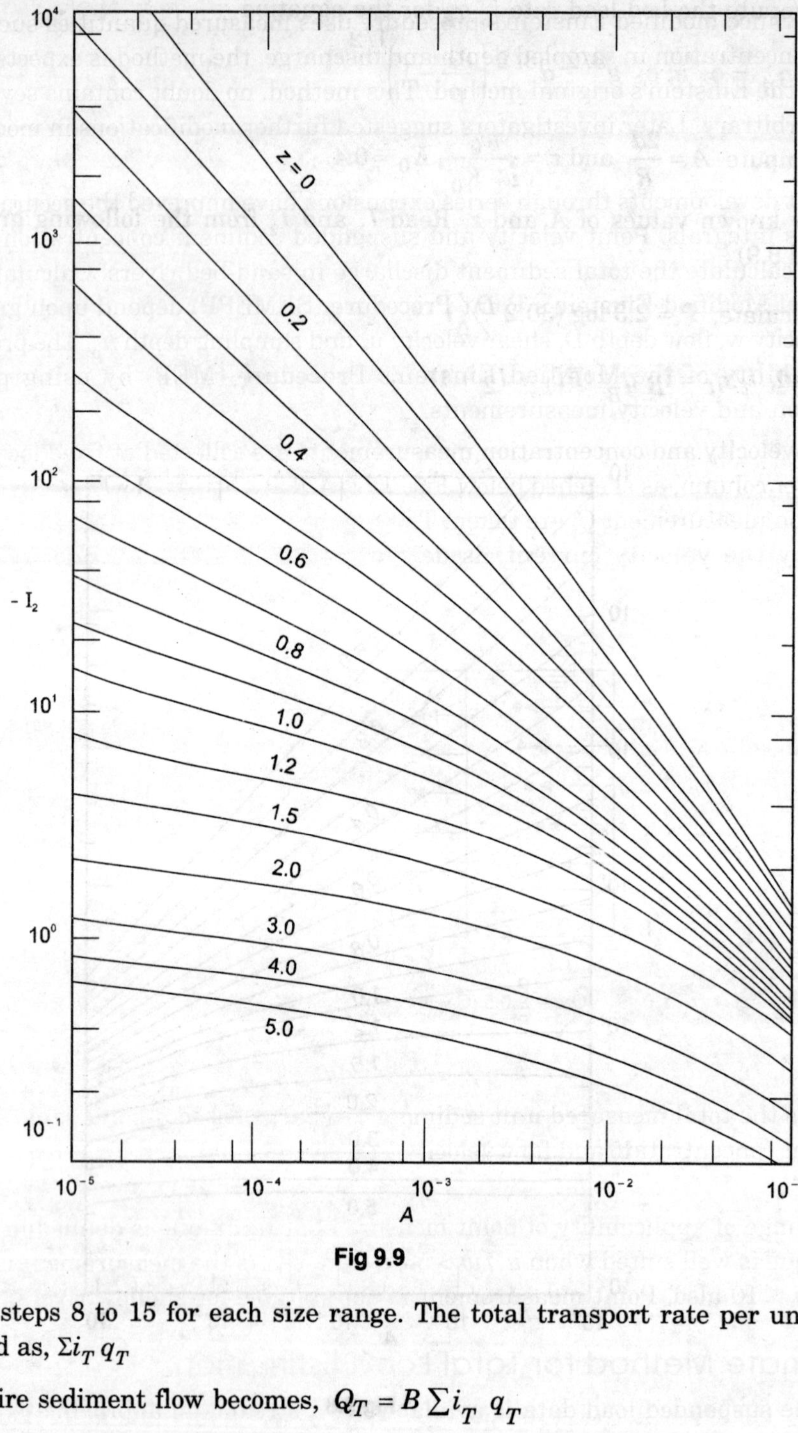

Fig 9.9

(16) Repeat steps 8 to 15 for each size range. The total transport rate per unit width is obtained as, $\Sigma i_T q_T$

$\therefore$ Entire sediment flow becomes, $Q_T = B \sum i_T \, q_T$

where B is the channel width.

Modified Einstein - Procedure: This method essentially based on Einstein's method as described above. However, it uses some of the hydraulic and sediment data collected from field study. Since modified Einstein's procedure uses measured quantities such as suspended sediment concentration in sampled depth and discharge, the method is expected to give better result then the Einstein's original method. This method, no doubt contains several corrections which are arbitrary. Later investigators suggested further modifications in modified Einstein's procedure.

Recent developments through series expansions have improved the accuracy of estimation of Einstein's integrals. Point velocity and suspended sediment concentration measurements are used to calculate the total sediment discharge in sand-bed rivers. Calculation with series Expansion of Modified Einstein's Point Procedure (SEMEPP) depend upon grain size d_s and settling velocity w, flow depth D, shear velocity u_* and sampling depth h_p. The procedure extends the applicability of the Modified Einsten's Procedure (MEP) by using point sediment concentration and velocity measurements.

Point velocity and concentration measurements are collected at fixed locations along the vertical water column, as sketched below Fig. 9.10. At each point i, flow velocity v_i and sediment concentration measurement C_i are taken. The sediment flux (sediment discharge per unit area imparted by the velocity current) is determined from the flow velocity and sediment concentration.

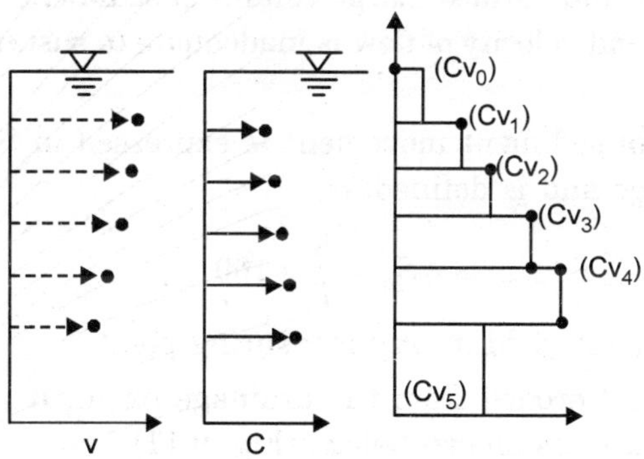

$$Q_{tm} = \sum_{0}^{p} 0.5\,(C_i v_i + C_{i+1} V_{i+1})\,(h_{2+1} - h_i)$$

Fig 9.10

where Q_{tm} is the total measured unit sediment discharge based p-point samples. C_i and v_i are the sediment concentration and flow velocity at a given point i, and $h_{i+1} - hi$, the vertical layer thickness.

The range of applicability of point measurement technique is defined in terms of u_*/w. The technique is well suited when $u_*/w > 5$. In deep rivers the measurement is most accurate where $u_*/w > 10$ also. Point measurement is not suitable for shallow rivers.

Approximate Method for Total Load Estimation

In case some suspended load data is available for a stream, an approximate estimate of the total load can be made. However, it must be realised that any approximate method should only be used when no other data is available or quick estimate is required.

(1) Colby suggested the unmeasured sediment load can be related with flow velocity as follows,

$$q_{sum} = 353.6\ V^{3.1}$$

where, q_{sum} = unmeasured sediment load in KN/day/m width, V = velocity in m/s. Colby found that total load correlates fairly well with the average velocity except at high velocity when antidunes are formed. In high velocity flows the total load will be a function of stream power (τ_0 V).

(2) Measurements in 11 rivers of USA, for an average value of sediment size of 0.2 mm, the average ratio of suspended load to total load is estimated as 0.67.

Sediment Yield from Catchments: Estimates of sediment yield are needed for studies of river morphology, soil and water conservation planning, design of erosion control structures and reservoir sedimentation. The process of soil erosion by rainfall and runoff mainly consists of detachment by raindrops and transport by runoff. It is reported that the surface of earth is eroded at an average rate of 30 mm per thousand years. Another estimate indicates that the world is now losing about 23 billion tons of soil from croplands in excess of soil formation.

Erosion from the catchment has a pronounced effect on the morphology of the streams in the catchment. It has to be realised that not all of the eroded material is effectively sent to the oceans. The rate at which sediment is discharged to the sea is much less than the rate at which it is eroded from the land surface. Large volume of sediment is deposited at intermediate locations where the runoff and velocity of flow is inadequate to sustain the transport of sediment particles.

The change in rate of sediment movement is expressed in Sedimentary Delivery Ratio S_D, expressed in percentage and is defined as,

$$S_D = \frac{S}{T} \times 100$$

where S is the sediment yield at any measuring point

T is the total material eroded from the drainage basin. It is obvious that as Area (A) increases, S_D would decrease, as shown below, (Fig. 9.11).

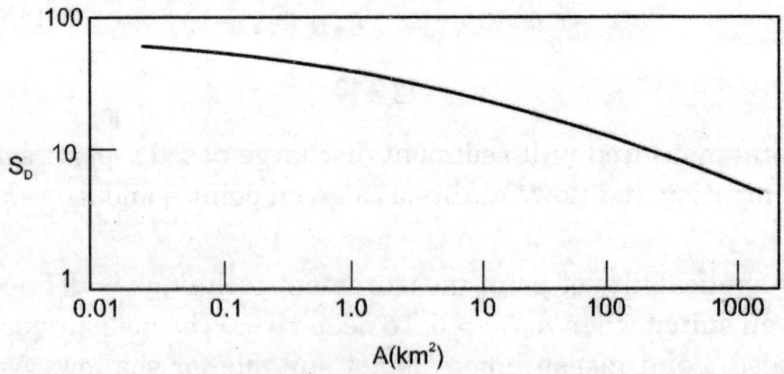

Fig. 9.11

Factors Affecting Sediment Yield

The rate of erosion, its quantity and its transport depend upon factors like climatic condition, topography, land use and geology of the catchment.

Climatic Factors: Include yearly rainfall its temporal distribution, intensity of rain and temperature variation.

Catchment Factors: Include its average slope, drainage density, area of catchment and land use pattern. With increase in slope velocity of flow, the shear stress on the land surface as well as the transport capacity increase. However, with increase in area the sediment yield per unit catchment area decreases. With increase in drainage density, the sediment yield also increases. Vegetation reduces soil erosion.

It has been reported that the erosion from agricultural land is about 40% of the total erosion followed by 26% from stream bank erosion (USA streams data).

Geology of catchment is also an important factor controlling upland erosion as well as channel erosion. Landslides increase sediment yield. The unconsolidated sedimentary rocks (young alluvium) are the most erodible material.

Formulae for Sediment Yield: Several sediment yield models have been developed for evaluation of sediment yield. The soil loss is calculated using Universal Soil Loss Equation (USLE) which gives Average Annual Soil Loss in t/ha (tonnes per hectare) as A,

$$A = R\,K\,L\,S\,C\,P$$

where, R is Index of Erodibility, K = Soil Erodibility Factor, L = Length of the Plot, S = Slope of the Area, C = Cropping Pattern Factor and P = Conservation Practice Factor. The USLE is in use for many decades. Several empirical equations have been developed for different regions.

Soil Conservation

Soil conservation technologies can prevent soil erosion with cost-effectiveness i.e. with small investment significant benefits can be obtained. There are several methods of controlling soil erosion. Construction of small bunds is an important method of controlling erosion. The erosion hazard is much more severe in hilly areas, where it can be checked by terrace farming and plugging the gullies. Afforestation plays the most important part in checking the soil erosion. Control on excessive grazing is also a popular method for control of erosion.

CHAPTER 10

SEDIMENT MEASUREMENT TECHNIQUES

Besides computation on sediment transport, measurement is also necessary for verification of theories and proper understanding of river behaviour. The techniques can be divided into two groups.

- Measurement with samplers
- Tracer Techniques

Sediment movement in streams and rivers takes two major forms – **Suspended sediment** is the finer particles which are held in suspension by the eddy currents in the flowing stream. Larger particles move along the bed and called the **bed-load**.

Measurement with Samplers

Due to the difference in mechanism of bed-load and suspended load there are different samplers for each type of transport.

(1) **Bed-Load Samplers:** Variation in bed-load transport and influence of bed forms will give large variations in results with samplers. For a significant value of the bed load a large number of observations are required to be taken.

A large number of bed-load samplers have been used in the past in various countries. Most of these were of box or basket type (Fig. 10.2) and consist of a pervious container. The earlier basket samplers were built with flat bottom. Some later ones were built with a bottom of loosely woven iron rings. This enabled the bottom to conform to the shape of the undulated bed. The efficiency of these bed-load sampler was not high and is only about 45% (for sediment size 5mm to 250 mm).

Other samplers are Pan or tray Type samplers and Pressure-Difference type samplers. The Pan or Tray type consist of a flat, wedge-shaped pan pointing upstream. They may be of a single slot or having number of slots. Their efficiency is even les than the box-type samplers.

The pressure-difference type are an improvement over the previous ones. In this diverging walls are provided at the rear in order to maintain the entrance velocity approximately equal to the stream velocity. The rear part is provided with a mesh. This type of sampler can be used to measure bed load of a wide range of sediment sizes.

Arnhem or Dutch sampler (Fig. 10.1) is the best known sampler in this category. It consists of rigid rectangular entrance to the rear of which is fixed a diverging rubber neck. A mesh basket (0.2 to 0.3 mm size) is fixed downstream of the rubber neck. Compared to the previous ones the efficiency is much higher about 70%. The frame has been added as an improvement.

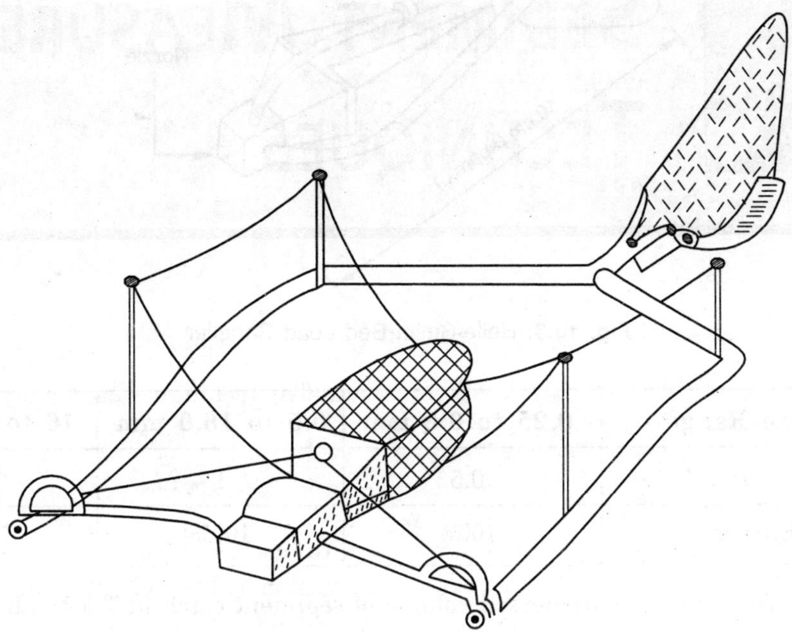

Fig. 10.1: Arnhem Type Bed Load Sampler

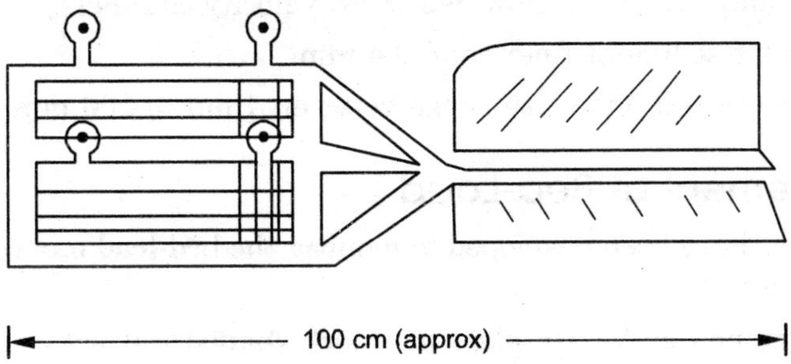

Fig. 10.2: Box Type Bed Load Sampler

A modified version of Arnhem Sampler has been developed by Helley and Smith Fig. 10.3 which is being used widely. A calibration has been developed by Emmet as follows to give bed load. For smaller particle size (0.2 to 0.5 mm) the efficiency is very high. For medium sediment size the efficiency is found to be 100%. For coarse sediment efficiency gradually falls down to 70%. The equation for q_B for Helley-Smith Sampler is,

$$q_B = \frac{\alpha\,(1-\lambda)\,\rho_S\; g\; Vs}{b\,T}$$

Where α is calibration factor given as:

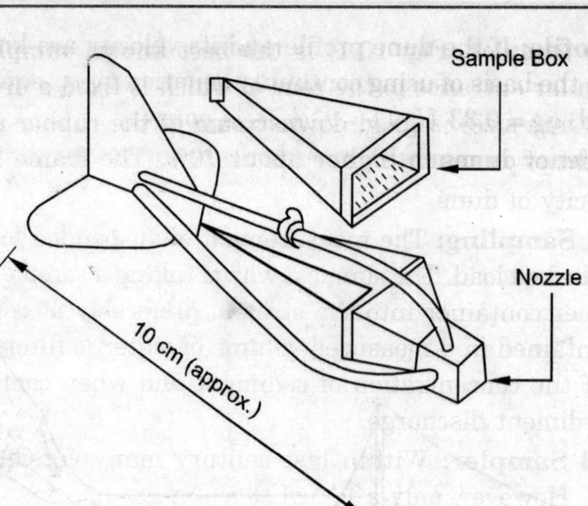

Fig. 10.3: Helle-Smith Bed Load Sampler

Size Range	0.25 to 0.5 mm	0.5 to 16.0 mm	16 to 32 mm
α	0.5	1	1.5
Efficiency	100%	100%	70%

Also, λ = porosity, Vs = Immersed volume of sediment catch in T seconds and b is the width of opening in (m).

Some other versions are also available for bed load measurement as follows:

Changjiang-78 samplers for shallow depth low velocity channels.

Sphinx sampler for sediment finer than 0.4 mm.

VUV -Sampler works on wide size range between 1mm to 100 mm.

Indirect Measurement of Bed-Load

A number of techniques have been developed to monitor the bed-load movement. Some of these are briefly described here.

(a) **Acoustic Instruments:** A base plate or a fork-shaped rod with microphone attached is lowered on to the stream bed. The impact on the plate is picked up by the microphone. This gives an idea of relative bed load. It is suitable for coarse bed material.

(b) **Radio-active Tracers:** The technique is to insert into the stream a radio-active tracer in a form similar to the bed load, it should have same size, shape and density as the natural sediment. The tracer should have a coating of radioactive material.

The movement downstream can then be monitored using portable detectors. In this method some health hazard is involved.

(c) **Ultrasonic Method:** Acoustic energy in the form of ultrasound is transmitted and the energy absorbed is correlated with the concentration. This method is suitable for fine sediment at high concentration.

(d) **From Dune Profile:** If the dune profile and its velocity are known, the bed-load can be estimated. On the basis of using continuity equation for q_B equation like the following can be developed, $q_B = 0.33\ U_w\ (1 - \lambda)\ h$, λ is porosity

h = height of dunes

U_w = velocity of dune.

Suspended Load Sampling: The measurement of suspended load is relatively simple and more efficient than the bed load. The simplest way of taking a sample of suspended sediment is to dip a bucket or other container into the stream, preferably at a point where it is well-mixed. The sediment contained in a measured volume of water is filtered, dried and weighed. This gives a measure of the concentration of sediment and when combined with the rate of flow gives the rate of sediment discharge.

Suspended-Load Sampler: Within last century many versions of Suspended-Load samplers were designed. However, only a few of these are in use now. The most popular are described below:

(1) **Depth Integrating Sampler:** A typical sampler consists of a glass bottle inserted in a fish-shaped frame mounted on a rod. The bottle is sealed by capping after the sample has been obtained. For the bottle to fill smoothly and evenly when below the surface it is necessary to have one nozzle or orifice for entry of sediment laden water, and a second pipe through which the displaced air is ejected. (Fig. 10.4)

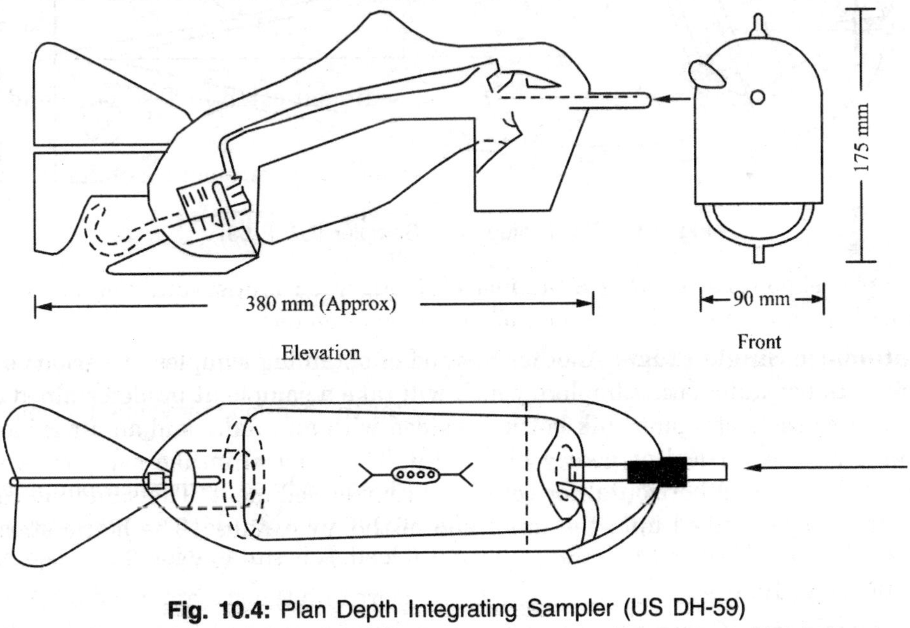

Fig. 10.4: Plan Depth Integrating Sampler (US DH-59)

The entry nozzle is usually designed with a slightly expanding cross-section behind the point of entry in order to reduce risk of back pressure which could interfere with the flow into the bottle.

In operation, the sampler is moved from the surface down to the bed and back upto the surface while sampling continuously. A few trial runs can establish how long is required to fill the bottle during the double journey. It is undesirable for any type of bottle sampler to continue to accept more inflow after the bottle is full as this can lead to an accumulation of sediment in the bottle.

In some depth-integrating samplers the bottle is lifted out of the flow when or just before it is filled; other types of sampler may have some device to stop further sampling once the bottle is full.

(2) **Point Integrating Sampler:** The point-integrating sampler remains at a fixed point to collect a sample which yields the mean concentration at that point in a vertical. It samples continuously during the time it takes for the bottle to fill. Opening and closing the valves of the sampler are controlled from the surface electrically or by cables. The sampler is constructed with an inner Chamber to hold the sample container surrounded by an air chamber having volume much larger than that of the sample container. The air chamber and the sample container are interconnected with air chamber has a permanent opening at the bottom. (Fig. 10.5)

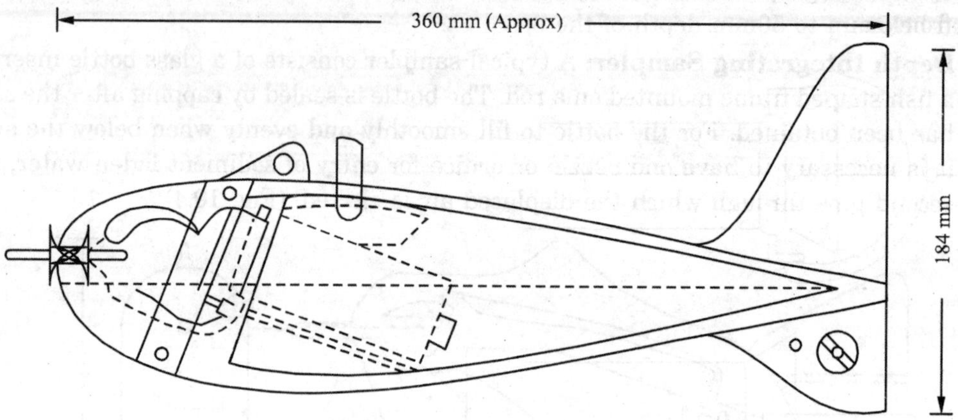

Fig. 10.5: Point Integration Sampler (US P-59)

Samples should be taken at a number of depth at each of several vertical sections as described in area-velocity method of flow measurement.

(3) **Automatic Single Stage:** Another method of obtaining samples at various depths of flow is to use automatic samplers which will take a sample at predetermined depth of flow. It consists of a pint milk bottle provided with an intake and an air exhaust. The intake can be vertical or nearly horizontal. The vertical intake sampler is used for fine sediment and horizontal for relatively coarser sediment. The sampling continues till the bottle is filled upto the inner end of the air exhaust. The bottle starts to fill when depth of flow reaches the crest of intake when the syphon flow starts into the bottle. (Fig. 10.9)

(4) **An Automatic Pump Sampler:** The pattern of rising and falling rates of flow, and the variations of sediment concentration at different flow rates, can to some extent be anticipated from observations, but even sophisticated automatic samplers cannot predict what is going to happen next. An automatic pump sampler may perform exactly as programmed. In these the intake velocity is maintained as the local flow velocity with the help of the pump.

A series of samples are required as the river rises, an automatic sampler can be set up as shown in the figure 10.10.

(5) **Optical Turbidimeter:** An optical turbiditimeter passes a beam of light through sediment-laden water from a source on one side of a channel to a sensor at the other side. For optimal sampling resolution the wavelength and the particle size must be of the same order. Similarly ultrasound waves can be used in turbidimeters.

(6) **Nuclear Gauges:** A similar principle is used in nuclear gauges which measure either the absorption or the scattering of gamma radiation instead of light. They are restricted only to specialised experimental measurement rather than routine monitoring.

Bed Material Sampling: The composition of bed material is required in computing discharge of bed material by analytical methods. The bed material samplers are of various types.

(1) **Drag Bucket Type:** It consists of a weighted bucket with a cutting edge. For sampling bed material the sampler is lowered to the bed and dragged in the upstream direction by a tow-line operated from the boat. They are able to collect about 1 kg of the sample from 1mm to 50mm depth of the bed. (Fig. 10.6)

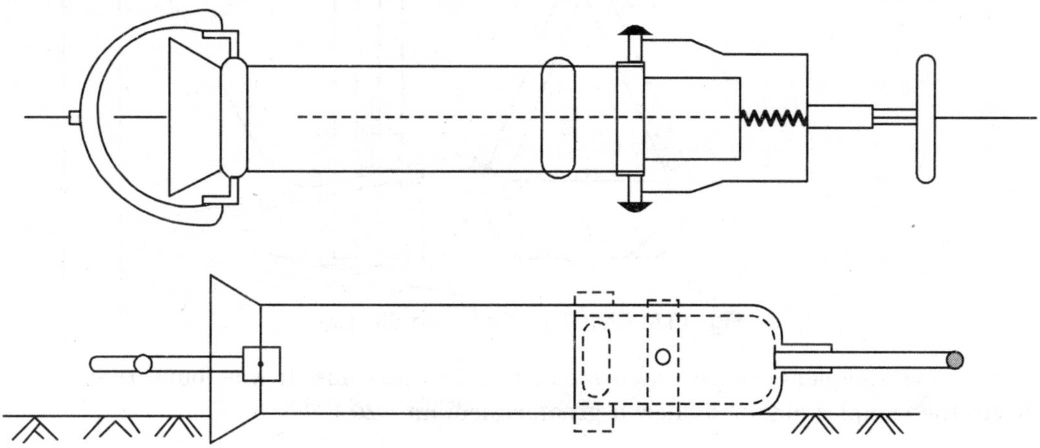

Fig. 10.6: Drag Bucket Type Bed Load Sampler

(2) **Scoop-Type:** It consists of a pipe-like unit, one end of which is closed and other bevelled to provide a cutting edge. A rod is attached to the top of the scoop. A hinged cover plate is placed over the cutting edge of the scoop. It is suitable to the streams upto 6m depth and it can collect samples upto 60mm depth of the bed.

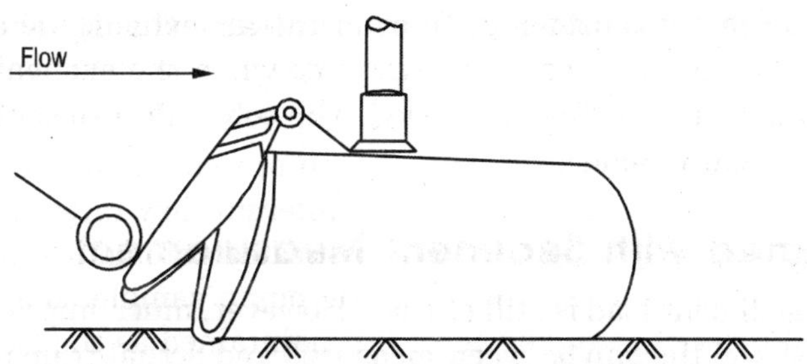

Fig. 10.7: Scoop-Type Bed Load Sampler

(3) **Grab-Type:** It consists of cupped jaws which are closed at the bed to trap the samples of bed material. The jaws are closed together either by pull on the auxiliary line or by a automatic spring arrangement. It can sample upto 5 kg of material from top 125 mm depth of the bed. (Fig. 10.8)

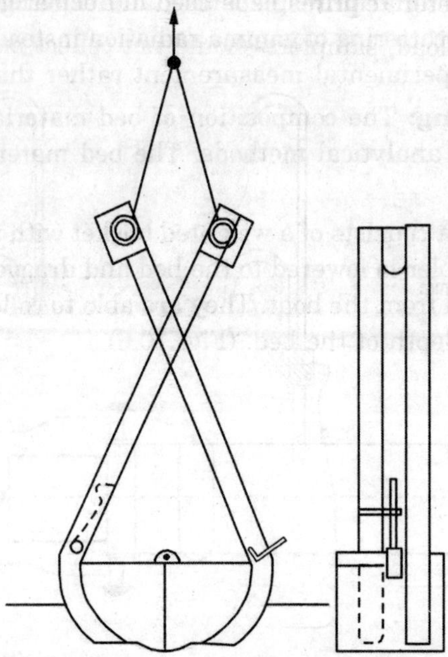

Fig. 10.8: Drag Type Bed Load Sampler

The above samplers can give good result in sandy streams. It was found that in gravel bed rivers the samples obtained show a greater medium size.

Laboratory Determination of Sediment Concentration

After the samples are collected, water and sediment has to be separated. For this either **evaporation** or **filtration method** is used. Evaporation method used where sediment concentration is high, filtration is suitable for lower concentration. In filtration method, the sample is filtered through a perforated crucible with a filter paper. The crucible is dried in a oven and weighed to determine the weight of sediment collected. The dissolved solid passes through the crucible, hence not considered. In evaporation method, the sample is allowed to stay for several hours so that solid particles settle down. The clear water is decanted. The remaining mixture of water and sediment is dried. The solid left also contains dissolved solid, for which suitable correction is made.

Problems Associated with Sediment Measurement

Exact measurement of sediment load is still elusive. However, much improvement in measuring techniques has occurred and the gap between measured and actual transport is slowly closing. Problems with sediment samplers use are,

(1) It is difficult to give the equipment a correct vertical are horizontal alignment with the bed.

(2) Samplers disturb the flow field, which may cause decrease in velocity. May cause deposition or erosion.

(3) Calibration of the meter requires expertise and experience.

(4) When collecting bed-load, samplers should not collect material during lowering.;

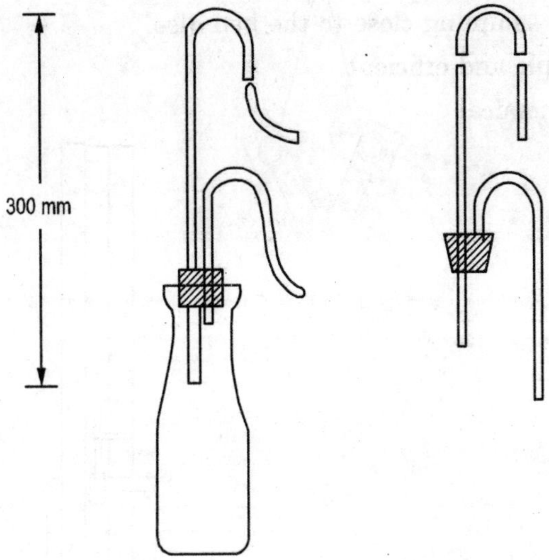

Fig. 10.9: Automatic Single Stage Suspended Sediment Sampler

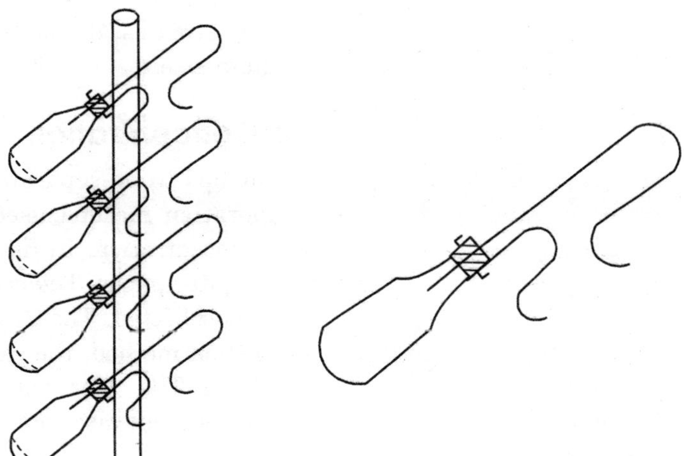

Fig. 10.10: An array of Samplers for Progressive Sampling

Requirements of an Ideal Sediment Sampler

An ideal sediment sampler should have following qualities.

(1) Velocity at entrance should be equal to stream velocity.

(2) The intake should extend to the upstream of the sampling location.

(3) The container of the sampler should be easily detachable and easy to attach.

(4) The sampler should be streamlined.

(5) It should permit sampling close to the bed also.

(6) It should be simple and efficient.

(7) It should be economical

PART III

- Methods of River Training
- River Gauging
- Flood and Flood Control
- River Ecosystem
- Interlinking of Rivers
- River Modelling

CHAPTER 11

METHODS OF RIVER TRAINING

River training in its broad aspects, covers
guide and confine the flow to river chan
configuration for effective and safe moven
aims at stabilizing a river within a suitable w
of purpose.

OBJECTIVES OF RIVER TRAINING

River training is an age-old practice resp
human ingenuity to correct vagaries of the
summarised below:

(1) Flood Protection (High Water T
property almost every year. River
or more of the following methods:

(a) By constructing levees or emba

(b) By increasing the discharge cap
straightening through dredg
reducing resistance to flow in

(c) By construction of reservoirs

(d) By providing escape channels

(2) Navigation (Low Water Training)
width required for navigation shoul
methods be adopted to achieve this

(a) Dredging the shallow reaches

(b) Using spurs to contract the

(c) By canalization accomplished b
Also sharp curves along the rive
movement of boats and ships.

CHAPTER 11

METHODS OF RIVER TRAINING

River training, in its broad aspects, covers all engineering works constructed on a river to guide and confine the flow to river channel, and to control and regulate the river bed configuration for effective and safe movement of floods and river sediments. River training aims at stabilizing a river within a suitable waterway and along a certain alignment for a variety of purposes.

OBJECTIVES OF RIVER TRAINING

River training is an age-old practice resulting in incessant development and application of human ingenuity to correct vagaries of the river. The various objectives of river training are summarised below:

(1) Flood Protection: (High Water Training) Floods cause enormous damage to life and property almost every year. River training for flood protection can be achieved by one or more of the following methods.

(a) By constructing levees or embankments to confine water in a narrower channel.

(b) By increasing the discharge capacity of natural channels by widening, deepening, straightening through dredging or smoothening the surface of the channel (Reducing resistant to flow i.e. reducing Mannings N)

(c) By construction of reservoirs.

(d) By providing escape channels or diversions from rivers

(2) Navigation: (Low Water Training) For a river to be navigable, sufficient depth and width required for navigation should be available even at low water period. Following methods be adopted to achieve this objective;

(a) Dredging the shallow reaches of the river

(b) Using **spurs** to contract the river channel, thus increasing the depth.

(c) By canalization accomplished by building a series of small dams, weirs or locks.

Also sharp curves along the rivers need to be eliminated for smooth unobstructed movement of boats and ships.

(3) **Sediment Control:** (Mean Water Training): It aims at attaining efficient movement of sediment load for keeping the river channel in a state of equilibrium. Spurs and pitched islands are normally helpful in training the river for sediment. This is the maximum bed building stage. Mean water training, therefore forms the basis on which both high and low water training are planned.

(4) **Guiding the River Flow:** Guide banks are provided to protect canal headwork, and communication structures such as bridges against outflanking and direct attack of flow. Main purpose is to make sure that water flows between the abutments. The spacing between guide banks conforms to the width required for the river to pass the design flood discharge.

If some portion of a bank needs to be protected it is done by constructing spurs projecting into the river from the bank in question.

(5) **River Channel Stabilization:** The river banks prone to erosion are protected by training methods which fall into two categories, soft armour and hard armour. For low velocities, soft armour (flexible or green techniques), consist of grass mats or geogrids (filled with soil) are provided which are cheap, easy to install and maintain. When the velocity is high hard armour as **rip-rap**, concrete or geosynthetic lining may be used.

River Training Practices

The planning and design of river training structures is done either on empirical methods or on intuition and judgment of experienced river engineers. These days model investigation is also resorted to before finalising the plan. Commonly used structural methods are as follows.

(1) **Levees (Embankment, Bund or Dike):** A levee is simply a man made embankment built to keep a river from overflowing its banks and protect the adjacent area from getting flooded. This is perhaps the oldest method used for flood protection. Levees generally follow the alignment of the river.

(a) Levees are kept farther apart considering the desirability of having high discharge capacity of river for a given stage.

(b) The requirement is that entire meander belt be within the levees so that they are not strongly attacked by the river.

Levees should also follow general curvature of the river to avoid attack by the river flow.

Design of Levees: The design of a levees is similar to that of an earth dam. It should, however, be realized that while the upstream face of an earth dam is exposed to water most of the time, that of a levee is exposed to water for a very short period, only during flood season.

Below is shown a typical cross section of a levee (Fig. 11.1). Recently, there had been great debate over the advantages and disadvantages of construction of levees. A large number of people feel that levees are more detrimental to us than beneficial. Besides the advantage of protecting surrounding areas from inundation, levees have several disadvantages also, as they deprive the flood plain of valuable sediment which is rich in nutrients. Levees can also fail by overtopping, underflow, slumping or erosion. Erosion is the most frequent reason for levee-failure. When it happens the disaster is much more severe than the flood without levees.

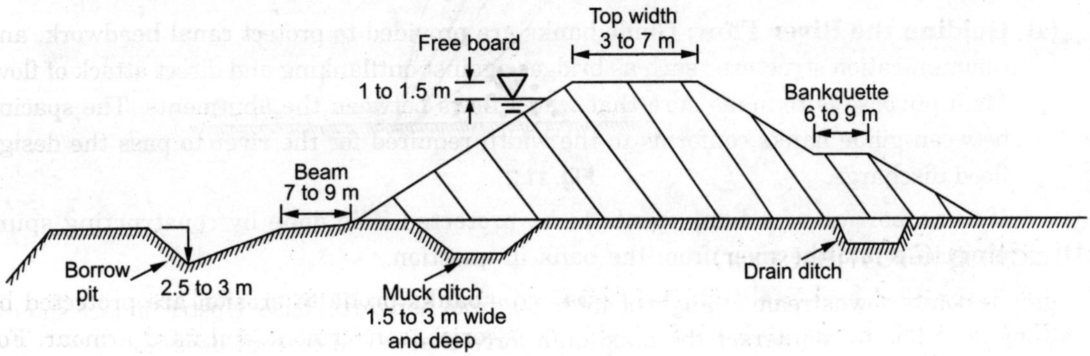

Fig. 11.1

(2) Spurs: (Groynes, Spur Dikes, Transverse Dikes)

Spurs are in the form of an embankment constructed transverse to the river flow extending from one of the river banks into the river. Spurs guide the river flow, promote scour or deposition of the sediment where desired, and trap the sediment load to build up new river banks.

Spurs help train a river to flow along a desired course by preventing erosion of the bank and encouraging flow along a channel with a more desirable width and alignment. They convert poorly defined streams into well defined channels. (Fig. 11.5)

The spurs may be aligned either perpendicular to the bank or inclined, pointing upstream or downstream. When a groyne points upstream then it is called a **repelling groyne** (Fig. 11.2). In this the river flow away from the bank. On the contrary, when a groyne points downstream, it is called an **attracting groyne** as it attracts the flow towards the bank (Fig. 11.3). The river flow thus remains along the bank permanently. If a groyne of short length is provided exactly at 90° to the bank, it only deflects the flow locally. Hence it is called a **deflecting groyne** (Fig. 11.4).

On the basis of model experiments some special types of groyne have been designed. These are hockey spur, inverted hockey spur and T-headed spur. According to the method and material of construction, the spurs may be permeable or impermeable. Some spurs are fully submerged in water.

Repelling Groyne (spur)

The groyne points towards upstream at an angle 10° to 30° from the line normal to the bank. A still water pool is created causing sediment deposition. Near the head (nose) of the groyne, scour may occur. The nose is therefore, should be strong to resist failure.

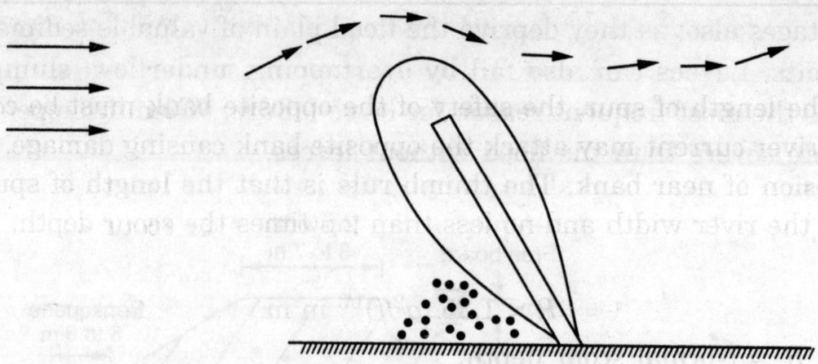

Fig. 11.2

Attracting Groyne (spur)

The groyne points downstream at angle of 45° to 60° from horizartal base. Upstream face should be strong as it has to counteract the maximum force there. The current does not attack the other bank of the river.

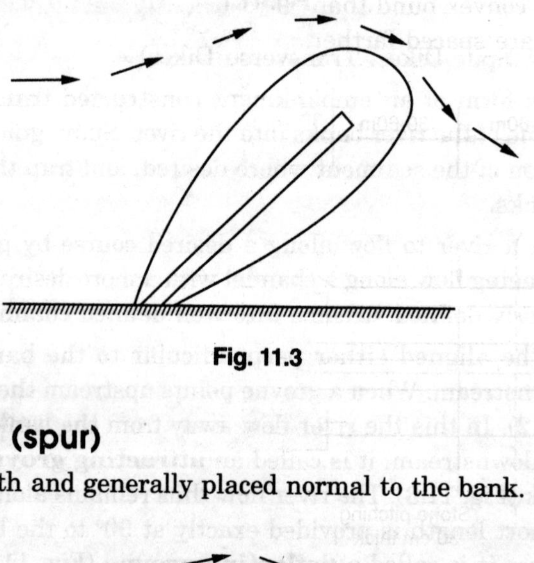

Fig. 11.3

Deflecting Groyne (spur)

It has much shorter length and generally placed normal to the bank. It only deflects the flow away from the bank.

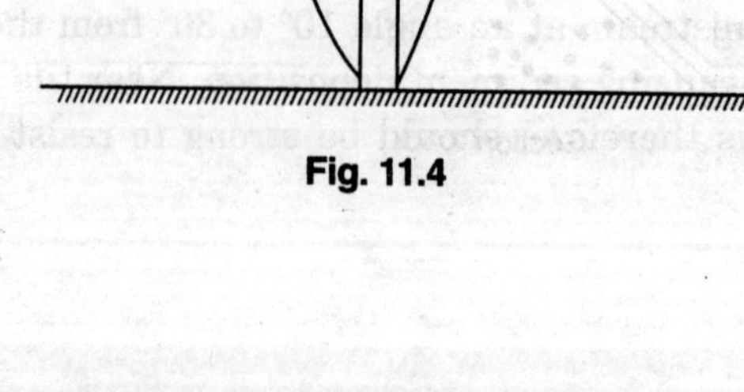

Fig. 11.4

Spur length

When choosing the length of spur, the safety of the opposite bank must be considered. If the spur is too long, river current may attack the opposite bank causing damage. If it is too short it may cause erosion of near bank. The thumb rule is that the length of spur should not be more than 1/5 of the river width and no less than 2.5 times the scour depth. The scour depth is given by,

$$R = 1.35\ (q^2/f)^{1/3} \text{ in m}$$

Where, R = Normal scour depth.

q = discharge intensity m^3/s per meter width

f = Lacey's silt factor, a function of grain size.

Silt factor varies from 0.4 for very fine sand to 1.0 for normal sand (size 0.323 mm). For medium sand (size 0.5 mm) f = 1.25 and 1.5 for coarse sand (size 0.725 mm).

Spacing of spurs: The general practice is to provide the spurs giving a space of 2 to 2.5 times its length. The spacing may vary according to the river's plan form. The spacing may be farther apart on convex bund than the concave bund, for wider river more spacing is given. Permeable spurs are spaced farther.

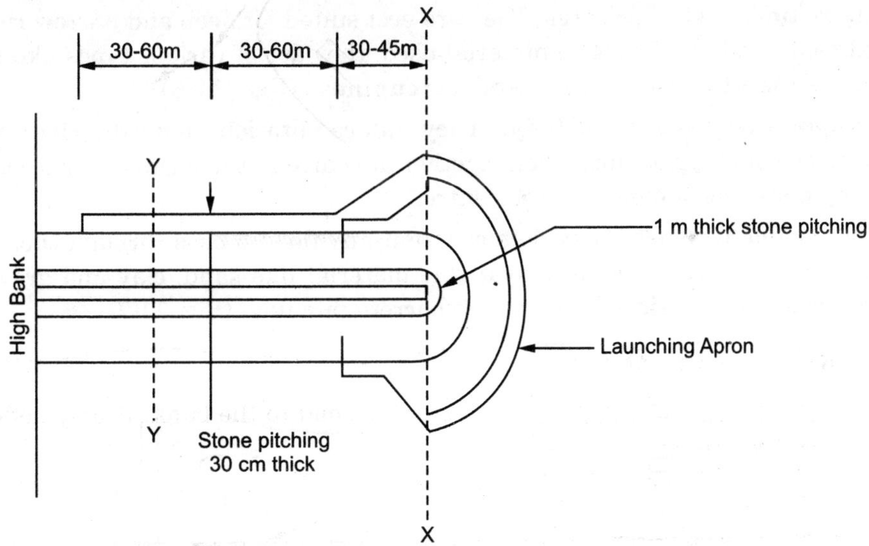

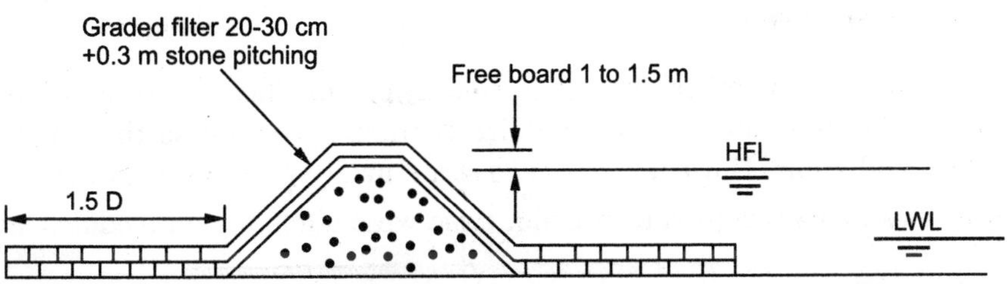

Section X-X

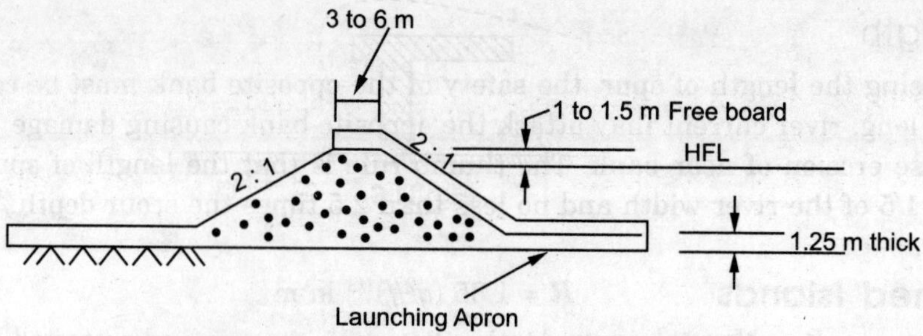

Fig. 11.5: Typical Sections of a Spur or Groyen

SPECIAL TYPES OF GROYNES

(a) Permeable and Impermeable Groynes

Permeable Groynes: They permit the water to flow through their body. The velocity of flow is dampened reducing the erosive action of the river. Because of partial obstruction of flow, they promote deposition of sediment as the flow is retarded. They are built of materials like bamboos, timber, steel or wires. They are best suited for deep and narrow rivers carrying heavy sediment load. According to material used, they are of various types like **tree groyens, pile groynes, bamboo cage spurs** and **porcupines**. (Fig. 11.6)

Percupines are popular in India. They induce siltation along the river banks. These are made of 3 to 6m long bamboos tied together at centre in the form of a space angle and are weighted by tieing some stones to the centre.

Impermeable Groynes: They do not permit any flow to pass through their body. These are constructed by a core of locally available material like sand, clay and gravel. They are heavily protected on the sides by stone or concrete pitching. (Fig. 11.7)

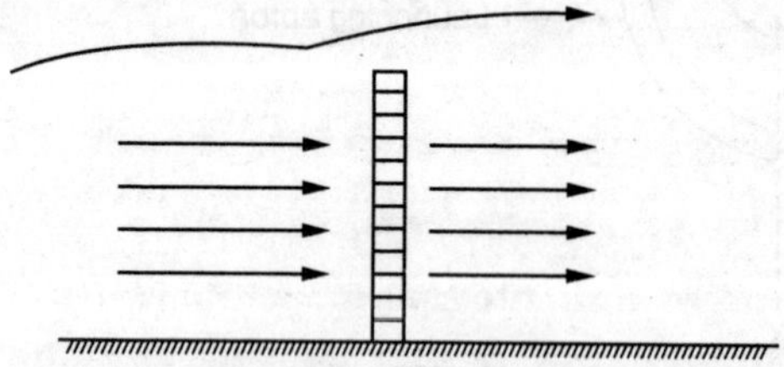

Fig. 11.6

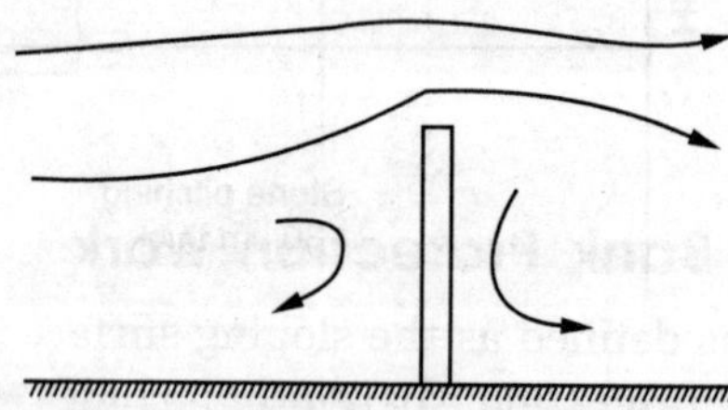

Fig. 11.7

The permeable groynes are cheap to construct and have a better performance than impermeable. It does not change the flow direction abruptly and so there is little chance of eddy formation and scour. However, they are structurally weak and cannot resist shocks.

Sometimes submerged groyens are also used which do not create eddies and turbulence.

(b) Denehy's Groyens

The head of this types of groyne is like a reversed 'L' as shown in Fig. 11.8. These are economical and have been used in India in some projects. The head has to be heavily protected.

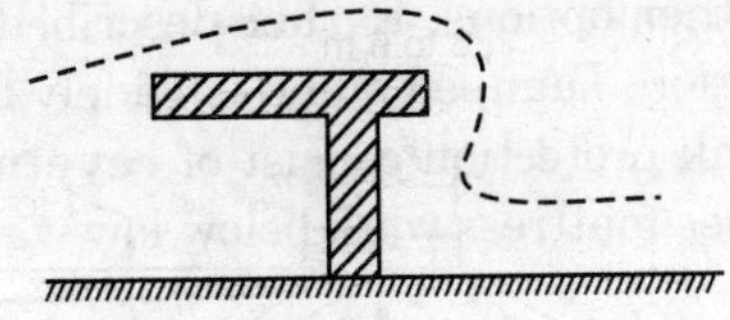

Fig. 11.8

(c) Pitched Islands

An island is created artificially on river bed with sand in its core and protected by stone pitching on all its sides is called **pitched island** (Fig. 11.9). This cause redistribution of velocity and tractive force. Deep scour is noticed round the island. Launching apron has to be properly designed. It serves the purpose of training the river for an axial flow and improving the channel for navigation.

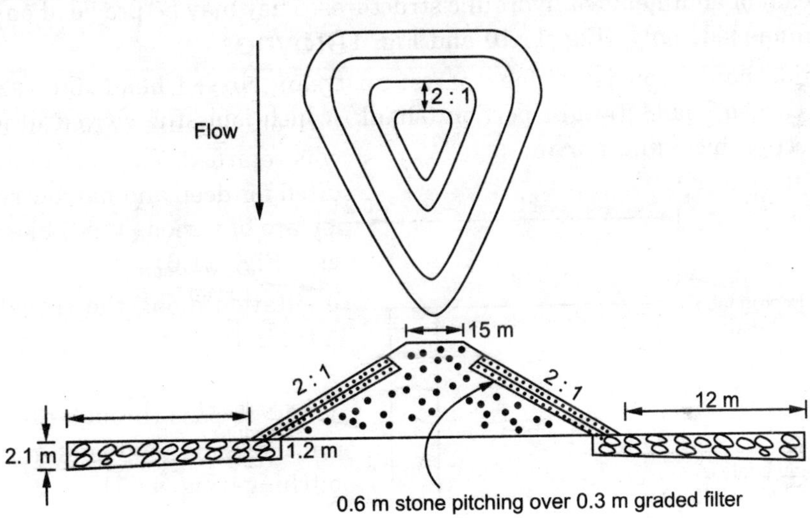

Fig. 11.9

(d) River Bank Protection Work

River bank is defined as the sloping surface of land coming into contact with a body of flowing water. Bank protection, therefore, includes any protective work that aims at maintaining the stability of land against the action of water. Generally speaking, the stability of sloping bank under the action of water is subject firstly to the static head of water which induces seepage and saturation and second to the erosive force of running water, which changes the form of the slope and in turn affects its stability.

Bank protection is necessary to check erosion of bank by current, to check sliding of slope, to prevent undermining of the toe, to prevent piping and to check sliding due to sudden drawdown.

Various methods are used for bank protection, where the current is mild, bank can be protected by turfing or sodding. Low growth of shrubs and willows can be an effective cover in this case. However, when the current is strong , stone pitching is an important option, asphalt or articulated concrete are other options. Earlier described spurs and groynes are important methods of river bank protection. Dumped stone is widely used method of bank protection. In many rivers of the world, bank protection consist of **revetment** along the concave side of the bends. The revetment comprises mattress work below low water line and grading and riprapping above that line.

(e) Guide Banks

Guide banks are structures built to guide a stream or river through any hydraulic structure like bridges and weirs. Since it is very expensive to construct the structure spanning whole width of the river, to economise some training work is normally provided to confine the flow of water within reasonable waterway. Guide banks are such structures constructed all over the world. These are known as Bell's bunds named after their designer. The guide banks are made parallel or approximately parallel to the direction of flow. They extend both upstream and downstream of abutments of hydraulic structures. They may be provided on either side or sometimes on one side only. (Fig. 11.10 and Fig. 11.11)

The guide banks consist of four parts: upstream curved head (impregnable head), downstream curved head, straight portion (shank) which joins the curved heads, and slope and bed protection including **apron**.

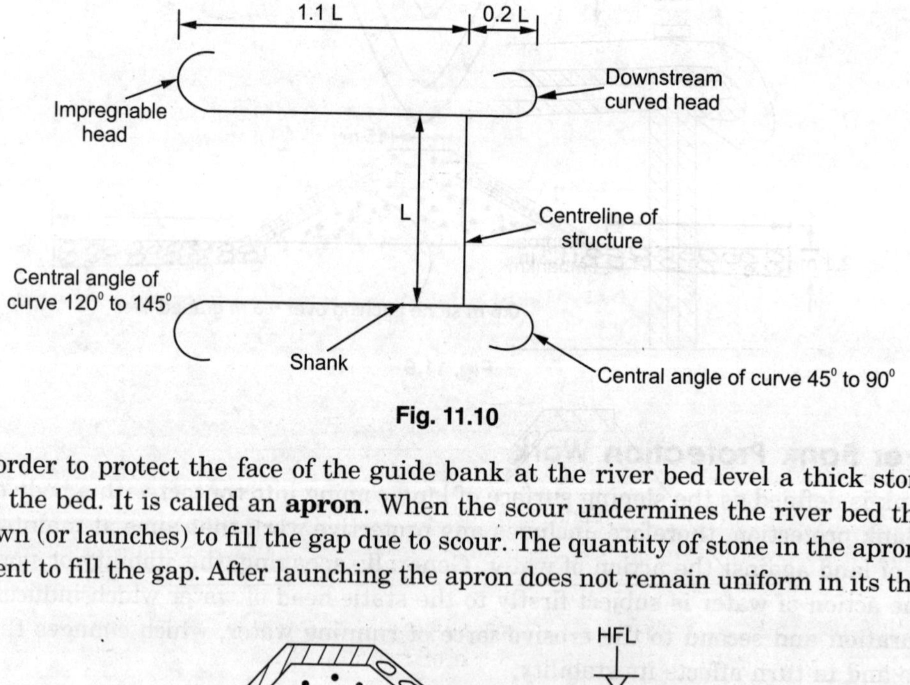

Fig. 11.10

In order to protect the face of the guide bank at the river bed level a thick stone cover is laid on the bed. It is called an **apron**. When the scour undermines the river bed the apron comes down (or launches) to fill the gap due to scour. The quantity of stone in the apron should be sufficient to fill the gap. After launching the apron does not remain uniform in its thickness.

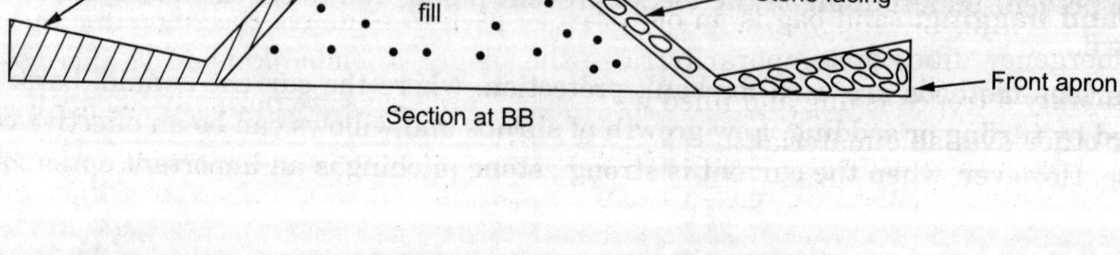

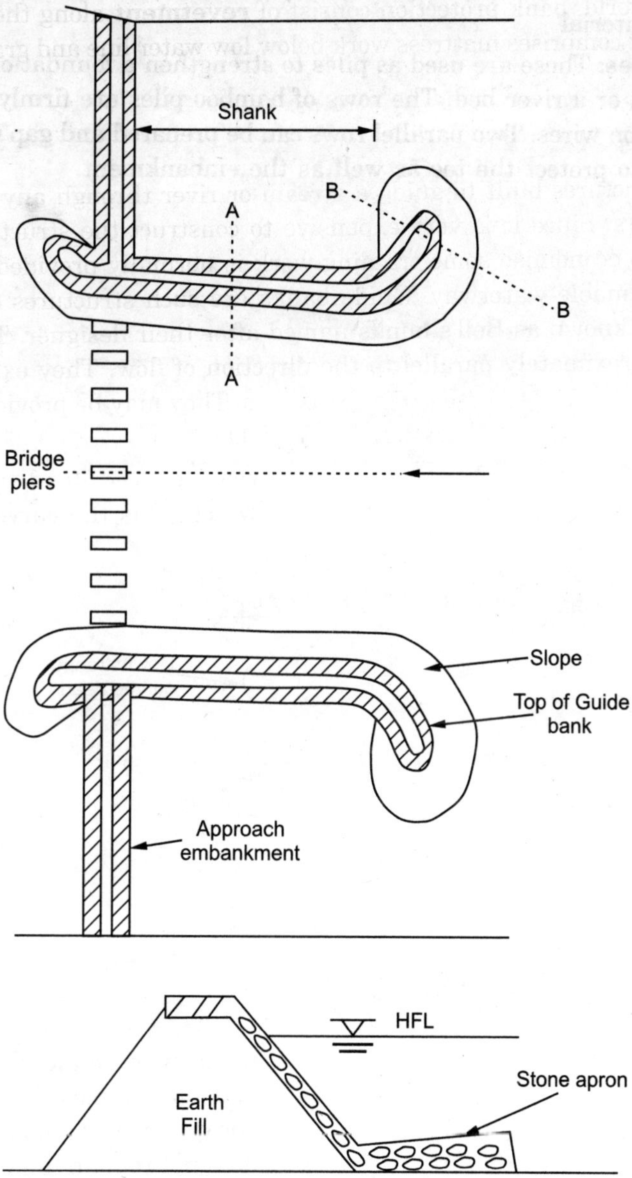

Fig. 11.11

(f) Other Protection Structures

(a) **Sand bagging:** sand bag is an old practice used to reinforce the structure and build emergency dikes or temporarily raise the height of embankment. To increase the stability a trench is dug and filled with bags. These bags are normally filled with sand or other available material.

(b) **Channel Lining:** It is provided to protect banks and bed against erosion. It helps in increasing the flow velocity ensuring easy sediment transport. These can be made of variety of material.

(c) **Bamboo Piles:** These are used as piles to strengthen a foundation or stabilize a flood embankment or a river bed. The rows of bamboo piles are firmly fixed with the help of ropes or iron wires. Two parallel rows can be prepared and gap is filled with pebbles or boulders to protect the toe as well as the embankment.

CHAPTER 12

RIVER GAUGING

River or stream gauging is the process of measuring the water discharge (flow) at a particular location on the channel. Area-velocity method is the most popular method for this purpose. In this method of stream gauging **depth** and vertically averaged **velocity** measurements are taken at successive locations along a stream cross-section and are numerically integrated to obtain stream flow discharge.

For the purpose of discharge measurement, the river cross-section is divided into a large number of subsections by verticals as shown in Fig. 12.1.

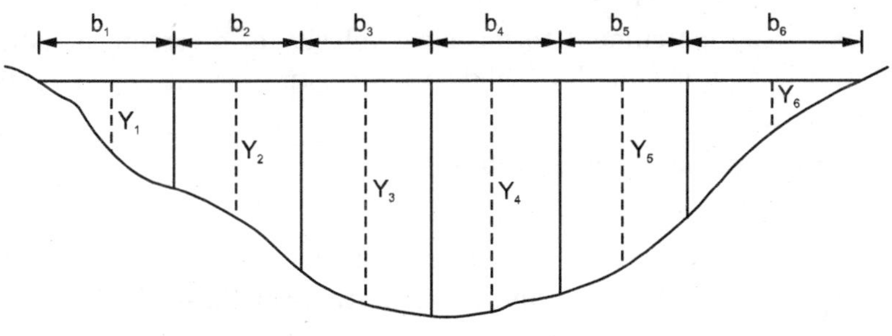

Fig. 12.1

Each of the section is denoted by width (b) and depth (y). The area of each section is calculated as $b_1 y_1$, $b_2 y_2$............ $b_n y_n$ for (n) number of sub-sections.

Locating Observation Points

This is done by Pivot Flag method. As shown in the figure 12.2 a line normal to the bank abc is drawn and divided in as many numbers as the sub-sections are desired. Flags are fixed at the pivot A and points *D, E* and *F*. A flag is carried on the boat *C*.

To keep the boat carrying velocity measuring device straight across the cross-section *x-y*, ranging is done between *D, E* and *F*. For fixing the distance from y ranging is done between *A, b* and *C*. For other locations, using the geometry of similar triangle, points on line *AC* are fixed and then ranging is done. The boat is anchored at each location.

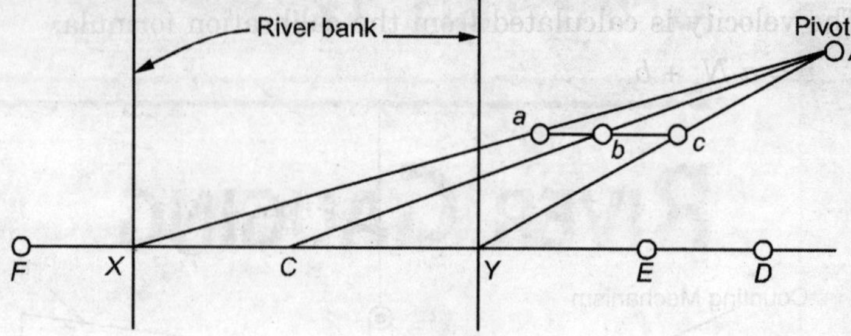

Fig. 12.2

Measurement of Depth

The depth at various locations is measured by sounding rods or sounding weights. If the depth of the stream is large, the electroacoustic instrument called **echo-depth-recorder** or **echo-sounder** is used. High frequency sound wave is sent down by a transducer kept immersed at water surface and the echo reflected by bed is also picked up by the same transducer. The time interval (t) between the transmission of signal and the receipt of the echo is recorded in the instrument. If (d) is depth of the river

then, $2d$ = velocity of sound in water × time (t).

Measurement of Velocity

The most commonly used instrument to measure velocity of a stream is called a **Current meter** (Fig. 12.3 and 12.4). It is a mechanical device consisting essentially of a rotating element. These are of two types,

(i) Cup type (Price) vertical axis currentmeter

(ii) Propeller type a horizontal axis currentmeter.

The rotating elements consisting of cups or propellers and these are calibrated to get a relation between stream velocity and number of rotations of these elements.

As already discussed the average velocity in a vertical occurs approximately at 0.6 depth below the water surface,

$$\text{or } v_{\text{average}} = v_{0.6}.$$

This gives good result for shallow channels upto a maximum depth of 3 m. For deeper streams, velocities are measured at 0.2 depth and 0.8 depth and the average velocity in the vertical is taken as,

$$v_{average} = \frac{v_{0.2} + v_{0.8}}{2}$$

For rivers in spate, having flood flows, surface velocity is measured and average velocity is found by,

$$v_{\text{average}} = Kv_s, \quad v_s = \text{surface velocity.}$$

K varies between 0.85 to 0.95.

Velocity Measurement by Currentmeter: Currentmeter having sounding weight is hanged below the water surface at required depth (0.2 *d*, 0.6 *d* or 0.8 *d*) with cups or vanes facing upstream. The velocity is calculated from the calibration formula,

$$v = a\,N_s + b$$

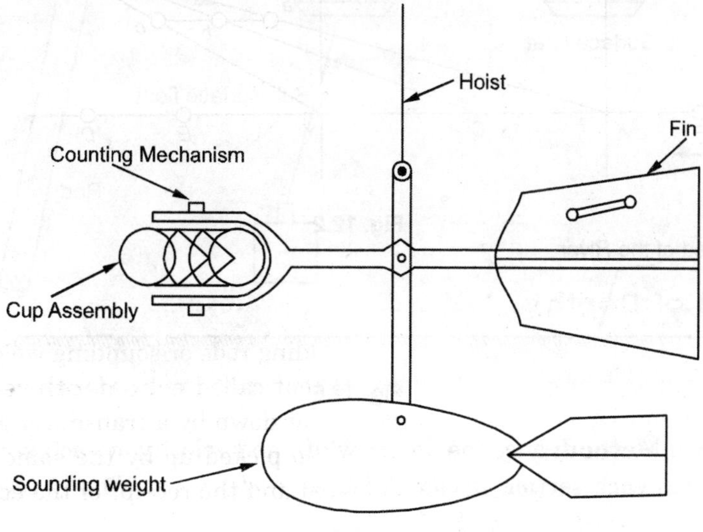

Fig. 12.3

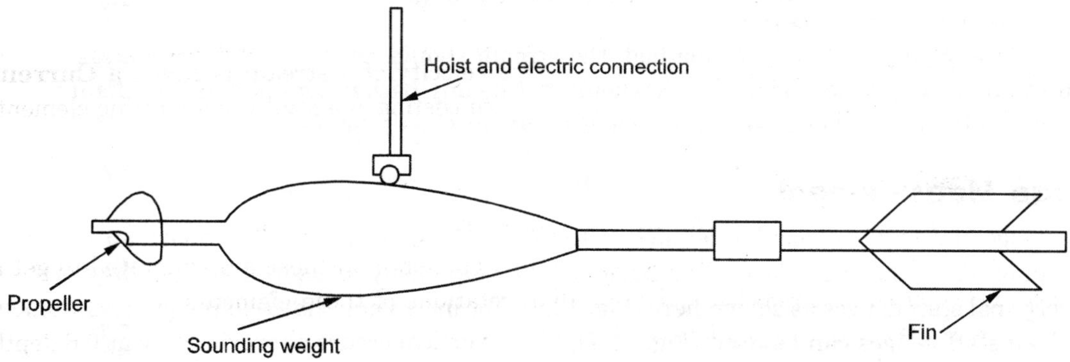

Fig. 12.4

Where, v is the stream velocity and N_s revolutions of the cups or vanes per unit time, a and b are constants of meter, (normally a and b values are provided by the manufacturer of the currentmeter). The range of velocity measured by currentmeter is between 15 cm to 4 m/s.

Surface Velocity Measurement

Normally surface velocity is measured with the help of floats. A simple float is made to move on the stream surface (surface float). Two locations are selected on the river bank. From upstream some distance float is released, the time taken by the float between two points is recorded with the help of stop watch. The surface floats may get affected by wind. To avoid this special floats are used like **canister floats** and **rod floats** (Fig. 12.5).

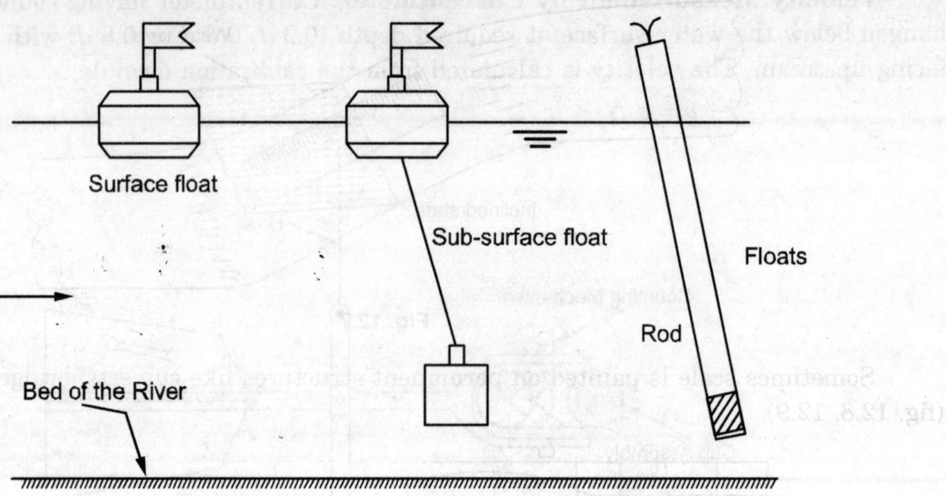

Fig. 12.5

Area-Velocity Method: once the depth, width and velocity at each section is measured, discharge (q) through each section is calculated as $q = b \times y \times v$. Finally the discharge (Q) is calculated as,

$$Q = \sum_{i=1}^{n} q_i \quad \text{Where, } q \text{ is the discharge in the } i^{\text{th}} \text{ section.}$$

For applying area-velocity method, the stream should have a well defined cross-section and should be easily accessible. There should not be any backwater effect in the channel. For better result the number of sections should be as large as possible.

Stage Measurement

The stage of any river may be defined as the *R.L*, of the water surface above an arbitrary datum or above mean sea level. The stage can be very easily measured by installing vertical or sectional staff gauges as shown here (Fig. 12.6). For increasing the accuracy in measurement inclined staff gauges can be used (Fig. 12.7).

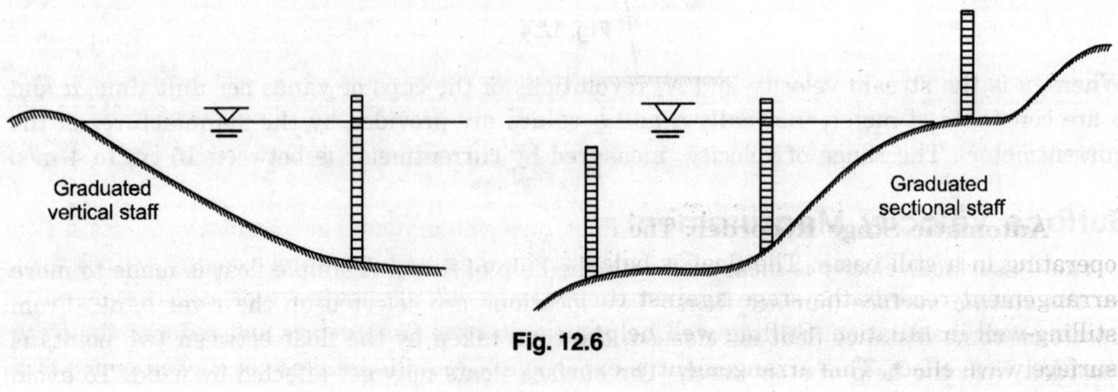

Fig. 12.6

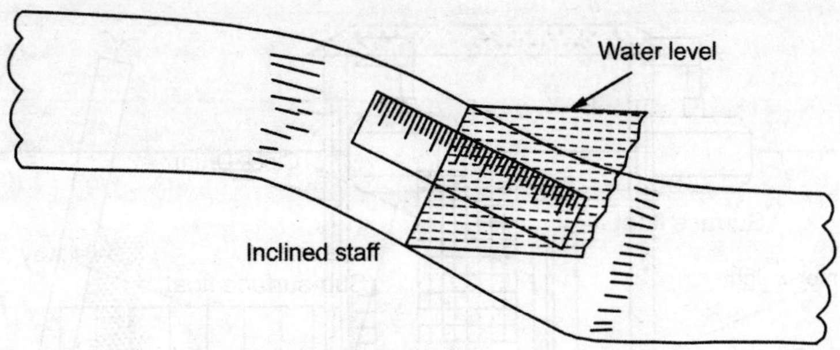

Fig. 12.7

Sometimes scale is painted on permanent structures like culverts, bridge piers or steps (fig. 12.8, 12.9).

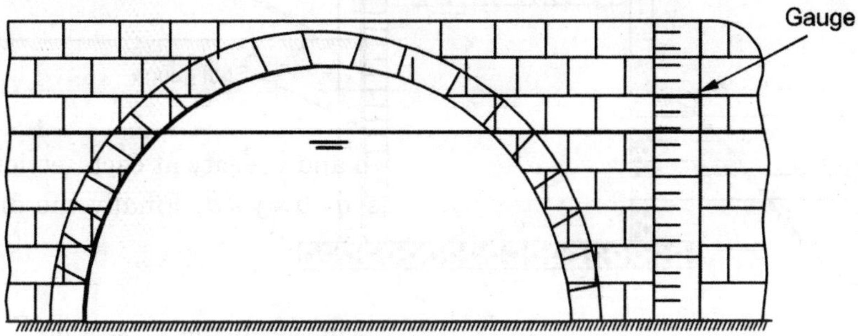

Culvert

Fig. 12.8

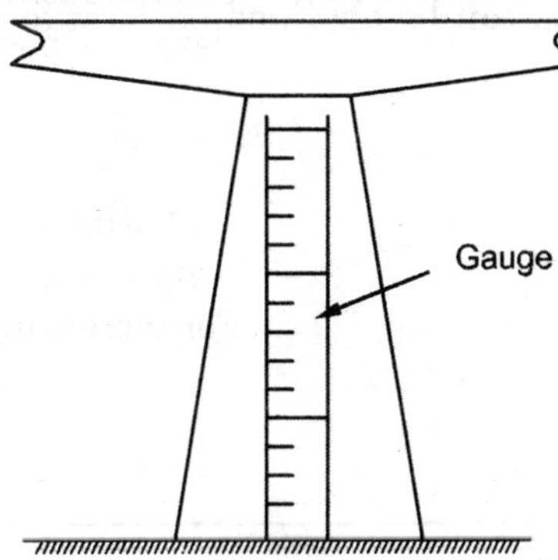

Bridge Pier

Fig. 12.9

Automatic Stage Recorder: The float type automatic stage recorder requires a float operating in a still basin. The float is balanced by means of a counter weight. A clock-drum arrangement records the stage against time. Figure 12.10 shows a typical arrangement of stilling-well installation. Stilling well helps in protection from debris and reduces the water surface wave effect. This arrangement is expensive. Often the intakes get choked which need to be cleared periodically.

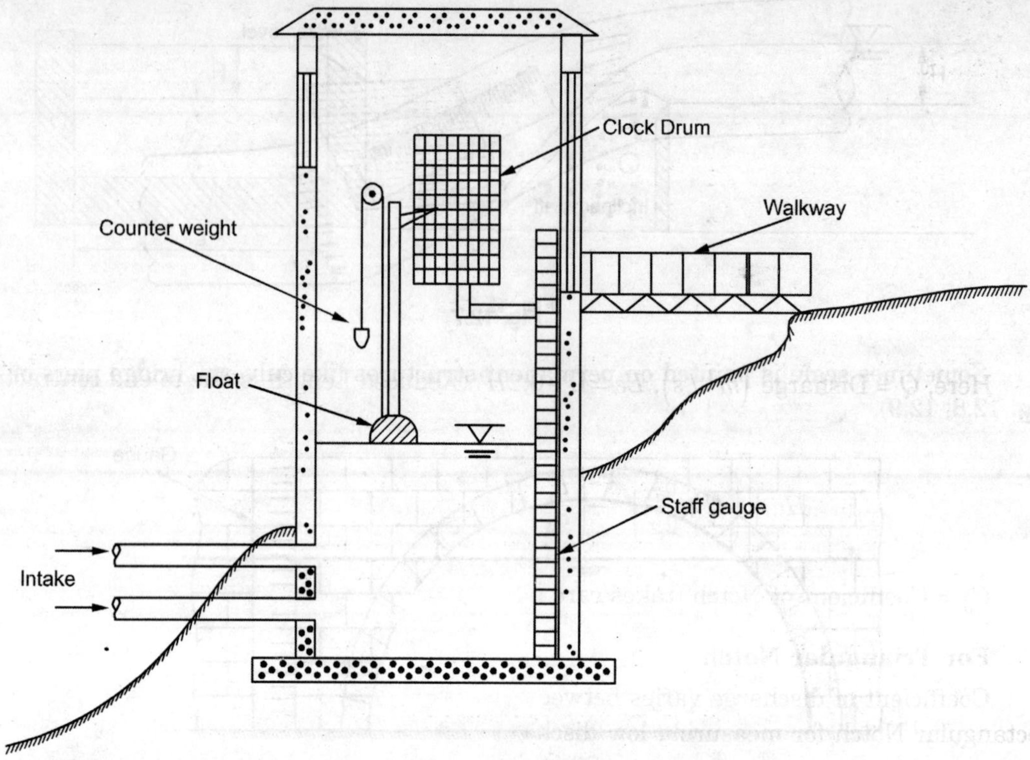

Fig. 12.10

From this system stage data can be obtained on minute to minute basis in the form of a stage hydrograph (Fig. 12.11).

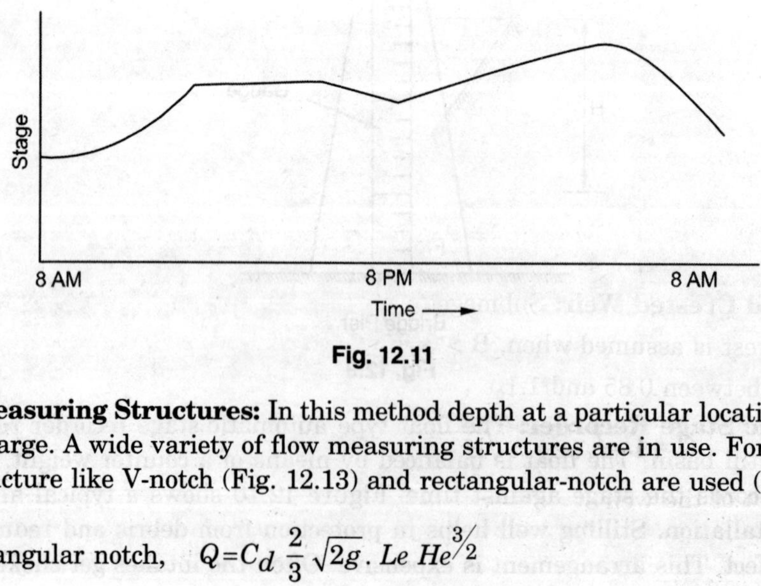

Fig. 12.11

Flow Measuring Structures: In this method depth at a particular location is correlated with the discharge. A wide variety of flow measuring structures are in use. For small streams thin-plate structure like V-notch (Fig. 12.13) and rectangular-notch are used (Fig. 12.12).

For rectangular notch, $Q = C_d \frac{2}{3} \sqrt{2g}\,.\, Le\, He^{3/2}$

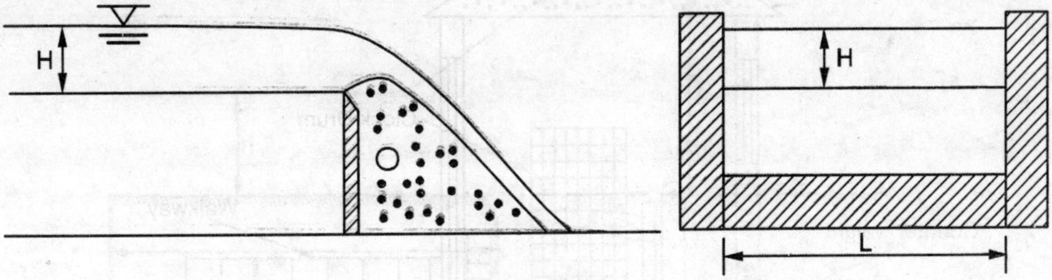

Fig. 12.12

Here, Q = Disharge $\left(m^3 / s\right)$, $Le = L - 0.2H$ (Reduced Length is due to end contractions)

$$He = \left[\left(H + \frac{v_a^2}{2g}\right)^{3/2} - \left(\frac{v_a^2}{2g}\right)^{3/2}\right], \quad V_a = \text{ Velocity of Approach}$$

C_d = Coefficient of Notch (takes care of friction loss) = 0.62 (approx.)

For Triangular Notch

Coefficient of discharge varies between 0.58 to 0.68 Triangular Notch is preferred over Rectangular Notch for measuring low discharges.

$$Q = C_d \frac{8}{15}\sqrt{2g}\tan\frac{\theta}{2} H^{\frac{5}{2}}$$

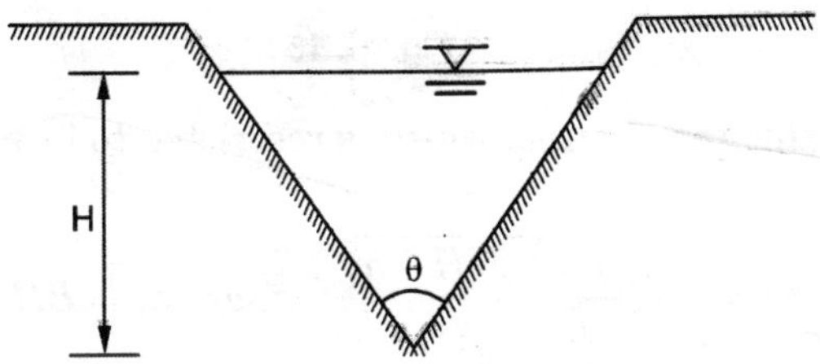

Fig. 12.13

For Broad Crested Weir: Submeged weir (Fig. 12.14).

A broad crest is assumed when, B > 3H

Cd varies between 0.85 and 1.1.

$$Q = C_d L\sqrt{2g}\, h\sqrt{H - h}$$

L = Length of the weir

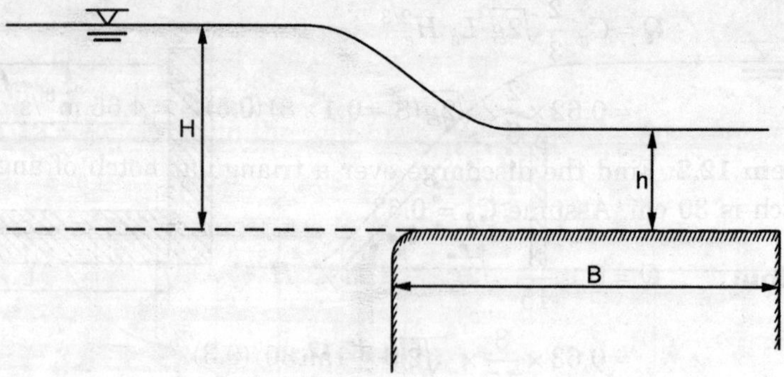

Fig. 12.14

Cippoletti Notch: This is a trapezoidal notch and does not need correction for end contraction. The slope is 1:4 (fig. 12.15)

$$Q = C_d \frac{2}{3}\sqrt{2g}\ L H^{3/2}, \qquad C_d \approx 0.63$$

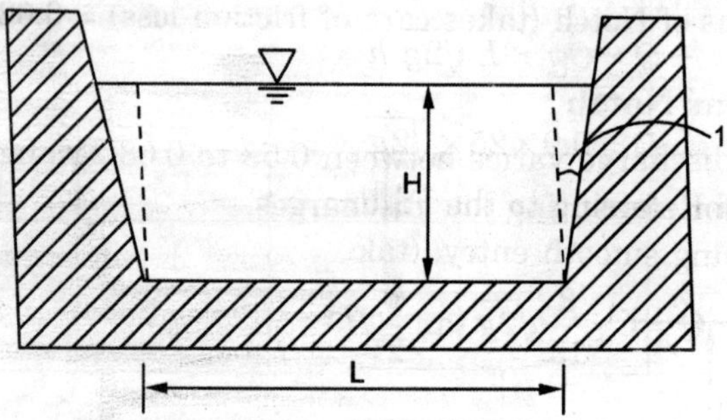

Fig. 12.15

Meter Flume: In this the channel width is restricted to form a throat with smooth entry and exit.

$$Q = \frac{C\, a_1\, a_2 \sqrt{2g(H-h)}}{\sqrt{a_1^2 - a_2^2}}, \text{ where } a_1 = BH;\ a_2 = bh$$

Problem 12.1: A rectangular notch (weir) 8m wide is divided into 4 bays by 3- vertical posts each 30 cm. wide find the discharge at a head of 0.5m.

Solution:

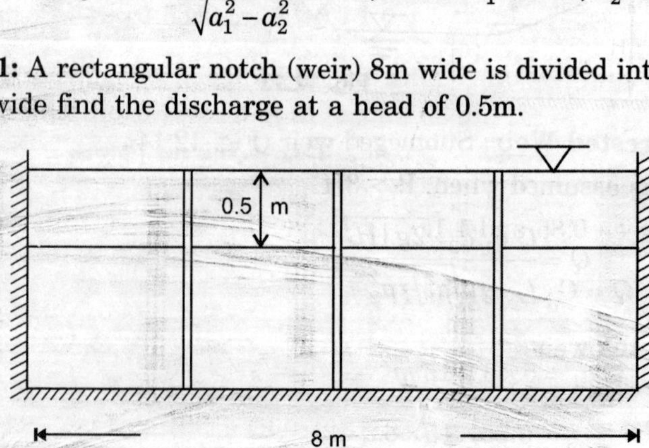

Fig. 12.16

$$Q = C_d \frac{2}{3}\sqrt{2g}\ L_e\ H_e^{2/3}$$

$$= 0.62 \times \frac{2}{3} \times \sqrt{2g}(8 - 0.1 \times 8)(0.5)^{3/2} = 4.65\ \text{m}^3/\text{s}$$

Problem 12.2: Find the discharge over a triangular notch of angle 60° when the head over the notch is 30 cm. Assume $C_d = 0.63$.

Solution: $$Q = C_d\ \frac{8}{15}\ \sqrt{2g}\quad \tan\theta/2\ H^{5/2}$$

$$= 0.63 \times \frac{8}{15} \times \sqrt{2g} \times \tan 30^\circ (0.3)^{5/2}$$

$$= 0.63 \times \frac{8}{15} \times 4.429 \times 0.57 \times 0.049 = 0.0415\ \text{m}^3/\text{s}$$

Prob. 12.3: A broad crested weir 25m in length has water head over the crest of 0.5m. Find the maximum discharge if upstream head is 1.5m.

Solution: Assume $C_d = 0.9$

$$Q = C_d \times L\sqrt{2g}\ h\ \sqrt{H - h}$$

$$Q = 0.9 \times 25 \times \sqrt{2g} \times 0.5 \times \sqrt{1.5 - .5} = 49.8\ \text{m}^3/\text{s}$$

Problem 4: Referring to the Figure below if H = 3m, h = 2m; B = 5m, b = 4m, Find the discharge, assuming smooth entry, (take C = 0.85).

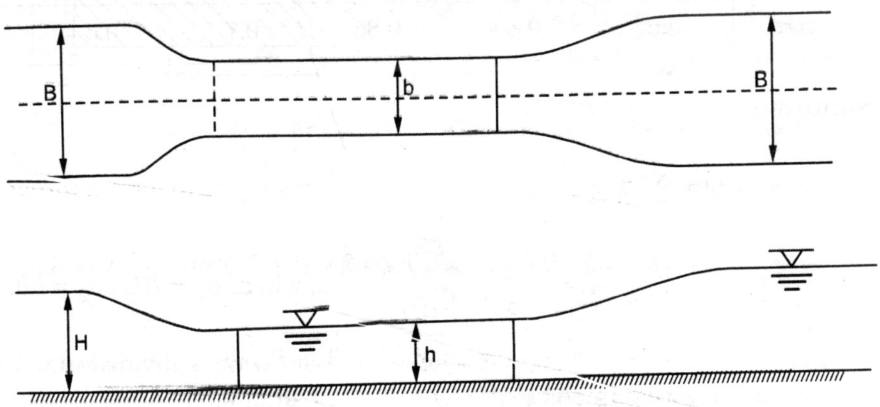

Fig. 12.17

Solution: $$Q = \frac{C\ a_1\ a_2\sqrt{2g\,(H - h)}}{\sqrt{a_1^2 - a_2^2}}$$

Now, $a_1 = 5 \times 3 = 15\ m^2 \qquad a_2 = 4 \times 2 = 8\ m^2$

$$Q = \frac{0.85 \times 15 \times 8 \times \sqrt{2 \times 9.81 \times 1}}{\sqrt{225 - 64}}$$

$$Q = \frac{0.85 \times 15 \times 8 \times 4.429}{12.688} = 35.6\ m^{3/s}$$

Problem 12.5 Referring to the following figure find the discharge in the river.

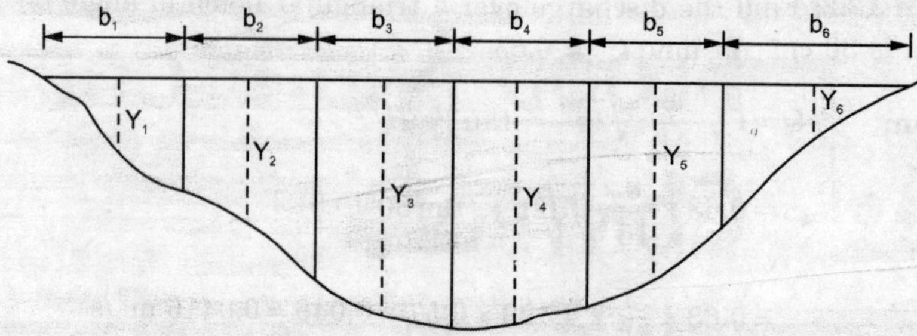

Fig. 12.18

b	b_1	b_2	b_3	b_4	b_5	b_6
m	12	12	12	12	12	8
y						
m	2.1	5.1	7.5	3.9	1.5	0.7
v						
m/s	0.6	0.8	0.85	0.7	0.5	0.4

Solution:

$$Q = \sum_{z=0}^{z=6} b_i\ y_i\ v_i$$

$$= 12 \times 2.1 \times 0.6 + 12 \times 5.1 \times 0.8 + 12 \times 7.5 \times 0.85 + 12 \times 3.9 \times 0.7$$

$$+ 12 \times 1.5 \times 0.5 + 8 \times 0.7 \times 0.4$$

$$= 12 \times (1.26 + 4.08 + 6.375 + 2.37 + 0.75) + 8 \times 0.7 \times 0.4$$

$$= 12 \times 15.195 + 2.24$$

$$= 182.34 + 2.24 = 184.58\ \text{m}^3/\text{s}$$

CHAPTER 13

FLOOD AND FLOOD CONTROL

Flood control is the art or technique of controlling river flow so as to minimize the occurrence of flood and to reduce the effect of inundation.

FLOOD

A flood is an overflow of water that submerges the land that is usually dry. Flooding may occur as an overflow of water from water bodies, such as a river, lake or ocean, in which water overtops the banks or breaks levees.

In rivers when the flow rate exceeds the capacity of the river channel, the flood situation occurs. Some floods develop slowly, while others such as flash floods and flood due to failure of embankments can develop in just a few minutes and without visible signs of rain.

Etymology: The word 'flood' comes from the old English **flod**, a word common to Germanic languages (German-Flut, Dutch-Vloed from the same root as seen in flow, float; also Latin- fluctus, flumen). Deluge myths are mythical stories of great floods sent by a **deity** or deities to destroy civilization as an act of divine retribution, and they are featured in the mythology of many cultures.

Main Types of Flood

Areal floods happen on flat or low-lying areas when water is supplied by rainfall or other causes more rapidly than it can either infiltrate or runoff. The excess accumulates in places, many times to hazardous depths. Reduced infiltration capacity is due to saturation of soil, concrete paving and frozen ground. Areal flooding begins in flat areas like floodplains and in local depressions not connected to a stream channel, because the velocity of flow is small in mild slopes.

Riverine or channel flood occurs in all types of river and stream channels, from the smallest ephemeral streams to the world's largest rivers. Localized flooding may be caused or worsened by drainage congestion due to landslides, rail and road embankment and land-use pattern. Slow-rising floods commonly occur in large rivers with vast catchments. Rapid flooding events more often occur on smaller rivers. The main cause may be localized convective precipitation or sudden release of water from an upstream impoundment.

Flash Floods are most common flood type in normally dry channels in arid zones. The first flood water to arrive is depleted by infiltration. The leading edge of the flood thus advances more slowly than later and higher flows. As a result the rising limb of the **hydrograph** gets steeper, ifiltration becomes insignificant.

Estuarine and coastal floods are caused by high upstream river flow and sea-tidal surges. The rise in water level can cause extreme flooding in coastal areas particularly when storm surge due to cyclone coincides with normal high tide, resulting storm tides of upto 6-7m. or even more in some cases. Extreme case may occur due to **tsunami**.

Urban flooding which is now rapidly increasing is defined as the inundation of land or property in the built-up environment, mainly in densely populated areas, caused by rainfall overwhelming the capacity of drainage system, such as storm sewers. Urban flooding is a condition, characterized by its repetitive and systematic impacts on communities even when they are not living in designated floodplains or near any body of water. The flood flow in urbanized areas constitutes a hazard to both population and infrastructure.

Flood flows in urban environment are being studied now after some catastrophes of the kind almost all over the world.

Catastrophic riverine flooding usually associated with major structural failures like the failure of a dam, or by drainage modification from a landslide, earthquake or volcanic eruption. In this category Tsumani can cause major devastation in coastal flooding, which most commonly results from undersea earthquakes.

Effects: The primary effects of flooding include loss of life, damage to buildings and other structures, including bridges, sewerage systems, roadways, and canals.

Methods of Flood Control

Man has always tried to protect himself from the fury of floods. Some methods of flood control have been practised since ancient times. These methods include planting vegetation (aforestation) to retain flood water, hillside terracing to slow down the flow and also increase infiltration, confine flow between levees and dikes, store water in reservoirs created by construction of dams and retention ponds to hold extra water.

Advantages of Floods

Besides disruptive effects of flooding on human settlements and economic activities, flooding can bring benefits also, such as making soil more fertile by providing nutrients in which it is deficient. Also, the viability for hydrologically based renewable sources of energy is higher in flood-prone, regions.

Floods can also play an important role in maintaining ecosystem functions and biodiversity. The river and surrounding land gets linked, it recharges groundwater systems, fill wetlands, increase the connectivity between aquatic habitats, and move sediment and nutrients around the landscape and into the marine environment. For number of species, floods trigger breeding events, migration, and dispersal.

Disadvantages of Floods

In general floods cause significant damage to the economy, infrastructure, property and environment. We all understand that the immediate impacts of flooding include loss of human life, damage to property, destruction of crops, loss of livestock and deterioration of health conditions owing to waterborne diseases.

Communication links and infrastructure such as power plants, roads and bridges are damaged and economic activities come to standstill. Most of the time people have to be shifted to higher locations and have to live in relief camps, which provide only life-saving service.

There is disruption to industry which lead to loss of livelihood. Long term impacts include disruption to supplies of clean and potable water, wastewater treatment, electric supply, transport system, communication, education and health care.

The consequences of floods, vary greatly depending on their location, duration, depth and speed, as well as the vulnerability and value of the affected natural and constructed environments.

Flooding in main agriculture production areas can lead to widespread damage to crops and loss of livestock. Crop losses through rain damage, waterlogged soils, and delays in harvesting are further intensified by transport problems due to damaged roads and inundation.

Floods also traumatise victims for long periods of time. Loss of dear ones can have deep impacts, particularly on children. Displacement from own home, loss of property, disruption in business and social affairs cause continuous stress. For most of the victims the impact is long lasting.

Areas that have been highly modified by human activity tend to suffer more serious effects from flooding. Floods accelerate degrading of the system.

It is now universally accepted that floods cannot be stopped altogether and can be controlled only to the extent justifiable by benefits accrued. Therefore, instead of using the term flood control, the term flood mitigation or damage mitigation seem to be more appropriate.

Popular methods of Flood Control

(1) **Construction of Dams:** Dams generally serve the primary purpose of retaining water, while other structures such as levees or floodgates or dikes are used to prevent water flow into specific land areas.

Reservoirs created by dams not only suppress floods but also provide water for various other purposes such as irrigation, human use, industrial use, aqua-culture, navigation and recreation. Hydropower is often used in conjunction with dams to generate electricity. It is well understood that Dams were built for water storage, irrigation and power generation. Recently dams are also built solely for the purpose of flood control. Groups of dams built on the headwaters of streams allow for retention of heavy runoff which can then be released during the dry periods. Dams which are constructed solely for the purpose of flood control are sometimes known as **dry dams.**

(2) **Construction of Diversion Canals:** Diversion Canals or floodways are man-made channels built to provide a different route for excess water to flow further mitigating the effects of flooding and restoring rivers to their natural water level. Typically diversion channels are made around communities or economic centres to prevent

extensive flood damage. These channels are only used in times of need. Through diversion channels water is routed to the temporary holding ponds or other bodies of water with lower risk or impact of flooding.

Redistribution of water from one region to another region which is facing drought can help in mitigating the effect of drought.

The environmental impacts of diversion channels, downstream of where water is diverted include loss of habitat and impact on bio-diversity. There is also probability of transfer of flood from one watershed causing flood to other region.

(3) **Floodplain Groundwater Replenishment (Recharge):** As there is excess depletion of groundwater the floodwater can be used for groundwater replenishment by diversion onto land that can absorb the water at faster rate. This method can reduce the impact of later droughts by using the ground as a natural reservoir. In many countries areas which are least damaged by inundation are identified and floodwater is spread in such areas which results in replenishment of groundwater and reduction in flood.

(4) **Jacketing of Rivers:** In many countries large numbers of rivers are prone to floods. To manage these floods defenses such as levees, bunds, reservoirs and weirs are used to prevent rivers from bursting their banks. Sometimes river jacketing proves to be disastrous. Though river's flow could be controlled but there is no way to check the resulting siltation. This has complicated matters. In the event of breach of embankment there is large scale loss of life and assets.

Experts argue that building embankments allowed too much silt deposition in a shorter stretch, leading to devastation.

Coastal Floods Remedy: Coastal floods occur when normally dry, low lying land area is flooded by seawater. This type of flooding occurs along the edges of oceans, and is driven by storm surges and waves. Normally, these are connected to hurricanes, tsunamis or tropical storms.

It is now well understood that one way to prevent flooding of coastal areas now and into the future is by reducing global sea rise. In addition more immediate measures of engineered and natural defences are construction of hard engineering structures such as **seawalls** and **levees**. Structures like groynes and breakwaters and artificial headlands promote the deposition of sediment on the beach, thus helping to buffer against storm waves and surges.

Temporary Methods: When permanent defenses fail, emergency measures such as sandbags, hydrosacks, flood barriers etc. are used. Aqua Fence, a transportable, removable, and reusable flood barrier which uses the water's weight against itself.

Flood Estimation: Various methods for estimation of flood peak are in use all over the world. Mainly surface runoff is the cause of flood, which depends upon various factors like soil porosity and degree of saturation of the soil in the catchment area; the shape and slope of catchment area; obstacles to flow; degree of vegetation; state of cultivation; rainfall intensity and evaporation. For estimation of Runoff Empirical Formulae, Rational Method, Unit Hydrograph technique and Flood-Frequency studies are popular methods.

Empirical Formulae: These are essentially regional formulae based on statistics correlation and important catchment characteristics. Most of the empirical relationships describe Peak Discharge (Qp) as a function of Area of the Catchment (A),

$$Q_p = f(A).$$

Among the vast number of this kind proposed for various parts of the world, one of the oldest and still popular is Dicken's Formula (1865),

$$Q_p = CA^{3/4}$$

where Q_p = Peak Discharge in m^3/s

A = Catchment Area in Km^2

C = Dicken's constant with value between 6 to 30

Note: Other empirical formulae can be found in any standard book of Hydrology and water Resources Engineering.

Rational Method: Rational Formula is one of the simplest method to determine peak discharge from a drainage basin. Consider a rainfall of Uniform Intensity and long duration over a basin. From the start of rainfall the runoff increases till the time of concentration (t_c) (which is defined as the time taken by a drop of water from farthest point of catchment to reach the outlet) is reached.

The normal form of the formula in commonly used units is given below:

$$Q_p = C.I.A/3.6$$

where, Q_p is the Peak flood flow in Cumec.

I is Mean Rainfall Intensity in mm/Hour for a duration equal to t_c and an exceedence probability p.

A is Area of Basin in Km^2

C is Runoff Coefficient depending on Basin characteristics.

Formulae for Time of Concentration (t_c)

Number of formulae are in use to find out the time of concentration. Z.P. Kirpich's formula is popular for finding out t_c.

$$t_c = 0.00032\ L^{0.77}\ S^{-0.385}$$

where, t_c is time of concentration in Hours

L is the maximum length of travel of water from the farthest point in the basin to the outlet (Gauging Station) in meters.

S is Slope of the basin.

Formula for Rainfall Intensity (I) (Known as Intensity-Duration – Frequency Relationship): Intensity I is given by

$$I = \frac{KT^x}{(D + a)^n}$$

where, K, x, a and n are the constants for a given catchment. T is the Return Period (=1/P, P is Probability) and D is duration of Rainfall.

(**Note:** Values for constants have been found by Central Soil and Water Conservation Research and Training Institute Dehradun. D and T relations have been prepared by I.M.D for the whole country).

Value of Runoff Coefficient

The Runoff Coefficient C represents the integrated effect of catchment losses and hence depends upon the nature of the surface, state of the land and of course the rainfall intensity. Value of C has been estimated for various types of areas. For example C is given as 0.3 to 0.5 for residential areas, 0.5 to 0.95 for industrial areas and 0.1 to 0.5 for agricultural land.

(**Note:** Detailed list can be found on any standard hydrology book)

Sometimes, a non-homogeneous catchment may be divided into sub-areas and C is calculated by the following formula,

$$C = \sum_{i}^{N} \frac{C_i A_i}{A}, \text{ where } C_i \text{ coefficient of } i^{\text{th}} \text{ area.}$$

Problem 13.1. Information on a 50-year storm is given below:

Durations (Minutes)	15	30	45	60	180
Rainfall (mm)	40	60	75	100	120

A Culvert has to drain 200 ha of land with a maximum length of travel of 1.5 km. The general slope is 0.0015 and its runoff coefficient is 0.22. Estimate the Peak flow by Rational Method for designing the culvert for 50 years flood.

Solution: By Kirpich's Formula, Time of concentration.

$$t_c = 0.00032\ L^{0.77}\ S^{-0.385}$$

$$= 0.00032 \times (1500)^{0.77} \,.\, (0.0015)^{-0.385} = 1.09 \text{ hours}$$

for tc = 1.09 Hours (or 65.5 minutes)

Rainfall = 101.6 mm. (By interpolation)

$$\therefore \quad I = \frac{101.6}{1.09} = 93.2 \text{ mm/Hour}$$

$$Q = \frac{1}{3.6} \times 0.22 \times 93.2 \times 2 = 11.39 \text{ m}^3/\text{s}$$

Problem 13.2. A basin is divided by l-h isochrones (lines joining points having equal time of travel of surface runoff) into four Sub-areas of size 200, 250, 350 and 170 ha from the upstream end of the outlet respectively. A rainfall of 5-h duration with intensities of 1.7 cm/hr for the first 2h and 1.25 cm/h for the next 3h occurs uniformly over the basin. Assuming a constant runoff coefficient of 0.5. Find the peak rate of runoff.

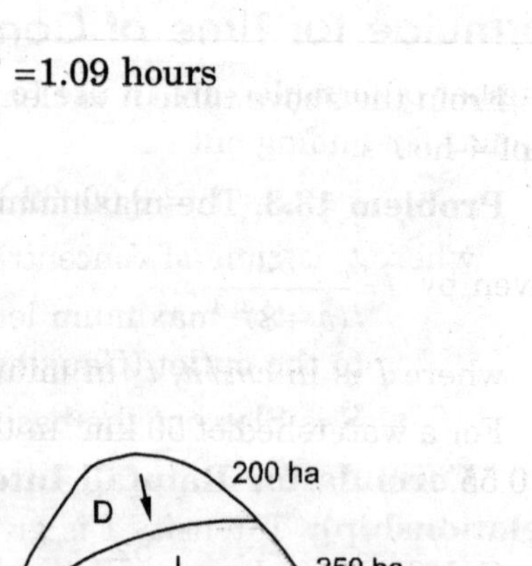

Fig. 13.1

Solution: The contribution to runoff would occur as follows,

Time (h)	*Rainfall (cm / hr)*	*Sub Area*
1st h	1.7 cm/hr	On A
2nd h	1.7 cm/hr	On A and B
3rd h	1.7 cm/hr, 1.25 cm/h	On C and B and 1.25 cm/h on A
4th h	1.7 cm/hr, 1.25 cm/h	On D and C and 1.25 cm/h on B and A
5th h.	1.7 cm/h, 1.25 cm/h	1.7 cm/h on D, and 1.25 cm/hr on C,B and A.

The discharge at the end of various intervals is calculated by Rational Formula, $Q = \frac{1}{3.6} \times C \times I \times A.$

At the end of	Q_A	Q_B	Q_C	Q_D	*Total Q* (m^3/s)
1 h	4.014				4.014
2 h	4.014	8.256			12.27
3 h	2.95	8.256	6.076		17.28
4 h	2.95	6.076	5.91	4.72	19.656
5 h	2.95	6.076	4.34	4.72	18.08

From the above table it is clear that Peak Rate of Runoff = 19.656 m^3/s and occurs at the end of 4-hours.

Problem 13.3. The maximum rainfall intensity of 50 years return period over a region is given by $I = \frac{52}{(t_c + 8)^{0.4}}$.

where I is in cm/h, t_c in minutes

For a watershed of 50 km^2 in this region with t_c = 2h, eastimate the flood Peak, assuming C = 0.55.

Solution: $I = \frac{52}{(120+8)^{0.4}} = 7.466$ cm/h

$$Q_p = 2.78 \text{ CIA}$$

$$= 2.78 \times 0.55 \times 7.466 \times 50 = 570.77 \ m^3/s$$

Unit Hydrograph Technique

Probably the most popular and widely used method for predicting flood hydrograph resulting from a known storm is the **unit hydrograph method**. The method was propagated by L.K. Sharman in 1932 and has undergone many revisions since then.

A unit hydrograph (UH) of any drainage basin can be defined as a hydrograph of direct runoff resulting from unit (1 mm or 1 cm) of rainfall excess generated uniformly over the basin at uniform rate during specified period of time (called Unit Duration).

Note: A D-Hour Unit Hydrograph for a basin would mean a hydrograph of direct runoff resulting from a D-hour long storm producing a direct runoff of 1 mm (or 1 cm).

Limitations of Unit Hydrograph Theory

The theory of Unit Hydrograph is based on the following assumptions.

(a) The rainfall is uniformly distributed over the whole area of the basin.

(b) The intensity of rainfall is constant for the whole period of storm.

(c) The base period of the unit hydrograph for a given drainage basin remains constant for a particular duration of rainfall irrespective of the rainfall intensity.

(d) The ordinates of the hydrograph are directly proportional to the ordinates of the unit hydrograph and are obtained by multiplying the unit hydrograph by the amount of rainfall excess. This assumption is termed as "assumption of linear response".

(e) The Unit Hydrograph represents the lumped (combined) response of the catchment and thus reflects all the physical charactristics of the basin.

In the light of the above assumptions it may be concluded that the unit hydrograph theory is limited to use for short duration rainfalls over comparatively smaller basins of compact shape. This theory cannot be applied to snow-fed basins.

How to Derive a Unit Hydrograph: The direct method for deriving a unit hydrograph involves the analysis of a simple hydrograph resulting from an isolated unit storm that produces reasonably uniform effective rainfall rates within its duration. Following procedure is adopted in determining unit hydrograph from a simple hydrograph.

Step I: From the past records select some unit period of intense rainfall duration corresponding to an isolated storm uniformly distributed over the area.

Step II: From the records of the river discharge for the above storm plot the storm hydrograph for some days before and after the rainfall of the given duration.

Step III: Separate the base flow and direct runoff.

Step IV: Calculate the Volume of Direct Runoff (in cm or mm.) as follows:

$$\textbf{Direct Runoff} = \frac{\text{Total Volume of Direct Runoff}}{\text{Area of the Basin}} = \left[\frac{\Sigma O \times t \times 60 \times 60}{A \times 10^6}\right] \times 100 \text{ cm}$$

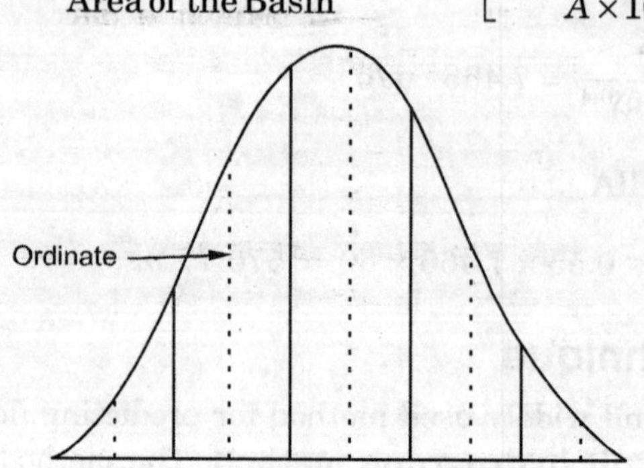

Fig. 13.2

where, t = time interval between successive ordinates

A = Area of Basin in Km^2

ΣO = sum of discharge ordinates in Cumecs.

Step V: Calculate the ordinates of the unit Hydrograph by dividing ordinates of the Direct Runoff Hydrograph by Direct Runoff (in cm or mm) as calculated in Step IV.

Problem 13.4. The following are the ordinates of the hydrograph of flow from a catchment area of 770 km^2 due to a 6-h rainfall. Derive the ordinates of a 6-h unit Hydrograph. Make Suitable assumptions regarding the base flow.

Time from Beginning of Stoms (h)	0	6	12	18	24	30	36	42	48	54	60	66	72
Discharge m^3/s	40	65	215	360	400	350	270	205	145	100	70	50	42

Solution: Depth of Direct Runoff $= \left[\dfrac{\Sigma O \times t \times 60 \times 60}{A \times 10^6}\right] \times 100\,\text{cm.}$

$$= 0.36\,\frac{\Sigma O \times t}{A} = \frac{0.36 \times 1781 \times 6}{770} = 5 \text{ cm}$$

$$\text{Ordinates of Unit Hydrograph} = \frac{\text{Ordinates of Direct Runoff}}{5} \qquad \text{(column 5)}$$

Time (hour) (1)	*Ordinates of Flood Hydrograph m^3/s (2)*	*Base flow m^3/s (3)*	*Direct Runoff Hydrograph ordinates m^3/s (4)*	*6-hour unit Hydrographs ordinates m^3/s (5)*
0	40	40	0	0
6	65	40	25	5
12	215	40	175	35
18	360	40	320	64
24	400	40	360	72
30	350	40	310	62
36	270	41	229	46
42	205	41	164	33
48	145	41	104	21
54	100	42	58	11.6
60	70	42	28	5.6
66	50	42	8	1.6
72	42	42	0	0
			ΣO =1781	

Problem 13.5. The Ordinates of a 6-h unit hydrograph are given below,

Time (h)	0	6	12	18	24	30	36	42	48	54	60	66
Ordinates of 6-h Unit Hydrograph (m^3/s)	0	20	60	150	120	90	66	50	32	20	10	0

If two storms, each of 1 cm rainfall excess and 6-h duration occur in succession, calculate the resulting hydrograph of flow. Assume base flow to be uniform at 10 m^3/s.

Solution:

Time (h)	*Ordinates of 6-h unit Hydrograph* m^3/s	*6-h unit Hydrograph lagged by 6 hr*	*Direct Runoff Hydrograph*	*Base Flow* m^3/s	*Storm Hydrograph* m^3/s
0	0		0	10	10
6	20	0	20	10	30
12	60	20	80	10	90
18	150	60	210	10	220
24	120	150	270	10	280
30	90	120	210	10	220
36	66	90	156	10	166
42	50	66	116	10	126
48	32	50	82	10	92
54	20	32	52	10	62
60	10	20	30	10	40
66	0	10	10	10	20
72		0	0	10	10

Problem 13.6. The Ordinates of a 6-h unit hydrograph are:

Time (h)	**0**	**3**	**6**	**9**	**12**	**18**	**24**	**30**	**36**	**42**	**48**	**54**	**60**	**66**
6-h Unit Hydrograph Ordinate (m^3/s)	0	150	250	450	600	800	700	600	450	320	200	100	50	0

A storm had three successive 6-h intervals of rainfall magnitudes of 3.0, 5.0 and 4.0 cm. respectively. Assuming a ϕ -index of 0.2 cm/h and a base flow of 30 m^3/s, determine the resulting flow-hydrograph.

Solution:

Time (h)	0-6	6-12	12-18
Total Rainfall (cm)	3	5	4
Losses 6 × ϕ (cm)	1.2	1.2	1.2
Effects Rainfall (cm)	1.8	3.8	2.8

Time (h)	*6-h Unit Hydrograph Ordinates m^3/s*	*Rainfall Excess I Storm 1.8 cm*	*Rainfall Excess II Storm 3.8 cm*	*Rainfall Excess III Storm 2.8 cm*	*Base Flow (m3/5)*	*Flood Hydrograph Ordinates m^3/s*
0	0	0			30	30
3	150	270			30	300
6	250	450	0		30	480
9	450	810	570		30	1410
12	600	1080	1710	0	30	2820
18	800	1440	2280	700	30	4450
24	700	1260	3040	1680	30	6010
30	600	1080	2660	2240	30	6010
36	450	810	2280	1960	30	5080
42	320	576	1710	1680	30	3996
48	200	360	1216	1260	30	2866
54	100	180	760	896	30	1866
60	50	90	380	560	30	1060
66	0	0	190	280	30	500
72			0	140	30	170
78				0	30	30

SYNTHETIC UNIT HYDROGRAPH

For developing a unit hydrograph rainfall and river flow data are essential. For ungauged basins no records are available. To obtain unit hydrograph for such basins, selected basin characteristics are related to typical shape of unit hydrograph. Once such relationship is established between the basin parameters and unit hydrograph features for the basins with sufficient data, the same relations are applied to get unit hydrograph of ungauged basins of similar characteristics as that of gauged basin. The unit hydrograph thus obtained is known as **Synthetic unit hydrograph.**

Out of the many methods available Snyder's method is most popular. Snyder in 1938 analysed a number of hydrographs from drainage basins of USA and selected three parameters for the development of unit hydrograph. These parameters are,

The base period or base width (T)

The peak discharge (Q_p)

The lag time or the basin lag (t_p)

He proposed the following empirical equations for the above three parameters.

$$t_p = C_t \; (L.Lca)^{0.3} \text{ in Hours}$$

where, C_t is a regional constant representing average slope of the watershed and other parameters (varies between 1.0 to 2.2)

L is the length of mainstream from basin outlet to the remotest point on upstream boundary.

Lca is the distance along the mainstream from the basin outlet to a point on stream nearest to the centroid of the basin in km.

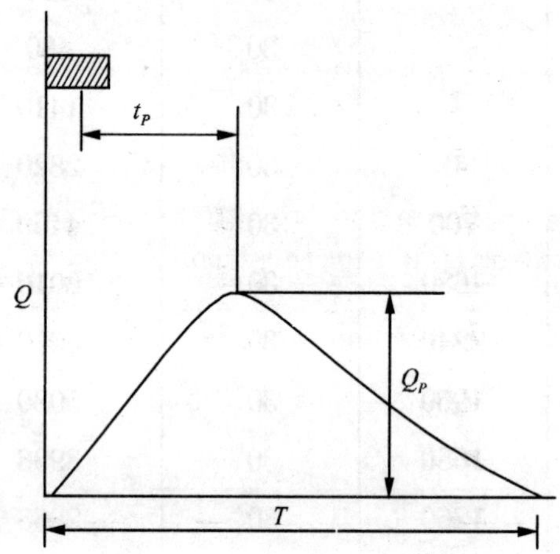

Fig. 13.3

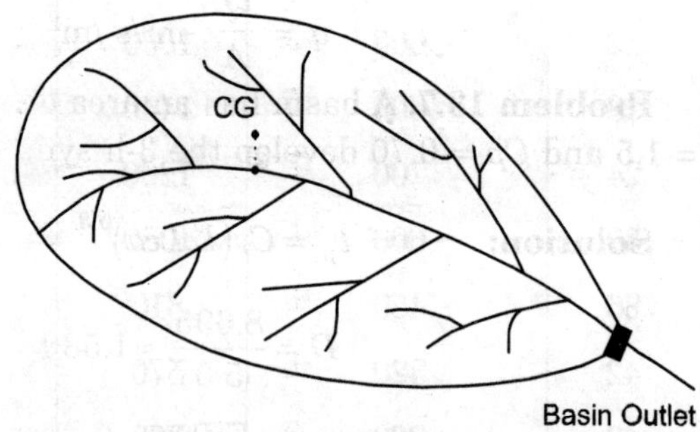

Fig. 13.4

$$Q_p = \frac{2.78\, C_p.A}{t_p}$$

where, C_p is a regional constant varying between 0.56 and 0.69

A is catchment Area in km^2

and $$T = 3 + 3.\frac{t_p}{24}.$$

where, T is the base period in days.

Standard Duration for the resulting unit hydrograph is estimated as,

$$D = \frac{t_p}{5.5}$$

In case a non-standard duration D′ is adopted instead of D, the value of basin lag is affected. The modified basin lag is given by,

$$t'_p = t_p + \frac{D' - D}{4}$$

where, t'_p is the basin lag in hours for an effective duration of D′.

∴ The Peak Discharge now will be

$$Q_p = \frac{2.78\,CpA}{t'_p}$$

and $$T = 3 + 3\frac{t'_p}{24} \text{ days.}$$

For plotting a reasonable unit hydrograph, the width of unit hydrograph at 50% and 75% of the peak have been suggested as,

$$W_{50} = \frac{5.87}{q^{1.08}} \text{ and } W_{75} = \frac{W_{50}}{1.75}$$

where, W_{50} is the width of unit hydrograph in hours at 50% Q_p.

W_{75} is the width of unit hydrograph in hours at 75% Q_p.

$$q = \frac{Q}{A}, \text{ m}^3\text{/s /m}^2$$

Problem 13.7. A basin has an area of 400 km^2, L = 35 km and Lca = 10 km. Assuming Ct = 1.5 and Cp = 0.70 develop the 3-h synthetic unit hydrograph for this basin.

Solution: $$t_p = C_t\,(L.Lca)^{0.3} = 1.5(35\times10)^{0.3} = 3.695 \text{ hours}$$

$$D = \frac{8.695}{5.5} = 1.58 \text{ h}$$

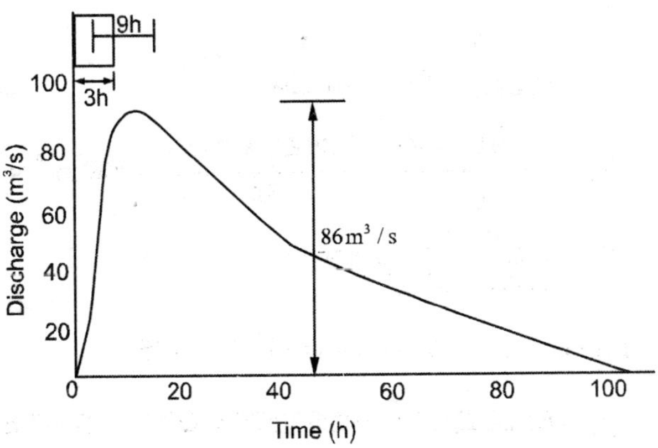

Fig. 13.5

Using $$D' = 3h\,;\; t'_p = 8.695 + \frac{3 - 1.58}{4} = 9.05 \text{ h}$$

∴ $$Q_p = \frac{2.78\times0.7\times400}{9.05} = 86 \text{ m}^3\text{/s}$$

$$W_{50} = \frac{5.87}{(86/400)^{1.08}} = 30.8\ h,\ W_{75} = \frac{30.8}{1.75} = 17.6\ h$$

Base period, $T = \left(3 + \frac{3 \times 9.05}{24}\right) 24 = 99$ hours

Problem 13.8. Characteristics of two catchments *M* and *N* measured from a map are given below. For a 6-h unit hydrograph in catchment *M*, the peak discharge is at 37 h from the start of the rainfall excess and its value is 200 m³/s. Assuming catchments M and *N* are meteorologically similar, determine the elements of a 6-h synthetic unit hydrograph for catchment N by using Snyder's Method.

Item	*Catchment M*	*Catchment N*
L_{ca}	76 km	52 km
L	148 km	106 km
A	2718 km²	1400 km²

Solution: Considering catchment *M*

$$D = 6\text{ h},\ \frac{D}{2} + t_p = 37$$

Or $\frac{6}{2} + t_p = 37$

∴ $t_p = 37 - 3 = 34\ h$

we know that $t_p = C_t (L.La)^{0.3}$

∴ $34 = C_t\ (148 \times 76)^{0.3}$

or $C_t = \frac{34}{(148 \times 76)^{0.3}} = \frac{34}{16.418} = 2.07$

also, $Q_p = \frac{2.78 C_p \times A}{t_p} = \frac{2.78\ C_p \times 2718}{34} = 200\ m^3/s$

∴ $C_p = \frac{200 \times 34}{2.78 \times 2718} = 0.9$

Considering Catchment N, $C_t = 2.07$ and $C_p = 0.9$

$$t_p = C_t\ (L.Lca)^{0.3} = 2.07(106 \times 52)^{0.3} = 27.43\ h$$

$$D = \frac{t_p}{5.5} = \frac{27.43}{5.5} = 5\ h$$

Using, $D' = 6\text{h}$

$$t_{p'} = t_p + \frac{D' - D}{4} = 27.45 + \frac{1}{4} = 27.68\,h$$

$$Q_p = \frac{2.78 \times 0.9 \times 1400}{27.68} = 126.54 \text{ m}^3/\text{s} = 127 \text{ m}^3/\text{s(say)}$$

$$W_{50} = \frac{5.87}{\left(\frac{127}{1400}\right)^{1.08}} = \frac{5.87}{0.0748} = 78.5\ h = 75\ h(say)$$

$$W_{75} = \frac{78.5}{1.75} = 44.8\ h = 45\ h(say)$$

$$\text{Base Period,} \quad T = 3 + 3 \times \frac{t_{p'}}{24} = 3 + \frac{27.68}{8} = 6.46 \text{ days} = 155\ h.$$

Flood-Frequency Studies

Like empirical formula and unit hydrograph methods, another approach to the prediction of flood flows is the statistical method of frequency analysis.

Frequency analysis deals with the analysis of flood flows at a station or at a particular location. The primary objective of frequency analysis is to obtain relation between the magnitude of an event and its probability of exceedence or recurrence interval. The analysis is made by either empirical method or by analytical method.

Empirical Method of Frequency Analysis

The values of annual maximum flood from a catchment area for large number of successive years constitute a hydrograph data series called the **annual series**. The data are arranged in decreasing order of magnitude and probability (P) of each event is calculated by any of the following formulae.

Formula Name	*Formula for Probability*
Weibull Formula	$\frac{m}{N+1}$
California Formula	$\frac{m}{N}$
Hazen Formula	$\frac{m-0.5}{N}$
Chegodayev Formula	$\frac{m-0.3}{N+0.4}$
Bloom Formula	$\frac{m-0.44}{N+0.12}$
Gringorten Formula	$\frac{m-3/8}{N+1/4}$

An order number 'm' is assigned to each value i.e., for first entry $m = 1$, for second $m = 2$ and for the Nth value $m = N$ (where N is the total number of observations).

The Return Period or Recurrence Interval then can be calculated as, $T = \frac{1}{P}$

After calculating P and T for all events from anyone of the above formulae, the variation of runoff magnitude is plotted against corresponding T on semi-log or log-log paper.

By extrapolating the above plot, the runoff magnitude of specific duration for any recurrence interval can be estimated.

Problem 13.9. The record for annual flood peaks of a stream for a period of 30 years from 1981 to 2010 in m^3/s are given below,

900	705	528	520	436	697	624	496	589	598
359	686	726	527	310	408	721	814	459	440
632	343	634	464	373	289	371	522	342	446

Construct the probability plot for annual flood magnitude with a return period of 50 years and 100 years.

Solution: First the data is arranged in descending order and their ranks mentioned. The return periods of floods are computed by Weibull's formula,

$$P = \frac{m}{N+1} \text{ and } T = \frac{N+1}{m}$$

Year	*Flood Peak* m^3/s	*Flood Peak in Descending Order* m^3/s	*Order* m	*Return Period* $T = \frac{30+1}{m}$
1981	900	900	1	31
1982	705	814	2	15.50
1983	528	726	3	10.33
1984	520	721	4	7.75
1985	436	705	5	6.20
1986	697	697	6	5.16
1987	624	686	7	4.42
1988	496	634	8	3.87
1989	589	632	9	3.44
1990	598	624	10	3.10
1991	359	598	11	2.82
1992	686	589	12	2.58
1993	726	528	13	2.38

1994	527	527	14	2.21
1995	310	522	15	2.06
1996	408	520	16	1.93
1997	721	496	17	1.82
1998	814	464	18	1.72
1999	459	459	19	1.63
2000	440	446	20	1.55
2001	632	443	21	1.47
2002	343	442	22	1.41
2003	634	436	23	1.34
2004	464	408	24	1.29
2005	373	373	25	1.24
2006	289	371	26	1.19
2007	371	359	27	1.14
2008	522	342	28	1.10
2009	342	310	29	1.06
2010	446	289	30	1.03

From Fig. 13.6 The return Period of 50 years, Q_{max} = 960 m^3/s and for Return Period of 100 years, Q_{max} = 1070 m^3/s.

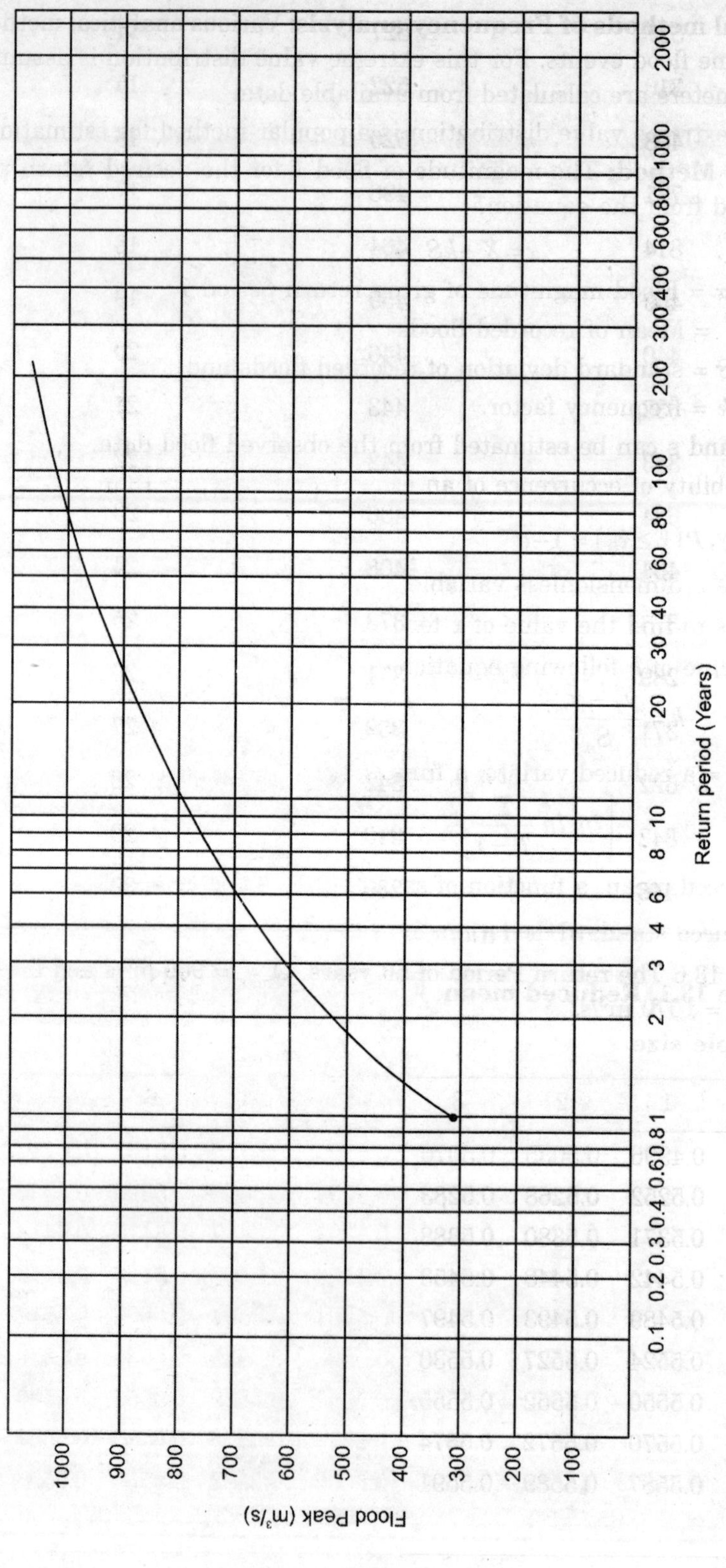

Flood Peak (m^3/s)
100
200
300
400
500
600
700
800
900
1000
Return period (Years)
0.1 0.2 0.3 0.4 0.6 0.81 2 3 4 6 8 10 20 30 40 60 80 100 200 300 400 600 800 1000 2000

Fig. 13.6

Analytical methods of Frequency analysis: Various analytical methods are available to predict extreme flood events. For this extreme value distribution is assumed and required statistical parameters are calculated from available data.

Gumbel's extreme value distribution is a popular method for estimation of flood peaks.

Gumbel's Method: The magnitude of flood x for the desired return period of T years can be estimated from the equation,

$$x = \overline{X} + kS$$

Where, x = Flood magnitude of given return period T

$\overline{X}$ = Mean of recorded floods

S = standard deviation of recorded floods and

k = frequency factor.

Here $\overline{X}$ and s can be estimated from the observed flood data.

The probability of occurrence of an event equal or larger than a value x_0 is,

Probability, $P(x \geq x_0) = 1 - e^{-e^{-y}}$

Where y is a dimensionless variable.

Our aim is to find the value of x for a given P.

For the value of k following equation can be used.

$$k = \frac{y_T - \overline{y}_n}{S_n}$$

where, y_T = a reduced variate, a function of T given as,

$$y_T = -\left[ln.ln \frac{T}{T-1}\right]$$

$\overline{y}_n$ = reduced mean, a function of sample size (N) as given in table 13.1.

S_n = reduced standard deviation, also a function sample size as given in table 13.2.

Table 13.1. Reduced mean $\overline{y}_n$ in Gumbel's Extreme Value Distribution

***N* = sample size**

N	0	1	2	3	4	5	6	7	8	9
10	0.4952	0.4996	0.5035	0.5070	0.5100	0.5128	0.5157	0.5157	0.5202	0.5220
20	0.5236	0.5252	0.5268	0.5283	0.5296	0.5309	0.5320	0.5332	0.5343	0.5353
30	0.5362	0.5371	0.5380	0.5388	0.5396	0.5402	0.5410	0.5418	0.5424	0.5430
40	0.5436	0.5442	0.5448	0.5453	0.5458	0.5463	0.5468	0.5473	0.5477	0.5481
50	0.5485	0.5489	0.5493	0.5497	0.5501	0.5504	0.5508	0.5511	0.5515	0.5518
60	0.5521	0.5524	0.5527	0.5530	0.5533	0.5535	0.5535	0.5538	0.5540	0.5543
70	0.5548	0.5550	0.5552	0.5555	0.5557	0.5559	0.5561	0.5563	0.5565	0.5567
80	0.5569	0.5570	0.5572	0.5574	0.5576	0.5578	0.5580	0.5581	0.5583	0.5585
90	0.5586	0.5587	0.5589	0.5591	0.5592	0.5593	0.5595	0.5596	0.5598	0.5599
100	0.5600									

Table 13.2 Reduced standard Deviation S_n in Gumbel's Extreme Value Distribution

N	0	1	2	3	4	5	6	7	8	9
10	0.9496	0.9676	0.9833	0.9971	1.0095	1.0206	1.0316	1.0411	1.0493	1.0565
20	1.0628	1.0696	1.0754	1.0811	1.0811	1.0915	1.0961	1.1004	1.1047	1.1086
30	1.1124	1.1159	1.1193	1.1226	1.1255	1.1285	1.1313	1.1339	1.1363	1.1388
40	1.1413	1.1436	1.1458	1.1480	1.1499	1.1519	1.1538	1.1557	1.1574	1.1590
50	1.1607	1.1623	1.1638	1.1658	1.1667	1.1681	1.1696	1.1708	1.1721	1.1734
60	1.1747	1.1759	1.1770	1.1782	1.1793	1.1803	1.1814	1.1824	1.1834	1.1844
70	1.1854	1.1863	1.1873	1.1881	1.1890	1.1898	1.1906	1.1915	1.1923	1.1930
80	1.1938	1.1945	1.1953	1.1959	1.1967	1.1973	1.1980	1.1987	1.1994	1.2001
90	1.2007	1.2013	1.2020	1.2026	1.2032	1.2038	1.2044	1.2049	1.2055	1.2060
100	1.2065									

$$S = \sqrt{\frac{\Sigma(x-\bar{x})^2}{N-1}}$$

Problem 13.10: Following table gives observed annual flood values in a North Indian river. Estimate the flood peaks with return period of 50, 100 and 1000 years by Gumble's method.

Year	1993	1994	1995	1996	1997	1998	1999	2000	2001	2002	2003	2004	2005
Flood Discharge m3/s	3210	4000	1250	3300	2480	1780	1860	4130	3110	2320	3480	3405	1820

Solution: $\bar{x} = \frac{35145}{13} = 2703.5$

$$S = \sqrt{\frac{95,98,817.75}{12}} = 894.3\ , \quad N = 13$$

From the table 13.1

For N = 13, $\bar{y}_n = 0.507$ and

From the table 13.2

$Sn = 0.9971$

Now, $y_T = -ln.ln\left(T/_{T-1}\right)$

T years	y_T	*K*	$x_T\ (m^3/s)$
50	3.9	3.4042	5762.5
100	4.6	4.105	6392.2
1000	6.907	6.4186	8444

Note: There are other methods also available for finding out the peak flow for different recurrence intervals like log-normal distribution, log-Pearson Type 3 distribution, etc. which are available in any standard hydrology text book.

Flood Routing

Flood routing is the process of computing probable effects on the flood hydrograph due to passage of a flood through a reservoir. As the flood wave enters a reservoir the reservoir level rises, resulting in temporary rise in the reservoir stage. The outflow through spillways and sluices also increases due to increased head.

When the peak is reached, the inflow begins to drop but there is gradual reduction in outflow until the inflow and outflow are equal. Thereafter the outflow is more than the inflow.

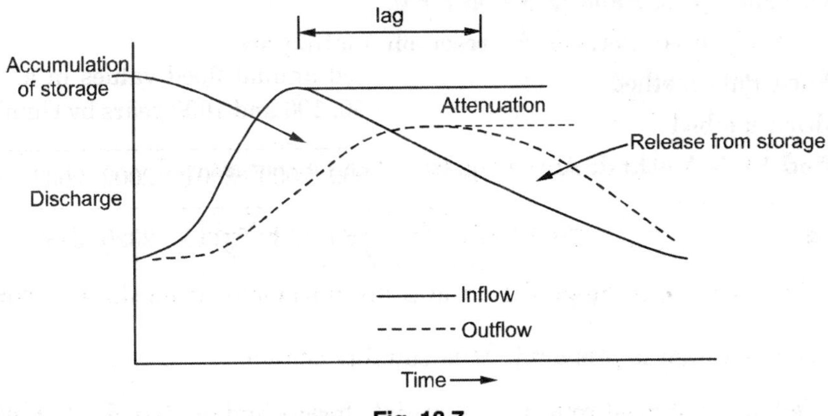

Fig. 13.7

The water which is stored temporarily in the reservoir is called **Flood Absorption**. The resulting hydrograph of outflow will have much lower peak depending upon the amount of storage in the reservoir.

The lowering of flood peak by passing through the reservoir is known as **flood moderation**.

(Note: The channel storage also provides similar effect.)

The Routing Process: The passage of a flood hydrograph through a reservoir or a channel reach is an unsteady-flow phenomenon. The equation used in all hydrologic routing is the continuity equation.

$$I - Q = \frac{ds}{dt}$$

where, I and Q are inflow and outflow rates respectively. We may express the above equation as,

$$\bar{I}\,\Delta t - \bar{Q}\,\Delta t = \Delta s$$

where, $\bar{I}$ is average inflow in time Δt

$\bar{Q}$ is average outflow in time Δt

Δs is change in storage.

Further, for a small reach, we may write,

$$\frac{I_1+I_2}{2}\Delta t - \frac{Q_1+Q_2}{2}\Delta t = S_2 - S_1$$

In practice, I_1, I_2, Q_1 and S_1 are known. We have to evaluate Q_2 and S_2, for this two equations are required against only one available. This necessiates either a trial solution or relating Q_2 or S_2 with some known parameters.

For reservoir routing, following data have to be known,

1. Storage volume Vs Elevation of Reservoir.
2. Water surface elevation Vs outflow i.e. storage Vs outflow.
3. Inflow hydrograph, $I = I(t)$
4. Initial values of S, I and Q i.e. at $t = 0$.

Two commonly used methods for reservoir routing are,

(a) Modified Pul's method

(b) Goodrich method

Modified Pul's Method: Above equation can be reorganized as,

$$\left(\frac{I_1+I_2}{2}\right)\Delta t + \left(S_1 - \frac{Q_1\,\Delta t}{2}\right) = \left(S_2 + \frac{Q_2\,\Delta t}{2}\right)$$

From the known storage-elevation and discharge-elevation data, a curve between $\left(S_1 + \frac{Q\Delta t}{2}\right)$ and elevation is prepared. Δt is suitably chosen.

At the beginning of flood routing, the initial storage and outflow discharges are known. Hence, all the terms on left hand side are known at the beginning of time step Δt. Therefore, the value of the function on the right hand side $\left(S_2 + \frac{Q_2 \times \Delta t}{2}\right)$ at the end of Δt can be found out.

Now water-surface elevation corresponding to $S_2 + \frac{Q_2 \times \Delta t}{2}$ is found from the graph. The step is repeated.

Goodrich Method

This is another popular method for reservoir routing, writing, the equation,

$$\left(\frac{I_1+I_2}{2}\right)\Delta t - \left(\frac{Q_1+Q_2}{2}\right)\Delta t = S_2 - S_1$$

and rearranging as follows:

$$I_1 + I_2 - Q_1 - Q_2 = \frac{2S_2}{\Delta t} - \frac{2S_1}{\Delta t}$$

or, $$(I_1 + I_2) + \left(\frac{2S_1}{\Delta t} - Q_1\right) = \left(\frac{2S_2}{\Delta t} + Q_2\right)$$

For a given time Step, left hand side value can be calculated, which gives right hand side value as $\left(\frac{2S}{\Delta t} + Q\right)_2$. Now with the help of $\left(\frac{2S}{\Delta t} + Q\right)$ curve, discharge, elevation and storage are obtained

Problem 13.11. The Storage, Elevation and Outflow data of a reservoir are given below:

Elevation (m)	*Storage (10^6 m^3)*	*Out flow Discharge (m^3/s)*
299.5	4.8	0
300.2	5.5	0
300.7	6.0	15
301.2	6.6	40
301.7	7.2	75
302.2	7.9	115
302.7	8.8	160

The spillway crest is at elevation 300.2 m. The following flood flow is expected into the reservoir.

Time (h)	0	3	6	9	12	15	18	21	24	27
Discharge (m^3/s)	10	20	52	60	53	43	32	22	16	10

If the reservoir elevation is at 300.0 m at the start of inflow, route the flood to obtain (a) outflow hydrograph and (b) reservoir elevation Vs time curve.

Solution: Using Goodrich method choose a time interval,

$$\Delta t = 3h = 10{,}800\ s = 0.0108 \times 10^6\ s$$

Following table is prepared.

Calculation,

$$\text{First}\ \frac{2S}{\Delta t} = \frac{4.8 \times 10^6}{.010800 \times 10^6} = 888.88$$

$$\text{Second}\ \frac{2S}{\Delta t} = \frac{2 \times 5.5 \times 10^6}{.0108 \times 10^6} = 1018.5$$

$$\text{Third} \quad \frac{2S}{\Delta t}+Q = \frac{2\times 6}{.0108}+15=1126.1$$

Calculation is shown in table below

S.No.	*Elevation*	*Q* (m^3/s)	$\frac{2S}{\Delta t}+Q$	*Rounded Value*
1	299.50	0	888.90	890
2	300.20	0	1018.50	1020
3	300.70	15	1126.10	1130
4	301.20	40	1262.20	1260
5	301.70	75	1408.30	1400
6	302.20	115	1578.00	1580
7	302.70	160	1789.60	1790

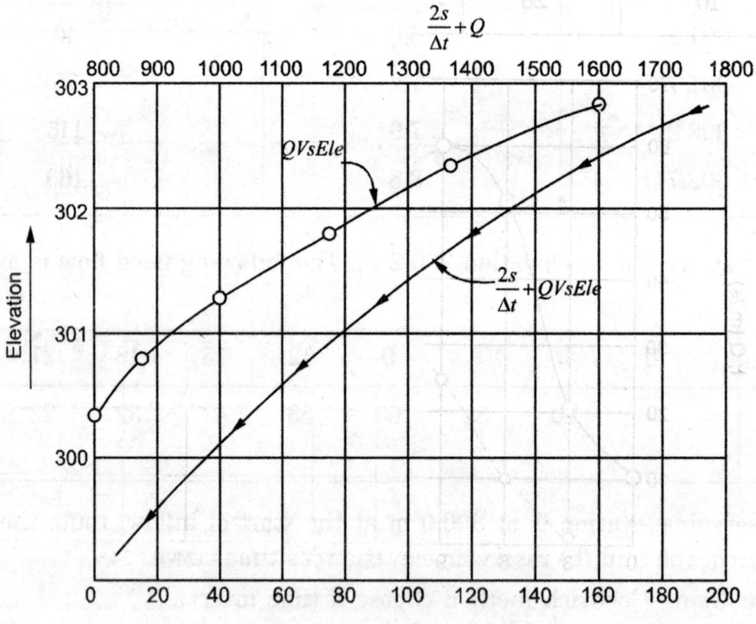

Fig. 13.8

Calculation by Goodrich method,

Time (h)	*T* (m^3/s)	$I_1 + I_2$	$\frac{2S}{\Delta t} - Q$	$\frac{2S}{\Delta t} + Q$	Elevation (m)	Q (m^3/s)
0	10			995	300.00	0
3	20	30	995	1025	300.30	1.0
6	52	72	1023	1095	300.45	10.0
9	60	112	1075	1187	300.85	26
12	53	113	1123	1236	301.03	36
15	43	96	1164	1260	301.15	43
18	32	75	1176	1251	301.08	38
21	22	54	1175	1229	301.00	34
24	16	38	1161	1199	300.90	29
27	10	26	1141	1167	300.75	22

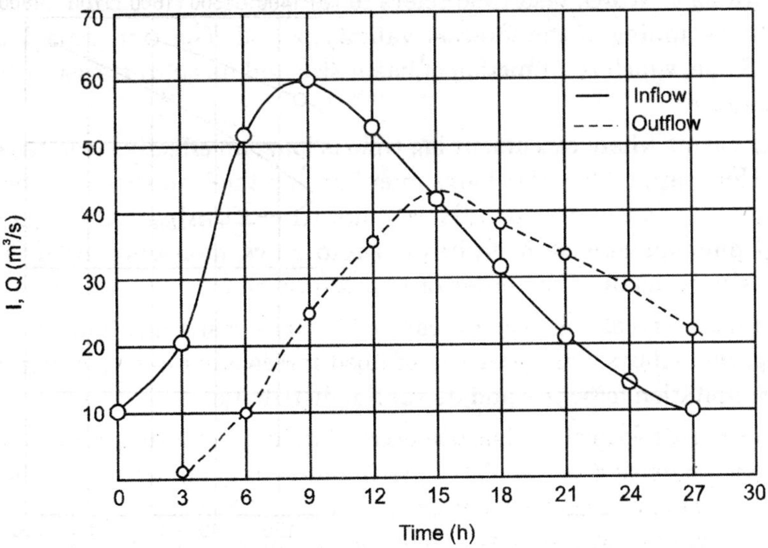

Fig. 13.9

From the inflow and outflow diagrams it can be seen that inflow curve is higher than the outflow curve. The area between the two curves indicate the accumulation of flow as storage. Also there is difference in peaks which is called **attenuation** or fall in the peak flow.

Note: there are examples of other methods also, which can be seen in any standard hydrology text book. However, Goodrich method seems to be widely used method.

Flood Forecasting

For a river engineer, flood forecasting is one of the most challenging and difficult problem. At the same time it is most important due to its critical contribution in reducing damage to property, and loss of life and degradation of environment. Forecasting of floods in advance enables a warning to be given to the people likely to be affected and further enables civil-defence measures to be organized. However, flood warning is meaningful if it is provided well in advance. It must be realized that erroneous warnings may cause loss of faith in the system.

- In India, the flood forecasts have been based on gauge-to-gauge correlation method. The gauge-to-gauge relationship has a limitation of waiting for the forecast to be made till the flood is observed through the gauge of the base station upstream of the forecasting station. Therefore, in the process, the possible travel time available in the form of catchment lag upto the base station is lost that can be added to the total forecast lead time.

Reliability of forecast carry great value. Fortunately, reliability of forecasts has increased in recent years due to the integration of meteorological and hydrological modeling capabilities, improvements in data collection through Satellite observations, and advancements in knowledge.

Among the various products, of the most useful output of Flood Forecasting and Warning System (FFWS) are river elevation, extent of inundation, and time of occurrence of Peak discharge. According to WMO, lead time refers to the period of time between the issue time of forecast and the beginning of the forecast validity period. The lead time depends upon the catchment Lag Time, which is a function of basin size and its characteristics like shape, slope and drainage pattern.

For larger basins where catchment lag time is long, an effective lead time can vary from hours to days. Here rainfall forecast helps in enhancing the lead time. On the other hand for smaller catchments, especially in hilly regions where flash floods associated with the meteorological phenomenon, dam failures, rapid snow melts etc. occur frequently, the catchment lag is very small of the order of minutes or hours.

Advanced flood forecasting systems can reduce flood risk and allow emergency response for better mitigation efforts. The accuracy of flood forecasts is highly determined by skill of quantitative precipitation forecasts and its spatial distribution.

Most modern hydrological models use precipitation inputs from various sources like rain gauges, radar, remote sensing, or simulated precipitation from numerical weather models. High-resolution satellite data are used for Weather Research and Forecasting (WRF) model to provide high-resolution precipitation forecasts. These are capable of forecasting daily precipitation amounts and facilitate early and accurate forecasting.

Reliable forecasting of weather, in particular rainfall, can allow advance warning and forecasting of floods. Weather forecasts for the next one to seven days rely on increasingly accurate computer models supported by accurate data availability due to satellite observations. It is now possible to have 3-days-ahead forecasts of heavy rain, consequently the flood forecasts.

Real Time Data Aquisition System (RTDAS)

The concept of implementation of RTDAS, on which technical specifications and special conditions are based intends to combine the advantage of modern Data Collection Platform

(DCP), data storage, processing and data communication technologies with the requirements of high availability and sustainability required for applications like flood forecasting.

Forecast Models: Mathematical models are used to predict future developments of the water resources situation in the river basins on the basis of real time information (short-term information) or analyses of historical data and developments (long-term forecasting).

Wide range of models have been produced by Government agencies, private companies and universities with a aim to transform precipitation into channel flow. The type of model employed in particular application depends largely upon the primary processes that produce runoff and their spatial and temporal extent, spatial coverage and resolution of data and catchment features.

Hydrological models for flood forecasting are either **deterministic** or **stochastic**. For deterministic models precipitation is a critical input and runoff and depth are the main outputs. The performance and efficiency of these models depend not only on selected model but also on how the catchment is represented and the extent and quality of available data. Stochastic models are data driven as they depend upon the statistical relationship between hydrological variables without considering the physical processes that underline the relationships.

Forecast updating: In flood forecasting a model may not be able to completely represent the complex processes in a basin. As a result, the simulated hydrograph may not match with the observed hydrograph, mainly due to uncertainties in input data and change in catchment characteristics over time. Therefore, continuous updating of forecast model is required by comparing the predicted hydrograph and observed hydrograph. This will result in minimising the uncertainties in prediction.

Note: Flood Forecasting Modelling is discussed in details in chapter 16.

CHAPTER 14

RIVER ECOSYSTEM

An ecosystem is a community of living organisms in conjunction with the non-living components of their environment, interacting as a system. These biotic (living) and abiotic (non-living) components are linked together through nutrient cycles and energy flows.

River ecosystems are flowing waters that drain the landscape, and include biotic interactions amongst plants, animals and micro-organisms, as well as abiotic physical and chemical interactions of its many parts. River ecosystems are part of larger watershed networks or catchments, where smaller streams drain into mid-size streams, which progressively drain into larger river networks.

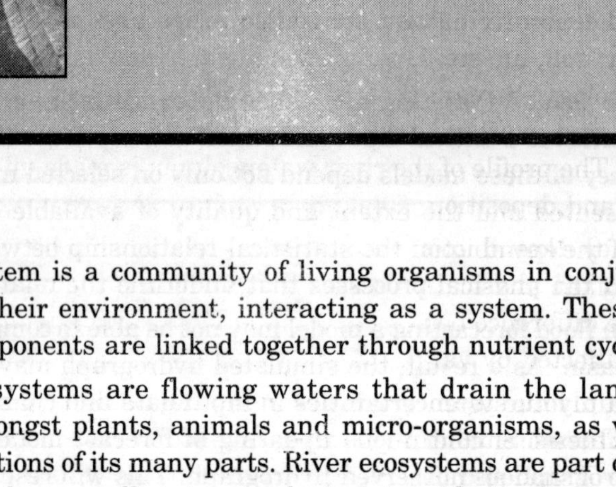

Fig. 14.1

A classification system of streams starts from smallest permanent streams, which are said to be of the **first order**. Two of these combine to form a wider stream, called a **second order** stream. Two streams of order (n) combine to form a stream of order (n + 1). The trunk stream (main stream) is not changed and remains of the same order as long as there are only addition by lower order streams, but if a tributary of the same order joins it, the order is increased. Some ecological studies have also correlated stream order with river characteristics such as input of particulate matter, primary and secondary production, species richness and abundance of functional groups.

River eco-systems are prime example of **lotic** ecosystems. Lotic refers to flowing water. Lotic ecosystems can be contrasted with **Lentic** ecosystems, which involve relatively still terrestrial water such as lakes, ponds, and wetlands. Together these two ecosystems form the most general study area of freshwater or aquatic ecology.

Abiotic Factors : The non-living components of an ecosystem are called abiotic components like stone, water, soil, air etc. Unidirectional water flow is the key factor in lotic systems influencing their ecology. Stream flow is the result of the summative inputs from groundwater, precipitation, and overland flow (Surface runoff). Flow of water is strongly determined by the bed slope. The profile of the river water column is made up of three primary actions : erosion, transport, and deposition of sediment and organic matter.

Temperature is one of the key abiotic factor. Water is heated through radiation. Shallow streams are typically well mixed and maintain a relatively uniform temperature. In deeper streams there is considerable difference between the bottom and surface temperature. Species like poikilotherms may get affected by varying temperature.

Light is very important to lotic systems, because it provides necessary energy for primary production through photo-synthesis. Smaller streams surrounded by trees get lesser light, while in large streams the influence of shade is minimised. Also, the amount of solar radiation received declines logarithmically with depth.

Among the dissolved gases **Oxygen** is the most important element of lotic systems, as all aerobic organisms require it for survival. Oxygen enters the water body through diffusion at the water-air interface. Solubility of oxygen in water depends upon pH and temperature. As the pH and temperature increase, solubility decreases. Turbulence tends to increase oxygen content. It may decrease if activity of lotic animals is high, or if there is large amount of organic decay occurring.

In river ecosystems **water chemistry** depends upon dissolved solutes and gases present in the stream. These may include, dissolved inorganic matter and ions, dissolved inorganic nutrients, suspended or dissolved organic matter, gases and traces of metals and other pollutants. Stream water chemistry is also influenced by precipitation, and addition of pollutants from human sources. Basically, water chemistry is determined by inputs from the geology of its catchment area.

The **Substrate** of lotic systems is composed of the geologic material supplied by erosion of catchment, transported, sorted, and deposited by the current. Inorganic substrates are classified by size ranging from big boulders, to pebbles, to gravel, to sand and to silt. The substrate particle size decreases downstream with larger boulders in mountainous regions to sandy and silty formations in lowland rivers. Substrate can also have some organic matter. Substrate deposition is not necessarily a permanent event, as it is subjected to larger modifications during floods.

Biotic Factors : The living component of an ecosystem are called the biotic components. The body of rivers have numerous types of biotic organisms including bacteria, primary producers, insects and other invertebrates, as well as fish.

Algae, diatoms, fungi, bacteria, plankton, and variety of small **microorganisms** exist in a film (biofilm) alongwith streambed (benthos). The biofilm assemblages are complex and therefore add to the complexity of streambed.

Bacteria in lotic waters is present in large number. Free living forms help in decomposing organic matter, biofilms and vegetation-suspended in water column.

Primary producers like **Algae** consisting of **Phytoplankton** and **Periphyton** are the most significant sources of primary production in most rivers and streams. As phytoplankton float in the water column and thus are unable to maintain population in fast flowing streams. In slow moving steams and backwaters they multiply considerably.

Plants are not comfortable in fast flowing water. Some plants like water **hyacinth** float, while others are rooted and submerged. The rooted plants are flexible, with elongated leaves offering minimum resistance to flow.

For plants living in flowing water is beneficial to plants and algae because current is usually well aerated and nutrient rich. Algae and plants are important to lotic systems as source of energy, forming micro-habitats that shelter other fauna from predators and also as food resource.

In lotic systems upto 90% invertebrates are insects. They exhibit high degree of diversity and adapt to cope with the physical harshness of the stream environment. Some of them even fly out of stream under adverse situation. Like most primary consumers lotic invertebrates rely heavily on flowing water to bring them food and oxygen.

Among the best-known inhabitants of lotic systems are the **fish**. Continuous swimming expends a large amount of energy and, therefore, fishes spend short periods in full current. Instead, they remain close to bottom or banks, behind obstacles, and sheltered from the current, swimming in the current only to feed or change location. A peculiar thing about some fish is that they spawn in fresh water and live in oceans, such as **Salmon** variety. On the contrary **Eels** live in fresh water but migrate to spawn in ocean waters.

River Dolphin

Other vertebrates that inhabit lotic systems include **amphibians**, such as reptiles, some bird species and mammals. With the exception of a few species, these vertebrated are not tied to water like fish, and spend part of their lives in terrestrial habitats. Many of the fish species are prey species to the larger vertebrates.

Energy Inputs : Energy sources are derived both from inside and outside the lotic systems. Energy inputs from within a river is referred to as **autochthonous**, while energy that is imported from stream banks is termed **allocthanous**. The amount and kind of energy input determines the biological nature of each river. In aquatic communities, the autochthonous input is provided by photo-synthesis of larger plants and attached algae and in shallow waters by microscopic phytoplankton.

In open waters, a substantial portion of the organic matter in aquatic communities comes from allochthonous material that arrives in rivers via groundwater or is blown in by the wind. the allochthonous source of organic material in an aquatic system depends upon the dimensions of water body and the types of terrestrial community that deposit organic material into it. The organic matter can also enter the lotic system by wind, surface runoff and bank erosion. Also dissolved organic material comes from canopydrip and surface flow.

River Continuum Concept (RCC)

River continuum concept provides a single framework to describe the function of temperate lotic ecosystems from the headwaters to the larger water bodies and relate key characteristics to changes in biotic community. The physical basis for RCC is size, location and order of the stream.

Low order sites are small shaded streams where allochthonous inputs of CPOM (Coarse Particulate Organic matter > 1 mm) are a necessary resource for consumers. At mid-ordered sites, energy inputs are required to be changed. Necessary sunlight should reach the bottom to support periphyton production. The main channels have much current and resulting turbidity. Here the phytoplankton is the only input. Photosynthesis rates also fall. In main channels, allochthonous inputs are primary energy source.

Microbial decomposition plays the biggest role in energy production for low-ordered sites and large rivers, while photosynthesis, in addition to degraded inputs from upstream are essential in mid-ordered systems. As mid-order ones receive the largest variety of energy inputs, they host the most biological diversity.

Human Activities and Their Impact

The effect of pollution generated by human activities can reduce ecosystem functioning, limit ecosystem services, reduce stream biodiversity and impact human health. River pollution may include : increasing sediment export, excess nutrients from fertilizer or urban runoff, sewage and septic inputs, plastic pollution, nano-particles, pharmaceuticals, synthetic chemicals, inorganic contaminants (like heavy metals) and even heat as thermal pollution.

Urban and rural centres both release considerable amount of pollutants at various locations along the length of the stream. Agricultural fields often deliver large amount of sediment, nutrients, and chemicals to nearby rivers and streams. Urban centres drain sewage into the streams, alongwith solid waste. Acid rain caused by sulphur and nitrogen oxides which are released from factories and automobiles is also a pollutant. This results in lowering the pH of these sites, affecting all trophic levels from alage to vertebrates.

Flow Modification : Whenever any obstruction is made in free flow of river, modification in flow occurs. For example by construction of a dam, water regulation and extraction, channel modification, and destruction of flood plain and adjacent riparian zone may occur. Immediate below a dam may show decline in species richness due to overall reduction in habitat heterogeneity. Fish migration is also obstructed.

River Ecosystem

Invasive species : The invasive species in lotic systems can affect native species via competition, for both prey and habitat, predation, habitat alteration, hybridization and introduction of harmful diseases and parasites. Once these guest species get established it is impossible to dislodge them. These are especially harmful in areas that contain endangered biota.

Upland and Lowland Rivers : Upland and lowland rivers are categorised as those above 200m to 500m of Mean Sea Level and those below 200 m of MSL respectively. Upland habitats are cold, clear and rocky and rivers are fast flowing, lowland habitats are warm with slow-flowing rivers found in relatively flat lowland areas, the water here is turbid containing sediment and organic matter. The two types of river habitat are very different, and usually support very different population of fish and invertebrates.

The upland rivers encourage fish species with limited temperature tolerance, high oxygen needs, strong swimming ability and specialised reproductive strategies to prevent eggs or larvae being swept away. In slow moving waters with fine sand beds, the lowland rivers encourage fish species with broad temperature tolerance, greater tolerance to low oxygen levels and ecologies revolving around habitats such as submerged woody debris or water weed.

River Restoration

River restoration refers to large variety of ecological, physical, spatial and management measures and practices. These are aimed at restoring the natural state and functioning of the river system in support of biodiversity, recreation, flood management and landscape development. River restoration improves the resilience of the river system and provides the framework for the sustainable use of rivers and streams.

River restoration describes a set of activities that aim to improve the environmental health of a stream or river. Improved health is indicated by expanded habitat for diverse species and reduced stream bank erosion. Enhancement may also include improved water quality i.e. reducing pollution levels and increase in Dissolved Oxygen (DO) level. Also achieving a self-sustaining, resilient stream system that does not require periodic human intervention, like dredging or construction of anti-erosion structures. Stream restoration also increases the value and quality of life in adjacent areas.

It is being realised that stream restoration is a vital exercise in water resources management, due to the serious degradation of many aquatic systems resulting from uncontrolled human activities.

Restoration Techniques

Two broad approaches to stream restoration have been defined : form based restoration and process based restoration. Whereas the former focuses on the restoration of structural features, the latter is based on the restoration of hydrological and geomorphological processes, such as sediment transport and connectivity between channels, and flood plains.

(a) **Form-based Restoration :** Form-based stream restoration promotes the modification of the stream channel. This may target at :

(i) Improvement in water quality.

(ii) Enhanced fish habitat and abundance

(iii) Increases bank and channel stability.

The measures can include installation of in-stream structures, bank stabilization and channel reconfiguration. Reconfiguration efforts may focus on - sinuosity and meander characteristics, cross-section and channel slope. These alterations affect the energy dissipation, flow velocity and turbulence in turn affecting water surface elevation, sediment transport, scour etc.

This method relies on construction for desired morphology, and its stabilization with natural materials such as boulders and vegetation to limit erosion and channel mobility.

(b) **Process-based Restoration :** Contrary to the form-bases restoration, this focuses on restoring the hydrological and geomorphological processes that influence streams alluvial and ecological dynamics. Process-based restoration includes restoring lateral as well as longitudinal connectivity which might be impacted by construction of dams, control structures and flood protection measures. In general process-based restoration aims to maximise resilience of the system, thus minimising the maintenance requirements.

The connectivity of streams to their adjacent floodplains and their entire length plays an important role in the equilibrium of the river system. Streams are shaped by flow of water and sediment. Any alteration in these results in change in cross-sectional geometry, as well as modification of the aquatic and riparian ecosystem. Removal or modification of levees/dams can allow a better connectivity between the river and floodplain.

(c) **Some Indirect Methods of River Restoration :** These include revegetation or reforestation efforts preferably with native species, adopting best agricultural management practices to minimize erosion, adequate treatment of sewage, and improved stormwater management to minimize pollution migration. Better storm water management can be achieved by developing : Bioretention systems and rain gardens, wetlands, Infiltration basins and retention basins.

CHAPTER 15

INTERLINKING OF RIVERS

On Interlinking of rivers various proposals have been mooted over the time. First of all it was from Arthur Cotton during British colonial rule in India. Post- independence, it was from Dr. K.L. Rao, who proposed a "National Water Grid". He proposed that surplus water from North Indian rivers be diverted to water deficient Southern States.

India's Ministry of Water Resources came out with a report titled "National Perspective for Water Resources Development" (1980). Two years later India set up a Committee of experts, through National Water Development Agency (NWDA), mainly to study the feasibility of inter-linking peninsular of south to the Himalayan component. NWDA brought forward various proposals. Obviously, none of these could be translated into action. These proposals were shelved on the plea that the proposals will be disastrous in terms of cost, environmental and ecological damage, water table and many unseen dangers.

A Public Interest Litigation (PIL) was lodged in the Supreme Court of India (2002). The SC disposing it (2012) directed the Ministry of Water Resources to constitute an experts committee to pursue the matter with the Government as no party had pleaded against Rivers Interlinking Project.

IMPORTANCE OF INTERLINKING OF RIVERS

Rivers linking is a project of linking two or more rivers by creating a network of manually created canals and providing water to the land areas that do not have river water access and reducing the flow to the sea. The principle involved is that surplus water in some rivers can be diverted to water deficient rivers by a network of reservoirs and canals. The advocates of interlinking of rivers find multiple benefits from interlinking. These are summarised below,

(a) **Irrigation:** Vast areas of land which do not get sufficient water for agricultural purpose will be largely benefited.

(b) **Prevention of Floods and Drought:** Surplus water which causes flood will be diverted resulting in fall of river stage. Water deficient areas will be made free of droughts.

(c) **Navigation:** With enough depth available in rivers new routes can be opened for free and cheap navigation compared to other transport mediums.

(d) **Hydroelectricity Generation:** For proper interlinking of rivers new dams and canals will have to be constructed which will facilitate generation of electricity as a byproduct.

(e) **Drinking Water Supply:** Large areas of India are deprived of potable water. Availability of water in these areas will increase. Hence, majority of population will get water at reasonable distance from their habitat.

(f) **Other Benefits:** There will be large scale job-generation, the G.D.P. will grow and Government revenue will increase. Tourism industry will be greatly benefited.

OBJECTIONS TO INTERLINKING OF RIVERS

Most of the environmentalists are of the opinion that interlinking of rivers will result in ecological disaster. Possible negative effects may be,

(a) **Ecological Disaster:** As there would be a decrease in downstream flow which will jeopardise the aquatic life and also infringe upon the water rights of the riparian population.

(b) **Land -use changes:** Creation of canals, dams and reservoirs will require large areas of land resulting in large scale deforestation in many locations. This would also require displacement of people and rehabilitate them in new areas.

(c) **Change in River Course:** Historically rivers have been changing their course. If this happens after interlinking, can create huge practical problems for the projects.

(d) **High Cost of the Project:** Huge amount of money is required for implementing the project which may affect the economy of the country. At 2017 level the cost per kilometer of Inter-linking can be as high as 30 to 40 thousand crores.

(e) **Lack of Knowledge among Engineers:** Engineers and others involved in managing our rivers lack the technical knowledge in river hydraulics and sediment transport as these two topics are given only fractional knowledge at undergraduate level.

(f) **Vested Interests:** While handling huge amount of money; people involved develop, interest in illegal earning resulting in failure of the projects.

INTERLINKING OF RIVERS: INDIA

Looked after by Ministry of Water Resources, River Development & Ganga Rejuvenation, interlinking rivers (ILR) programme is visualised as a programme of national importance and has been taken up on high priority. The mission of the programme is to ensure greater equity in the distribution of water by enhancing the availability of water in drought prone areas.

Under the National Perspective Plan (NPP) prepared by the Ministry, National Water Development Agency (NWDA) has identified 14 links under Himalayan Rivers component and 16 links under Peninsular Rivers Component for inter basin transfer of water based on field surveys and detailed study. Out of these, Feasibility Reports of 14 links under Peninsular component and 2 links (Indian Portion) under Himalayan component have been prepared. Draft Feasibility reports of 7 link projects (Indian Portion) of Himalayan component have also been completed.

Consequent to Supreme Court's order (2014), the Government of India constituted a Special Committee for ILR. This committee held a series of meetings, last one on Aug. 20, 2018 at New-Delhi. Vigorous efforts have been taken up for generating consensus with development of alternative plans and also setting up of road maps for implementation of projects.

The special committee constituted four specific sub-committees which have been meeting regularly and their assigned work is in progress. Some regional conferences were also held to discuss various water related issues.

Besides these activities, Task Force for ILR, Group on Inter-State River Links, Group on Legal Aspects (under Task Force), Group on Financial Aspects (under Task Force) were also involved in preparing proposals..

Interlinking Proposals

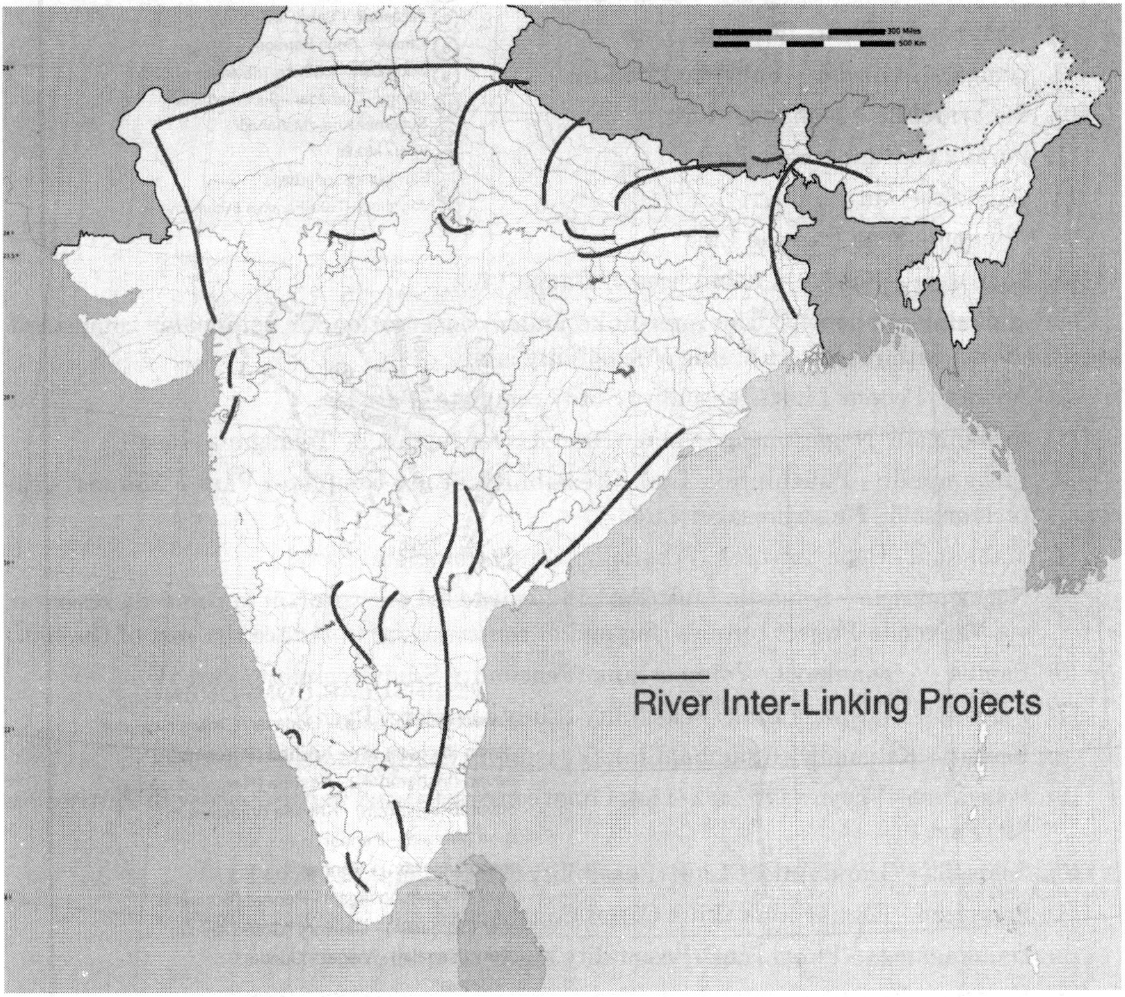

Himalayan Component: Himalayan River Development envisages construction of storage reservoirs on the main Ganga & Brahmputra and their principal tributaries in India and Nepal to transfer water from Eastern part to Western part. According to some estimate it will help in providing irrigation to 22 million hectares and generate 30 million kilowatt of hydro-power.

Fourteen Inter-links are under consideration (2015) as detailed below:

1. Ghaghra – Yamuna Link (Feasibility study completed)
2. Sarda – Yamuna Link (Feasibility study completed)
3. Yamuna – Rajasthan
4. Rajasthan – Sabarmati Link
5. Kosi – Ghaghra Link
6. Kosi – Mechi Link
7. Manas – Sankosh – Tista – Ganga Link
8. Jogighopa – Tista – Farakka Link
9. Ganga – Damodar – Subarnrekha Link
10. Subarnrekha – Mahanadi Link
11. Farakka – Sunderbans Link
12. Gandak – Ganga Link
13. Chunar – Sone Barrage Link
14. Sone dam – Southern tributaries of Ganga Link.

Peninsular component: The inter-links under conservation for peninsular component are as follows, with respective status of feasibility study:

(1) Almatti -Pennar Link (Feasibility Study complete) Part I
(2) Inchampalli -Nagarjunsagar Link (Halted construction by Telangana) Part I
(3) Inchampalli - Pulichintala Link (Feasibility Study complete) Part I Merged with Inchampalli - Nagarjunsagar Link
(4) Mahanadi - Godavari Link (Feasibility Study Complete) Part I
(5) Nagarjunsagar - Somasila Link (Part I). Remodelled as Srisailam to Somasila reservoir via Veligonda Project tunnels (fag end of construction) to reduce the cost of the link.
(6) Pamba - Anchankovil - Vaippar Link (Feasibility Study complete) Part IV
(7) Par-Tapi - Narmada Link (Feasibility Study complete) Part II
(8) Parbati - Kalisindh - Chambal Link (Feasibility Study complete) Part III
(9) Polavaram - Vijayawada Link (Link Canal constructed and partly in use with Pattiseema lift) Part I
(10) Somasila - Grand Anicut Link (Feasibility Study complete) Part I
(11) Srisailam - Pennar Link (Link Canal Constructed and is in use) Part I
(12) Damangamga - Pinjal Link (Feasibility study complete) Part II
(13) Kattalai - Vaigai - Gundar Link (Feasibility study complete) Part IV
(14) Ken-Betwa Link (Feasibility Study complete) Part III
(15) Netravati - Hemawali Link, Part IV
(16) Bedti - Varada Link, Part IV

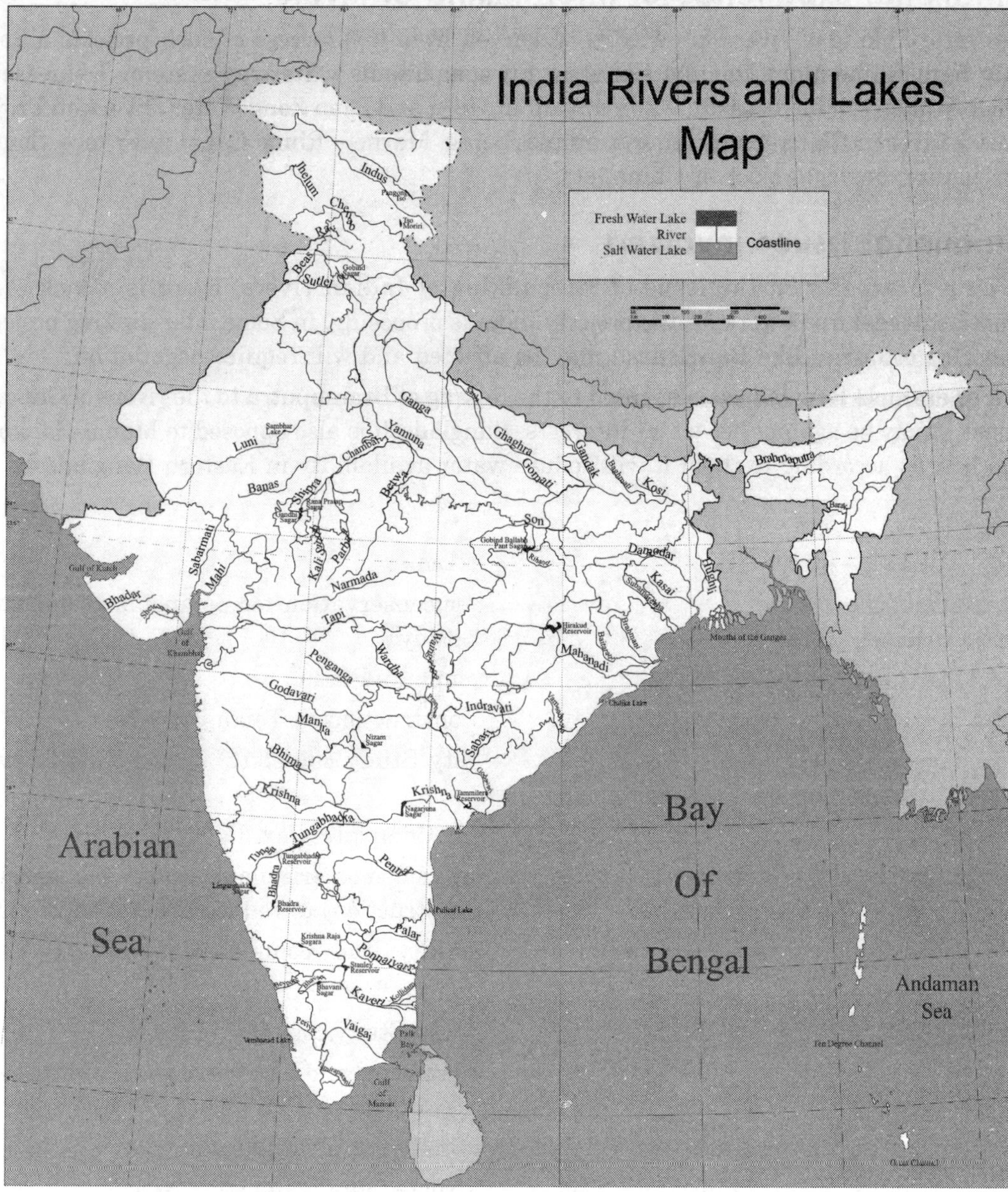

Interlinking within the State (Intra-State)

The state Government of Bihar proposed 6 Inter-linking Projects, Maharashtra 20 projects, Gujrat 1 project, Orissa 3 projects, Rajasthan 2 projects, Jharkhand 3 projects and Tamilnadu 1 inter-linking project. NDWA has completed feasibility study of many of these proposals. Some of these are still under study.

However, there is considerable disagreement among Indian States over some proposals. Odisa is not enthusiastic about linking Mahanadi with Godavari in Andhra Pradesh.

International Experience of Inter-linking of Rivers

India's inter-linking of rivers knowledge is derived from the success of such projects abroad. Mainly from Rhine-Main-Danube Canal in Europe; Illinois waterway system, Tennessee – Tombigbee and Gulf intracoastal waterway all in USA; and Dian Zong Water Diversion Project in Jinsha River in China. Some other examples being, Marne – Rhine Canal in France, South–North water transfer project in China, etc.

International Issues Involved

According to experts on the issue of interlinking of Indian rivers, there is a lack of an international legal framework for the projects India is proposing. In Some inter–linking projects, neighboring countries like Bangladesh may be affected and will require negotiation.

For example Bangladesh is opposed to the linking of Brahmputra to the rivers of Gangetic plains as it may be against her water interests. Bangladesh is also opposed to Manas-Sankosh-Ganga link as according to them it will reduce water availability in Eastern Bangladesh.

VIEWS EXPRESSED ON INTERLINKING OF RIVERS

By Dr. Dinesh Mishra

Interlinking of rivers (ILR) got a fresh lease of life when Hon. Supreme Court gave a judgment in its favour in October, 2002. Assam and Bihar were earmarked as surplus water states that will feed some other states suffering shortages of water. This scheme estimated to cost ₹ 560,000 crores(1998 estimate) was supposed to alleviate shortages in water starved states, prevent floods in the flood prone states and produce enough power to support many other activities.

Without going into the debate discussing pros and cons of the scheme that was supposed to have been completed by 2017 over years there are many questions to be answered in this context.

1. Is it possible to transfer the Ganga water to western India without lifting the same. If yes, what has been the performance of pump canals already made almost all over the country. Hardly any lift canal in so called surplus state of Bihar meets its stated objective.
2. Studies show that not an inch has been added to irrigated area of the country during 1990-2006 and the flood prone area of the country during the plan period is almost doubled up to the 12th Five Year Plan. It shows that the investment in the irrigation field is much off the target that the technocracy has fixed for itself. The scenario in the flood control sector is even worse as the flood prone area of the country has doubled during the plan period.
3. The drainage mechanism of the donor states will suffer adversely and go beyond repairs when the canals transferring water to western India are laid.
4. ILR will displace millions of people from their home and farmlands. Resettling them will be a gigantic task. Given the track record of the government to rehabilitate project affected people in engineering projects, it is suspected that a large number of people will remain unattended and left to fend for themselves into miserable conditions.
5. ILR is said to be the last and final solution to the ailing water scenario in the country. One can obviously ask what was the objective of constructing earlier schemes and why those objectives were not met? Has any lesson drawn from their failures? Were they not built to meet certain targets? What if the technocracy fails in dealing with its 'last and final solution' The basic problem is of accountability which is sadly missing historically.
6. Then there are problems with Nepal and Bangladesh which needs to be dealt separately.

Dr. Dinesh Mishra : *An engineer from IIT Kharagpur, has laid the foundation for an extensive knowledge base on floods in rivers. He believes that India's flood control policy revolves around embankments resulting in severe environmental problems. His work is a confluence of solid grass root level contacts, extensive knowledge of local traditions, topography, geography and hydrology, robust field research and unique analysis.*

ON INTERLINKING OF RIVERS

Professor Triyugi Prasad's Remakrs

Interlinking of rivers is generally talked about in the popular and populist context of linking of supposedly water surplus rivers with water deficit rivers or basins. The conceptual, technological and economic aspects of interlinking are, to say the least, complex and complicated and need comprehensive examination and analysis. Also, the impact and implications of such a massive scheme would be of far-reaching significance and largely irreversible. Taking only a simplistic and superficial view of the technology involved in pursuing a pious and ideal national objective would be woefully inappropriate. Massive effort and national commitment required for achieving an objective which inspires hopes and aspirations of suffering masses can ill-afford to be based on subjective perceptions and on gross inattention to the grave impacts and implications. As indicated by the case study of Bihar vis- à-vis interlinking of rivers, the perception of Bihar as a water surplus region simply because its north Bihar plains are subject to recurrence of floods, is erroneous and is based on deficient understanding of the physical phenomena of flood occurrences themselves as well as disregard of both the current status and the future prospects of integrated water resources development which can ensure realisation of a very high agro-potential of the region. If solution of the flood problem afflicting Bihar is not sought in the framework of highly prospective comprehensive intra-basin water resources development and instead inter-basin transfer of water through interlinking of rivers is depended upon for the purpose, not only will Bihar remain deprived of its legitimate opportunity of economic emancipation and feasible prosperity but the nation will be denied a contribution of feasibly high order of magnitude to its economy. The envisaged benefits to water-deficit regions of the country through interlinking of rivers will have to be assessed and anlysed in terms of economic, environmental and ecological as well as social cost involved and in the context of options and alternatives.

In any case, the theoretical, scientific and professional exercise that should precede and form the basis of such a massive scheme that has prompted the highest judiciary of the country to make epoch-making pronouncements for its speedy, time-bound implementation; has appealed to the slogan-loving politicians to take it as a national and popular cause; has captivated the imagination of the people; has lured many institutions and individuals to ride the band-wagon of interlinking; has lulled the suffering masses into vague hopes of deliverance on account of this new found panacea; has evoked dismay among intellectuals at the unseemly haste with which it is being pushed; has raised nightmarish apprehensions among certain quarters about its disastrous consequences; has led to protests and demonstrations against its implementation; and has given rise to intense debate about its desirability and acceptability has not been done. If it has, then civil society is grossly ignorant about it. Before the nation is committed intellectually, financially, legally and otherwise to this giant endeavour, it is imperative that such an exercise is carried out comprehensively and transparently.

Dr. Triyugi Prasad : *Having done research under the guidance of world renowned hydrologist Professor Ven Te Chow, Dr. Prasad has also been trained in Water Resources at Moscow University and Harward University. He has more than hundred research papers to his credit. He had been worried about the poverty situation in India and has opined on several occasions that proper Water Resources Development of India could be one answer to the problem.*

CHAPTER 16

RIVER MODELING

In river engineering physical as well as mathematical model have been used for solving various problems encountered concerning rivers. While physical models have been used extensively since long for finding reasonable solutions of complex river problems, the use of mathematical models for solving problems in rivers with movable beds is recent.

Physical Models: As described by Garde and Raju, whenever a certain phenomenon is to be studied with the help of a model, one must know the governing differential equations or at least the variables influencing the phenomenon. The differential equation is developed in dimensionless form in terms of dimensionless parameters. Dimensional analysis is a good tool to obtain complete set of dimensionless parameters in form of following equation,

$$A = \phi\,(B, C, D, E, F\ \ldots)$$

Where B, C, D, E, F. etc. are independent dimensionless parameters and A is the dependent dimensionless parameter.

If the values of independent variables are maintained same in the model and the prototype, it would mean that complete similarity is obtained, the value of A will also be same in the model and the prototype.

Distorted Model: If one or more of the independent variables differ in the model and the prototype, the model is known to be a distorted model. In a geometrically similar model the corresponding lengths in the model and prototype have the same ratio. If these ratios are not identical for all the parameters, the model gets distorted. In river models it is almost impossible to get a geometrically similar model as it becomes necessary to adopt different scales for vertical and horizontal lengths. The river models are compulsorily distorted models.

Besides geometrical distortion there may be **material distortions** and **force distortion** in alluvial streams (rivers), one of the parameters is $\Delta\gamma_s / \gamma_f$ which will have different values in model and prototype. In model lighter material is required to be used to ensure adequate sediment movement. This is called material distortion. Force distortion occurs when dimensionless ratios involving forces assume different values in the model and the prototype. Froude number and Reynolds' Number are important parameters governing gravitational and viscous forces. Due to distortion in the model the value of dependent variable A, will not be same both for model and prototype.

Model Designing : For designing of models following conditions should be satisfied,

(1) The continuity Equation : For a prismatic channel, Discharge

$$Q = A \times V = L \times h \times v$$

$\therefore$ For Prototype and Model, $\dfrac{Q_p}{Q_m} = \dfrac{L_p}{L_m} \cdot \dfrac{h_p}{h_m} \cdot \dfrac{V_p}{V_m}$

Or $\quad Q_r = L_r\, H_r\, V_r$

Where, Q_r = Scale ratio for discharge

L_r = Scale ratio for horizontal distance

h_r = Scale ratio for vertical distance and

V_r = Scale ratio for velocity

(2) Dynamic Equations: The river flow is maintained by the gravity force, equality of Froude Number is essential for reproducing the model correctly. The importance of Froude Number in scour problems further emphasizes the need for its equality.

$$\frac{V_p}{\sqrt{g_p L_p}} = \frac{V_m}{\sqrt{g_m \times L_m}}$$

Or $$\frac{V_p}{V_m} = \sqrt{\frac{g_p}{g_m} \times \frac{L_p}{L_m}}, \qquad \text{Since } g_p = g_m$$

Or $$V_r = \sqrt{L_r} \qquad \text{Or} \qquad \frac{V_r}{\sqrt{L_r}} = 1$$

(3) Resistance Law: According to Garde and Raju, the resistance law can be written as,

$$\frac{V}{\sqrt{\Delta\gamma_S d/\rho}} = K\left(\frac{R}{d}\right)^{2/3}\left(\frac{S}{\Delta\gamma_S/\gamma_f}\right)^{1/2}$$

This would mean that

$$V_r = \frac{h_r^{2/3}\, S_r^{1/2}}{d_r^{1/6}}$$

Where, Sr = Scale ratio for slope

dr = Scale ratio for sediment Size.

(4) Criterion for Sediment Movement: In this the incipient motion condition as given by Shields and the sediment transport law have to be considered. for complete similarity the following law should be satisfied,

$$\lambda = \frac{\beta\, h_r\, S_r}{\left(\Delta\gamma_s/\gamma_f\right)_r d_r} = 1 \qquad \text{Where,} \qquad \beta = \frac{R_r}{h_r}$$

Also if d/δ, is same in both model and prototype the sediment starts moving at corresponding shear stresses in both cases.

(5) The time scale: Time scale is applied for flow and bed variation. The controlling equations are **(a)** For flow $t_r = L_r / V_r$

(6) For morphologic Process $\frac{\partial Z}{\partial t} + \frac{1}{(1-n)}\frac{\partial q_T}{\partial x} = 0$ Where n is porosity. On solving, the time scale for bed variation is given by, $T_r = \frac{L_r h_r (1-n)_r}{q_{Tr}}$,

$$\left[\begin{array}{l} Z_r = hr \\ q_T = \text{Rate of Total load transport in weight per unit width.} \end{array}\right.$$

It was found by Zwamborn that morphological time scale Tr is about 10 times the hydraulic time scale tr.

(7) Slope Law: Simply, $S_r = \frac{h_r}{L_r}$

However, this simple relation does not work in movable beds because of distortion in $\tau_0 / \Delta\gamma_s d$ value to attain equality. Therefore, a coefficient η is applied to give

$$S_r = \eta \frac{h_r}{L_r}, \qquad \eta > 1$$

This will mean a steeper slope in the model.

(8) Perimeter Law: If Lacey theory is considered then $L_r = Q_r^{0.5}$. However, it does not consider other effects on perimeter. Following equation is suggested by Velikanov,

$$\frac{W}{d} = K_3 \left[\frac{Q}{d^2 \sqrt{\Delta\gamma_s dS / \rho}}\right]^m$$

m was found to be 0.42, K_3 = 2.7 to 3.0.

Which was converted into dimensionless form as, $L_r = Q_r^m \; S_r^{m-2} \; d_r^{(1-2.5m)} \; (\Delta\gamma_{s/\rho})_r^{-m/2}$

(9) β-Values: The value of β depends upon the shape of stream's cross-section and ratio L_r / h_r. For a rectangular cross section and ratio, L_r / h_r, β is given as, $\beta = 2\left(\frac{h}{w}\right)\frac{L_r}{h_r} + 1$

In natural channels $\frac{h}{w}$ is normally 0.01 to 0.04 and L_r / h_r equal to 2 to 7. Therefore, β is of the order ≤ 1.2

Note: When planning a physical model for movable bed channel the use of above conditional equations should be made. Depending upon the equations used and number of unknowns, one can find the number of scale ratios that can be chosen freely. The methods differ depending on the nature and number of equations considered, very few data is available regarding the success of river models.

Garde and Raju have listed nine conditional equations based on the study by Einstein and Chien as mentioned below,

(1) Manning – type resistance law.

(2) Equality of sediment transport parameter.

(3) Equality of shear parameter ψ_* involving hydraulic radius with respect to grains

(4) Equality of ratio of sediment size to laminar sub-layer thickness.

(5) Equality of q_T/q_B

(6) Equality of Froude Number

(7) Definition of time scale $t_r = \frac{L_r}{V_r}$

(8) Definition of time scale for morphological process.

(9) $S_r = \frac{h_r}{L_r}$

Garde obtained, considering various aspects, Scale Ratios for various parameters as mentioned below,

Scale	a_1 in $L_r^{a_1}$	a_2 in $d_r^{a_2}$	a_3 in β^{a_3}
Q_r	2.444	0.257	– 0.60
U_r	0.414	0.087	– 0.20
h_r	0.170	0.830	– 0.40
S_r	–0.276	0.276	– 1.20
q_{Tr}	2.480	– 0.980	–11.70
λ	0.552	– 0.552	0.60

Note: These scale ratios have been founds for $\Delta\gamma_s/\gamma_f = 1, k_r = 1$

APPROACH USED IN INDIAN SUB-CONTINENT

In this region the scales in alluvial river models are based on Lacey's Regime Equations and subsequent variations suggested by Blench. According to Garde, the longitudinal scale ratio Lr is fixed depending on the space available, facilities available in the laboratory, purpose of model studies and accuracy desired.

In Indian practice L_r is taken to be $Qr^{0.5}$ in accordance with the meander length and meander belt. Other scales are determined by Lacey's equations for R, S and silt factor f_1 as follows.

$$Q_r = L_r 2$$

$$R_r = \beta h_r = \left[\frac{Q_r}{f_{1r}}\right]^{1/3}$$

$$S_r = f_{1r}^{5/3}\ Qr^{1/6} \quad \text{and} \quad f_{1r}^2 = dr$$

For simplicity β can be assumed to be unity. The remaining unknowns are Q_r, h_r, f_{1r}, dr and Sr. For these unknowns four equation, as mentioned above are available. One can choose two ratios Lr and dr according to situation present and others can be computed.

Some Comments on Physical Modeling of Alluvial Rivers: Scaling considerations

It is desirable for the scale to be kept as large as feasible to maintain the maximum visual sense of similitude possible for use of the model as a visual display tool. Issues in achieving realistic similitude in sediment transport rapidly become insurmountable problems as model size is diminished. At the same time, the scope of prototype conditions being simulated causes the model to rapidly approach limits of space and discharge availability as the scale is increased. Model geometry scales of 1:2, 1:4 and 1:15 are considered to be practical.

Sediment Modelling: Good similarity of sediment movement is difficult to achieve. In prototype sediment moves both as suspended and bed load. Suspended load is very fine grain material that can remain in suspension for long periods. Suspended load is very difficult to accurately model. Therefore, only bed load is simulated.

The bed load is assumed to be largely non-cohesive sand. Modelling bed load transport is based on providing similarity between prototype and model for several key parameters like particle fall velocity, dimensionless shear and channel roughness, both grain and form roughness/resistance.

Summary : Scale model studies for any proposed system can be effective only when requirements for hydraulic similitude are met. Idealistically, this would require matching of the ratio of appropriate pairs of forces in both scale model and prototypes that play significant roles in physical processes being examined. Often of interest is the ratio of inertial force to viscous force (Reynolds Number) as well as the inertial force to gravity force (Froude Number) in both model and prototype. These dimensionless numbers are expressed as, $R_e = \frac{Vy}{\nu}$ and $F_r = \frac{V}{\sqrt{gy}}$.

In practical applications, meeting both criteria would require scaling of not only physical dimensions, but scaling of fluid properties like fluid viscosity - which can almost never be achieved due to the fact that fluids with suitably scaled properties almost never exist.

For sediment movement, the hydraulic scale of interest is at bed sediment particle diameter. It is well known that particle movement is a function of shear force $\tau_o = \rho\sqrt{g\ y\ s}$ and $\text{Re} = \frac{u_* d_s}{\nu}$

Generally, it is not feasible to simply reduce particle size according to geometric model scale. As particle size reduce, cohesiveness properties may change dramatically.

Problem : 16.1 : Considering Froude Number $\left(Fr = \frac{V}{\sqrt{gy}}\right)$ **as the criterion for dynamic similarity for an open channel flow situation, Work out the scale factor for velocity, time, discharge and force in terms of scale factor for length.**

Solution : Let, $Lr = \frac{Lm}{Lp}$ is the scale factor for model and prototype. L is the Linear Dimension.

(i) Scale Factor for Velocity: $\frac{Vm}{\sqrt{L_m g_m}} = \frac{V_p}{\sqrt{L_p g_p}}$

$$\therefore \quad \frac{Vm}{Vp} = \sqrt{\frac{Lm}{Lp}} = \sqrt{Lr} = L_r^{0.5} \; (g_m = g_p)$$

(ii) Scale factor for time : $T_r = \frac{Tm}{Tp} = \frac{L_m / V_m}{L_p / V_p} = \frac{Lm}{Lp} \times \frac{Vp}{Vm} = \frac{Lr}{Lr^{0.5}}$

$$= L_r^{0.5}$$

(iii) Scale factor for Discharge: $Q_r = \frac{Qm}{Qp} = \frac{Am\ Vm}{Ap\ Vp}$, $\quad Q = A \times V$

$$\therefore \quad = \left(\frac{Lm}{Lp}\right)^2 \times \frac{Vm}{Vp} = Lr^2 \times Lr^{0.5}$$

$$\therefore \quad Q_r = L_r^{2.5}$$

(iv) Scale factor for Force $F_r = \frac{Fm}{Fp} = \frac{Mm \times a_m}{Mp \times a_p} = \frac{\rho Lm^3 \times a_m}{\rho Lp^3 \times a_p}$

$$= \frac{\rho Lm^3 . Vm / Tm}{\rho Lp^3 . Vp / Tp} = \frac{Lm^3}{Lp^3} \times \frac{Vm}{Vp} \times \frac{Tp}{Tm}$$

$$= \frac{Lr^3 . Lr^{0.5}}{Lr^{0.5}} = Lr^3$$

$\therefore$ Force Ratio $(F_r) = L_r^3$

Problem: 16.2: A shallow river is 1500 m wide and the maximum depth of flow in it is 5.0 m. It carries a discharge of 3,300 m³/s, the velocity of flow is 1.5 m/s. The model is constructed to the horizontal scale of 1:750 and the vertical scale of 1:50. If Manning's N = 0.025 for river material, find N for model bed material. Assume a wide channel.

Solution: $\quad Q_p = A_p \times V_p = 3{,}300$

$$\therefore \quad A_p = \frac{3{,}300}{1.5} = 2{,}200 \; m^2$$

Depth of flow, $\quad Dp = \frac{Ap}{Bp} = \frac{2{,}200}{1{,}500} = 1.466 \; m$

$$Bm/Bp = \frac{Lm}{Lp} = \frac{1}{750} \qquad B = \text{width.}$$

$$\therefore \quad Bm = \frac{Bp}{750} = \frac{1500}{750} = 2m$$

Also, $$\frac{Dm}{Dp} = \frac{1}{50}, \qquad D = \text{Depth of Flow}$$

$$\therefore \quad Dm = \frac{Dp}{50} = \frac{1.466}{50} = 0.029m$$

Considering Manning's Equation, $V = \frac{1}{N} R^{2/3} S^{1/2}$

In terms of scale Ratios, $Vr = \frac{1}{Nr} Rr^{2/3} Sr^{1/2}$

$$\therefore \quad Nr = \frac{Rr^{2/3} Sr^{1/2}}{Vr}$$

According to Froude Law, $Vr = Dr^{1/2}$, $\qquad Rr = Dr$

$$Sr = \frac{Dr}{Lr}$$

$$Nr = Dr^{2/3}\left[\frac{Dr}{Lr}\right]^{1/2}, \qquad \frac{1}{Dr^{1/2}} = \frac{Dr^{2/3}}{Lr^{1/2}}$$

$$= \frac{(750)^{1/2}}{(50)^{2/3}} = \frac{27.386}{13.571} = 2.0$$

$$Nm = Np \times Nr$$
$$= 0.025 \times 2 = 0.05$$

This shows that model has to be rougher than the prototype.

Velocity in the model Vm

$$Vm = Vr \times Vp$$

$$= \left(\frac{1}{50}\right)^{1/2} \times 1.5 = 0.212\ m/s$$

MATHEMATICAL MODEL

A mathematical model is a description of a system using mathematical concepts and language. The process of developing a mathematical model is termed Mathematical Modelling. These models are used in almost all fields of pure science, social sciences and engineering.

Mathematical models help in explaining any system and to study the effects of different components, and make predictions about behavior. In engineering mathematical models are used to maximize a certain output. The system under consideration will require certain inputs.

A Priori Information

Mathematical models are often classified into (1) Black Box and (2) White Box models, depending upon the magnitude of Priori information on the system is available. A black box model is in which no priori information is available. On the contrary a white box model (also known as glass box or clear box) is a system where all necessary information is available.

Practically, all systems are somewhere between the black-box and white-box models. Usually it is preferable to use as much priori information as possible to make the model more accurate. Sometimes it is useful to incorporate subjective information into a mathematical model. This can be done based on intuition, experience, or expert opinion.

The Simple and Complex Models

Generally, model complexity involves compromise between simplicity and accuracy of the model. The simplest models are most desirable, added complexity may improve the accuracy of a model. However, it can make the model difficult to understand and analyze. According to Vent Te Chow "A simple model can be solved easily by mathematical methods, but it must be noted that the results so obtained should be considered approximate. On the other hand, a relatively complicated model may delineate the system better and yield more exact results, but it may be difficult to solve,"

Flood Forecasting Methods and Models

Meteorological Phenomenon are the prime natural causes of flooding either as rainfall or snow and snowmelt. Clearly the ability to forecast critical events, in both time and space and also quantitatively, is of significant value in flood forecasting and warning.

Hydrometeorological statistics, primarily rainfall are vital to flood forecasting and warning operations. The purpose of the data and statistics is to estimate the severity and probability of events. Long term records are essential and this requires robust network of raingauge network both manual and automatic. Among these a representative proportion of the raingauge network is linked to the forecasting and warning control centres by telemetry.

Forecast Lead Time : The lead time of any forecast is the period from the time of making the forecast, i.e. the time of origin of the forecast, to the future point in time for which the forecast applies. The forecast lead time that it is possible to achieve is mostly related to the type of catchment. The basic principle involved for assessing lead time requirements is minimum period of action to be taken effectively. There are no hard and fast rules regarding the provision of lead time for warning. Principally it depends upon - the size of the catchment, the nature of risks and impacts. The lead time may vary from few hours to few days. For example in United States of America, a lead time of 2 and 48 hour is generally be considered a short-term forecast, between 2 and 10 days a medium - term forecast, while a long - term forecast would be one for which lead time exceeds 10 days (WMO - No. 49, vol. III, 2007).

Steps for a Flood Forecast Model

The expectations for Flood forecast have increased with time as past methods of simple extrapolation of forecasts from gauged sites are no longer sufficient in terms of magnitude and timing of the event.

The steps needed in creating a suitable flood Forecasting Model are illustrated in fig. 16.1.

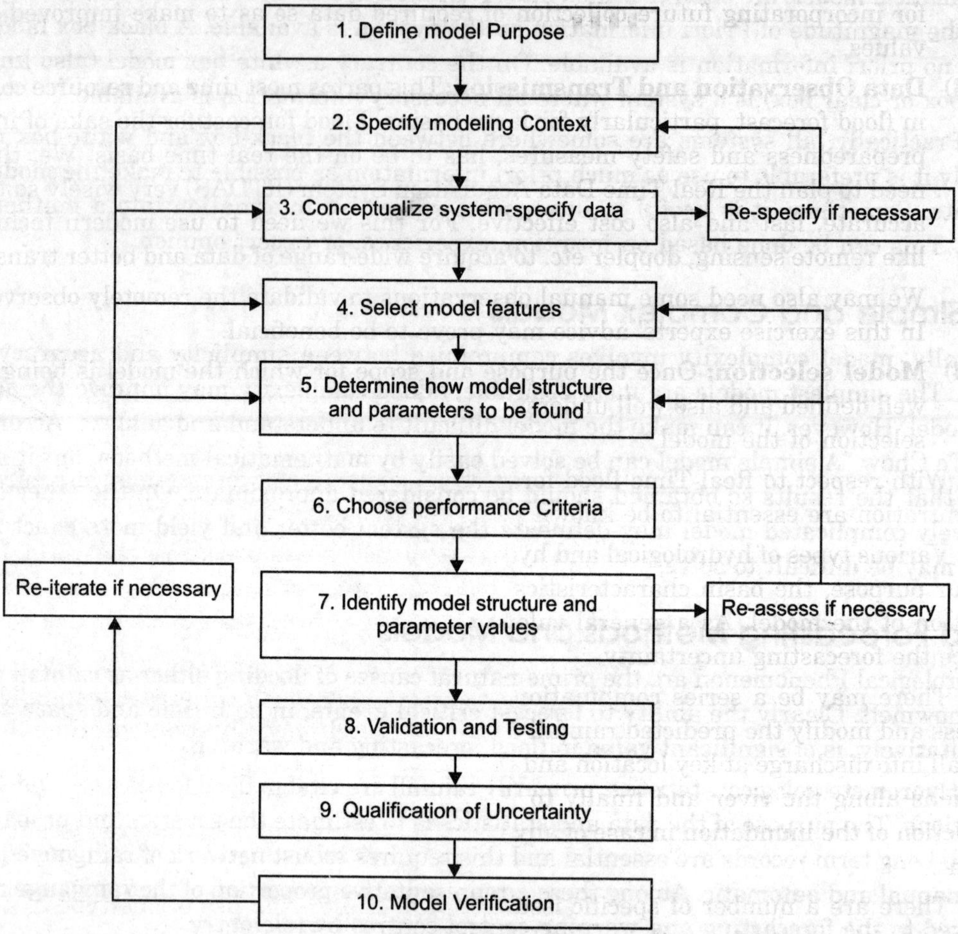

Fig. 16.1

A flood forecast is an estimate of the future state of flood phenomenon including flow rate, cumulative volume, stage level, area of inundation etc. at a particular geographical location or channel section.

To be useful, the selected forecasting models must satisfy certain objectives, depending on the requirements of the stakeholders and the end-users of the forecasts.

Important Issues: There are various issues and challenges in flood forecasting exercise.

(1) Types of Forecast: Here it is discussed that which is the appropriate type of forecast one should go for. Whether the forecast of water level only or both water level as well as discharge should be considered. What should be the lead-time. Flood forecast for a large lead time is likely to have less accuracy and vice-versa.

(2) Data Requirement: Data is the most important part in the hydrologic and hydraulic modeling. In general, a sophisticated mathematical model used for the output of high accuracy requires large quantity of input data of good quality. However, data limitation quality wise as well as quantity wise is a real hard proposition. Thus model selection should be in accordance with the data available presently having reasonable flexibility for incorporating future collection of required data so as to make improved forecast values.

(3) **Data Observation and Transmission:** This part is most time and resource consuming in flood forecast, particularly for large basins. Flood forecast for the sake of improved preparedness and safety measures, has to be on the real time basis. We, therefore, need to plan the Real Time Data Acquisition System (RTDAS) very wisely so that it is accurate, fast and also cost effective. For this we need to use modern technologies like remote sensing, doppler etc. to acquire wide-range of data and better transmission. We may also need some manual observations to validate the remotely observed data. In this exercise experts' advice may prove to be beneficial.

(4) **Model selection:** Once the purpose and scope for which the model is being built is well defined and also well understood, it is the availability of data that conditions the selection of the model.

With respect to Real-Time flood forecasting, the choice of forecasting time and time of concentration are essential to be known while choosing a model.

Various types of hydrological and hydraulic models are in use across the world. Basically for our purpose, the basin characteristics and availability of past records (data) dictate the selection of the model. As a general rule of thumb, the forecasting model must be used to reduce the forecasting uncertainty.

There may be a series combination of several models-one to predict rainfall, then to process and modify the predicted rainfall data using the ground observations, then to convert rainfall into discharge at key location and then to predict water levels (river stages) at various locations along the river and finally to map the expected inundation on the countryside. Prediction of the inundation in case of any breach of the embankment at given location is also sought.

There are a number of specific issues that may limit the use of one type of modeling approach with respect to another one. Here three types of models are discussed for different situations.

(1) Data - Driven Models: (DDM)

Data driven modeling method has proven its applicability to various problems related to river basin management: modeling, short-term forecasting, classification of hydrology-related data and even automated generation of flood inundation maps based on aerial photos. The DDM models should be preferably used where, predictand (That which has to be predicted), namely the quantity of interest to be forecast, is at a gauged river section. In DDM extension of their use to ungauged cross-sections is practically impossible. The forecasting span is relatively short compared to time of concentration.

(2) Conceptual (hydrological) Models

These are the most widely used for flood forecasting as they are easily understood due to the fact that they try to describe rationally the different components of the hydrological cycle. Conceptual hydrological model, sometimes called gray-box models are precipitation-run-off models built based on observed or assumed empirical relationships among different hydrological variables. In conceptual models the dependency on stream flow data for model calibration is considerably reduced. Here also the predictand is at a gauged river section, extension of which to ungauged section is often difficult. The required forecasting span is of the same order of magnitude as the time of concentration.

(3) Physical-Process Models

In physical-process models, the different parts of the hydrologic cycle are more specifically represented by mathematics of physical process. These are used when sufficient geomorphologic and hydro morphological data are available. The computational time is short to allow for timely forecast. The rainfall is available in spatially distributed form. There may be large variability over different parts of the catchment. The forecast can be extrapolated to suit ungauged locations.

LUMPED VERSUS DISTRIBUTED MODELS

A lumped model is one in which the dependent variables of interest are a function of time alone. In general, this will mean solving a set of ordinary differential equations. A distributed system is one in which all dependent variables are function of time and few spatial variables. In this partial differential equations have to solved.

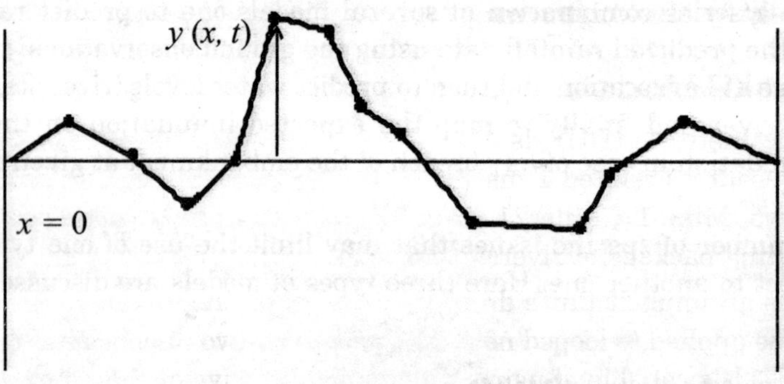

Fig. 16.2

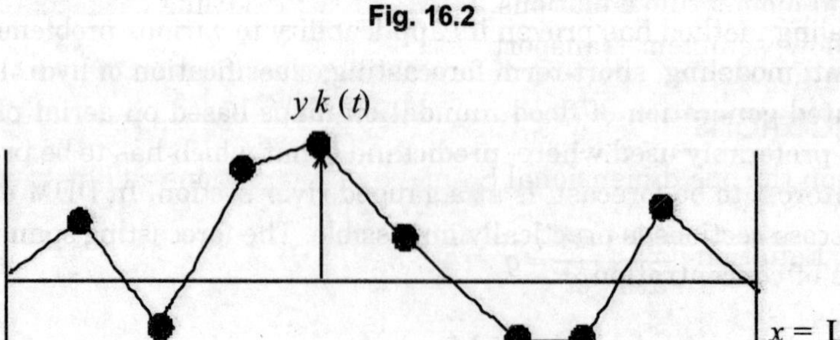

Fig. 16.3

The first system is a distributed system, consisting of an infinitely thin string, supported at both ends; the dependent variable, the vertical position of the string y(x, t) is indexed continuously in both space and time.

The second system, a series of **beads** connected by massless string segments constrained to move vertically, can be thought of as a lumped system, an approximation to the continuous system.

Obviously the lumped system is able to cut computational costs as it requires to solve ordinary differential equations at few points, rather than a full partial differential equations. (Fig. 16.3)

FLOOD MODELLING EXAMPLE

Floods occurs due to natural as well as man-made causes. Major causes of floods in India include intense precipitation, inadequate capacity within riverbanks to contain high floods, and silting of riverbeds. Wise application of engineering science has afforded ways of mitigating the ravages due to flood and providing reasonable measures of protection to life and property. Hence an efficient flood-Forecasting and advance warning systems are necessary in order to evacuate the life and movable goods.

Many conventional flood forecasting methods are in use like by using flood routing technique, by using inflow-outflow correlation curves, forecasting the time of travel and duration of peak, use of electrical analogy model, computer simulation etc. The hydrologic routing is carried out traditionally by Muskingum method.

Modeling with MIKE Models

The Danish Hydraulic Institute (DHI) is one of the world's leading software developers for incorporating water-resources related Time-Series data into modeling. The DHI has provided Mike zero, Mike Hydro, Mike-11, Mile 21, Mike 3, Mike 21/3 and Mike - flood which is an integrated flood modeling package of rivers (MIKE - 11).

The MIKE -11 is an implicit finite difference model for one dimensional unsteady flow computation and can be applied to looped networks and quasi-two dimensional flow simulation on flood plains. MIKE-11 is capable of using Kinematic, diffusive or fully dynamic, vertically integrated mass and momentum equations. MIKE-11 is a modeling package for the simulation of surface runoff, flow, sediment transport etc.

Governing Equations

MIKE-11 is based on the one dimensional Saint-Venant equations as illustrated below,

- Continuity Equation $\dfrac{\partial Q}{\partial x}+\dfrac{\partial A}{\partial t}=q$

- Momentum Equation: $\dfrac{\partial Q}{\partial t}+\dfrac{\partial\left\{\alpha\dfrac{Q^2}{A}\right\}}{\partial x}+g\,A\dfrac{\partial h}{\partial x}+\dfrac{g\,Q\,|\,Q\,|}{c^2 A\,R}=0$

Where, Q - discharge (m^3/s)
A - Flow area (m^2)
q - Lateral inflow ($m^3/m/s$)
h - Stage above datum (m)
R - Hydraulic Radius (m)
C - Chezy's resistance coefficient.
α - Momentum distribution Coefficient

The four terms in the above equation of momentum are, local acceleration, convective acceleration, pressure and friction. In MIKE-11, a network configuration depicts the rivers and flood plains as a system of interconnected branches. Water levels and discharges (h and Q) are calculated at alternative points along the river branches as a function of time as shown in fig. 16.4.

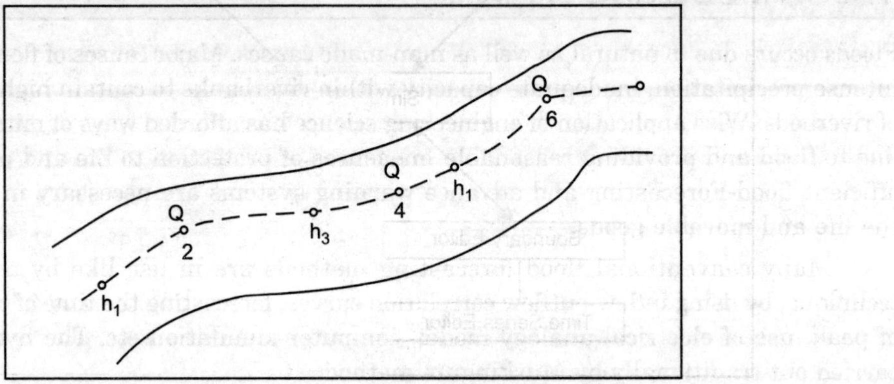

Fig. 16.4 : Channel section with computational grid.

It operates on basic information from the river and flood plain topography to include manmade features and boundary conditions.

Solution scheme in MIKE-11

The finite difference scheme used in MIKE -11 is 6 point Abbot scheme. A graphical view of the method is shown in the figure 16.5. As can be seen at $n+\frac{1}{2}$ Step the model bring data from n and $n + 1$, so unknowns will obtain simultaneously for each time step.

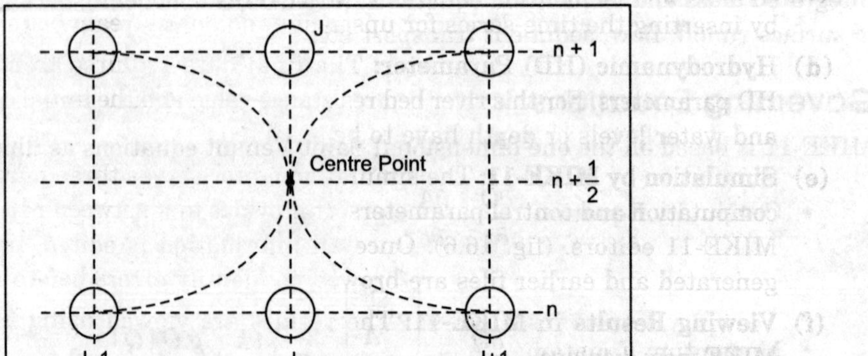

Fig. 16.5: 6-point Abbott seheme

MIKE-11 model is fully implicit method to solve the problems and usually there is no limitation about computational steps.

The Model setup

MIKE-11 includes multiple Editors, each operating in different types of data. The integration and exchange of information between each of the individual data editors is main task of MIKE-11 simulation Editor.

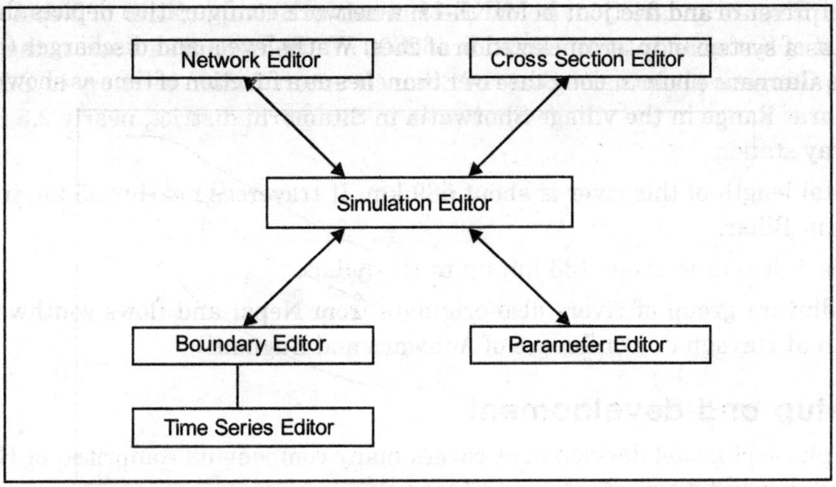

Fig. 16.6

Following steps have to be followed in order to setup the one - dimensional model.

(a) Defining the River Cross - Section: It has an xy co-ordinate system, allowing the model to import and export data. It allows to define the river network, reference cross-sections, and control structures to the network and to obtain a graphical overview of model information in the current simulation.

(b) Inserting River cross - section: The geometry of cross-sections obtained from field-surveyed data. These are entered into MIKE-11 cross-section file,

(c) Boundary Cross - Section: Boundary conditions can be defined for the river reach by inserting the time-series for upstream and downstream boundary condition.

(d) Hydrodynamic (HD) Parameter: The final data required to run simulation is the HD parameters. For this river bed resistance value and the initial conditions of discharge and water levels or depth have to be specified.

(e) Simulation by MIKE-11: The simulation editor serves three purposes i.e, simulation, computation and control parameters. It provides link between network editor and other MIKE-11 editors. (fig. 16.6). Once all information is edited, new simulation file is generated and earlier files are browse, to identify errors before running simulation.

(f) Viewing Results in MIKE-11: The results are viewed using MIKE view program. MIKE view displays.

(i) Longitudinal profile animations of both stage height and discharge from unsteady simulation.

(ii) Stage height at any given cross-section.

(iii) Rating curves at specified locations along the river network.

(iv) Time series results of stage heights at cross-section locations.

(v) Time series results of discharge at mid points between two cross-section locations.

Example : Flood Forecast Model for Baghmti-Adhwara basin in Bihar.

Introduction of Basin

The Bagmati River originates just below the summit of Shivapuri Hill of Nepal at about 16 km north-east of Kathmandu at an elevation of 2800 m. The river drains across the Mahabharat Range to the Gangetic plain in the State of Bihar. It enters Indian territory in Bihar through the Mahabharat Range in the village Shorwatia in Sitamarhi district, nearly 2.5 Km north of Dheng railway station.

The total length of this river is about 589 km. It traverses nearly 195 km in Nepal and rest 394 km in Bihar.

The reach length is about 133 km up to Hayaghat.

The Adhwara group of rivers also originate from Nepal and flows southward to meet with Bagmati at Hayaghat. (confluence of Adhwara and Bagmati)

Model Setup and development

- The phase of model development covers many components comprised of Hydrological Model, Hydrodynamic Model, and Flood Forecasting etc.
- Hydrological modelling has been developed using NAM (Rainfall-Runoff) module and Hydrodynamic using MIKE11 (1D) module.

Input Data for Flood Forecast Model

- Rainfall data
- Water level data
- IMD rainfall forecast data
- Cross sections

Rainfall Stations of Bagmati

Adhwara catchment

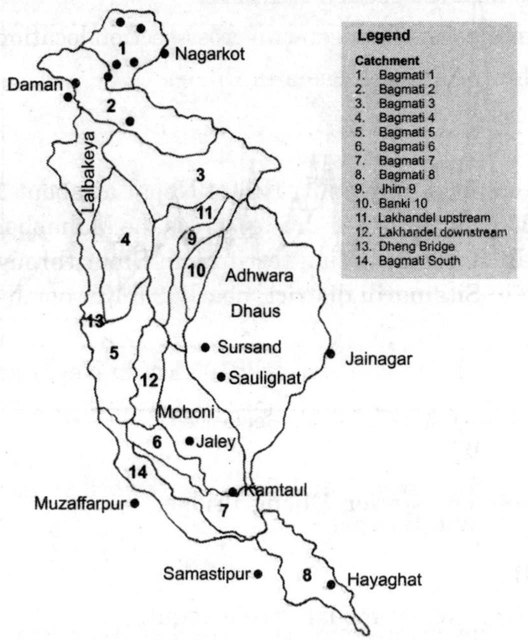

Water level stations

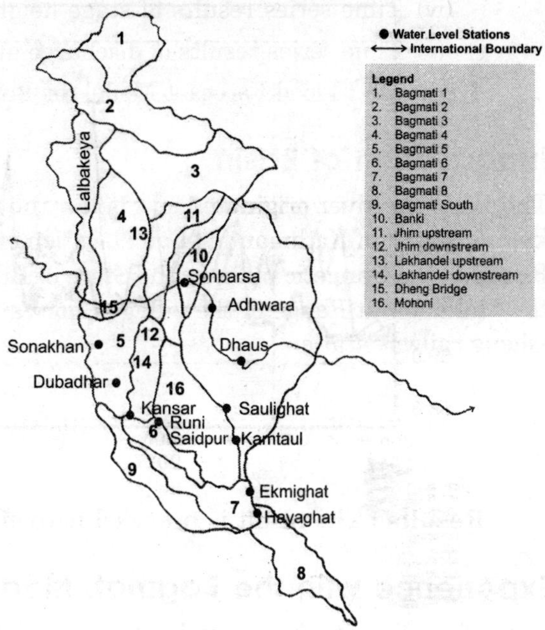

Rainfall Forecast data from IMD in (9 × 9 km) Grid

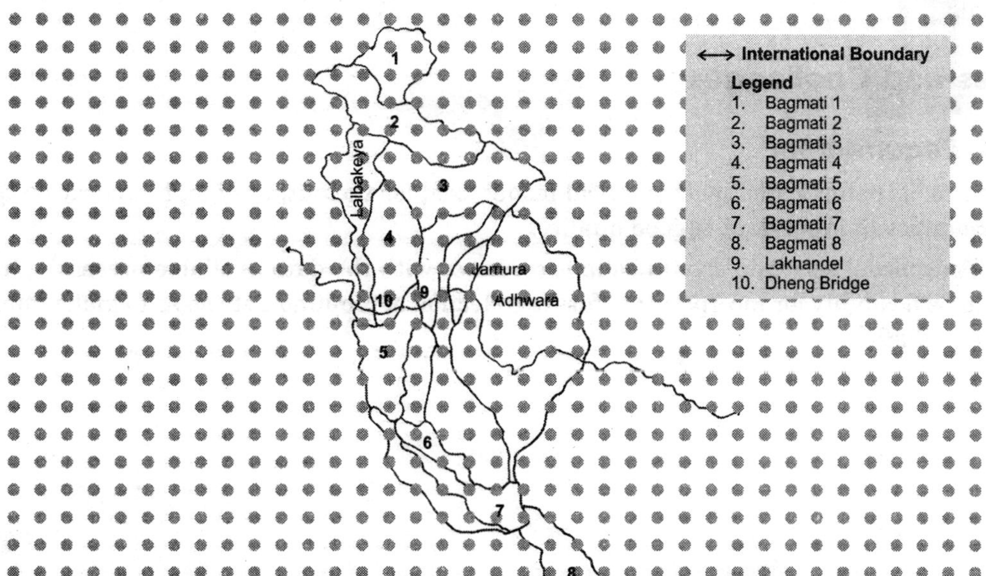

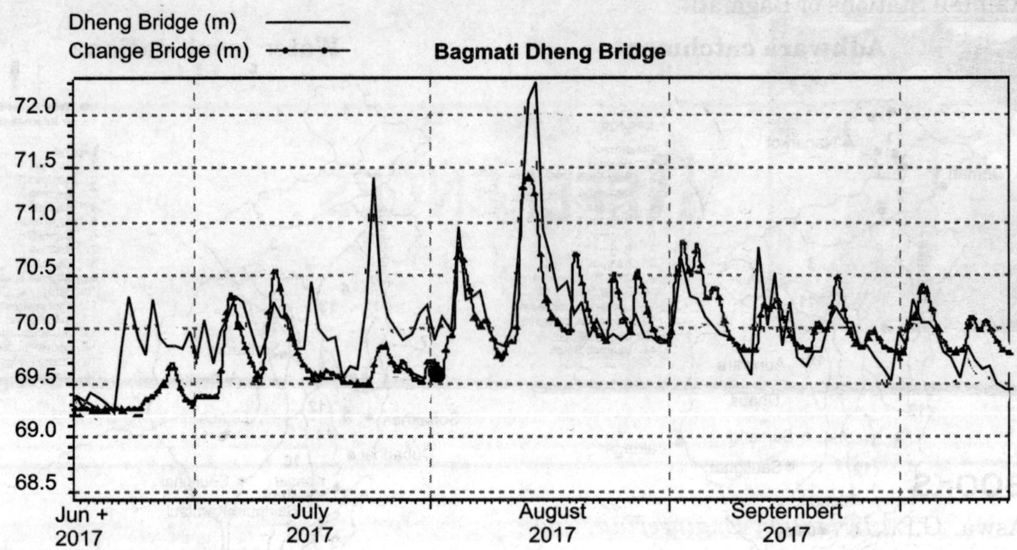

Results : The result is provided here of only one station Dheng Bridge.

Experience with the Bagmati Model

Need of quality data was found a pre-requisite for a robust model development.

Lack of historical hourly rainfall and discharge data made the work more cumbersome.

Due to dynamic character of river morphology, river cross sections need update at closer intervals.

Issues and Challenges

Data Requirement

In general, a sophisticated mathematical model used for the output of high accuracy requires large quantity of input data of good quality.

Thus model selection should be in accordance with the data available presently, having reasonable flexibility for incorporating future collection of required data so as to make improved forecast values.

REFERENCES

BOOKS

Aswa, G.L., *Irrigation Engineering*, 2nd ed., New Age Int. Pub., New Delhi, 1996.

Central Water Commission, *Estimation of Design Flood Peak*, Report No. 1, Flood Estimation Directorate, CWC, New-Delhi, 1973.

Central Water Commission, *Water Resources of India*, CWC Pub., No. 30/88, CWC, New-Delhi, 1988.

Chow, V.T., *Handbook of Applied Hydrology*, McGraw-Hill, New-York, NY, 1964.

Garde R.J., Raju, K.G.R; *Mechanics of Sediment Transportation and Alluvial Stream Problems*, 3rd ed., New Age Int. Pub., New-Delhi, 2015.

Graf, W.H., *Hydraulics of Sediment Transport*, McGraw-Hill, Book Co., Inc. New York, 1971.

Leliavsky, S., *An Introduction to Fluvial Hydraulics*, Constable and Co. Ltd. London, 1954.

Linsley, R.K. and Franzini J.B., *Water Resources Engineering,* 3rd ed., McGraw-Hill Inc. New Yourk, 1979.

Linsley, R.K., et al. *Applied Hydrology*, Tata McGraw-Hill, New-Delhi, 1975.

Peterson, M.S., River Engineering, Prentice-Hall, 1986.

Punmia B.C., Pande, B.B.L., *Irrigation and Water Power Engineering*, Laxmi Pub. (P) Ltd., New Delhi 12th ed., 2007.

Rouse, H., *Elementary Mechanics of Fluids*, John Wiley & Sons, 1946.

Scheidegger, Adrien E, *Morphotectonics*, Springer, 2004.

Subramanya, K., *Engineering Hydrology*, 2nd ed., Tata McGraw-Hill Pub. Company, Ltd., New Delhi, 2005.

Subramanya, K., *Flow in Open Channels*, Tata McGraw-Hill, New-Delhi, 1991.

Varshney, R.S., *Engineering Hydrology*, 4th ed., Nem Chand & Bros., Roorkee, India, 2012.

RESEARCH PAPERS

Agrawal V.C., *Studies and Characteristics of Meandering Streams*, Ph.D. Thesis, Univ. of Roorkee 1983.

Albertson, M.L., Simons D.B., Richardson E.V., *Discussion*, JHD, Proc. ASCE, Vol., 84, No. HY-1, Feb. 1958.

Amarsinghe, U, the *National River Linking Project of India, Some Contentious Issues*, Water Policy Research, IWMI-TATA, Water Policy Program, 2012, (www.iwmi-tata/apm2012)

Bell. H.S., *Density Currents as Agents for Transporting Sediments*, Jour. of Geo, Vol. 50, No. 5, 1942.

Blench, T, **Regime Behaviour of canals and Rivers.**, Butter worth's Scientific Publications, London, Chapter VII 1957

Brooks A., Shields, F. Douglas (ed) : *River Channel Restoration : Guiding Principles for Sustainable Projects* : John Wiley ISBN 978-0-471-96139—0.

Brooks, *Channelized Rivers : Perspectives for Env. Management.*, John Wiley, ISBN 978-0-91979-7, 1989.

Buchanan, T.J. and Somers, W.P., *Discharge Measurement at Gauging Stations* : USGS Techniques of Water-Resources Investigations, Book 3, 1969.

CBIP. **Manuel on Rivers Behaviour, Control and Training,** Pub. No. 60, 1971.

Colby B.R. and Hubbell, D.W., *Simplified Methods For Computing Total Sediment Discharge with Modified Einstein Procedure Geo.*, Survey, Water Supply 1593, U.S. Govt. 1967.

DHI (2013) River model setup and Model Application Manual, Training Exercise, Danish Hydraulic Institute, Horsholm, Denmark.

Einstein and Barbarossa, *River Channel Roughness*, Trans. ASCE, Vol. 117, 1952.

Einstein H.A., *The Bed Load Function for Sediment Transportation in Open Channel Flows*, USDA, Tech. Bull. No. 1026, Sept. 1950.

Einstein, H.A. and Ning Chien, Similarity of Distorted River Models with Movable Beds. Trans, ASCE, Vol. 121, 1956

Engelund, F. and Hansen, E., *Investigation of Flow in Alluvial Streams, Bull.;* No. 9. Hyd. Lab, Tech. Univ., Denmark, 1966.

Friedkin J.F., *A Laboratory Study of Meandering of Alluvial Rivers*, U.S. Waterways Experiment Station, Viksburg, Miss, (USA), 1945.

Galay V.J., *Causes of River Bed Degradation*, Water Resources Research. 19(5), 1057-1090, 1983.

Garcia, Celso, et al., *Process of Initiation of Motion Leading to Bed load Transport in Gravel Bed River*, Geophysical Research Letters, Vol. 34, American Geo. Union, 2007.

Garde R.J. and Hasan S.M., *An Experimental Investigation of Degradation in Alluvial Channels*, Proc. IAHR, 12th Conference, Fort Collins, Vol. 3., 1967.

Garde R.J., Albertson M.L., *Sand Waves and Regimes of Flow in Alluvial Channels*, Proc., IAHR, 8th Congress Montreal. Vol. 4, 1959.

Garde R.J., and Raju K.G.R., *Resistance Relationships for Alluvial Channel Flow*, JHD, Proc. ASCE, Vol. 92, No. HY-4, July 1966.

Garde R.J., Shaikh A.A. and Diette S., *Armouring Process in Degrading Streams*, J.H.D., Proc. ASCE, Vol. 103 No. HY-9, 1977.

Garde, R.J. Analysis of Distorted River Models with Movable Beds. JIP (India), Vol.25, No.4, Oct. 1968.

Garde, R.J. and Raju KGR, *Regime Criteria for Alluvial Streams,* JHD, Proc. ASCE, vol. 89, HY-6, Nov. 1963.

Garde, R.J. **Physical Modelling of Alluvial River Problems.** Proc. of Int. Workshop on Alluvial River Problems, Univ. of Roorkee, India, March 1980.

Garde, R.J., *Initiation of Mohan on Hydrodynamically Rough Surface-Critical Vel.* Approach JIP (India) Vol. 27, No. 3, July 1970.

Gilbert, G.K., *The Sufficiency of Terrestrial Rotation for Deflection of Streams*. National Academy of Science U.S., Vol. 3, 1884.

Gumble E.J., *'Flood Estimation by Probability Method'* Jour. Engineering New Record, Vol. 134, No. 24, June 14, 1945.

Hamed, M.A., Karima Atia and El-Bahrawy, *Bed Form Types and Dimensions at El Ekhsas Gauge Station from Field Measurements*, Nile Basin Water Science & Engineering, Jour, Vol. 3, Issue 3, 2010.

Helle, E.J. and Smith W., *Development and Calibration of Pressure Difference Bed Load Samplers*, USGS, Open file Report, 1971.

Hold, Rinchart & Winston 2001. *Earth Science*, 1120 South Capital Texas Highway, 787446-6487 :. ISBN 0-03-055667-8.

Holy Forrest M., Karim M. Fazzle, *Simulation of River Bed Degradation*, Jour. of Hyd. Eng. 112:497, 1986.

Ilo, G.C., *Analytical and Experimental Investigation of River Bed Degradation*, Ph.D., Thesis, I.I.T. Bombay, India, 1976.

Inglis, C.C., *The Behaviour and Control of Rivers and Canals* (with aid of models), Pt. 1, CWINRS, Research Pub. No. 13, 1949.

Joglekar D.V., CBIP Manual on *River Behaviour, Control and Trianing* (Vol., 1) Pub. No. 204 (India), 1989.

Joglekar, D.V., *Silting of Resservoirs, Inst. of Engrs (India),* Vol XI, No. 8 Part I, April 1960.

Kennedy, J.F., *Formation of Sediment Ripples, Dunes and Antidunes*, Annual Review of Fluid Mech., Vol. 1, 1969.

Khasturia, R.M., *How and Why Rivers Meander*, CWPRS, Pune, 2010.

Lacey, G., *Stable Channels in Alluvium*, Min. Proc. ICE (London) Vol. 229, 1930.

Lane E.W. and Kalinske, *Engineering Calculations of Suspended Sediment*, Trans. AGU, Vol. 22, 1941.

Lane, E.W. : *Report of the subcommittee on Sediment Terminology*, Trans, AGU, Vol. 28, No. 6, 1947.

Laursen, E.M., *Observation on Nature of Scour*, Proc. 5th Hyd. Conf. lowa 1952.

Leopold, L.B. and Wolman, M.G., *River Meanders*, Bull., Geo. S.A., Vol. 71, 1960.

Leopold, L.B., and Maddock T, *The Hydraulic Geometry of Stream Channels and some Physiographic Implications,* USGS Professional Paper No., 252, 1952.

Liu, H.K., *Mechanism of Sediment Ripple Formation*, JHD, Proc. ASCE, Vol. 83, No. HY-2, April 1957.

Marra, W.A. et. al., : *Near Bed and Surface Flow division Patterns in Experimental River Bifurcations*; Water Res. Research 50(2), 1506-1530. ISSN 0043-1397 (2014).

Mehta, P.J., Garde R.J. and Raju K.G.R., *Transient Bed Profiles in Aggrading Streams*, Proc. of 2nd Int. Conf. on River Sedimentation, Nanjing, China, 1983.

Meyer-Peter. E., and Muller, R., *Formula for Bed Load Transport* IAHR, 2nd Conf., Stockholm, 1948.

Neu, H.A., *Transverse Flow in a River Due to Earth's Rotation, J.H.D.* Proc. ASCE, Vol. 93, No. HY-5, Sept. 1967.

Paris, E., New Criteria for Predicting the Frictional Characteristics in alluvial streams : a Comparision, IAHR syposium on River Engineering and its Interaction with Hydrological & Hydraulic Research, Belgrade, 1980.

Patnaik P.C., Vittal N. and Pande P.K., *Lift Coefficient of a Stationary Spheres in Gradient Flow*. J.H.R. Vol. 30, No. 3, 1992.

Patnaik, P.C., Vittal, N. and Pande P.K., *Drag Coeff, of a Stationary Sphere in Gradient Flow*, J.H.R. Vol. 30, No. 3, 1992.

Prasad, T; *Interlinking of Rivers for Inter-basin Transfer,* Economic & Political Weekly, March 2004.

Serban, P and Askew A.J. Hydrological Forecasting and Updating Procedures, IAHS Publ. 201:357-369, 1991

Shields, A, Anwendung der Aehnlichkeitsmechanik und der Turbulenzforschung auf die Geschiebebewegung. Mitteilungen der Pruessischen Versuchsanstalt für Wasserban and Sehiffbau, Berlin, 1936.

Singh, Bharat, *Bed Load Transport in Channels*, JPP (India), Vol. 18, No. 2, Feb. 1961.

Snyder, F.F., *Synthetic Unit Hydrograph*, Trans Am. Geophysical Union, Vol. 19, 1938.

Soni J.P., Garde R.J. and Raju K.G.R., *Aggradation in Streams due to Overloading*, J.H.D., Proc. ASCE, Vol. 106, No. HY-1, Jan. 1980.

Swamee P.K. and Ojha C.S.P., *Drag Coeff. and Fall Vel. of non-spherical Particles*, J.H.E. Proc. ASCE, Vol. 117, No. 5 May, 1991.

Swamee P.K., *Analysis and Experimental Investigation of Stream Bed Variation Upstream of a Dam*, Ph.D. Thesis, Univ. of Roorkee, 1974.

Van Rijn, C.L., *Manual, Sediment Transport Measurements*, Delft Hyd. Lab., The Netherlands, March 1986.

Velikanov, to 9th Congress IAHR, 1961

Warner, P.W., *On the Origin of River Meanders*, Trans AGU, Vol. 32, No. 6. Dec. 1951.

White C.M., *The Equilibrium of Grains on the Bed of Stream*, Proc. RSL, Series A, Mathematical and Physical Sciences No. 958, Vol. 174, Feb. 1940.

Yang, C.T., *Incipient Motion and Sediment Transport*, JHD, Proc. ASCE, Vol. 99 No. HY-10 Oct 1973.

Zwamborn J.A., Reproductibility in Hydraulic models of Prototype River Morphology. Houille Blanche .No. 3, 1966

Journals

CBIP Pub., Design of Spurs (Groyens), Tech. Report No. 39, Research Scheme Applied to River Valley Projects, July, 1987.

CBIP, *Manual on River Behaviour, Control and Training*. Pub. No. 60, 1956.

CWC, GOI, *Manual of Estimation of Design Flood*, March 2001.

European Centre for River Restoration, Utrecht, Netherlands; *What is River Restoration* 2014.

Lynch, David, Earth Science Picture of the Day : *The confluence of Rivers*, Jan. 13, 2014.

Scour and Deposition in Rivers and Reservoirs. HEC 6, U.S. Army Corps of Engineers, User's Manual, Aug., 1993.

UNO/WMO, *Assessment of Magnitude and Frequency of Flood Flows*, United Nations Pub., Water Resources Series No. 30, 1967.

INDEX